W9-BHN-919

Solo
by •
Choice

**How to Be the Lawyer
You Always Wanted to Be**

Solo
by
Choice

**How to Be the Lawyer
You Always Wanted to Be**

CAROLYN ELEFANT

DB **DecisionBooks**
Seattle, Washington

Published by DecisionBooks
DecisionBooks is an imprint of Niche Press,
A division of Avenue Productions, Inc.

Copyright © 2008 Carolyn Elefant
All Rights Reserved

Printed in the United States of America
No part of this book may be reproduced, stored in a retrieval system, or transmitted
in any form or by any means, electronic, mechanical, photocopying, recording, or
otherwise, without the prior written permission of DecisionBooks/Niche Press

Interior design by Rose Michelle Taverniti
Cover image: Leap Worklounge chair by Steelcase (*www.Steelcase.com*)

DecisionBooks are available at special discounts for bulk purchases. For more
information, write to Special Markets, DecisionBooks, 4701 SW Admiral Way
#278, Seattle WA 98116, or email us at info@decisionbooks.com

Library of Congress Cataloging-in-Publication Data
Elefant, Carolyn.
Solo by choice : how to be the lawyer you always wanted to be / Carolyn Elefant.
p. cm.
Includes bibliographical references.
ISBN 978-0-940675-58-2
1. Solo law practice—United States. 2. Lawyers—United States. I. Title.
KF300.Z9E44 2007
340.023'73—dc22
2007036684

For my beloved daughters,
Elana Joy Israel and
Mira Justine Israel.
May you follow your dreams
and find passion in whatever
you pursue.

ACKNOWLEDGMENTS

Like so much of what I do, this book started as a whim, one that seemed like a good idea until it collided with reality—the raising of two daughters, the demands of a thriving solo law practice, and my blogging responsibilities at *MyShingle* and *LegalBlogwatch*. So, I'm grateful to my publisher for sticking by this project notwithstanding the delays, and coaxing the best possible voice out of my drafts.

I thank my parents, Milton and Eleanore Elefant for their unparalleled devotion as grandparents. They enrich my daughters' lives with their constant presence and generosity, and as a consequence, make my own life easier. And to my husband, Bruce Israel, my deepest gratitude for never doubting that I would finish this book or that my law firm would succeed. He was right on both counts. For Bruce, it was never a matter of "if" but when, and that support made all the difference.

I may have authored a book, but I'm a practicing attorney first... a solo by choice. And each day, I am privileged to work alongside thousands of other solo and small firm lawyers who improve our legal system by helping clients—from ordinary individuals to behemoth corporations and government entities—to solve problems or to find justice, and who do so zealously, professionally and with pride.—*CE*

CONTENTS

Back when you were in law school, you had dreams. Maybe it was standing before a jury, passionately arguing on behalf of a desperate client...or winning an appeal that would link your name to a new legal precedent...or pulling off a dramatic 11th hour deal that would give your struggling technology client a life-saving infusion of capital.

But what happened?

Here it is two, five, eight years out of law school—maybe more, maybe less—and most of those dreams are unrealized:

- You work 60-hour weeks in BigLaw, researching narrow legal issues for clients you never met, toting a partner's briefcase to court and watching him argue a motion you drafted nights and weekends, and which you *know* you could argue better given the opportunity.
- Or, you're a government prosecutor or Justice Department attorney whose litigation experience is the envy of your large-firm colleagues, but where the work no longer challenges you and you can't move up any higher without political connections. Or you want to move to the private sector, but your limited tenure won't bring sufficient value to the firm.
- Or, you were let go from a firm because you weren't *partnership material,* and now you're temping at document-review jobs that barely pay the bills.
- Or, you enjoy your work but you're plagued with guilt about leaving your children with a nanny five days a week.
- Or, you just passed the bar, and the prospect of paying off your student loans by slaving away the next seven, eight years on the chance you *might* make partner has you popping antacid in the middle of the night.

Of course, your own situation might not be all this grim, but you're still haunted by the thought there ought to be greater satisfaction practicing law.

Believe me, there is.

This book is dedicated to every lawyer who ever wanted to run the show but worried that going solo was career suicide...every lawyer who wanted to solo but didn't know how to set up the office and make it work...every lawyer who never set foot in a courtroom but dreamed of one day practicing law their way. In short, this book is dedicated to becoming the lawyer you always wanted to be.

Solo practice has always been a tough sell. But it isn't the dead-end that some lawyers have made it out to be. Just the opposite; more and more lawyers—from new grads to senior lawyers colliding with mandatory age policies—are giving the most serious consideration to opening their own shop because of changes in the legal environment.

For example:

- Institutional clients are thinking twice about retaining large firms because of the explosive growth of large law firms and the increase in fees.
- The drive to maximize profits is impacting the law firm collegiality.
- BigLaw mergers favoring larger, more lucrative clients are sending smaller clients into the arms of solo or small firms.
- The diversity requirements of corporate clients are creating new opportunities for women and minority-owned firms.
- Technology has made it cheaper than ever to start a law firm and to build a marketing platform.
- And in an entrepreneurial age, solo practices are more often seen as start-ups with a potential of enormous success.

Maybe the practice of law hasn't turned out for you the way you dreamed. What are your options?

You can stay put and, like so many other lawyers, rationalize that no job is perfect and that financial security trumps youthful aspirations. Or, if you've already been fired from one firm and can't find work—or you haven't been able to find a law firm job after graduating—you could leave the law altogether, always wondering whether you might have become the lawyer you envisioned as a first-year law student.

Or you could take a third path. Realize that no matter what stage you're at in your legal career, it's not too late to follow your heart. Once upon a time, author Henry David Thoreau, the quintessential American idealist, wrote, *Go confidently in the direction of your dreams. Live the life you imagined.* Maybe starting a solo law practice is the path you were intended to take all along.

—Carolyn Elefant, October, 2007

I. The Decision

CHAPTER 1

Six Reasons to Solo

"Everyone told me that the first year, even the first two, would be slow. And they were right. But now six months after going solo, my phone rings constantly, I get a more steady stream of higher quality referrals, I have interesting work, and I enjoy what I'm doing." —Sergio Benavides, solo

Whether it's derogatory comments by large-firm lawyers, or the legal media's spotlight on the ethical foibles of a few solos, our profession is regularly bombarded with negatives about solo practice. But you rarely hear why you might want to start your own law firm. In fact, solo practice remains one of the best-kept secrets of the legal profession because no one ever bothered to make a strong case in its defense. Until now. In this chapter you'll find six powerful motivators for starting your own firm:

1. Autonomy

When I ask solos to identify the strongest reasons for starting their own practice, the one at the top of nearly everyone's list is…autonomy. It doesn't surprise me. In contrast to other professions, a law practice, by its very nature, demands deference: as lawyers, we serve clients, we're bound by precedent, we're constricted by a code of professional ethics. So, when you add such factors as the bureaucracy of a large firm or government practice…firm hierarchy and the rigidity of a partnership track…and the ego-driven tendency of many lawyers to want to do things "my way," it's only natural that lawyers would crave the freedom that comes with solo'ing:

Freedom to choose cases—Above all, starting a practice liberates lawyers from the overbearing bureaucracy of practicing law in any kind of a large entity, be it a big firm, inside a corporation, or at a government agency. Within these organizations, most lawyers have no control over the cases they're assigned, and usually the younger or less-favored attorneys wind up either with the duds or more mundane tasks within a matter. Associates don't get much relief even when they take the initiative to drum up their own clients. Even when an associate gets a nibble from a potential client, he or she still needs to discuss the prospect with a supervisor or write up a proposal to a committee to justify taking on the client. And many times, firms turn away the types of clients that younger associates attract, either because the clients can't afford the firm fees, or they create a conflict with the firm's larger, institutional clients.

By contrast, solos don't have this problem.

Solos can pick exactly the types of cases they want to handle, and develop their very own strategy to handle them. And at the end of the day, even though lawyers with their own practice may need to consult with their partners, or decide to seek guidance from a more experienced lawyer in making decisions about the merits of a case or pursuing a particular strategy, the decision to accept a case is theirs alone.

Not only does autonomy eliminate frustration and sense of powerlessness, it also gives solos an edge over their large-firm counterparts.

In just one example, small-firm lawyer Tom Goldstein, who specializes in Supreme Court litigation, beat out several other large firms to snag a compelling death penalty matter. Why? Goldstein was able to decide to accept the case after consulting with his law partner, who happened to be his wife. In fact, Goldstein was already on a plane to Tennessee to meet the client while the large firms were still deliberating over whether to accept the matter[1]. (Note: Goldstein has since moved to a large firm, where he serves as partner while his wife continues to operate their former practice with another lawyer).

Lawyers in solo practice can also structure a firm that's conducive to the types of cases they want to take on. For example, one lawyer I know started his own firm after he grew tired of his BigLaw employer turning down potentially precedent-setting appellate matters that he brought to the practice because the prospective clients couldn't afford the firm's hourly rates. As a solo, the lawyer opened an office in a suburban location closer to his home, and invested in the right combination of hardware and software that he could manage most administrative tasks without a full-time assistant. As a result, he was able to take on cases that his former firm declined as unprofitable. Even more satisfying, he's earning more money than he ever did at the firm.

Freedom in handling a case—These days, most large organizations don't exactly encourage recommendations on case strategy from associates. In fact, conventional wisdom (see *From Appealing to Scary: The Zen of Partner Contact*; Fulton County Daily Report, June 2005), advises associates to refrain from offering suggestions about potential case theories since the partners have likely already considered them anyway. In my own case, I frequently witnessed the same junior attorneys-should-be-seen-not-heard rule applied in government practice. Once, as a new, eager-to-please junior attorney for a federal agency, my boss reprimanded me after a meeting for volunteering some ideas on how to resolve a dispute without getting her approval first. Later, in an effort to placate me, she explained that even her deputy general counsel—someone with the agency some 40 years—needed her permission before expressing his view at meetings! Solo practice liberates you from just this sort of foolish, often degrading, demonstrations of hierarchy and power, leaving you free to exercise your own independent judgement and actually practice law, not interoffice politics.

Freedom over the smallest matters—While most solos revel in their autonomy over substantive matters, sometimes it's just the freedom to make decisions about the smallest, most trivial things that makes the biggest difference. When I started my own practice, I made a point of choosing office supplies distinct from the standard issue at my former law firm—such as choosing Post-Its in bright pink instead of corporate yellow; expensive pens not cheap ball-points; business cards with blue print-on-cream rather than black-on-white. Not necessarily because I preferred them...but because I could.

2. Practical Experience

One reason the number of pro bono programs has surged in recent years is not because law firm attitudes are more enlightened. Firms are desperately searching for ways to get hands-on training for their associates. A partner at one well-known large firm told me one day that even their junior litigation partners were chomping at the bit to handle a *pro bono* matter just for the experience of getting in front of a jury for the first time. When you start a law firm it's you who gets the experience. For example, if you bring a business client with you from your former firm, you—and not the partner—will negotiate and draft the company's next contract. If it's an appellate matter, it's you who will write the brief and argue the case. And when the client calls for advice—on anything from a pressing strategic decision to how to dress for a deposition—it's your advice he wants because there's no one else. Solo practice also gives you opportunities to gain practical experience in new fields. When I started my firm, I'd been out of law school for five years and had never set foot in a courtroom except to observe. However, my practice specialty...energy regulatory work...didn't give me opportunity for trial work since most regulatory disputes are resolved on the papers or perhaps at an administrative hearing. So, to get the court time I craved, I signed up for court-appointed criminal cases. Within six months, I had a bench trial and argued a couple of motions, and within a year had my first jury trial. I never would have had those opportunities if I remained at a law firm, especially in my practice area.

3. To Feel Like a Lawyer

Back in the 19th Century, Karl Marx, the social revolutionary and father of Communism, decried the Industrial Revolution for alienating workers from the product of their labor. He argued that where once craftsmen built a product from start to finish, the assembly line had atomized the process for the sake of efficiency, robbing the working class of the satisfaction of their craft. Sound familiar? It should. Because in some ways, modern American law firms resemble the assembly lines that Marx so vigorously condemned. At large firms, lawyers—primarily associates—work only on portions of a case, often never speaking with a client or even being privy to the entire matter. In fact, many lawyers today feel like paper-pushers[2], sleep-walking through their jobs rather than being vibrant professionals with an ability to solve problems and make a difference in people's lives. More than anything, solo practice makes you feel like a real lawyer, the kind of lawyer you imagined you would be back in law school. And each time you introduce yourself in the court room or boardroom, each time you reassure a nervous client, each time you explain to prospective clients what you can do for them, you reinforce the image of yourself as an autonomous, can-do professional with the tools to solve problems, resolve disputes, and even improve the legal system. And that feeling of being a lawyer never goes away, even when you're handling such administrative tasks as photocopying your own briefs or sending out bills late at night, because those tasks aren't the central focus of your job, but merely incidental to work as a real lawyer.

4. Work Flexibility

Many solo and small-firm lawyers, especially those just starting out and working full-time, may put in nearly as many hours as their large-firm colleagues. But solo practice allows you to set your own schedule, spreading out the work in a way that works best for you. For instance, suppose that your son or daughter has important after-school soccer matches that you don't want to miss. Back at BigLaw, you'd probably be too embarrassed to cut out early more than once for a family event, and if you worked in government you'd have to use up personal leave. On your own, you can simply get an earlier start on your work day, or make up the time after the match when your kids are in bed. Sure, there will be days when you have a conference or a court hearing you can't postpone. But generally speaking, you have far more control over your own time when the law firm has your name on the door.

Moreover, when you run your own shop, you avoid many of the inefficiencies and superficialities endemic to any large employer. As you know, there are all sorts of practice group meetings, sensitivity training, ceremonial lunches, and office happy-hours that cut into the day without relieving you of deadlines or billable quotas. In addition, at large firms, face-time is paramount to success; simply being seen by your colleagues is just as important as actually getting the job done. So, if your assigned partner prefers to remain at the office until eight...you can count on staying until after eight most nights even if you'd rather arrive at dawn to get home by dinner. Then there are the non-billable demands. Though most associates believe their salaries more than compensate for long hours at the office, the actual calculations prove otherwise. A well-known study by the Yale Law School Career Office (*law.yale.edu/documents/pdf/ CDO_Public/cdo-billable_hour.pdf*) shows that with various non-billable work day interruptions, an associate working a 60-hour week will bill only 42.5 hours, barely meeting a 2,000-hour minimum billable requirement. Spread out over a 60-hour work week, (and assuming three weeks for vacation) that $160,000 salary amounts to roughly $55 an hour, which doesn't seem so bad until you consider that it amounts to just 25 percent of a large firm associate's billing rate!

And for lawyers who want or need to work part-time, few if any other alternative work situations can match the flexibility of solo practice. Though lawyers choose part-time employment for many reasons, the most common is to enable lawyers to stay home with their children. For many years, law firms have been grappling—mostly unsuccessfully—with ways to accommodate new parents, primarily mothers, who want a part-time schedule. But at law firms, part-time often means working almost similar hours on less interesting projects at drastically reduced pay.[3] Moreover, part-time frequently involves "work seepage", or at least an implicit understanding that a lawyer must drop everything when a case emergency comes up.[4] As a result, some women don't take advantage of part-time programs even when firms make them available.[5] You can't blame law firms or government organizations for not accommodating women any better. Not surprisingly, the partners give priority to their own financial well-being and the perceived needs of their clients over the desires of a handful of women asking for alternative schedules.

When you start your own firm, though, you're the boss…and your needs come first. And you have complete freedom to design a schedule and a practice tailored to your specific family situation.

5. To Own Not Loan Your Talent

Lawyers toiling away at firms lose a substantial portion of their earnings to firm overhead and partner profit. By way of example, a firm might bill a second-year associate at $250 an hour, and collect $500,000 based on a 2,000-hour billable year. Of that, the associate receives only $160,000 a year, or roughly a quarter of the firm's take. Granted, the remaining $340,000 isn't all firm profit; the

AUTHOR'S NOTE

When my first daughter was born, I knew that I wanted to spend as much time with her as possible. At the same time, I'd been solo for three years, and with my practice firmly established and growing, I was reluctant to close it entirely. My practice wasn't particularly high-volume, so I didn't need to cut the number of cases as much as change the nature of some of the work I was handling.

For starters, I phased out my court-appointed criminal work and referred or closed out several civil litigation matters because trial work, with its spur of the moment hearings and frequent meetings with clients and opposing counsel, was too time-consuming and unpredictable to provide enough time with my daughter. In place of these matters, I found a steady stream of energy regulatory work on a contract basis for a couple of other busy solos, and continued to handle a couple of appellate matters. Initially, I was able to squeeze my work responsibilities into early mornings, late nights, naps and weekends. When my daughter got older, I hired a nanny for a few mornings a week. Two years later, with the birth of my second daughter, I cut back even further, eliminated childcare, and capped my schedule at 15 hours a week.

These days, with both daughters settled in school, I'm free to work a nearly full-time schedule until I meet my girls at the bus stop at 4 p.m. That pick-up time is set in stone, and I won't alter it except in unusual situations like an out-of-town trip or a deposition that runs late (in which case, my husband or parents stand in). I realize that my afternoon curfew would brand me as inflexible or unreasonable if I worked for someone else's firm. Fortunately, I don't. ●

firm covers your benefits (i.e., retirement contributions and health insurance), training and office space. But even deducting a generous $100,000 a year for these expenses leaves the firm with a quarter-million dollars in profit. By contrast, if you were to start your own firm and generate 1,000 billable hours a year—that is, 20 hours a week at an average rate of $150 an hour—you would still come out roughly the same as if you had stayed at the firm, but working far fewer hours! Just as we realize the advantages of owning rather than renting home, lawyers should think carefully about the benefits of owning versus loaning their talents.

To be sure, solo practice has its ups and downs. After all, if you don't take care to adequately diversify your practice, or if you don't market your practice with vigilance, you could find yourself without any paying clients before too long. But consider: if you choose not to solo in these tumultuous times, you might be find yourself coping with a variety of grim scenarios: getting ejected from your law firm's partnership track after five years...getting unceremoniously booted from the law firm when you get too old...or, if you're working at a government agency, getting relegated to low-level cases when a new political appointee comes into power. What would you have to show for yourself then?

6. Career Satisfaction

More than any other career in law, solo practice offers great personal satisfaction. From one day to the next, you never know whether the next client walking through the door will bring that case that catapults you into the limelight, earns you enough to retire, or makes you a subject-matter expert in an area of law you never anticipated entering.

It certainly was true in the case of solo Donna Newman.

A few years ago, Newman was just another hard-working solo picking up occasional court appointments for indigent defendants on federal charges. In May, 2002, a federal judge appointed her to represent Jose Padilla, an ex-Chicago gang member and Muslim convert on charges of helping Islamic extremists. In time, the Bush Administration classified Padilla as an enemy combatant and sent him to a military prison. On her client's behalf, Ms. Newman fought all the way up to the United States Supreme Court (*Rumsfeld v. Padilla, 124 S. Ct. 2711 (2004)*, setting historic precedent in the process and establishing her as an expert on novel areas of constitutional, human rights and military law. Her story (New York Times, Feb. 11, 2003) bears out what I've long observed about solo practice: the most amazing opportunities for solo and small firm lawyers to soar often come by sheer accident.

It's no coincidence that this kind of accidental celebrity would involve a solo practitioner. Solos run their own ship, and they're the best situated to act quickly when a novel or new matter crosses their path. And because most successful solos have a propensity for risk, they're also not scared off by the prospect of taking a case that involves an area of law with which they have little or no experience. Contrast the solo mentality to that of a large firm, where a new client matter involving a unique or complicated legal question of first impression would require an endless litany of conflict tests, committee meetings, and preliminary (but still exhaustive) associate research before the firm would make a decision on whether to accept the case. By that time, the client would probably have sought other counsel.

AUTHOR'S NOTE

Truth be told, if I hadn't gotten up the nerve to start my own firm, I would probably not be practicing law at all.

Five years out of law school, I was informed by the managing partner at my firm that I wasn't partnership material! I was given six months. With the deadline at my back, though, I still hadn't found a new position, and my only alternatives were unemployment or starting my own firm. But, as luck would have it, my husband and I had just closed on our first home, and the mortgage was based in part on what I was earning as an associate. Between the mortgage and my student loans, unemployment was not an option; I needed to work. As if that wasn't enough impetus, I was angry. Though I had just been fired, I knew deep down that I had it in myself to be a good lawyer if only I could find the right opportunity. Anyway, I certainly wasn't ready to be forced out of the legal profession before I'd argued a real case in court.

I left my firm the last week of October, 1993. By the first week of November, I opened for business in a makeshift home office and a virtual office in downtown Washington D.C. In my first two years of practice, not only did I finally argue that case that I'd long coveted (before the esteemed D.C. Circuit no less) but numerous others followed. I also took scores of depositions, first-chaired five jury trials, and represented at least a half dozen clients in multiple administrative hearings. Even better, within three years I had exceeded the miserly salary that I'd been earning at my former firm. After leaving my firm, both the economy and my practice specialty of energy regulation picked up nicely. And while other firms have serenaded me, I've never been tempted.

Maybe *your* career hasn't taken the path you'd hoped... maybe logging long hours at a big firm have been miserable... and maybe, without even realizing it, your unhappiness or desperation or nervousness has impacted your performance to the point where you got yourself fired. But honestly: *are you ready to leave the law?* If your answer is yes, you can put the book down. But if you are still committed to the same ideals that attracted you to law, or if you want to squeeze your money's worth out of the degree you worked so hard to attain, then don't let a lousy boss or the dysfunctional and unyielding hierarchical law firm system force you out of the legal profession. Sure, starting a law firm may not be your first choice. But give it time. You just might discover that going out on your own gives you that second chance to find satisfaction and fulfillment as a lawyer. ●

Of course, one of the best known examples of someone enjoying the fullest opportunities of solo practice is David Boies.

Before starting his own firm— originally six attorneys but now a large practice (*Boies, Schiller & Flexner*)—Boies worked as a partner at *Cravath, Swaine and Moore*. Respected by his BigLaw colleagues, Boies was virtually unknown to the general public until he started his own shop, which enabled him to represent the Department of Justice in its antitrust action against Microsoft and to argue *Bush v. Gore*. In so doing, Boies became famous. Had he stayed at Cravath, he would no doubt have enjoyed wealth, continued success, and respect amongst his peers. But he would have missed out on an exciting career, and the chance to leave a permanent mark on the law. Starting a law firm gave Boies enormous possibilities, well beyond the narrow margins of his former employer, one of the largest law firms in the world.

Some of the best advice on starting a law practice comes from the real experts: solos themselves. This the first of nine sidebars in which solos of all levels of experience offer their personal insights. You'll find the complete interviews in Appendix 6.

Q: Why did you open a solo practice?

- Walter James III (class of 1987)—"I got tired of not getting compensated for the amount of business I was bringing in. I was among the top-five in business generation but not anywhere near the top-five in compensation! And I also got tired of the hours, tired of the commute."

- Spencer Young (class of 1995)—"I wanted to work for myself, and get paid completely and fully for my own efforts…I had a desire for freedom in my day, and the cases I chose…I wanted to self-test my business and legal skills…I had a risk/reward rush…I wanted to learn how to run a business…and I thought I could as well or better than lawyers who were not as bright as me (and had no MBA) doing great on their own. The list (of reasons) is endless."

- Scott Wolfe (class of 2005)—"Why did I want to solo? I have a strong background in business. My family is full of entrepreneurs, and throughout high school, college and law school, I was self-employed. My personality has never allowed me to work for any companies or organizations, and so I knew upon starting law school that I would be going solo. Beyond it, I wanted to solo for the usual reasons: the ability to make my own schedule, the power of controlling my job security and destiny, the benefit of not having a promotional ceiling, the rewards of being in business for yourself, etc."

- Denny Esford (class of 2003)—"I had no other choice (but to solo). I graduated in the middle of the pack, and, as a new lawyer at age 46, I knew no one would hire me unless I was willing to work for $30–40K, which was unacceptable for someone a family with a home, a wife and two teenagers."

- David Abeshouse (class of 1982)—"I wanted to sink or swim on my own, do things in my own fashion, rather than abide by the often-interminable partnership meeting/committee/sub-committee process of decision-making."

- Brian Rabal (class of 2005)—"For me, some of the factors (about going solo) were the ability to spend more time with family, the costs of commuting…also the fact that I have never been good with office politics."

To read the complete interviews, go to Appendix 6. ●

CHAPTER 2

The Big Decision

"I opened the doors of my own firm a little over a year ago, and it's been quite a roller-coaster ride. But the challenges of running a solo practice keep my blood pumping, and keep me learning new things on a daily basis." —Amanda Benedict, solo

Good lawyers need to understand a client's motives to successfully represent them. For example, the wealthy client intent on destroying the reputation of a business partner who betrayed him. Without understanding the client's motives, the lawyer might fail to make a case for accepting a generous settlement when the issue is really a desire for retribution. Once the motive is understood, other strategies are possible. As you embark on your own firm, you likewise need to understand your motives. Because whatever they are—a need for autonomy, flexibility, security, career satisfaction—they will drive your expectations and—ultimately—your success and satisfaction.

What follows are the five commonly cited motives for starting a firm:

1. You've always dreamed of starting a law firm. Without question, having the drive and desire to start a law firm will contribute to your potential success. But you can't allow your enthusiasm to lead you to careless decisions or to underestimate the commitment needed to get started. I've known a few lawyers so keen on hanging a shingle that they've invested precious resources for posh office space, mahogany furniture, and expensive technology without really thinking about the cash flow needed to cover that kind of overhead. Other lawyers have been so blinded by the urge to help clients find justice, that they're naively lured into representing every troubled, needy client with a sympathetic story and no cash on hand. Still others believe that by working conscientiously and acting honorably, cases will simply come, not realizing how much time they need to devote in those early years to marketing, making social contacts, and establishing a reputation to guarantee steady work over time.

Bottom line: Be careful that your judgment is not clouded by enthusiasm. It can lead to imprudent choices or poor timing in the opening of your new solo practice.

2. You work at a large firm (and are desperately unhappy). More and more, dissatisfaction with large firm life is motivating unhappy associates to explore solo practice... or to leave the law entirely. But why should a bad experience drive you out of a profession you worked so hard to enter? After all, even if you hate certain aspects of BigLaw—like the tedious checking of briefs—these mundane tasks aren't so bad when you're doing it for yourself.

At the same time, some of the issues driving you from large-firm practice don't magically vanish when you open your own shop. Launching a law firm demands many non-billable hours networking at bar events, writing articles, or meeting with potential referrals…on top of whatever client commitments you have. No, you won't have 60-hour weeks, but unless you're planning a purely part-time practice (and a part-time salary), expect to invest at least 45 hours a week to build your practice. And that if you have low tolerance for difficult personalities, solo practice won't solve things. True, you won't have to kiss up to an arrogant junior partner for choice assignments, but you may have an annoying client calling frequently, questioning your legal strategy. And what about that nasty opposing counsel, who constantly accuses you of unethical conduct to intimidate you from zealously representing your client? In many ways, dealing with an aggressive adversary is just as stressful as working for an overbearing law firm partner.

Don't confuse problems inherent in the practice of law with your unhappiness at your firm. When you practice law, you can't avoid dealing with jerks, whether they're opposing counsel, judges, or even your own clients.

Bottom line: When you consider leaving BigLaw for "YourLaw," make sure the gripes you have about large firm practice are specific to your firm and not to the practice of law in general. If the latter is true, you won't find satisfaction starting your own firm.

3. You want to be a stay-at-home mom.

After slaving long hours at a firm and being a weekend parent, you may fantasize about starting a part-time practice, working on memos at the dining room table while the kids play at your feet.

As I mentioned earlier, starting your own firm makes sense from a parenting or family perspective simply because it gives you the flexibility and control that working at a firm or government agency simply cannot match. But creating and sustaining a part-time practice while you raise young children isn't nirvana. For one thing, you won't have the amount of time usually available to stay-home parents for organizing play groups, or serving as class parent, or participating in the PTA. And a part-time practice demands that you cap your work hours, which means you might have to forego a promising networking opportunity, or to accept chunks of contract work that can be managed more easily on a tight schedule but pays less. And even though part-time practice does allow you to get to meet your child's bus at 3 p.m., that privilege may cost you an occasional all-nighter or weekend at the library to meet a tight deadline. After all, just because you put your family first doesn't mean your clients will.

And a part-time practice can be frustrating. You're still working hard, and you may not earn job as much or advance as quickly as your full-time peers. Nor will you get much sympathy from either full-timers who envy your flexibility, or stay-home parents who haven't found a way to keep a foot in the working world. All things considered, a solo practice offers one of the best ways to balance family and work. Striking the right balance won't be easy; it can take months or even years of experimentation before you hit the right equation that works for you and your family.

Bottom line: As a part-timer, what you gain in flexibility you may lose in earning power, and you may feel suspended between the working world and the stay-at-home-mom world.

AUTHOR'S NOTE

A layoff or termination is a real blow to the ego. Some lawyers who lose their job question their ability to start a practice, wondering how they can successfully manage their own clients when they couldn't even cut it working for someone else. Others harbor so much anger and bitterness they can't function productively.

If you've been laid off, here are some things to keep in perspective from someone who's been there:
In my case, the managing partner walked into my office without warning and told me that I wasn't "partnership material", and that I had six months to find a new job. I was stunned, the say the least. I was too proud to beg for my job (to be honest, I'd been fairly unhappy and uninspired by the work for some time), and yet I felt that I had to say something. Before I knew it, these words tumbled out: "*I know that the firm's decision to let me go has nothing to do with my abilities. I know that I am a good lawyer. I was good enough for you to hire two years ago, and I'm just as good now. No matter what you think, I am a good lawyer and that I will succeed at whatever I do.*" I remember the managing partner just nodding at me with a mildly amused look, and then retreating as fast as he could out of my office.

In the months that followed, I struggled with feelings of failure as I looked for work. And whenever I felt ready to quit…and I did…it was always a faith in myself and my abilities that carried me through the really dark times.

If something similar happened to you, remember this: you had the capability and talent to finish three years of law school, pass a grueling bar exam, and convince an employer that you were worth hiring. That makes you as good a lawyer as anyone. Circumstances may have put you in an unfortunate situation: perhaps you were fired or laid off because the work didn't interest you…or you took a little longer to catch on than your peers…or your personality didn't mesh with your boss…or your firm just hit an economic downturn and management had to make some choices. You can't let those external forces detract from your belief in yourself, and you can't let them derail you from the career that you've worked so hard to attain."

4. You were fired. Losing a job can be humiliating. Most of us feel too ashamed to admit we've been fired, and too honest to lie about why we left our former job. What to do? If, after losing your job, you decide to start your own firm, you can keep it to yourself that you had been fired. No one has to know. Most would never ask why you decided to go out on your own, and many assume it was by choice. For those who do inquire, say—truthfully—that solo practice offered far more professional opportunities and challenges than your former position…and leave it at that.

As angry as you may be, don't burn any bridges. Put your emotions into your morning jog or your journal (*not* a blog; this is one situation where a blog is not the smart play).

Even if your firm considered your performance sub-par (and you acknowledge that you did make some stupid mistakes), that doesn't mean you won't succeed on your own. Whatever you do, don't—repeat, *don't*—badmouth your firm or attempt revenge. For whatever reason you were let go, do nothing that would compromise the possibility that your old firm might one day give you referrals. In my own case, lawyers from my former firm (which had asked me to leave) helped me to prepare for my first appellate argument after I'd started my own practice, they referred me several small energy regulatory matters, and they provided sufficiently positive references that enabled me to land several lucrative contract matters. As time has passed, my relationship with some of the firm's lawyers has grown more cordial. I even attended the firm's anniversary celebration, and shared a terrific time with my old colleagues.

Bottom line: Though starting a firm after losing your job may not be your first choice, you can increase your chances for success by focusing on making a fresh start and letting go of whatever animus you have toward your former employer.

5. You want to practice law your way.

Perhaps you're not advancing as quickly as you'd like because of the struggle to manage your workload and keep pace with your peers. Lawyering is a struggle, but starting a firm can actually help you master new skills because—for the first time—you're able to modify your workload to learn at your own pace free of comparison to others. Many years ago, I was part of a team of six attorneys hired by a government agency for a long-term contract position. Because the position involved an obscure area of law, the agency provided a two-day training session. At the end of the session, one of our team members confided that she hadn't understood any of the material. So, when we got assigned our cases, she always asked us how to respond to a particular pleading, and what questions to ask during a deposition. As the job continued, she eventually caught on and closed out her cases as quickly as the rest of us. What's more, by asking questions, she had grown acquainted with the other temp attorneys as well as the full time attorneys at the agency, and knew exactly where to turn for specific problems. Before long, she became the go-to attorney in this area of law. As a result, the agency chose her as its project manager, and eventually hired her permanently.

Bottom line: Don't be hard on yourself; people learn at different rates. Even if you're not a quick study you can—with hard work—catch up and even surpass your colleagues.

A Personal Assessment

After giving careful thought to your motives, you still need to consider whether solo practice suits your personality and temperament. Consider:

Do you crave independence? The most satisfied solos prefer to operate without affiliation to a larger controlling unit, and don't require others for guidance in conducting their business.

Are you comfortable wearing many hats? Successful solos act as project manager, office manager, HR director, business manager, strategic planner, VP for business development, and general worker bee, all of which can consume as much as half your day. You don't have to like all of these roles, but you do have to be willing to assume them if you can't afford to delegate them. As a solo, tasks like collecting payment from clients, cold-calling potential clients, or scanning documents, aren't any more enjoyable than the busy work that's demanded at almost any job. The upside is that you get to practice law the way you want.

Do you thrive when you're in charge? The most successful solos readily accept responsibility for failure as long as they can take all the credit for a good result.

Are you enterprising? In my experience, the most successful solos have a talent for spotting opportunities and taking advantage of them. For them, networking is a regular and enjoyable part of every week, and they don't rely on telephone ads to keep their operation afloat. Note: Shyness is often cited as a reason not to seek out business. But some of the most effective lawyer-marketers are introverted, and it only compels them to approach networking in a more disciplined, systematic manner.

What is your tolerance for risk? There's the possibility of great payoffs and then you might run into days (even weeks) without billables. As a solo, you won't know when or whether business will come, or how long you'll have it, or if it will generate a living wage. In order to experience satisfaction, you must be comfortable with the part of you that is willing to take a leap of faith…or willing to diversify your practice instead of focusing on a single practice area (such as bankruptcy or real estate, which are especially sensitive to changes in the law and economic recession).

Are you a self-starter? Successful solos don't need someone looking over their shoulders; they're motivated to do what needs to be done. Look back at your childhood. Were you one of those kids who complained about being bored when left to your own devices? Or were you someone who could amuse yourself for hours? Note: if you're concerned about your ability to get motivated, consider working in a shared space rather than a home office. Working in the company of others can have the effect of forcing you to be more conscientious.

Are you resourceful? The most successful solos are good at finding answers quickly, and are unafraid of asking questions, requesting input, and seeking help. Over the years, what I've learned is that solo practice requires you to unlearn some of the bad habits you picked up in law school and on the job. Asking a question isn't a sign of weakness but a form of empowerment. Admitting what you don't know can make you feel stupid but it also opens yourself up to learning more and making yourself a better lawyer. Besides, if the questions that your clients bring to you were already resolved, they wouldn't need you anyway.

How Much Do Solos Earn?

Even though the federal government posts GS-pay scale charts for lawyers, and BigLaw firms publicize the pay of incoming associates, there is no definitive answer on how much solos typically earn. This is true for several reasons:

- Solos are a disparate group, and gathering a sufficiently wide data sample is difficult.
- Solo practices vary so widely that salary charts offer little guidance even for the same

geographic area (for example, a solo who practiced employment law at a large firm for institutional clients, and who continues on the same matters when she starts her own firm, will likely earn more than a family law attorney who represents consumer clients).

- And, in contrast to large firms, where associates often bill 2,000 to 2,200 hours a year, solos have more control over their schedule, their overhead expenses... and their income. If you cap your work week at 40 hours to spend more time with your family, you will earn less than a solo who works 60 hours. And if you gross $100,000 and trim your overhead costs to 20 percent of your gross revenues, you 'll earn $80,000 before taxes, whereas a colleague who prefers to have a secretary and Class A office might wind up with only $40,000 or $50,000 at the end of the year.

Susan Cartier Liebel (*susancartierliebel.typepad.com*), a solo practice coach, says of lawyer salaries:

... A solo's income is dependent upon numerous variables, but the metric remains the same: solos sell their time regardless of their billing model, and there is only so much time they can sell. They can choose to sell all of it or part of it. And when they reach their individual maximum, they can choose to bring on another and sell that person's time and take a percentage. Or they can increase their profits by increasing their rate and/or reducing their overhead. Or they can do all three. Not all solos choose to make millions or build empires, but simply want to sustain themselves in the lifestyle with which they are happiest.

Still, there are some ways to ballpark what you can expect to earn.

Comparing apples to apples. Some bar associations do publish data on solo earnings.

In Florida, a solo's median income in 2005 was reported to be $105,000 (source: Florida Bar News, *tinyurl.com/32j68u*), while in Texas that same year a solo's median income was reported to be $88,604 (source: State Bar of Texas, Department of Research and Analysis, Private Practitioner 2005 Income Report). What's important to remember about salary study data—even bar association data—is that it often relies on a sampling of only a few hundred attorneys ranging from solos to large firm practitioners. Still, if you compare apples to apples, the data may provide a rough estimate of potential salary.

Consider: The Florida bar breaks out its data by years of experience. So, while the overall median salary was a reported $105,000 a year, it was only $65,000 for lawyers with less than three years of experience, and $85,000 for those with six-to-eight years of experience. In Texas, the Bar breaks out salary data by years of experience and by practice area. The median salary for a more traditional solo practice areas (such as family attorney) was reported to be $81,588. By contrast, the median salary for environmental attorneys was \$124,000. So, a mid-level associate at a large firm in Texas who is considering solo practice should not assume that he would earn under \$100,000 merely because that's the median for a solo with a consumer-oriented practice.

Needless to say, the "apples-to-apples" rule also applies to geographic location. Solos located in a small, rural community with five years of experience will earn less then their counterparts in a major urban area in the same state because rural clients can't afford to pay as much (although the salary gap might even out because the cost of living in a rural area is probably substantially less).

Where to find salary advice. Many lawyers are circumspect about how much they earn, so you may not have much luck obtaining earnings information from them. But if you're really determined to locate specific data on what you can expect to earn as a solo, contact your bar's law practice management advisor (most bar associations now have an LPM expert on staff). LPM advisors consult with lawyers on starting and ramping up their practices, and often have access to information about how much particular types of solos earn. If an LPM advisor has assisted a lawyer with a profile similar to yours—e.g., a former BigLaw attorney with 15 years of corporate experience, or a recent graduate with a criminal practice—he could provide information that proves more meaningful. LPM advisors can also inform you about practice trends that may impact earnings. For example, they might be aware that immigration attorneys have been experiencing an uptick in earnings due to increased demand for service, or that earnings for personal injury attorneys have been depressed by tort reform.

Previous employment as a baseline. Reference to your previous employment, or to comparable private sector employment, can also offer a decent baseline for predicting future earnings (at least in the first few years of practice).

As a general rule, lawyers who come to solo practice by way of a law firm or government position…and who bring with them few, if any, clients…may find their net solo earnings are 25 to 80 percent less during their first year in practice, and some may earn only enough to cover expenses during their first year of practice. By the second year, though, a solo is likely to be close to matching their previous salary, and, by the third year, most solos will exceed what they earned before leaving a law firm or government position. Lawyers who manage to take at least one or two decent "anchor" clients (e.g., clients with enough steady matters to provide a base-load revenue stream to your practice) typically experience only a downward earnings "blip" of 10 or 20 percent compared to their earlier job, and frequently exceed their previous salary by Year Two. Moreover, those lawyers who bring one or two small corporate clients find that those clients who come with them may actually send them more work because as solos they can offer more affordable rates. As for solos fresh out of law school, they generally manage to cover their expenses within six months of starting their practice if they've been vigilant about minimizing their start-up costs. And by Year Three their earnings can equal those of law firm associates or government attorneys with comparable practice areas and similar geographic areas.

A few caveats. For experienced lawyers, baseline comparisons only work when your new solo practice is in the same practice area as before. When you change practice areas, it's as if you're a solo just out of law school because you're learning a new practice area and just beginning to make contacts. As a result…depending upon the practice area you select, and your previous employment…you may never match your prior salary.

For example, let's say an eighth-year associate earning $250,000 as an associate at an AmLaw 100 firm handling corporate transactions decides to open a solo practice specializing in consumer bankruptcy or family law. Their first-year earnings will dip substantially; indeed, he or she may never come close to his salary from his law firm days. And yet, the associate's solo earnings would compare favorably to other law-related career options, such as government, academia or in-house positions at a small company, not to mention that the associate would be working fewer hours and have greater flexibility than before. It bears noting that if this same associate decided to continue his corporate practice instead of changing to a consumer-oriented fields, his earnings potential as a solo would be greater. And with outsourcing or hiring associates or clerks to leverage earnings, the associate could reasonably match or increase his law firm salary. In this example, a large portion of the senior associate's revenue drop in moving to solo practice derives from the change from a corporate to a consumer-oriented practice, and not exclusively from the decision to go solo.

For salary projections, the apples-to-apples comparison is even more important when the issue is part-time vs full-time. Consider the example of Joanne Sternlieb, a trusts and estates lawyer who works from home. During her first two years of solo practice, she earned two-thirds percent of her salary at a major New York law firm where she worked 40 hours a week (full-time was 60 hours). Anticipating the shortfall when she went solo, Sternlieb supplemented her income by working part-time on a contract basis. Now, after several years, Joanne works a flexible 40-hour week from home, and her salary is equivalent to what she earned in BigLaw (source: *jdbliss.com/ e_article000563621.cfm?x=b11,0,w*).

A Financial/Economic Analysis

From a financial perspective, the thought of starting a firm can be daunting (see Chapter 6). Not only must you replace the lost stream of income, but you carry the burden on everything from computer equipment and supplies to malpractice, health insurance and retirement contributions. What follows are some of preliminary financial considerations:

What are your business prospects? Even as you start thinking about starting your own firm, it's important to analyze any immediate business prospects that you may have. Of course, you can't solicit firm clients when you're still working at the firm (more on that in Chapter 5), but you need to look critically at which, if any, clients, are likely to follow you to a new practice. In addition, consider what other possible sources of revenue are available. Perhaps you've got good relationships with other attorneys who might refer cases to you or send you contract work. Maybe you'll be approached by friends or family with legal matters that were too small to handle while at a law firm, but which could generate revenue at your own practice. Don't worry if you don't have a single client on the horizon, because you really don't need many billable hours to get started. Let's say that starting out you can find only one day's worth of billable work a week. At $125/hour, that's $1,000/week (or more, depending on the billable rate in your area). Granted, that's gross revenue; you've still got taxes and overhead. But if you trim your costs, you should be able to capture some profit from Day One. Moreover, by marketing yourself four days a week during the first few months, you should be able to generate leads for future cases.

Should you start a practice part-time? To make ends meet, many new solos consider working part-time at a law-related job while their practice is getting off the ground (see Chapter 17). Whether you jump fully into solo practice or not is a personal decision. Some argue that a solo law practice requires full-time commitment for success, and that working at it part-time compromises that commitment. Whether it's true or not in your own case, the revenue from part-time work will provide some financial security as you get your practice off the ground. And with that (along with some other revenue stream), you may feel less pressured to take any case that walks in the door, or to recommend a less-than-ideal settlement just so you can get paid.

What does it cost to open a law practice?

Years ago, when my husband and I were remodeling our kitchen, we were astonished at the range in cost of labor and materials. Considering all the combinations of appliances, cabinetry and surface treatments, the remodel could have cost us from $15,000 to $100,000. In the same way, the cost of starting a solo law practice can vary widely. And despite what you may have read or heard, the barriers—financial or otherwise—to opening your own practice have never been lower! As legal tech guru Dennis Kennedy (himself a solo and BigLaw expatriate) has noted, *Leasing, other payment plans, and the continuing drop in technology costs make it possible for big firm lawyers to equip themselves with better technology than they now have at their firms, for a very small initial outlay of capital. As a result, the financial barriers to moving to a solo or small firm practice have been greatly reduced.* Bottom line: you can open a solo law practice for a capital outlay of $3,000 or less to cover the basics: a valid bar license, a computer, a phone, an Internet connection, some type of online presence, business cards and malpractice insurance.

In my opinion, the biggest mistake a solo can make is to take on too much overhead at the beginning. For example, the strain of having to cover the cost of leased space AND a secretary could lead to foolish decisions such as accepting a case outside your expertise for less than your billable rate... or worse, borrowing money from client trust accounts to pay bills! In your first year or two, I suggest you grow into your needs.

- Work exclusively from home
- Work partly from home and maintain a virtual space, arranging with a local business center to provide a local phone number and mailing address, as well as appointment access to office space and support services.
- Sublet space from a firm or another attorney
- Join forces with a couple of other lawyers

There are those who would argue that you might not be taken seriously working from a home office, and that you should lease space to impress clients. Would this be true for your practice? I know several attorneys with successful regulatory or IP practices who serve a national clientele. Even though they could easily afford a downtown space, they maintain a home office because their clients never visit, and because leased space would be an unnecessary cost. For additional thoughts on the matter, see Chapter 6.

What are your financial obligations?

Student loans. If student loans are your main financial worry, you have several options: you can try to extend your payment period to decrease the amount that you pay each month. Of course, this means you might not finish paying off loans until 20 years after you've graduated... at a time when you may want to focus on a college fund for your children. Most student loans allow you to defer payment for some period of time. During this period, you could take the money that you would ordinarily spend on loan repayment and put it into your firm. By the time the deferral period ends, it's likely you would have enough business to cover the loans yourself. You might also inquire whether your law school offers a loan-forgiveness program. Many law schools repay several thousands of dollars in loans to students who hold public-interest jobs. Starting a solo practice isn't likely to qualify; still, if you've chosen a practice area like consumer law, criminal defense or another with a public interest bent, you could make a plausible argument for seeking loan-forgiveness. If you're currently working, and think you may want to start a practice in the future, do your best to pay down as much of your loans as you can now. That way, when you do start your firm, you'll have one less expense to worry about.

House as piggy bank. Depending on prevailing interest rates, a home-equity credit line or mortgage refinance offer two options for generating money for living

SHOULD I FIRST SAVE A YEAR'S LIVING EXPENSES?

Some law practice management experts caution against solo'ing without having saved at least a year's worth of living expenses. Sensible in theory, but most practicing solos (myself included), might never have hung out a shingle if we followed that advice.

If you ask me, the one-year rule depends on your type of practice. For example, if you intend to handle only large class-actions, or personal injury matters, on an exclusively contingency basis, then, yes, you'll need enough savings to see you through to a settlement or verdict. But unless you're planning to handle only contingency matters, and you're unwilling to take any billable work, a sizeable nest egg—certainly a year's worth—isn't as important. And let's be honest, the one-year rule just isn't feasible for some lawyers. Those who were unexpectedly laid off, or who are working in dead-end, low-paying jobs, don't have the luxury of setting aside that much cash, and these are precisely the individuals who would benefit the most from starting a practice.

One more thought: unless you're independently wealthy or have a high-paying job, the process of setting aside a year's worth of expenses takes time…months, even years…during which you may get so discouraged and depressed about your existing job that your work suffers and you get fired anyway! Or, your spouse grows unhappy with his or her own job and quits first, thus preempting you from making your own break…or your courage fails you, and by the time you recover, your life circumstances are different…or you have another child or one on the way, or a larger mortgage, or you need to establish a college fund. Any or all these changes in circumstance could preclude, or at least delay, your going solo. Having a year's worth of expenses would definitely ease your mind and reduce your risks when you start out. But waiting until you reach the one-year benchmark carries risks of its own. ●

expenses. A line of credit can provide a safety net if you need it; you pay back only what you actually use. With refinancing, you might obtain a lower interest rate on your mortgage that decreases your monthly payments and frees up money for your firm. Or, you can increase your mortgage and cash out some of your home's equity during refinancing and use that money for start-up expenses. When you draw on your home equity, you can also deducting the interest at tax time.

Other sources of financing.

Credit cards and small business loans are other sources of financing for getting a law firm off the ground. Just as with overhead, you've got to be careful not to overextend yourself. Before you take out a business loan or rack up credit card debt, make absolutely sure that you can't eliminate anything else from your budget. Also, limit your draw to the bare minimum.

Getting a Second Opinion

Back in law school, when you were trying to decide whether to take a clerkship, or which firm you should join, you could always consult with a professor, a career advisor, or an alum. And the chances were good that someone knew, or had heard about, a judge who had a clerkship to offer or who had contacts at the firms you were considering. But where do you turn if you're thinking about starting your own small practice? The legal profession has grown so stratified that many large-firm or government attorneys don't know any colleagues who've started their own practice. In fact, there are many excellent resources, and more all the time.

Below, are just a few of those you will want to seek out…and those you will want to avoid:

Bar and LPM programs. Many local bar associations have Law Practice Management (LPM) advisors able to offer a wealth of information on starting a law firm. Typically, you can set up a meeting with an LPM advisor by contacting the bar. There's usually no cost for an initial meeting. An LPM advisor can fill you in on many of the details unique to starting a practice in your jurisdiction, and may be able to refer you to other attorneys who you can call for advice. You can also learn about various support groups or mentoring programs that are available to solos through some local bars. For a roster of JD-trained career counselors and coaches around the country, go to *DecisionBooks.com* or *LawyerAvenue.com*.

Friends or colleagues. When I started out, I was fortunate enough to have a close law school friend who, along with a partner, started a general practice about a year earlier. Though I intended to focus on a different area of law, it was inspiring to talk things over with a peer who'd already taken the plunge. A year later, I was able to pass along the favor to another friend who was thinking about starting his own criminal defense firm. If you don't know any other solo practitioners, join a solo practitioner's listserv (i.e., the ABA's *solosez.net*), or seek out the growing number of blogs that focus on starting a practice. Of course, sometimes destiny takes a hand. I remember flipping through the Yellow Pages for an attorney who could help me decide whether to file suit over my dismissal from my law firm. As it turned out, the lawyer with whom I consulted had graduated law school the same year as myself, and had started his own practice a year earlier. In the course of the consultation, he shared some of the ups and downs of a new solo. He was the right person at the right time, and the experience helped me imagine what my own practice might be like...and I liked what I saw.

My advice is to seek out a broad sampling of solo attorneys:

- Someone who started a firm when they were at the same place in life that you are now.
- Someone who shares your particular practice area, and who can help you analyze the viability of your business plan or to tip you off to related fields where you can expand.
- Someone a little older who can provide a wealth of advice on such practical issues as dealing with clients, resolving ethical dilemmas, and generally keeping things in perspective.
- Someone, perhaps an expatriate from government or BigLaw, who can share their own early struggles to become a solo practitioner.

Your spouse. In solo practice, you're in charge...but never forget the one partner with whom you must consult (again and again and again) is the partner with whom you live. Make no mistake, solo practice can be hard on a marriage or live-in arrangement. And if your spouse or significant other isn't on board 100 percent with your desire to open a law practice, it will make things difficult for both of you. Some of the impacts are predictable: the family will probably need to trim expenses—at least for awhile—as the practice gets off the ground. Then, too, roles and responsibilities are certain to change. For example, just because your new schedule is more flexible, it might be assumed you can do more things around the house, or that you have the responsibility of picking the kids up from school. You, of course, will want to focus all of your available time on building your new firm, and you believe it would be unrealistic to take on all kinds of new household chores. Or, maybe you feel so guilty for requiring your partner to make so many sacrifices that you overcompensate, and start spending even more time on household matters to the detriment of your new practice. Opening a new practice is one of a couple's biggest challenges. So, when you and your spouse or partner sit down for a frank discussion, talk about everything; avoid surprises down the line. Starting a solo practice is challenging enough without adding domestic stress.

Should You Reveal Your Plans at Work?

Unless one of your colleagues at work is a personal friend, it's best NOT to reveal your plans prior to leaving (the obvious exception being if you discover that another colleague wants to solo, and you decide to partner up).

Once a firm hears of a possible departure, the partners assume the worst and usually activate all their defense systems to secure clients, supplies, and other firm resources. Why would a firm be afraid of you going solo? Because law firms are one giant living ego, and any threat—no matter how remote—usually raises suspicion. So be discrete. The other reason to be less than candid about your plans is the naysaying from colleagues. Just at a time when your deliberations are fresh and your optimism high, your colleagues may try to convince you that your plans are nothing less than career suicide. Or, if you work for a government agency or claims department, where risk-averse co-workers bide their time in dead-end jobs, they might be quick to point out the folly of leaving the security of a solid job. You might even encounter naysaying from solos themselves. Disgruntled or unsuccessful solos may try to discourage you from starting a firm because they can't stand the idea that you might succeed where they could not.

Note: The foregoing advice assumes a) that your firm shows no indication of letting you go, or b) that it doesn't suspect that you're considering leaving. Any change in the status of A or B—i.e., you're notified that you will be terminated, or the firm learns you wish to leave—will trigger automatic changes in your relationship at the firm. Under these circumstances, there would be only minimal risk if you floated the possibility of looking for other opportunities, including starting your own firm.

Three Essential Questions

In the final analysis, the decision to start your own law firm may be more art than science, more instinct than reason. After you've examined your motivation, analyzed your business prospects, and engaged in exhaustive self-reflection and self-evaluation, the answers to three essential questions may well determine whether your new solo practice succeeds... or not:

1. Are you willing to do what it takes to establish your firm?

Solo practice makes the greatest demands in areas where you have the greatest... and the least... competency. You will have make cold-calls in search of new business, reason with unreasonable clients, and, as a newcomer, face humiliation in court. You may find yourself photocopying documents at two in the morning, or searching the library for digests to find a case not available through LEXIS. Every solo can tell you stories about the most desperate thing they had to do to salvage a case or keep their firm afloat. If you're willing to do what it takes, chances are good you will succeed.

2. Are you confident with your lawyering skills?

A solo practice puts so many nonlegal demands on your plate ...from marketing and administrative arrangements to hand-holding clients...that your legal abilities have to be a given. Having the legal ability to start a firm doesn't really depend on your actual skills, *i.e.*, whether you've actually deposed a witness or drafted articles of incorporation. Rather, it is having the belief that you can handle any case with the training you had in law school, at your previous job, and with any follow-up research. No doubt, more practice will perfect your lawyering skills, but, at a minimum, you need to believe that

---

MAKING THE LEAP

Wayne Cohen, a well-known personal injury lawyer in Washington D.C., began his career as an associate at a major D.C. law firm, and years later wrote what it was like to transition from BigLaw to a solo practice (So You Want to Be A Trial Lawyer; Washington Legal Times, May 26, 2003):

"When I began my legal career at Shaw Pittman, a large firm based in Washington D.C., I would have given 1,000-to-1 odds to anyone who wanted to bet that one day I'd become a "personal injury lawyer." The idea never crossed my mind. And why would it? Even as a first-year associate, I enjoyed the benefits that a major firm had to offer: a well-equipped gym, a wonderful dining area, a squash court and a secretary. (But) the reality of life in a large firm is that young lawyers don't see courtrooms. They see their offices...they see libraries...they see rooms filled with documents. But they don't see courtrooms. So, to go from the prestige of one of the largest law firms in Washington to the obscurity of a solo practice focusing on personal injury cases was a big leap. Shortly after I gave notice, I overheard a few colleagues commenting that maybe I had gone mad. *'Is he really going to be a P-I lawyer?'* someone asked. *'That's disgusting...nuts,'* said another. Partners at the firm came to me to persuade me to stay, and even my assigned mentor spent hours trying to get me to change my mind: *'Wayne,'* he said, *'You're on track to have an excellent career here. Don't do this. Don't throw all it away.'* I didn't listen. I knew that I wanted to try cases. I wanted to right some wrongs; I wanted to help people who truly needed my help. So I gave notice, and hung out my shingle. I had no money, no cases, and no immediate prospects. But I had the chance to be the kind of lawyer I had dreamed about."

Note: A decade later, Cohen's solo practice has grown into a seven-lawyer firm (Cohen & Cohen), and—one year alone—he tried 18 jury trials. ●

---

with hard work you can perform a serviceable job every time out of the gate. However, if you see law as rocket science—something that takes years of practice—solo'ing will be difficult because you'll always feel unsure and obsess over each document before going on to other matters.

3. Will you regret it? Social science tell us that human beings suffer regret only for experiences we want but do **not** yet have…not for experiences we have had regardless of their outcome. So, if, after extensive consideration, you're still on the fence about starting your own firm, you might as well go for it. Of course, it carries the inevitable risks; after all, you're leaving behind security, stability, and probably a decent group of colleagues. But even if starting your own firm turns out to be a disaster, you'll have the satisfaction that you had the courage to try. You'll only experience regret if you don't grab for the brass ring.

IN THEIR OWN WORDS

Q: Who was the biggest help when you were just starting out?

- Scott Wolfe (class of 2005)—"My attorney friends. Specifically, an attorney who represented my father in the past. He was one of my father's attorneys, and he and I had become friends from that relationship. He fielded all of my questions, and was a great ear for some of my rookie problems. Also, it should not go unmentioned that I subscribed to a few e-mail solo lists. I was able to ask practically any legal question to these e-mail lists and get a quality answer back within minutes."

- Walter James III (class of 1987)—"A couple of lawyer friends of mine helped me steer the shoals of what software to get, what hardware to buy, what to lease, and how to get a line of credit. Those guys were also great from a morale standpoint as well."

- Denny Esford (class of 2003)—"I have a mentor I met during a law school internship, and a couple of other attorneys that I do litigation work for periodically, and they have been a good source of substantive help with the law and moral support. I recently joined the ABA's *solosez.net* that I use to get quick answers and point me in the right direction when I am stumped or feeling a bit overwhelmed.

- Jill Pugh (class of 1994)—"Spouses are KEY in having a solo practice. I know this from both ends of the spectrum. My first husband was not supportive at all, and also did not pick up any household chores, so I was pretty much in charge of everything. It was a terrible drain and hindered my ability to grow my practice. My second husband has been terribly supportive—in terms of helping me think like a business person, in terms of marketing, helping the technology side of my practice, and helping make sure the household chores are done. I have so much more energy to devote to my practice with a supportive husband!"

To read the complete interviews, go to Appendix 6. ●

CHAPTER 3

Solo'ing Out of Law School

"Think carefully about whether you're the solo type.
Not only should new grads prefer to be their own
boss, they must also be disciplined for it. The legal
and business requirements will come with time and
effort, but to be a successful solo comes down to an
ability to be one's own boss, and to feel confident
enough to put your money and future on the line."

—SCOTT WOLFE, SOLO

Many new grads feel that if they want to establish their own practice eventually, then why not solo right out of law school?

And some do, and they go on to build a lucrative practice. But is it the best choice for you?

It depends.

If you've come to law from another career, starting your own firm right away might make sense. You probably have existing business contacts who could serve as clients, and your financial situation is no doubt more secure than that of a new grad. Also, fair or not, law firms often discriminate against older or second-career lawyers, preferring to hire younger and, presumably, more impressionable graduates.

But if you come to law as a first career, there are different issues: it's not so much your lack of practical experience. After all, many lawyers employed for years at a large firm or a government agency have most likely never filed a complaint, served a subpoena, or taken a deposition on their own. What new graduates usually lack are the references, the social contacts, the connections, the professional exposure, and the reputation that a previously-employed attorney has developed through legal networking, participation in bar associations, and writing articles. Such activities, far more than actual work experience, matter most when a young attorney starts a practice. Even a good word from a partner at a prestigious law firm, or a judge for whom you've clerked, might help you bring in a contract work to pay your bills while you work on drumming up a client base. In my own case, some of my earliest referrals, including a couple of appeals at the DC Circuit, came from an energy attorney whom I had helped a couple of times while working at a federal agency. When I started my practice, he returned those favors many times over by sending assignments my way.

While solo'ing directly out of law school has undeniable heroic appeal, the young new lawyers who spend even a year or two at a post-law school job reap other benefits:

For starters, there are financial considerations. Because the results of the summer bar exam typically don't issue until fall, lawyers solo'ing right out of school lose a couple of months while awaiting admission. By contrast, most clerkships and government or law firm jobs don't require bar admission, which means that by late August a new graduate who's accepted employment can start collecting a paycheck and get a jumpstart on paying down student loans. Furthermore, by working for a year or two and living frugally, you can put a considerable dent in your student loans, relieving the financial pressure one typically experiences in the early days of solo practice.

Moreover, law firm jobs and clerkships give young attorneys many opportunities to learn about practicing law, even if they don't provide any hands-on experience. A new graduate who clerks for a trial or federal district court has the chance to make contact with local attorneys and to observe their different courtroom techniques. And clerks on the appellate level, through their review of countless briefs, gain a solid feel for what qualifies as persuasive legal writing.

Even grinding away as an associate, frantically tracking down obscure case law for a minor point in a 100-page memo... or proofing a document several times over... can teach skills that you'll use in solo practice. Working at large firms trains lawyers to meet deadlines and work accurately under pressure, and helps them develop an instinct for distinguishing between the tasks that impact the outcome of the case and those that are just busy-work designed to build up hours. As a result, when former BigLaw associates eventually go solo, they can tackle sophisticated matters and deliver the same top results at a fraction of a large firm's cost simply through their ability to prioritize tasks and focus on the essentials for getting the job done .

So if you're a new graduate who can't wait to get started on your own, weigh very carefully whether taking a position even for a year or two might help you attain even more success in the long run.

Solo'ing Out of Law School: The Pros & Cons

Pros:

No golden handcuffs. When you solo right out of law school, you don't suffer the loss of a six-figure income, or the sacrifice of such BigLaw perks as a secretary, BlackBerry, and expense-account that comes with firm life. As an ex-student, you're already accustomed to living frugally, and more likely to take in stride such cost-cutting sacrifices as sharing an apartment with roommates or subsisting on top ramen noodles until you get your practice off the ground. Moreover, with the exception of your student loans, you're less likely to have the sort of major financial expenses—e.g., mortgage, car loan, family health insurance policy—that often deter more settled lawyers from starting a law firm later on.

It may be the best option. Solo'ing right out of law school makes sense if you can't find a job as a lawyer. After three years in law school and passing the bar, you are fully qualified to practice as a lawyer. So, why waste your newly acquired skills working as a paralegal, or—if you're a second-career lawyer—returning to a position where a law degree isn't required because it's the only job you could find? Better to start your own practice now, and get your money's worth out of your law degree.

It's easier to seek help. As a new grad, you're less likely to feel awkward asking for help, or seeking out mentors than more experienced lawyers who might feel some embarrassment about reaching out for support.

The most direct route to what you want. Some argue that if you're really certain you want to start your own law firm right away, working for others only postpones the dream. And there's some logic to that: after all, if you take a law firm job and resent it, you might perform badly and get fired.

Cons:

Financial pressure. Even without a mortgage or other financial burdens, you may still have as much as $100,000 or $150,000 in student loans. And while you can defer—or spread out—your loan payments, there is no escaping the reality that your new solo practice will need to generate revenue right out of the gate. In this situation, you may feel pressure to take on unattractive cases or large amounts of low-paying, document-review projects just to pay rent. By contrast, if you work for someone else for a couple of years and live frugally, you can make a substantial dent in your student loans before opening your practice. And don't forget, many schools now provide loan-forgiveness for grads going to government sector or legal aid groups (in some cases, as much as $5,000 or $10,000 a year), so you needn't feel compelled to work for BigLaw to start paying down your loans.

Lack of contacts. You need time to build up an established network of professional contacts to serve as a source of referrals and references. In fact, it's generally accepted that most new solos need as many as three years to establish a network (which is why most new solos don't truly hit their stride until their third year of practice). By contrast, if you start your legal career working for a firm, the government, or some other employer, you can use the time for networking—participating in bar activities, attending conferences, and meeting other lawyers through your job. Then, when you're ready to start your own practice, your network will have been set up.

You may not be taken seriously. Most clients don't ask or particularly care about how much experience you have. But other lawyers are more particular; they may inquire about your level of experience when considering whether to refer you cases or to hire you for contract work. The fact is, many lawyers hesitate to refer good cases to a lawyer straight out of school because they have no assurance the work will be performed competently. But if you go to work for a few years, particularly for a well-known firm or judge, other lawyers may feel more comfortable about sending you cases, and then—

In reply to a student's online post about solo'ing right out of law school, law practice management expert Jim Calloway, wrote:

"...There are no shortage of 'experts' who would urge you to jump into solo law practice right after graduation, or people like myself who would urge you to be cautious. There is much to recommend the lifestyle of a solo practitioner. But the question is, *'What is the best way for you to get there?'* I strongly disagree with your suggestion that if solo'ing after graduation doesn't work out, you can always try to get a job. That simply doesn't reflect real life or the marketplace. In my opinion, your employment chances are far greater right out of law school than if you were to apply after a year or two of solo practice. There are always exceptions to the rule, but, generally speaking, if you open a solo practice right out of law school...and then apply for positions a year or two later...you may be viewed as someone who didn't succeed with the practice. Not only by the large firms, but many medium and small firms as well.

"I would be more optimistic if you said that you were going to move back to your hometown...or to a smaller city...to do family law, bankruptcy law, or to set up a general civil practice. But moving to (a large city in the Southwest) to do real estate and environmental law when you have almost no experience, no contacts, or potential clients, is a tall order. Certainly it can be done and it has been done, but the difficulty in doing it today is more than it was a decade ago or even a couple of years ago.

"The problem with starting a new solo law practice right out of law school is that you combine all of the challenges of starting a new business with a great deal of theoretical knowledge but little idea of how to do many legal tasks from beginning to end. A couple of years spent learning how to do some things, and then developing some client relationships (some of whom might even follow you to the new solo practice when it opens) could greatly increase your chances for success when you do open your law practice. So, if your ultimate goal is to set up a solo practice with a focus on real estate and environmental law, one way to get there might be to focus your job hunt on firms that do that sort of thing in your (target) city. And don't limit it to the larger firms that interview at the law schools. There are a lot of great opportunities with firms of 20 lawyers or less.

"...I don't mean to sound like a wet blanket, but I thought you deserved a more balanced response. My point is that no one with a large student loan debt, and no client prospects, should turn down a decent job offer right out of law school if one is forthcoming...and it doesn't have to be a six-figure salary either. (If you do decide to solo), the amount of starting capital will be a huge factor. It is possible to start on a shoestring, but it's more comfortable not to have to do so. Even for the lawyers I counsel who open a new practice in the small town county seat towns of Oklahoma, I suggest a minimum of $20,000. It would be a lot more in your city, and it's doubtful you would get a bank or SBA loan without pledging collateral.

"Just my opinions, along with my wishes for success with whatever path you choose."

Jim Calloway (jimc@okbar.org) is director of the Oklahoma Bar Association Management Assistance Program. ●

from time to time—you can ask for a referral from your former boss.

No safety net. If, despite your best efforts, solo'ing doesn't work out, or you don't enjoy the solo experience, it will be much tougher to find law-related employment without references from a prior employer (unless you can bring a significant amount of business to a new firm). As unfair as it may be, potential employers may assume that you started a firm directly out of law school because you couldn't find a job. By contrast, most lawyers who've previously been employed can generally find another job more easily even after having spent several years as a solo. Bottom line: if you want to leave yourself some options for other careers in the law down the line, you're better off working a few years for others before starting a firm.

Paths to Solo Practice

Suppose you do decide against going solo right out of law school, but you see yourself hanging a shingle sometime in the future. Some career advice:

Reject conventional wisdom. Think twice before going to work for another solo or small firm (three lawyers or less) if what you want is hands-on experience. Solos and small firm lawyers are very busy, and may not have time to mentor a new lawyer or the resources to send you to training or to CLE courses. Moreover, it's generally easier to move from a larger firm, or other legal employment position, to a small firm than the other way around. If, however, you decide to work for a small firm, make sure to find out how much training the firm provides.

Give preference to one-time opportunities. Some jobs, like judicial clerkships or government agency honors programs, are only available to new graduates and can help set you apart when you start your firm. For example, clerking at the trial level in a state or federal court gives you an opportunity to observe lawyers in court, and to get a sense of what practices are most effective. Moreover, as a law clerk (particularly on the trial level), you'll get to know some of the lawyers who practice before your judge. As for government positions—either at an agency honors program or a DA's or Public Defenders' office—you also have a chance to develop contacts with opposing attorneys. Moreover, government positions typically provide top-of-the-line training and great first-hand experience.

Make a name for yourself. No matter where you land after law school, it's never too early to start building your reputation. Take steps to get your name in circulation from the outset of your career—by starting a blog, or serving on a bar committee, or offering to co-author articles with a more experienced lawyer. Making a name for yourself will help advance your career whether you solo or not.

Don't be too quick to reject BigLaw. Large firms can be great stepping-stones for a future solo. For starters, a BigLaw salary can help you pay off a substantial portion of law school debt. In addition, large firms can afford to pay for multiple bar memberships for you, training programs, CLE courses, and industry-specific conferences to help you help establish a base of contacts. In addition, you can learn about marketing and career-building from the firm's marketing staff and associate outreach lawyers. Many firms also provide excellent pro bono opportunities from which you can get valuable hands-on experience. And while a large firm may not teach you about general practice areas like family law or wills and trusts, working in BigLaw can help you develop a specialization in areas you couldn't master on your own, such as health care law, copyright and intellectual property, and environmental law. To a solo, such specializations can be lucrative because they enable you to attract business clients (which generally pay better than consumers), or to provide "of counsel" services to other firms.

Don't wait too long. If you do accept employment right after law school, don't wait too long—no more than five to six years—before starting your own practice. After that, life may have other plans: house, family, the seductive appeal of a steady paycheck, and the possibility a spouse will lose their job or decide to stay home with the kids. And there's always the possibility that colleagues or co-workers may try to talk you out of starting a firm. Remember: just as there are risks to starting a firm too soon, there are risks that you won't start a firm at all if you work too long for someone first.

NETWORKING FOR YOUNG LAWYERS   *Jessica Adler, Esq.*

Q: What kinds of networking opportunities are open to young lawyers?

A: With so many different bar associations, it's just too expensive to join them all. It's better to be selective. Pick one, or a few, that you find interesting or relevant to your career path. In my own case, the Women's Bar Association of the District of Columbia turned out to be a great way to become involved as a young female lawyer. And since I specialize in family law, I have also joined the family law sections of the mandatory bars. Typically, bar associations make it easy to network. Some have reduced membership dues for young lawyers, while others have Young Lawyers sections. And then there are all the many *non-legal* networking opportunities: pro bono work, religious groups, alumni associations, or activities specifically targeted to your practice. For networking to be effective, though, you need to get involved, to circulate your name, and to meet people. In this way you earn their respect, their trust, and—hopefully—their referrals.

Q: What are the benefits of networking?

A: Over time, the benefits of networking are indisputable. The process of building personal relationships not only helps with client development but also with career opportunities. Once you are a trusted colleague, more people will want to refer business to you, hire you, or recommend someone else to you. My own career began at a very small firm, and then I moved to a slightly larger firm. While at both firms, I networked through the bar associations and through other organizations. Less than seven years after I graduated from law school, I opened my own solo firm practice. Networking has become my main source of clients.

Q: Many of the bar committees that I would like to join are headed by big firm partners. How can a young lawyer get his foot in the door?

A: Start small. Join a committee and show up regularly to demonstrate that you are dedicated. Volunteer to help or to assume a leadership role. Talk to as many people as possible. Invite some of the leadership to lunch or coffee, and ask about getting more involved in the committee. You may even find a mentor this way.

Q: As a junior lawyer on a committee, I'm worried I'll get stuck with grunt work. How can I avoid it?

A: You may get stuck with grunt work when you first get involved in a committee. But in doing so, you prove yourself as dedicated and hard-working. In time, you will work up to more substantive and meaningful assignments. If you do want to avoid the grunt work, get involved with smaller bars or sections. There are always bar associations and committees who are short on volunteers and would be thrilled to have the help. Study their newsletter or Web site to see where you are most needed and can get involved as a young lawyer. Try to come up with innovative ideas for a committee and volunteers to implement. Another option: partner up with someone more senior in order to get your name out, and you will then have access to the senior attorney.

Jessica Adler is a Washington D.C.-based solo.

Q: Will clients trust, or even hire, a new solo?

A: Yes, because most people don't know how little one is taught in law school. When I opened my practice, I always candid with prospective clients. I'd tell them, '*I've been practicing four months and haven't handled a case like this before, but this is the approach I would take*'. And then I would describe how I proposed handling their matter. When I finished, I'd say something like, '*I just want to let you know up front that because I'm new, I won't immediately know all the answers to your questions, but I will get the answers for you*'. And, then, depending on the size of the case, I might add: *... And if it looks like it's going to be a difficult situation, I won't be shy about asking a more experienced lawyer for help, or to call someone to take over the case if it's appropriate. I won't let pride get in the way. Handling your case correctly is the most important thing to me.* I used a variation of this, and it worked like a charm. People would say, *Okay. We'll go with you.* I was often sort of stunned, thinking, *Really? You will? Holy Cow!* It is my opinion that people want lawyers who will talk to them without talking down to them, who will work hard on their case, give them straight answers, and not charge them too much.

Q: What are the most important quality to succeeding right out of law school?

A: An entrepreneurial spirit. Skills can be learned, attitude can't. And then there's all the other ingredients to a lawyer's success that have nothing to do with the practice of law...like setting up and running an office. As the person in charge, you'll have to deal with the copier repair guy, the phone guy, the computer guy. You'll have to handle money issues, staff issues, upset or nonpaying clients, and make sure you reconcile your trust account on a monthly basis so it meets state reporting requirements. If you're thinking, *I don't want to deal with all that junk, I just want to be a lawyer*, you may not be solo material. If, however, you're thinking, *I can provide clients better service at a lower cost, and put more money in my pocket*, maybe you are cut out to be a sole practitioner.

Q: Do you know anyone who solo'ed right out of law school?

A: Yes, me. And, for what's worth, here's how I got my start: I went to law school in Ohio in the 1990s, and moved to South Carolina, where I took the Bar and opened my practice. My father had a business there, so I was able to work out of his office. That way I didn't need a copier, receptionist, conference room, or other office amenities. In the beginning, I did commercial leases, incorporation, real estate closings. I didn't have that much work (a good thing, too, because I didn't know what I was doing, and it took a long time to do even basic legal tasks). And after awhile, I learned I could handle most any matter as long as I was willing to spend three times as much time and effort as it would normally take with an experienced lawyer. As part of my education, I talked to, and lunched with, older lawyers. They threw me their scraps and cast-offs. Some of them were worthwhile and some weren't. In time, I learned what to look for. After six months, I hired a paralegal; within a year, I had two employees. We did a lot of real estate closings, and a fair number of car wreck cases.

David Swanner (info@davidvsgoliath) practices in Myrtle Beach SC. To read David's complete FAQ, go to Chapter 17.

Q: What would you tell new grads about solo'ing?

- Grant Griffiths (class of 1997)—"There is so much to cope with when you are a solo right out of law school. Sometimes I felt like I had no idea what I was doing. Not that it can't be done…just that you have to be careful not to allow yourself to be overwhelmed or think that you have to do everything yourself. That was my mistake. My advice: find a good paralegal or assistant. And, if you have a spouse/partner, listen to them and allow them to help. Don't do what I did; don't let your pride get in the way of accepting help and advice."

- Anonymous (class of 1993)—"If you think you might want to solo, go for it now (or early in your career), before the golden handcuffs go on."

- Jill Pugh (class of 1994)—"I think the biggest struggle for the solo practitioner is isolation. If you are a loner, I do not think you can truly succeed as a solo. You must have people you can brainstorm with, bounce ideas off, and ask for help. Certainly the era of the Internet and online listservs make this easier, but there still is no substitution for human contact. Not only do you need it to build your referral base, you need it so you have a shoulder to cry on when a judge or a client does something really stupid!

- Sergio Benavides (class of 2005)—"You need to have a good support network, and (considerable) savings to survive the slow times. Keep overhead low. Be choosy where you decide to invest your funds for building up the practice. And don't advertise. Most attorneys will tell you it doesn't pay off that well. I have found that to be true."

- Spencer Young (class of 1995)—"(What I would tell new grads) is that solo'ing may or may not be for them and that they should work in different environments…and know themselves…before making the decision. That they shouldn't solo by default (e.g. lay-off) or do it for the money. They should solo because they like the profession, have the guts, want to be their own boss, and they can deal with the ramifications of that decision."

- Sarah Meil (class of 2003)—"What I would tell new grads is, 'You can take on the big firms and you can beat them.'"

- Scott Wolfe (class of 2005)—"Think carefully whether you are the solo type. Not only should new grads prefer to be their own boss, but they must also be disciplined for it. There are a lot of benefits to being a solo practitioner…and a lot of responsibilities. The legal and business requirements will come with time and effort, but I think that to be a successful solo comes down to an ability to be one's own boss, and to feel confident enough to put your money and future on the line."

- David Abeshouse (class of 1982)—"There are two diametrically opposed schools of thought on the issue of whether to go solo right out of law school. For myself, I feel it was important that I had a good grounding in the substantive law via work experience, practice skills in general, and practice management, before I went solo. I'm sure I'd have made many more mistakes if I'd gone solo right from law school, and would have missed out on some excellent experiences. Others feel that a new grad can go solo, but I believe that it's much harder to concentrate your career in a given area or two if you do this (unless you had a previous career in a related area, such as if you were an insurance adjuster and then practice insurance law, or if you were a physician and then practice med-mal), and I believe that a broad general practice is far more difficult to succeed in than a practice with one or two focal areas of expertise."

To read the complete interviews, go to Appendix 6.

II. Planning the Great Escape

CHAPTER 4

A Course of Action

"If I'm going to work the hours of a litigation
attorney, I want to be the one who decides what cases
I take, and I want to reap the benefits without having
them go to a partner playing golf while I work all
weekend."—Jill Pugh, solo

Lawyers come to solo practice from different career paths and life stages, all of which impact the planning process. A lawyer who's spent a decade at a firm, and has already made the decision to solo, will plan differently than a second-year associate who's just been laid off. The more experienced attorney might try to establish a professional identity distinct from that of his firm, whereas a laid-off associate may decide to explore solo options while interviewing for a job. And what about lawyers, such as moms who've left the work force to raise a family, looking at solo'ing as a means to re-enter the legal field? They may have more time to launch a practice, but they also need to devote more time to establishing a professional identity after time off.

Whether you have 12 weeks or 12 months to get a practice off the ground, this chapter will help you identify and prioritize the tasks you need to accomplish.

Four scenarios

You're currently employed. You have the luxury of researching a solo practice and paying down your student loans while still collecting a paycheck. The downside is that you will be tempted to postpone your departure until you get that next bonus or bring in another client. If you're serious about starting a firm, give yourself six months to a year. If you still haven't left, you may wind up staying where you are.

You're not on a partnership track. You're either temping, or working full-time and have been notified you're not on the partnership track and will soon be downsized. In either case, the upside is that if you have decided to start your own firm, two to six months will be sufficient to get a bare-bones practice up and running. The downside is that you may not have decided you want to (or need to) start a solo practice. If so, expect to be splitting those precious last few months writing letters to, and interviewing with, prospective employers while *also* showing up at the office and doing a preliminary due diligence on starting a firm.

You've been terminated. You find yourself facing a sudden and unexpected termination. Either your firm has dissolved unexpectedly, or you committed an error that prompted your dismissal. In either case, you're probably too shell-shocked to ponder your next move. Right now, you must focus on what benefits (e.g., unemployment or health insurance) you can extract from your employer, and consider whether you have legal recourse for your termination. Once you come to terms with the situation (and get beyond the anger, frustration or depression), you will be able to start thinking more rationally about whether to start a law firm. The worst time to consider starting a firm is right after you've been fired. From personal experience, I can tell you that your confidence will be shaky and your abilities in doubt. If you have been let go, give yourself at least a few weeks to recover before thinking about your next steps.

You're not currently employed. In this scenario, you're currently a law student considering solo practice right out of law school, or perhaps a lawyer who voluntarily left the law to raise a family, and is now seeking to make a re-entry. In this case, you will have some flexibility to follow a slightly longer time-frame in planning a practice (particularly, if you're a new grad, since you won't even get your bar results until a few months after you take the bar).

When You Know You're Going to Leave:

The Countdown. Do you anticipate opening your firm in six to twelve months? If so, get to work now on raising your professional visibility.

If you're at a firm, don't worry that your firm might benefit from your efforts; your own benefit will be greater. For example, if you present a paper at a bar conference, a prospective client will call you not your firm. And if you've already left the firm, you're still ahead; the prospective client associates you—not your firm—with the speech. Prospective clients or referral sources always remember the person not the affiliation. Note: most of the opportunities to increase professional visibility have long lead times. The trade conference for which you wish to propose a paper might not be held for six, eight, even 12 months. And the blog you start next week might not attract a loyal following for a while. In short, many reputation-building activities may not pay off for months...maybe years. So don't use the excuse that you're still employed to postpone what you should have been doing: making a name for yourself.

There's nothing unethical about asking ask your firm to pay for bar dues, or the types of seminars it ordinarily would subsidize, so long as you make sure the firm accrues the same benefits from your attendance as it would if you were not leaving. Use discretion and common sense. Obviously, putting in a reimbursement form for a CLE class on *How to Start a Law Firm* or, *Defending Clients As a Court-Appointed Attorney* benefits only you personally. At the same time, asking the firm to cover costs associated with a course on issues within the firm's practice area is a fair request, provided that you summarize the proceedings in a memo to the file, or make sure that the firm gets a copy of the conference attendance list for its contacts database (though you can keep a copy for yourself). So long as the firm obtains value from its investment, you're not cheating the firm. Plus, if your business development pays off and you reel in a large client down the line after you leave, you can repay your firm by hiring it to help with overflow work.

Increasing your professional visibility

Send papers to conferences. Go online and start searching for the conferences in your practice area that have issued calls for papers. Most trade shows and conferences begin soliciting papers at least six months in advance, and all that is usually required at the beginning is a two-page abstract. Note: some big-name conferences extend preference to existing members who are active in the organization, but many are always looking for new names and ideas to fill the program. For details, see the section on *Speaking Engagements* (Chapter 14).

Write articles. Law reviews and monthly bar magazines once served as the only platform for lawyer-written articles. The Internet has changed everything; these days, it has never been easier to get published. You can still pursue law reviews and the legal trades to highlight your expertise. In the meantime, consider drafting 750-2,500-word articles or op-eds for web sites and online publications, in addition to weekly legal media and local or national newspapers.

Start a blog. These days, the fastest way for lawyers to make a name for themselves is by blogging. Consider the case of Howard Bashman, one of the blogosphere's legal luminaries. In 2002, Bashman launched a blog (*appellateblog.com*) devoted exclusively to appellate litigation. Though it began while he was still a partner at a BigLaw firm in Pennsylvania, Bashman's blog was a personal project he undertook on his own time. Within six months, his analysis, his prolific postings (several times a day), and his monthly feature—*20 Questions For an Appellate Judge*—generated several thousand hits a day from reporters, attorneys, federal judges, professors, and law clerks. Two years later, Bashman opened a solo practice, and his online visibility continues to generate business for his new firm and enhance his reputation as a nationally recognized appellate expert. It's never too soon to start a blog. Kevin O'Keefe recently posted about a law student who started a blog while still in law school about his dreams of solo'ing. As a result, the blog gave him national exposure and he wound up with a job at a law firm instead (see *kevin.lexblog.com/2007/05/lawyer-blog-success-stories/law-grad-lands-job-with-large-firm-by-blogging*). For blogging tips, read Grant Griffiths' *Top 10 Tips for a Successful Blog* (Chapter 15). And for information on a lawyer's blogs rights, go to Chapter 5 (*What's Theirs, What's Yours* and *Who Owns the Blog?*).

Networking. Of all the articles and books on business networking, you probably won't find reference to what I call *double-duty networking*. It's a high-value activity exclusive to lawyers who are still sorting out whether to go solo, but who are already making the rounds in search of work. Double-duty networking considers that every lawyer with whom you interview is a potential source of business or contract work down the road... if you *should* ever go solo. So, keep track of who you meet, and how they may be able to help if you do open a practice. Likewise, any classes you take can lead to networking opportunities. You might meet other lawyers with leads on inexpensive office space, or who are looking for others so as to qualify for a group discount for online legal research services or some type of billing or litigation software. You might also find lawyers with complementary practices with whom you can develop a relationship for cross-referral.

Changing your mind-set. At most of the BigLaw-dominated events that I attend, the large firm and government attorneys usually huddle together, showing little if any enthusiasm for conversation—let alone exchange business cards—outside their circle. Moreover, after events that involve a speaker, these same lawyers usually race back to their offices rather than introduce themselves to other attendees or the speaker. On the rare occasion I have been able to engage one in conversation, he or she comes across as bored and uninterested, or suddenly preoccupied with the pile of papers on their desk at the office. Talk about anti-networking! As you begin thinking about solo'ing, it is critical—really, absolutely critical—that you change your mindset about networking. If you see this sort of human interchange as an unpleasant task from which to retreat, you rule out serendipitous possibilities. As the clock ticks down towards starting your law firm, do find a way to get comfortable with this new perspective on networking... because it will make all the difference to your revenue stream.

Investigate new substantive areas

Starting a law firm isn't just a matter of procedure, as some how-to books on solo'ing would have you believe. You also need to prepare yourself substantively to serve clients, to avoid malpractice, and to diversify your skills so can expand your market. For example, if you're starting a firm and hope to gain some real litigation experience, or take on court-appointed work, you will probably want to sign up for training courses. If you have a narrow specialty that may not sustain a practice, explore related practice areas so you can leverage your existing experience. Of course, all this supposes you have some lead time. If not, put off the substantive preparation until after you open your doors. Better yet, squeeze in substantive classes while you're still employed, or, if you're a student, while waiting for your bar results. If you are still working somewhere, you can sign up for a relevant seminar on the firm's dime, though be sure to write up a summary so the firm shares in the benefit.

Below are some suggestions for substantive preparation:

Training courses. For basic training on wills and estates, domestic relations, bankruptcy and consumer credit, forego all those costly CLEs in favor of training courses offered for *pro bono* attorneys. Such classes are taught by practicing attorneys with years of experience in the field, and who can explain the law. More importantly, they can offer practice tips such as how to file a case, and the potential pitfalls not apparent from the statutes or regulations. In addition, many of your instructors will welcome an occasional phone call for assistance once you open a practice. Some of these *pro bono* trainings charge a *de minimis* fee, while others require you to agree to handle one or two small matters in exchange (though neither I nor anyone I know was ever actually sent a referral). If you plan on taking on court-appointed criminal work and lack experience, take a class. It will not only insulate your future clients from stupid mistakes, but the course will build your confidence, and help you make a better impression in the courtroom before the judge and other lawyers…all of whom are prospective referral sources. Sometimes, a public defenders' office or local bar section will offer a free or reasonably-priced course on criminal practice. Back when I started my firm, I took a free three-day sponsored by the public defenders' office and filled up 75 pages of notes, including a little *mantra to* recite when a client was arraigned.

Sign up for seminars in your practice area. Do you practice in a field where some important transition is underway? Perhaps a new law has been passed, or an agency has issued regulations that will bring about new changes. Such developments generate market opportunities: they create more work as clients scramble to deal with new uncertainty, and tend to level the playing field, giving younger attorneys a leg up on more established colleagues who no longer have the advantage of experience. Seminars, some of which can be costly, address these transitional issues. I suggest you sign up for the course while you're still employed and ask your firm to pay. Again, so long as you make a good impression for your firm while you're at the conference, and report back on what you've learned, the firm will get its money's worth. However, if you're unemployed or have just started a firm, approach a colleague and offer to attend the conference and provide written summaries in exchange for picking up or sharing the cost. Finally, see if any online webinars or lower cost local bar events will duplicate the more costly seminars. In my case, the DC Bar's Energy, Environment and Natural Resources Committee held bi-monthly brown-bag lunch talks on current topics in my field at a fraction of the cost of most industry-sponsored seminars.

Skills classes. At least in the early days of your firm, you'll probably perform most of the tasks, including court or deposition appearances, document-drafting, proofing, and document formatting. As time permits, you may want to take a course or find some training on, say, writing appellate briefs or using the electronic filing system down at the court. These are the sort of courses that you're usually too busy to take, but which can improve your practice. Where possible, make time to brush up on practice skills before you open your firm.

Fast cash solutions. Start exploring some of the fast-cash solutions discussed in Chapter 10. Some of these prospects may require some lead time; for example, you may need to take a training course which is only offered at certain times, or wait until projects are available. If you can put at least one or two fast-cash solutions in motion before you open your door, you'll help alleviate some of the financial stress you may feel once your salary comes to an end.

In which jurisdiction will you open your firm?

Ethics rules can impact your decision about where you can locate your office.

In my home state of Maryland, lawyers working from home must be licensed in Maryland, even if they only represent clients in those jurisdictions where they are licensed. So, suppose you're an attorney living in Maryland, and you are currently working at a large firm in the District of Columbia, where you're also licensed. If you wish to open a law firm, you have two options: a) open an office in the District of Columbia, or b) gain admission to the Maryland bar so that you can work from home. And if you choose b), there is another consideration: Maryland doesn't have reciprocity with other states, which precludes admission by waiver. So, to gain admission to practice in Maryland, lawyers must either take a full bar exam or the abbreviated practitioners' exam if they've practiced law for more than five years. Thus, a junior lawyer living in Maryland but licensed in D.C. faces a dilemma: do I invest the time and money to prepare for a full-blown bar exam so I can practice out of my house? Or, do I pay for office space in DC, and defer the decision about gaining admission to Maryland until I'm eligible for the practitioner's exam?

Ethics rules also need to be taken into account if you're thinking about waiving into another jurisdiction to expand your business opportunities.

Case in point:

Suppose you live in Washington DC and are licensed there and in New York, but you work at a national firm in DC whose clients are primarily in Northern Virginia? Up to now, the fact that you're not licensed in Virginia hasn't been an obstacle to representing Virginia clients because other lawyers in your firm are licensed there, and they sign off on the contracts you draft or they make an appearance with you in court. But now, after practicing for six years, you're thinking about starting a firm. You know that you must waive into the Virginia bar so that you can represent those Virginia clients. But what you may not know is that Virginia does not allow attorneys to gain admission by waiver *unless they provide evidence of their intent to maintain an office in Virginia* (such as providing an office address). Which means that if you want to work from your DC apartment and represent Virginia clients, you need to take the full bar exam. Or you can seek admission by waiver, but you'll have to set up shop in Virginia, which may not be particularly convenient if you're living in DC and don't have a car.

As you see, where you open your practice is no small decision. It's affected by where you live, where your potential clients are located, and the ethics rules of the jurisdictions where you practice. But in most cases, even though you still need to thoroughly investigate the applicable regulations, your current bar admissions will give you enough flexibility to get started (though you might still consider waiving into another bar in the future to expand your business opportunities).

SEVERANCE PAY VS. WORKING UNTIL THE END

Q: My firm just gave me notice that it will be downsizing some of its more senior associates, myself included. I have the option of staying on and working for four more months or taking a three-month severance pay with benefits. I'd probably like to look for a new job, but I am seriously considering starting a firm. Do I stay on for more cash...or take the money and run?

A: If you're ambivalent about starting a firm, my advice is to stay for the remaining months for several reasons. First, your firm may offer outplacement resources to identify potential employers (or prospective business opportunities, if you decide to go solo). Second, continued employment makes you more attractive to prospective employers, which will enable you to snag more interviews. Third, as long as you remain employed, albeit on your way out, your firm will most likely continue to cover your CLE, bar membership, conferences and other perks that will benefit you when you go solo. Finally, sticking around the firm and discretely mentioning the possibility of going solo along with other employment options could even lead to clients. In the last days at my firm, when I had announced that I'd be opening my own practice, someone working in the firm's supply room said he had a friend who needed an attorney for a misdemeanor matter. He hired me right a few days after I opened for business. Warning: remaining at a firm that's just fired you can be demoralizing. If staying on is too stressful, take your severance and leave. The extra month's pay and benefits just aren't worth your peace of mind. ●

What You Can Do Now?

If you're still on the fence about how to proceed...whether to solo or interview for another position...the circumstances in which you find yourself still demand action. It's the time when you need to move from blueprints to breaking ground. Which is why I believe you should not rule out job hunting at this juncture.

Here's why:

Many times when you interview for a job, a firm assumes that you're looking for full-time work, so it isn't likely to offer you part-time or *per diem* projects. But if, after going out on several interviews you still haven't landed somewhere, you can always approach firms where you've interviewed for that kind of work. That's what I did. After my firm handed me my notice, I hit the circuit, interviewing with most of the major energy regulatory shops in town. Though nothing panned out and I eventually started my own firm, I still kept contact with many of the lawyers I met on interviews. I sent an announcement to each of them when I opened my practice and followed up with annual holiday cards. A few years after I started my firm, I ran into one of the partners at a firm where I interviewed and re-introduced myself. Months later, the firm outsourced a lucrative piece of work to me on a contract basis.

And here's another benefit to interviewing now, especially if you practice in a specialized or niche practice area:

You can use the interview to get a sense of what other firms are doing and what other lawyers consider the "hot opportunities" for business development. You can use interviews to put your finger on the pulse of your industry, and to generate marketing ideas that you may want to pursue if you decide to start your own practice. Finally, interviewing for employment will help you solidify a decision on whether to start a firm. After you sit through one interview after another with lawyers who themselves can barely muster up any enthusiasm for describing their work, you just might experience that "aha moment" when you realize that you don't want to sign up for more of the same. If you've got three to six months until your current employment situation runs out and you remain ambivalent about going out on your own, I suggest you proceed on a parallel track: continue to explore the solo option even while you're sending out resumes. Just make sure that if you haven't found another job six weeks or so before the last paycheck, that you transfer most of your energy to getting your firm up and running.

Some additional thoughts about the best use of your time now (also see the Task Timeline in this chapter):

Spend now while you're earning. If you're still employed but on your way out, start making purchases for the new firm. Get your own laptop and business software, sign up for trade association or specialty bar memberships, purchase how-to guides, and subscribe to newsletters and journals relevant to your practice. If your firm typically pays for annual expenses like bar dues or licensing fees, try to time your departure so you won't have to pay these expenses for as long a period as possible. Also start paying down any outstanding loans to reduce future overhead.

Establish your business identity. Select a business name early that makes it easy to secure an Internet address. Select announcements and cards.

Set up your business entity. Most solos start out as sole proprietors and put off establishing a corporate structure until they've been practicing for a while (for details, see Chapter 6). However, if you decide at the outset that you want to set up a corporate entity (for example, if you're teaming up with another lawyer and you want protection against each others' possible acts of malpractice), you should form the corporate entity before you open for business. Some jurisdictions require disclosure of your corporate structure when using the firm name, so you'll need to have it in place to order your printed materials. Also, your corporate structure may dictate your record-keeping practices, and whether you need to register with a city or state licensing agency.

Identify office space. Whether you rent space or work from home, you need to settle that before you open for business. You needn't be wedded to your first location (see Chapter 6), but you do need to establish your mail, e-mail, and phone information for business stationery.

Set up bank and trust accounts. Your new checks should include your firm name, address and phone number. Your bar number, too, if you practice in a jurisdiction where your local court will only take law firm checks with a bar number. Your bank may also require a federal employee identification number (FEIN) to establish a business account. FEINs are issued by the Internal Revenue Service, and you can easily obtain one from the IRS Web site. Even if you're not sure that you'll hold money in trust for clients, you should set up a trust account when you open your bank account. The cost of setting up and retaining a trust account isn't significant, and if you do wind up requiring a retainer check from a client or receiving a settlement check, you'll have the account already in place so that you can cash the check without delay.

Purchase computer equipment. If you have a computer that is not shared with your spouse or your family, there's no reason you can't use it for your new practice…especially if you'll be working from home. If you decide to use an existing machine, set up a separate folder for law firm business, one that you back up regularly. If you decide to buy a new computer, make the purchase before you get start your practice, and stock it with whatever software packages you plan to use for word processing and billing.

Draft announcements. Draft a "new law firm" announcement for local bar publications, newspapers, and alumni paper. As soon as you open for business, drop the announcements into the mailbox or send them off via e-mail.

Prepare your Web presence. Law firms without a web site sacrifice credibility, even with less sophisticated clients. More importantly, they miss an easy opportunity to make a good impression on potential clients, and to give the appearance of being far more prominent and established than they actually are. Have your Web site operational from Day One. The site should be professional-looking, and include your resume and a few articles or simple "how to" lists and (if applicable) links to cases that you've handled. You may not have much to post on a Web site right away, but you can add materials as your firm grows (or start a blog as a companion to the site). At a minimum, you must have a Web site up and running from the day you open (see Chapter 15).

Establish your user accounts. If you practice before a court or agency that uses electronic filing, remember to set up user accounts and passwords in your law firm's name. Though you've probably used these accounts while still at your firm, you won't be able to continue to do so once you leave. And if your former employer relegated electronic filing to administrative staff, you'll want to sign up for a training or online tutorial. Electronic filing systems are typically user-friendly, but you don't to wait to test them out on the morning that you have a filing due. Setting up own registration right away will speed up the process of entering an appearance in ongoing cases for clients that you're able to take with you when you leave the firm.

Secure legal research service. You ought to have some online research service in place when you start. In some jurisdictions, lawyers have access to *Casemaker*, a legal research service that comes with the cost of bar membership. *Casemaker*, or *Versulaw*, a $20/month research service, supplemented by library research, may suffice for your initial research needs. In other jurisdictions, *LEXIS* or *Westlaw* are available free at the library, or can be purchased *per diem* on a project specific basis, which might allow you to forego purchasing those services for a while. Don't be shy about asking *LEXIS* and *Westlaw* reps for free trial subscriptions to test their service…and to accomplish some of your own research in the process. Though it may not be convenient to defer investment in online legal research, you'll be able to negotiate a better deal if you have a good sense of exactly what your needs are. While many of the sales reps for online research services are attorneys, many of them have never operated their own law firms and may misunderstand the needs of solo and small firm practitioners. Invariably, they will try to sell you an expensive package that bundles more information than you need, or they may pitch a special deal on a state specific law library which may not have much value if you focus on regulatory law. Worse, you might have to commit to a two- or three-year plan, which means that you're foreclosed from changing your plan if it turns out you decided on the wrong one. By waiting to procure online research service until you've been in practice for a couple of months, you'll be able to negotiate for an plan that's best tailored for your firm's unique needs.

Task Timeline

6 to 12 months in advance
- Join solo practice listservs (e.g., solosez.net).
- Read books, blogs, and Web sites on starting a law firm.
- Take a bar course on starting a practice.
- Read applicable ethics rules in your jurisdiction relating to starting a firm.
- Determine if you need to take another bar exam or to get a waiver process underway.
- Begin saving and paying down student loans.

3 to 6 months in advance
- *Priority*—If your departure is involuntarily, set up interviews even if you're undecided about whether to solo.
- *Priority*—Explore how to get your firm to pay for bar dues or insurance in the short term.

- *Priority*—Sign up for the next available bar course on solo'ing; meet with an LPM advisor.
- *Priority*—Investigate applicable bar dues and whether you need to gain admission or obtain a waiver.
- *Priority*— Read books on establishing a new practice.
- *Priority*—Develop an abbreviated business plan with preliminary ideas and goals.
- *Priority*—Investigate court-appointed programs.
- *Priority*—Get serious about saving and paying down loans.
- Identify potential clients within your firm; making yourself indispensable in their case.
- Register for CLE courses on potential practice areas.
- Investigate court-appointed programs, prepaid legal services, insurance company "counsel" lists.
- Increase your visibility in potential practice areas.
- Wait until your firm is established to start a blog or to write articles.
- Wait until just before your firm is established to take substantive training courses.

0-3 months in advance

- *Priority*—If you only have four months or less, and you've been fired/laid off, look into unemployment, student loan-deferrals, and other ways to stay afloat. Meet with an LPM advisor. And sign up for the local bar's next "how to start a law firm" workshop.
- Identify your office space and sign a lease if renting.
- Begin setting up your home office if you intend to work there.
- Set up a law firm bank account, and an IOLTA trust fund.
- Purchase computer and other office equipment.
- Secure your Internet address, and begin work on your Web site and/or blog.
- Order business cards and other stationery.
- Draft a firm announcement and identify places to send it.
- Draft a letter to potential clients.
- Give official notice to your employer, and leave all your cases in good order before departing.
- Wait on training, writing articles, and substantive courses until you're resolved to solo.

Resources

- Sign up for the ABA's *solosez.net*, an online forum for lawyers practicing alone or in a small firm setting, particularly those in firms of five or fewer lawyers. The ABA also publishes several books on the nuts and bolts of starting a practice, including *Flying Solo* (now in a 4th edition).
- Check out a few of the most active blogs for solos, including Grant Griffith's

Home Office Lawyer (*gdgrifflaw.com/home_office_lawyer*)...thepracticeblog.com, written by a team of three solos...Susan Cartier Liebel's blog (*susancartierliebel.typepad.com*)...Sheryl Schelin's blog (*theinspiredsolo.com*)...Chuck Newton's Third Wave Lawyer (*stayviolation.typepad.com/chucknewton*)...Rick George's Solo Lawyer (*futurelawyer.typepad.com/sololawyer*)...Enrico Schaefer's Greatest American Lawyer (*greatestamericanlawyer.typepad.com*)...Solo in Chicago (*soloinchicago.blogspot.com*)...and this author's own blog— *myshingle.com*.

- Sign up for seminars or workshops taught by a team of experienced solos in conjunction with the bar's Law Practice Management Advisor in your area. Bar classes are usually reasonably priced and held in the evening or on weekends. In addition to these classes, almost every bar publishes a practice-starting pamphlet or handbook which contains jurisdictional-specific information. Note: go to *myshingle.com/my_shingle/online-guide0505.html*. My blog has a list of state bar guides on starting a firm.

- Make an appointment with the law practice management experts in your area. They can help you sort out the issues common to new solos. How-to guides and conversations with solos in other jurisdictions will definitely help you decide whether or not to solo. But do set up an appointment with an LPM advisor from your state bar, and do take a course designed to launch a firm in the jurisdiction where you practice. In this way, you will be able to better comply with the jurisdictional laws where you're licensed.

- Note: if you need to gain admission to another state bar, put the process in motion early. And if you decide to waive into another state bar, you need to complete a lengthy application which will take several months to process. Of course, you will need to allow even more time if you need to take a bar exam in another jurisdiction. In addition to the time needed to study for the test, most bars ask that you register for the exam several months in advance.

See book updates at author's blog—www.MyShingle.com

Q: What role does risk play in a solo law practice?

- Jill Pugh (class of 1994)—"Risk and solo practice are synonymous. As rewarding as it is, solo practice is incredibly unpredictable and inherently risky. You bear the brunt of bad court decisions (especially in a contingency fee practice), and you bear the risk of clients who fail to pay."

- David Abeshouse (class of 1982)—"The prospective solo has to be able to stomach a fair bit of risk, because you ultimately have only yourself upon whom to rely. And that doesn't really change as long as you're a solo, although there are ways in which you can modify that effect (by using outsourcing judiciously, for example) over time."

- Traci Ellis (class of 1990)—"You have to be a risk-taker to own your own business…any business…but *especially* a law practice. In addition to cash-flow fluctuations, there is the added risk of malpractice claims by disgruntled clients."

- Sergio Benavides (class of 2005)—"My advice to new solos? Keep overhead low, build a good support network, and make sure you've got enough savings to survive the slow times."

Q: What legal or practice skills were you least prepared for?

- Arthur Macomber (class of 2003)—"Accounting."

- Sergio Benavides (class of 2005)—"Litigation. And the simple, day-to-day office management/secretarial skills."

- Spencer Young (class of 1995)—"The run-of-the-mill procedural stuff; the stuff they don't teach you in law school. Also, I had no idea how time-consuming it would be to track bills, deductions, expenses etc. Seems like that's half the job. It reminds me what one of my mentors once told me. He said, 'Spencer, start solo'ing when you're young. If I had learned how to run the business aspect of solo'ing at your age, I'd be a millionaire now.'"

- Jill Pugh (class of 1994)—"The first time I solo'ed, the skills I was the least prepared for were depositions. I had never attended a deposition much less taken one, and I had no idea what I was doing!"

- Scott Wolfe (class of 2005)—"I was very prepared for the business side of law. Ready for the accounting and bookkeeping, for the marketing, for the management of clients and employees and case load, and I had an intimate understanding of the bottom line. It's why I felt comfortable going into a solo practice straight out of law school. (But what I wasn't prepared for) was figuring out proper venue and jurisdiction…I had no idea how to actually file the paper with the clerk of court's office…and I didn't know how to properly request service—either in the sheriff's office or on a petition…"

To read the complete interviews, go to Appendix 6. ●

CHAPTER 5

The Great Escape

"When I first solo'd, I remember thinking, 'What have I done? I've just walked away from a six-figure salary plus bonuses.'" —Traci Ellis, solo

"My friends from law school were skeptical about my decision to solo. But I made it clear that because of my personality and my business background, I thought I would be more successful as a solo than in a firm environment." —Scott Wolfe, solo

Before you can make a fresh start, you need to sever ties with your existing employer.

Whether your departure is involuntary or voluntary, emotions and self-interest often contaminate the disengagement process. If you've been terminated, you may feel tempted to exact revenge by badmouthing the firm to clients or filching firm property; if you're leaving voluntarily, the firm may still try to lay claim to clients that you brought to the firm or serviced exclusively. When you disengage from your firm, you walk a thin line between protecting your rights and taking the high road. Of course, you should vigorously negotiate for what you're entitled to, whether it's a fair severance package if you've been terminated, or an assurance that the firm will promptly transfer files for clients who choose to follow you to your new practice. Whatever the circumstances, avoid lawsuits, badmouthing your firm, or skulking out with a pile of client files in the dead of night. Even in large metropolitan markets, the legal community is a much smaller place than you can imagine. In the long run, burning bridges or acting in an unprofessional manner will cost you many opportunities.

In this chapter, I discuss issues relative to disengaging from your firm, including involuntary departure (giving notice, negotiating benefits), voluntary departure, and the divisions of clients and assets.

Giving Notice

Involuntary departure. How you give notice depends primarily on whether your departure is voluntary or forced. Obviously, when the firm lets you go, your own notice is not as important since the firm already knows you're leaving. Under these circumstances, the only decisions you have are whether…and when…to announce that you are starting your own firm. During your final weeks, you should definitely mention the possibility of starting a firm as one of your options. If colleagues know you're thinking about solo practice, they may have ideas about other lawyers you might speak to, or may even have potential referrals. Many times, firms—or at least individual partners or associates—may feel badly or guilty about an economic-induced layoff, and will try to help you with possible leads. Firms sometimes make office space available on a temporary basis to a terminated lawyer who wants to start a firm. Even though you've been fired, assess the situation carefully. Don't make your plans for going solo sound too definite if you believe the firm may try to limit your access to client files, or worse, may contact your clients and tell them you've been let go, to prevent them from following you.

The voluntary departure. In many ways, departing a firm voluntarily is more difficult than if you'd been fired. Sure, you don't experience the same powerlessness and embarrassment as when you're told to leave. On the other hand, you still need to deal with colleagues who may feel betrayed by your departure, or who view your motives with suspicion, believing you want to steal clients or bring down the firm. Below are some do's and don'ts about disengaging. Note: leaving a government agency or in-house position is not as complicated because you don't have to address the issue of dividing clients or money, which is always the sticking point when lawyers leave a firm. At the same time, some recommendations, such as *always act professionally* apply no matter what position you leave:

Learn from others. Before you give your notice, investigate how your firm handled lawyers who left the in the past, and consult with a lawyer who has already left the firm. If that's not an option, make discrete inquiries about the firm's practices.

Consider the following questions:

- How has the firm treated departing lawyers in the past? Did it deal fairly, giving a reasonable time to clear out their offices and to copy their work product off the computer? Or did the firm have the departing lawyer escorted from the office soon after the announcement?
- How did the firm provide notice of an attorney's departure to existing clients? Did it send a joint letter with the attorney, or did the managing partner get on the phone to alert clients and discourage them from leaving the firm?
- How has the firm handled transition of clients who decide to follow the departing lawyer? Did it cooperate in transferring files for clients who followed a departing lawyer to a new firm, or did it insist on retaining files in the hopes of deterring clients from moving to your firm?
- Has the firm had a negative experience with a departing lawyer (i.e., someone who stole files and solicited clients even before he was out the door)?

Be prepared. It doesn't hurt to prepare for a worst-case scenario in which your firm sends you packing on the day you give notice. In this situation, the firm would close ranks, and deny you access to your computer and files by deactivating your security codes and password. Of course, this means you would lose the ability to save what's rightfully yours. So, before you give notice, save copies of all of your work product and e-mail messages, any client materials you're entitled to retain, and start bringing home the seminar materials, bar journals. and other publications that belong to you. As I discuss later, you must absolutely positively refrain from soliciting any clients while you remain part of the firm. But do have a pre-drafted e-mail announcing your departure to clients. So, if the firm does cut you loose upon giving notice, you can preempt the firm's announcement with one of your own. Note: some bar prohibit departing lawyers from contacting firm clients without authorization from the firm.

Have consideration. Give your firm the traditional two weeks notice…if not more! And, where possible, avoid giving notice in the weeks before a major trial or closing. Finally, assure your firm that you will remain around long enough to finish outstanding work, or to brief a new attorney on the matter. Of course, your firm might decline your offer; in fact, they might ask you to leave right away. But at least you can be satisfied at having acted professionally. This end-game can also end an up-note: a colleague told me that when he left his large firm, he wound up continuing to handle work for his employer for six months after his departure on a contract basis, which helped ease him into solo practice.

Act professionally. Resist the temptation to sneak into the office to collect client files, and to drop a letter of resignation on the managing partner's desk. Such conduct forecloses any future referral opportunities from your firm…not to mention the bad feeling it leaves with colleagues. I've spoken with several lawyers who were left in the lurch by departing associates who sneaked out with law firm files. Years later, these colleagues still refuse to refer clients to those former associates. Of course, if you do stoop to such conduct, lost referrals would be the least of your worries. Under the ethics rules of almost any jurisdiction, taking client files would invite a civil lawsuit or bar complaint by your former firm. Do you really want to spend your first few weeks or months of practice defending yourself against your former firm before a disciplinary committee? Put yourself in your employer's shoes; after all, someday, you may be in a position where some of your associates leave the firm your firm to hang out their own shingle. How would you feel if they left you with imminent deadlines and no information about outstanding cases? Leave your firm with the same professionalism and grace you'd expect from your own employees.

Negotiating Benefits

When you leave your employer, you may be entitled to certain benefits, such as compensation for vacation time or the right to purchase health insurance through COBRA. But in contrast to when you started your job and HR took care of all of these matters

When wronged, a lawyer's first impulse is to file a lawsuit, or at least to consider the possibility. If that's your reaction to your firm's decision to fire you, slow down. It's understandable that you might derive some pleasure at a process server charging into the managing partner's office to serve a summons. Before you declare war, though, consider whether a lawsuit will benefit you in the long run. Ask yourself:

Do I even have a case?

Firms terminate associates (and sometimes even partners) for a variety of reasons. In most cases, economics...not merit...drive a firm's decision. Firms don't pass lawyers over for partnership because they're not capable, but because the firm has grown so top-heavy that adding new partners would reduce profits for existing ones. The bottom line is that if you've been let go for economic reasons (even if the firm couches its decision as merit-based), you're not likely to succeed with your lawsuit. But let's not kid ourselves: law firms don't always behave lawfully when they fire attorneys. Many a firm has *constructively discharged* women returning from maternity leave, demoting them on cases that they once lead, relegating them to scut work, and generally making their lives so unpleasant that they're effectively forced out. In October, 2007, Chicago-based Sidley Austin, one of the nation's largest law firms, agreed to pay $27.5 million to 32 former partners to settle a closely watched age discrimination lawsuit. The federal Equal Employment Opportunity Commission had contended that Sidley violated the Age Discrimination in Employment Act when it forced the partners out of the partnership on account of their age.[1]

One lawyer I know was fired for reporting a colleague's excessive billing practices to firm management...even though the Code of Professional Responsibility obligates attorneys to disclose ethics violations committed by other lawyers. If, after consulting with an employment law attorney or the EEOC, you determine that your firm acted unlawfully, you should consider a lawsuit. Though you may face adverse repercussions, our profession will not change for the better unless lawyers treated unjustly step forward.

How will a lawsuit affect my career?

Bringing a lawsuit can prevent you from moving forward. After all, how are you going to get your new practice up and running if your day is consumed with filing motions and attending depositions in your own case? In addition, the legal community...even in major cities...is awfully small. And word of a lawsuit can circulate quickly, perhaps branding you as a litigious trouble-maker. Fair or not, many firms may decide against sending contract work or referrals to a lawyer whom they believe might sue them if a dispute over referral or contract fees ever arose. Note: a lawsuit against your firm would irreparably destroy the relationship. Though you might not care about ever dealing with a firm that just fired you, consider the impact that burning bridges would have on future opportunities.

When my own firm asked me to leave, I was humiliated and furious. I consulted with an attorney about a possible discrimination action (I was the only female associate at the firm), but I was advised that I didn't have a case. On my last day, I was tempted to march into each partner's office and deliver a "good riddance" speech. Instead (and after discussing it with my husband, who was able to think more objectively about my situation), I merely sent an e-mail around the office, wished everyone well and left for home. A few days later, I got on with my life; I started my practice and didn't have much contact with anyone from the firm for at least six months. By that time, I was scheduled to argue my first case at the DC Circuit, a small matter which had originated while I was at my former firm. With nothing to lose, I called one of my former firm partners who had done some appellate work, and asked if he'd help me out. He agreed and we set up a meeting, where he and two of the other partners spent about an hour giving me pointers and tossing practice questions at me. Working together broke the ice, and, later, the firm referred me a few cases and also served as a reference for some lucrative contract assignments. None of that would have happened if I gave in to my adrenalin, and vented my outrage before leaving. ●

for you, it's up to you to ensure that you receive all rightful benefits before you leave. Negotiate vigorously for what you deserve; every little extra bit of cash can help alleviate the financial stress of the early days of starting your own practice.

Benefits to actively negotiate.

Vacation/sick days. Many attorneys who leave a firm or the government find themselves with three or four weeks of unused vacation. It is important to fight for your rights. So, check with HR or your employee manual to determine whether your firm is required to pay for remaining vacation and sick days. And even if the firm maintains that it is not obligated, its position may be at odds with the labor laws in your state. Why bother? Because the compensation you receive for unused time can amount to the equivalent of almost another month of salary, a big help if you're starting out without a source of revenue.

Retirement contribution and bonuses. In contrast to vacation benefits, which accrue all year long, some benefits—like retirement contributions or bonuses—are distributed annually, usually in January or February for the previous year. If you're leaving voluntarily, you may be able to time your departure so that you're around when these benefits are dispensed. However, if you're asked to leave late in the year, you may miss out on these benefits unless you speak up. Again, consult your employee handbook and HR manual. If you've already met the criterion for a pension contribution or bonus, then make your case for receiving it.

COBRA. Federal law requires employers with 20 or more employees to provide employees and their dependents the right to continue health insurance coverage up to 18 months after leaving a job. Even though COBRA requires you to reimburse your employer for its share of your insurance premiums, COBRA coverage is generally lower than what you could procure on your own since you can take advantage of your employer's group rates. COBRA imposes strict deadlines for electing coverage so it's up to you to stay on top of the process to avoid missing a deadline.

Unemployment. If your separation is involuntary, you probably qualify for unemployment benefits. Don't be too ashamed or proud to take unemployment; after all, you've been paying into the system for as long as you've been working, so you might as well take what you've earned. Generally, most states allow unemployment so long as you certify that you are continuing to seek employment, something you can truthfully claim even after you start your firm (for example, it's likely that you might apply for contract work positions after you start a firm, which constitutes looking for other work). In addition, you must report any earnings you receive from a new jobs so that you do not exceed the maximum level of employment that you're entitled to by law.

See book updates at author's blog—www.MyShingle.com

After what you've been earning at your firm, unemployment doesn't amount to much, maybe $300 to $400 per week for three months. But that may be enough to cover some bills while you get your practice off the ground.

Other benefits. Believe it or not, even when you've been terminated from your position, you have some leverage in negotiating benefits. If your firm fears you might bring a lawsuit, it may try to avoid the possibility by placating you. Or, one or more of the partners may feel so guilty about your dismissal that they will try to ease their conscience by giving you what you ask for. For example, if you've been told to leave by May and the firm pays bar dues and other licensing fees in June, ask that they pay these costs for the year. If you're forced out in the last quarter of the year, maybe the firm will pick up the tab for health insurance premiums through the end of the year. This would be especially helpful if you intend to switch over to your spouse's plan, and you're not sure how long that process will take or whether you need to wait until the end of the year to put it in place.

Dividing the Assets.

Don't be surprised at how hard your firm fights to keep clients, even clients you brought to the firm yourself, or who originated with the firm but where you acted as managing attorney.

Nor is it hard to understand why, even in the case of a client whose matters you handled exclusively, or who only generated several thousand dollars in business. Clients are a firm's most important asset...for more reasons than money. Their retainers and fees serve as a law firm's sole source of revenue, providing the high six-figure incomes, the box seats at sports games, the expense-account dinners, the designer interiors. Even prominent clients with smaller matters bring prestige to the firm, enabling it to capture future business and ensure future growth. Thus, firms worry that news of a loss of even a few insignificant clients to, of all people, a lawyer going solo, might damage the firm's carefully cultivated reputation.

Ethics rules. As much as firms may want to keep clients, ethics rules impose some imitations that can level the playing field...at least a little.

In contrast to private corporations, law firms can't execute non-compete agreements to prohibit former attorneys from soliciting existing clients. Both the ABA Model Rules of Professional Responsibility, and every state bar, take the position that clients have an unfettered right to choose their attorney.[2] And any practice which restricts a client's ability to choose—whether it's a non-compete agreement, a law firm's ban on communications between a former attorney and firm clients, or a firm's refusal to turn over client files so that a client can transfer to another attorney—will not pass muster under ethics rules.

Still, law firms have some wiggle room.

Ethics rules don't stop a firm from offering an existing client all kinds of perks to remain with the firm.

In fact, ABA Opinion 06-444 held that a firm can ethically make retirement benefits contingent upon a lawyer's agreement to sign a non-compete clause (source: ABA Journal e-Report, May 25, 2007; *abanet.org/journal/ereport/my25ethic2.html*). Furthermore, ethics rules don't prohibit a firm from highlighting the disadvantages of being represented by a solo practitioner rather than the law firm whose very letter head causes opponents to quake in their boots. In addition, the rules impose limitations on departing lawyers. Both the ABA rules and most state ethics codes forbid lawyers, while still employed at their firm, from soliciting firm clients with whom they do not have a personal, working relationship. Some state codes go further, banning solicitation attempts between firm lawyers and all clients, even where a personal lawyer-client relationship exists. Law firm employment or partnership agreements may also prohibit pre-departure solicitation of clients, even if ethics rules don't.

Then there are, in the words of Dennis Kennedy, author of *Leaving a Firm: Guidelines to a Smoother Transition*, "the petty little games" that some law firms play.[3]

For example, one firm's refusal to turn over client e-mails on the grounds that they did not comprise part of the client file…or the firm that required departing lawyers to pay exorbitant rates to have client files copied so that they could retain the copies after transferring the files…or the firm that argued they were entitled to fees for the entire client matter even where the client moves to another firm in the interim! All such behavior interferes with the client's ability to remain with the departing lawyer. But don't expect to see any of the rules clarified in a way that benefits the departing lawyer. As long as the ABA and the state bars are dominated by large firm interests, any attempt to close these ethical gaps will be resolved in favor of the large firms.

Soliciting & Dealing With the Firm's Clients:

The Do's and Don'ts

DO refrain from actively soliciting existing clients while still employed at the firm. As previously mentioned, bar rules aren't completely clear on whether lawyers still employed at the firm can solicit existing clients with whom they have a personal relationship. Ethics rules generally preclude solicitation of clients where there's no personal relationship. But just to be safe, refrain from actively soliciting firm clients while you're still employed at the firm. The line between solicitation and ordinary small talk is awfully thin, though. ABA Rules and most codes define a solicitation as any kind of communication, motivated by pecuniary gain, concerning a lawyer's availability for employment. So, telling the client you're leaving to start a firm and asking him or her to come with you constitutes an impermissible solicitation, while merely floating the idea that you might want to start a firm probably is not (though here, you want to be careful that word doesn't get back to your firm which might send you packing sooner than you imagined). If a client said to you that she wished you practiced at another firm because your firm's fees are too expensive, it would be appropriate to say, "I'll give that some thought." But sending her a brochure and a proposed retainer agreement probably is not. Beyond ethics rules, use common sense and courtesy. Because at the end of the day, it's not worth to putting your firm on the defensive for clients that may come with you anyway.

DO have an ethically compliant letter to clients ready upon giving notice. When you give notice of your departure, you should have already drafted a letter informing clients of your departure and advising them of their right to remain with the firm or to come with you. Since your firm will probably want to notify clients themselves, having your own letter or e-mail already drafted gives you a chance to preempt the firm's announcement. Bear in mind that some jurisdictions may prohibit you from contacting former firm clients unless you transmit notice jointly with the firm, or if the firm pre-approves your announcement. Some rules may also restrict you from contacting clients with whom you did not have a personal relationship. Check your state ethics rules on departing attorneys, and consult with bar counsel before you send anything to existing firm clients. See Appendix 4 (Creating a Sample Forms Library) for links to sample departure letters.

DO settle unpaid balances for existing clients before you leave. The clients who follow you may have a variety of different billing arrangements with your existing firm. Some may owe outstanding balances for work that has already been completed; others may pay a flat, monthly retainer fee under an annual contract. If you're a partner in the firm, the partnership agreement probably provides for the percentage of disbursements that you're entitled to from clients as well as a provision for resolving division of profits when a partner departs with a client. Here, you need to determine whether it's worth it to fight for every last nickel that you're owed, or to simply cut a fair deal and get on with your life. As an associate, your rights to fees from existing clients may be more limited since you were paid a set salary rather than a share of profits. So if you take several contingency matters with you where the firm fronted significant costs, you (or your client) will have to compensate the firm for its investment in the case after you receive a judgment just as any other client would who switches attorneys midway through a contingency proceeding.

DON'T even think about swiping office supplies. You may think that you're saving yourself money by filching legal pads, pens or other office supplies from the firm before you leave. And the temptation to copy software licensed to the firm is probably even greater. In fact, if you've been fired, you may feel justified as compensation for unjust treatment. But the cost of office supplies is negligible, and if you poach licensed software you don't have access to the help desk or upgrades. It's just not worth it. Anyway, why lock yourself in to your firm's way of doing things? Make a fresh start. Your firm isn't likely to catch you sneaking supplies, but think how foolish you would appear if they did. What argument could you make? That you can't afford to buy software now that you're out of a job? Not the sort of impression you want to leave on a firm that you hope will send you referral business.

DON'T *use firm resources to solicit clients.* One Utah attorney learned the hard way that you shouldn't use firm resources to solicit clients. He used firm letterhead to solicit clients under the guise of being employed at the firm, then took the cases and handled them on his own. Use of firm resources isn't limited to stationery, however. Most firms maintain detailed data bases of clients, including client contacts and background information. That data belongs to the firm, which means you cannot take it and use the information to contact clients after you leave the firm.

DON'T *steal client files, but DO keep copies.* When you leave your firm, do not, under any circumstances, leave with client files, whether you worked on those matters or not. Under ethics rules, client files are either considered property of the client and held in trust by the firm. Taking files without permission is stealing, and that can expose you to ethical sanctions. If you're discovered taking files, don't expect your former firm to go easy on you, even where the client was likely to follow you anyway. Firms need to retain client files for malpractice purposes. By taking client files, you compromise your firm's ability to defend itself in future malpractice actions, creating problems for the firm with its insurance carrier. All of this would make your firm angry enough to file ethics charges against you…and the firm would probably prevail. At the same time, you should retain copies of client files, or at least key documents from those files, for matters in which you were personally involved. State ethics codes do not address the issue of copies, but copying files would probably pass muster as it does not compromise either the firm's or the client's ability to access the original files. More importantly, departing attorneys must keep file copies as a matter of self-preservation. Should malpractice claims arise in the future, an attorney must have proof where his involvement in the case terminated so that the firm does not attempt to transfer the blame for malpractice.

DON'T *badmouth the firm to get clients.* After you leave the firm, you may be tempted to convince one of the former clients to come with you by sharing some not-so-flattering information about your former firm. The information might be general in nature, (*e.g.,* a law firm policy that allows the firm to double-bill hours spent in travel to Client 1 and work done during that time to Client 2), or information that is specific to the client (*e.g.,* the managing partner calls the client *an annoying, pimply-faced dweeb*). Don't do it. Badmouthing can potentially expose you to a defamation action; also, it makes you look infantile and unprofessional. Further, badmouthing is not an effective marketing technique. Criticizing your old firm may give your client a reason to leave, but it won't give the client reasons to come with you.

What's Theirs, What's Yours?

While figuring out the division of clients, departing lawyers must also determine what property they can rightfully take, and what belongs to the firm.

In some instances, technological advancements have mooted the work-product question. Most federal courts, and many state courts and administrative agencies, have transitioned to electronic filing. Consequently, you don't need to concern yourself with the ethics of copying your firm's briefs and motions when you can readily access many of them online at the court's Web sites after you leave. But while questions about briefs and memos are easier to resolve, intellectual property issues complicate the question of who owns work product, according to Dennis Kennedy, a legal technology expert and BigLaw-attorney-turned solo:

TAKING CLIENTS WITH YOU: EXPECTATION VS REALITY

As you plan your departure from your firm, be realistic about which clients are likely to follow you. Obviously, you can't expect Corporation X, a 15-year client whose CEO is a close, personal friend of the managing partner, to jump ship. Especially when you've only handled his company's matters for three years and dealt with contacts as junior as yourself. At the same time, other more likely clients may also decline to come to your firm for one or more of the nine reasons outlined here by lawyer/author Dennis Kennedy:[4]

- The client you thought loved you and your work actually hates you and your work, or actually loves the paralegal or associate who is staying with your former firm.
- Your client contact does not have authority to take the work from your former firm.
- Your client contact is limited to an approved list of firms.
- Your client's choices include not only you and your former firm, but also other firms and moving work in-house.
- Your client requires technology or other infrastructure that you can no longer provide.
- You misread or misinterpreted what you hoped were positive signals from your client.
- Your former firm makes your client a better deal than you can.
- You walk into a conflict of interest that you did not see coming
- Unbeknownst to you, your former firm blackens your reputation in conversations with the client.

Since you do not have control over these factors, you should—at a minimum—anticipate that they may limit your ability to take clients with you. So be conservative in predicting future business when you start your firm. At the same time, being realistic in the short run doesn't mean that you should write off the prospect of luring in a former firm client entirely. The business of law is competitive and fluid, with companies constantly reevaluating and switching "dance partners." Down the road, a client may expand its list of "approved counsel" to include your new firm. Maybe the great deal that your firm extended to the client ended six months after your departure and the firm decides to look elsewhere. Maybe, the CEO of Corporation X retires and the new CEO appoints your once-junior contact as general counsel. One of these days, that ex-client just might give you a call after all. ●

See book updates at author's blog—www.MyShingle.com

. . . In the good old days, a lawyer leaving a firm took work product, forms and other materials. No one gave much thought to this common practice. Today, lawyers create articles, presentations, videos, forms, software applications, Web pages, databases, knowledge-management tools, and other pieces of intellectual property. Firms also realize the value of firm forms, brief banks, handbooks, and the like." [5]

Though intellectual property considerations do not necessarily bar you from taking presentations, forms and software applications that you created for your firm for your own fair use, they may preclude you from licensing or otherwise profiting from those materials. Kennedy notes that many firms have added intellectual property clauses to partnership agreements and advises that, "if you have specific uses planned for materials, be sure to address and document the intellectual property issues."

WHO OWNS THE BLOG?

As blogs increase in popularity, and gain acceptance as a way for young attorneys to establish their reputation in the legal field, the question of ownership may lead to disputes. In fact, in February 2007, Enrico Schaefer, a small firm attorney who authors the Greatest American Lawyer Blog (greatestamericanlawyer.com) reported that his former firm sued for the rights to the blog (see greatestamericanlawyer.typepad.com/greatest_american _lawyer/2007/02/blog_fight.html). Here's how a dispute might arise:

Suppose an associate at a large firm starts a blog on communications law. He writes it through his own efforts on an account he set up himself, but posts to the blog during the work day from his office computer. The associate informs the firm of his blog, and further indicates online that he is employed by the firm. Within a few months, the blog emerges as one of the go-to sites for the industry, generating positive buzz for both the associate and the firm. At that point, the firm links the blog at its own site, highlighting that its own associate runs the blog. A year later, the associate decides to leave the firm. Can the firm demand that the associate turn over his blog? In this case, the firm would probably not prevail. Though the associate blogged on firm time, he took responsibility for setting up the site and created all of the content without supervision or direction from the firm. Thus, the firm could not lay claim to the blog under a theory of "work for hire."[6] Moreover, if the firm continues to link to the blog from its Web site, the associate should ensure that the firm does not use the link to convey the impression that the associate still works at the firm, or that the firm plays a role in generating the content of the blog.

In one recent case, an associate sued his former firm for keeping his biography on the firm Web site, which the associate claims directed prospective clients to his former firm away from his new solo practice.[7] Of course, an associate who writes a blog established by the law firm won't have any rights to the site upon departure. At best, the associate could link to posts or articles that he wrote for the firm blog, though even that may not offer proof of expertise or writing skills, since most firm blogs attribute posts to the firm and not to the individual author.

If you're thinking about volunteering to start a blog for your firm, insist on attribution for posts, if not some entitlement to co-ownership, so that you have something that you can take with you, or at least link to, if you leave. ●

Equipment and materials. Chances are, your firm equipped you with a laptop, PDA, and/or a smartphone, the better to keep you tethered to the firm 24/7. Now that you're cutting the ties, expect the firm to cut your service and seek return of its property...though as a partner and part-owner of the firm, you—at least in theory—may have some claim to keeping some of your road warrior gear. As discussed earlier, be sure to copy all vital information from your PDA/cell/smartphone and your laptop before giving notice of your departure. As for law books, journals or directories, keep those that came your way by virtue of a bar membership or attendance at a conference. The firm will probably toss those materials anyway.

Special Considerations for Government Lawyers.

Lawyers leaving government service to solo don't face the same ethics dilemmas related to client solicitation that confront their colleagues in private practice. At the same time, government lawyers must deal with ethical restrictions on the "revolving door" between successive government and private employment:

> **ABA Model Rule 1.1,** *provides that government lawyers: shall not otherwise represent a client in connection with a matter in which the lawyer participated personally and substantially as a public officer or employee, unless the appropriate government agency gives its informed consent, confirmed in writing, to the representation.*

Most state bars apply a similar "personal and substantial" participation standard, though you should consult applicable rules and bar counsel for further guidance.[8] In addition, lawyers leaving positions with the federal government must comply with the requirements of federal conflict of interest statutes.[9] In addition, some agencies may have their own regulations in addition to restricting attorneys from actively courting clients with cases pending before the agency, or also prohibit attorneys from making personal appearances before the agency for a certain period of time after leaving for the private sector.

While it seems onerous, the "revolving door" regulations may restrict you from handling only a small number of cases.

If you worked as a junior attorney at a federal agency, you most likely dealt with small, finite matters that concluded before your departure so the players involved would not have a need to hire private counsel. The same is true if you are leaving a prosecutor's office: most of the defendants you prosecuted were probably incarcerated and won't need lawyers, while those in the middle of a case already have representation and, if not, would probably not want to hire the same person who indicted them. And even if you are subject to a bar on personal appearances before an agency for a set time, that still does not preclude you from advising clients on the agency's policies during that time-frame. Even though you are leaving government to start your own firm, consider how large firms deal with conflicts when they hire top agency personnel, a frequently occurring phenomenon.[10]

Government lawyers leave office for private firms all the time, but at a firm other attorneys can handle matters that come before the lawyer's former agency, even if the government lawyer is personally precluded from doing so. At the same time, the former government lawyer adds value, because he can educate other firm attorneys on the agency's regulations and identify appropriate contacts in the agency for further assistance.

In contrast to large firm practice, as a solo, you won't be able to pass off cases that you're disqualified from handling to other attorneys in your firm. But what you can do is establish affiliated networks with other attorneys, or even enter into an "of counsel" relationship. You can then refer clients to these attorneys in your network and provide general consulting and advice while you wait out any cooling period on appearances before the agency. Plus, you can use these affiliations to learn more about fields outside the expertise you gained at government, which will enable you to diversify your practice. *See* Chapter 17 (*From Government to Solo*).

CHAPTER 6

Seven Steps to Getting Started

"Keep your overhead low, build a good support network, and make sure you've got enough savings to survive the slow times." —SERGIO BENAVIDES, SOLO

1. Bar licensing/court membership

To practice law, you need to be a member in good standing of the bar in the jurisdiction where you practice.

The importance of having a current license seems obvious, but back at the law firm or government agency, your license probably did not matter much. If you were employed with the federal government, you were able to practice in any federal court irrespective of the jurisdiction where you're admitted to practice. And if you were at a large firm, you were probably never attorney-of-record, so where you were licensed was also of less importance. In addition, your employer most likely paid your annual licensing fees, even if you were admitted to multiple bars. Now that you're on your own, you bear the cost of keeping your licenses current.

Which licenses will you need?

The answer depends largely on your anticipated practice:

Must you be licensed in the state where your office is located? Some states, Maryland, for example, require lawyers practicing in the state to be a member of that state bar, though some exceptions apply (*e.g.*, attorneys with exclusively federal practices that do not require any specific state bar membership need not join the Maryland bar to work in Maryland). This rule applies even to lawyers working from home offices. If you practice in this type of jurisdiction, consult with the ethics office to determine what bar membership is required.

Should you be licensed in the state where you live? If you worked for a large firm located in one state, and lived in an adjacent state, chances are that you're only a member of the bar in the state where you worked. You may want to consider gaining admission to the bar of the state where you live. Depending upon your potential practice area, you may get referrals from neighbors or family members in your home state, and if you're not a member of the bar, you could lose out on prospective clients.

Will you have a federal practice? With a federal practice, sometimes you can get away with belonging to just one bar. That's because both the federal appeals courts and a number of federal district courts will allow you to gain admission to practice in that court even though you're not a member of the bar in the jurisdiction where the court is located. Generally, the only requirements are that a member of the appellate court where you're seeking admission sponsors you and that you are a member in good standing in the jurisdictions where you're licensed. Admission to other federal courts costs under $200, making it far less expensive and less time-consuming, than waiving into another bar (which can cost several hundred dollars) or worse, taking the bar in another state. Also, keep in mind that federal agencies generally do not require you to belong to any specific state bar. Thus, if you practice exclusively before federal agencies, you may be able to limit your number of bar licenses.

Does admission in another jurisdiction generate more work opportunities? In many tri-state regions comprised of smaller states, you'll find that most attorneys belong to the bar of the state where the largest city is located. For example, in the areas of New York, New Jersey, and Connecticut area, most lawyers practice in New York City and tend to be licensed in New York; in the areas of Massachusetts, New Hampshire, and Rhode Island, most lawyers practice in Boston and are licensed in Massachusetts; and so on. Moreover, if you previously worked at a large firm in Boston or New York, most of your colleagues will be more likely to know lawyers from Massachusetts or New York than from the adjacent states. Consequently, if you gain admission to the bar in an adjacent state like New Hampshire or New Jersey, you'll have less competition for referrals from your former colleagues.

Sometimes, you may need to gain admission to a particular state bar to qualify for temporary document-review projects, which is an option for some solos getting a practice off the ground. About a year ago, the D.C. Court of Appeals Committee on Unauthorized Practice of Law ruled that contract lawyers doing business in the District must have a D.C. Bar law. Since many temp attorneys in DC were licensed in other jurisdictions and had never taken the time to waive into the DC bar, a large number of attorneys who had previously handled contract matters were disqualified, opening up more jobs for lawyers with the foresight to gain admission to the DC Bar. In some instances, you can waive into another state bar by paying a hefty fee (about $500–$800), filling out lots of forms, and sitting for a day of ethics training. In states which do not have reciprocity, you may need to take a full bar exam. Other states, such as Maryland, offer a compromise; attorneys who have practiced for five years or more can take a "practitioner's exam" which focuses on Maryland practice rather than multistate or general bar issues. Taking a state bar, even a practitioner's exam can be costly and time-consuming. You'll probably need to pay for a review course, set aside time to study, and pay for the exam and admissions cost. But if it creates added financial opportunities, the extra bar is worthwhile.

2. Choosing a business structure

Which structure will work best for you?

Most solos start off as sole proprietorships, and then evaluate other options after they've been in practice for a while. There's no simple answer, but the DC Bar's *Online Guide to Starting a Firm* has this advice:

> ... *The form of business organization you choose will depend on your situation and needs. If you are a solo practitioner, you may decide to be a sole proprietorship, or form a professional corporation. If you are starting a firm, you may want to form a partnership. You may also choose to form a limited liability partnership or corporation. Deciding which one may be right for you may not be simple. Common issues to consider include liability for debts, contracts, and malpractice; income and employment taxes; availability of health insurance and insurance premium tax deduction; availability of retirement plans; bankruptcy of entity or partner/colleague; and the cost of forming and maintaining the chosen entity. Unless this is your practice area, you should probably consult a colleague familiar with entity choice and formation before you make this decision.*[1]

The business structures from which to choose include:

Sole proprietorship. An unincorporated law firm owned by one individual. It is the simplest business form, and most solos start out this way. In contrast to an LLC or partnership, in which you must form and submit for approval to the state, a sole proprietorship does not involve these steps. However, even as a sole proprietor, you may need to register your business in the city where you practice, so check local business laws to determine whether this requirement applies. For ordinary business owners, sole proprietorship is usually regarded as less advantageous than corporate formation which protects owners from personal liability. As a solo, however, your greatest potential from liability arises out of malpractice. *Note*: no corporate structure will shield an attorney from personal liability for professional malpractice (though it will protect you from other liability, *e.g.*, liability for breach of a contract or lease).

Limited liability company. A corporate structure that offers the protection of liability available to corporations but may be treated as a sole proprietorship for tax purposes.[2] An LLC will not protect lawyers from liability for acts of professional malpractice, but it will guard against personal liability arising out of contractual disputes or malpractice committed by employees, associates or partners. Some lawyers choose to incorporate as an LLC because it is a simple process but can give the appearance that the firm is a more established, formal entity. Frank Yunes, a Massachusetts solo, offers this advice:

> *Although we all have liability insurance, this protection isn't enough in some cases. The creation of a legal entity is an additional layer of protection that might be appropriate depending on your practice area. The single member LLC is a perfect fit for attorneys in solo practice; in addition to the obvious liability protection, it is treated as a 'disregarded entity' for personal income tax purposes. This means that a formerly sole proprietor can continue to file Schedule C with their personal income tax*

return for as long as the entity is a law firm of one. The process of forming an LLC is remarkably easy. Where I practice, it takes a few minutes to create one at the Secretary of State's Web site, and to obtain a tax ID number at the IRS Web site.

Source: guest post at *myshingle.com/my_shingle/2006/01/guest_llc_.html.*

Professional corporation. A corporation formed for the sole purpose of rendering professional services. Generally, a professional corporation is taxed the same way as a standard corporation.

Partnership. A partnership may be appropriate for two or more lawyers who choose to form a law firm. In a general partnership, each individual partner is liable for all actions of the partnership as well as each partner. If you wish to form a partnership, be sure that you know and trust your partners. And invest in enough malpractice insurance to cover not only your potential malpractice but that of your partners as well.

3. Selecting a name for your firm

Once you decide on your firm's business structure, you need a firm name. While naming the practice after yourself (*Law Office of John Smith*) is not original, many lawyers—weary of the obscurity and anonymity that comes with working at a large firm or government agency—are eager for the chance to put a personal stamp on their practice. And why not? This is one time you shouldn't feel embarrassed to follow the crowd. So, proclaim ownership of your firm; you deserve it. And don't be modest. Remember, you are a law firm of one, not merely an attorney. Why settle for *Jane Doe, Attorney at Law*? That's what you were the day you graduated law school. Today, you are a law firm...and your name should reflect that.

As more firms develop niche practices, a trend has emerged towards descriptive trade names. A few years ago, one Atlanta law firm got some attention by calling itself Red Hot Law, a name that helped distinguish the firm apart from its competitors, and reflected a commitment to their fast-paced, cutting-edge practice, and innovative way of practicing law.[3] Solo Jay Fleischman, who practices bankruptcy and consumer credit law, calls his firm the Debt Relief Law Center of New York, which describes the service that he provides to his clients. If you practice in a competitive field, consider a trade name that sets your firm apart.

A cautionary note. Most bar associations are sensitive about law firm names, and believe they can be confused by the most benign designations. Take note: some state bars do not permit lawyers to use trade names, finding them to be inherently deceptive. Other bars will allow a trade names so long as they do not imply that the firm is actually a government-sponsored agency or legal aid organization. Thus, a bar might express concern over a firm that calls itself *The George Smith Legal Aid Clinic* or *The Employment Law Help Center*. Bars are also concerned about deception where a firm uses a name that gives the impression that it is larger than it actually is (though, the bar apparently sees no deception where 700-lawyer firms like *WilmerHale* are known by a two-person name, giving the impression that they are smaller, more congenial or less expensive than they are). So, don't call your firm *Jane X and Associates* or *The X Law Group* if you do not have associates or other lawyers in the firm, because the name would suggest to clients that you employ other attorneys. Also beware of a prohibition against the phrase *and associates*, which may apply to law firms employing virtual associates offsite. In 2005, the South Carolina bar disciplined a former state senator who, in the name of his law firm, used *and associates* when his associate was an out-of-state attorney who researched and drafted pleadings on a contract basis. The bar held that the phrase applies only to staff not contract attorneys [*Greenville News*, June 5, 2005]. If it's your intent to employ virtual associates offsite, seek guidance from the bar.

As a solo, you may even run into problems by referring to yourself as a "law firm." In Opinion 332 (November 2005), the DC Bar concluded that a solo could call herself the X Law Firm, in which she was the sole member,[3] finding that the use of the term "firm" by a solo was not presumptively misleading. Of course, that the bar would even suggest that a solo's use of the term law firm could ever be misleading insults those of us solos who take our business as a "law firm of one" as seriously as a law firm of thousands. Bottom line: if you're not sure about the ethics of using a law firm name, read the bar rules for yourself, and if it's still unclear, seek advice from the bar.

4. Purchasing malpractice insurance

One absolute rule I have for new solos is that they *must* purchase malpractice insurance. In the interest of full disclosure, though, I do admit to not following my own advice during my first three years of practice! Back then, I was young and cocky, and I calculated that my potential exposure was low given my regulatory practice, my "long shot" litigation matters and criminal defense work.

I assumed legal malpractice insurance was as costly as health insurance and probably couldn't afford it. I had a nothing-to-lose attitude back then, figuring that if anyone sued me I'd simply pack up my firm and walk away. I see things differently now with my practice well under way. I have so much invested in my practice that I am unwilling to sacrifice my firm if a client sues me. Also, after a couple of close calls, I realize that—despite my diligence—I am only human, and capable of mistakes that could morph into a grievance or a malpractice action. Once I understood this, the purchase of malpractice insurance to protect myself from future claims was better than berating myself for my mistakes, or worse, waking in a cold sweat in the middle of the night. When I finally shopped around for malpractice insurance and spoke with other solo and small firm lawyers, I discovered that it was not as expensive as I had thought. Of course, this is just my story.

Read what a solo in family law wrote to the ABA's *solosez* listserv about an experience that happened to them:

I've heard it said that if you have never had a client file a claim against you, you haven't been practicing long enough. By this measure, I have now been practicing law long enough.

Several years ago, a disgruntled former client filed a complaint with the Attorney Discipline Office. The claims specialist assigned to my case offered insight, provided a sounding board, reviewed my response and other documents, and confirmed that I could either handle this pro se, or with counsel. For a variety of reasons, I handled it pro se. The ADO dismissed the complaint, and concluded that this was merely a matter of differing opinions. The former client then filed suit in court... also suing his former spouse, the judge, the guardian ad litem, the parenting counselor, and advised the screening officer and chair of the ADO that he would be suing them, too.

I am absolutely delighted that I can leave this in the hands of my attorney, and I am absolutely delighted that my insurance company rejected a settlement offer from the Plaintiff for half the policy limits (which means they feel quite strongly that a judgment will either be in my favor, or for an amount less than half the policy limit). And I am absolutely incensed that my attorneys will be spending at least $5,000 worth of time on my behalf, which means that a judgment in my favor will still cost me $5,000 (my deductible). But I am thankful that I was not practicing 'bare', which would have deprived me of the advice I received in the ADO matter, and would have seriously interfered with my ability to defend myself in this suit. I am not a bad attorney. I don't deserve this. But this is part of practicing law. Please, please, please think long and hard before going bare.

Here are some of the factors you should consider in purchasing malpractice insurance as well as suggestions on how to procure the best plan for your firm:

Does your state require malpractice coverage or have a mandatory disclosure policy? You may not even have a choice about whether to get legal malpractice insurance or not. In fact, one state, Oregon, requires all lawyers to buy malpractice insurance. Other states, including South Dakota, Alaska, Ohio, and others, have "mandatory disclosure" rules that require attorneys to reveal to prospective clients whether they have malpractice coverage. As a practical matter, a mandatory disclosure rule has virtually the same effect as a mandatory requirement. In a mandatory disclosure jurisdiction, lack of malpractice coverage gives prospective clients the impression that you're running a fly-by-night operation, and they'll likely pass on hiring you. On the other hand, if you don't disclose a lack of malpractice coverage, you run the risk of disciplinary reprimand if your concealment is later discovered. You might as well avoid all of these hassles in a mandatory disclosure jurisdiction at the outset by obtaining malpractice coverage.

Do you need malpractice insurance for business opportunities? Another factor to consider is whether you need malpractice coverage for business opportunities. Some referral services will not refer cases to lawyers who do not carry sufficient malpractice coverage. Many times, an RFP (request for proposal) for legal services also require coverage. Even law firms and attorneys who retain lawyers for *per diem* or contract work often require some amount of malpractice coverage. In short, malpractice insurance is a worthwhile investment economically if it allows you to take advantage of lucrative opportunities that would not otherwise be available in the absence of coverage.

How much does your degree of exposure matter? Quite frankly, your own assessment of your degree of malpractice exposure should not serve as the deciding factor in your decision regarding coverage. Because even though the chances of client actually *winning* a malpractice action against you and collecting a judgment are probably low, it doesn't take much for a client to initiate such an action in hopes of pressuring a quick settlement—or worse, to file a bar complaint which, if unfavorably resolved, can cause damage to your reputation and lead to a suspension. These days, many legal malpractice plans cover the cost of defense both in malpractice actions in court and, equally importantly, in grievance procedures where lawyers who are represented almost always fare better than those who participate *pro se*. Thus, malpractice insurance buys you the peace of mind, and gives you one less thing to worry about when that client who initially seemed so reasonable starts threatening a grievance. Moreover, if your risk of exposure is low anyway, you'll probably be able to find a relatively inexpensive coverage plan.

What can you afford? Even though malpractice insurance is a good investment, cost matters when you're just starting out. There are some practice areas (such as certain IP matters) where malpractice insurance can be prohibitively expensive. But if you expect that IP will generate substantial revenue for you, bite the bullet and write the check. On the other hand, if you're only intending to handle a smattering of IP work and focus on other areas, you might consider dropping that practice area or figuring out other ways to do it—maybe on contract basis for another firm—that will limit your exposure and the concomitant costs of coverage.

How to purchase malpractice insurance. Many state bar associations have an insurance company that is designated as a "preferred provider" or bar association sponsor. Be wary of these designations; they do not necessarily guarantee that the company offers the lowest cost or is the most reliable. In fact, as I discovered when I signed up to use the DC Bar's preferred provider, the opposite was true. In my case, the provider charged roughly 20 percent more than my current insurer and also went out of business a year after I signed up. Essentially, a preferred provider is nothing more than an insurer which has paid the bar a certain amount of money in exchange for exclusive billing.

A preferred provider may in fact offer the lowest price; just don't automatically assume that it will.

- To find potential malpractice companies, seek advice from other attorneys who have personally procured the plan and who practice in the same jurisdiction. Getting advice from an associate at a firm that uses, say, Ajax Insurance, isn't much value since the associate won't know the terms or cost of coverage. Likewise, information about a cheap plan in California won't do much good if you practice in Florida. Your best bet is a recommendation from a fellow attorney with a

See book updates at author's blog—www.MyShingle.com

similar practice, who can share his or her personal experiences with the provider, and perhaps even give you a sense of what he or she pays for the policy. Once you've gathered a list of two or three prospective providers, shop around for quotes. Ask for a range of costs depending on variables such as the size of your deductible or coverage per claim.

- Most legal malpractice plans are claims-based, which means that coverage applies for any claim made during a specified period. In addition, even if you've gone "bare" for several years, you may be able to negotiate insurance for "prior acts," past incidents that pre-dated your plan but for which no claim has yet been filed. And when shopping for a plan, make certain that it will cover defense costs, both in civil suits and disciplinary actions. Also ask what other benefits the plan offers. Some plans might offer a free legal research package or discount pricing, others include risk- management training with a discount on the cost of insurance to those who participate.

The ABA has an entire Web site devoted to purchase of malpractice insurance at *abanet.org/legalservices/LPL/home.* It includes some reasonably current information on purchasing malpractice insurance and statistics, reporting claims and minimizing malpractice risk.

5. Establishing your financial accounts

Before you open your practice, you need to establish a law firm bank account and to order business checks. Many courts do not accept personal checks, but will honor checks from attorneys. Make sure your checks include the name of your law firm.

Lawyers who plan to hold money for clients even for a short time (such as funds received from the proceeds of a settlement pending disbursement by the attorney) must deposit the money into a trust account. Bar rules prohibiting commingling of lawyer and client funds are stringent; even an *accidental* deposit of client funds into your law firm account that you report immediately thereafter could earn you a reprimand.

Bars have different rules about whether a retainer or advance fee belongs to the attorney (in which case it can be deposited directly into the law firm's operating account), or whether these fees belong to the client until such point that work is performed (in which case the money must go to the trust account). Some bars reason that a retainer fee belongs to the attorney because it compensates the lawyer to secure his availability for the duration of the case. Other bars take the position that a retainer is like an escrow fund that provides assurance of future payment. As such, it belongs to the client until such time as the attorney renders services and is entitled to payment from the retainer amount. The point is that even an action as frequent as acceptance of a retainer fee can trigger questions about appropriate trust account treatment. So, study the applicable bar rules.

Client trust accounts must comply with the applicable bar's IOLTA (Interest On

Lawyer Trust Account) rules. Under IOLTA programs, participating banks forward the interest on certain lawyer trust accounts (i.e., those where client funds are nominal or held for too short a period to warrant establishment of a separate account) to the state's IOLTA program, which distributes the money to legal services organizations. Since their inception, IOLTA programs have generated millions of dollars in support for legal aid programs.

According to the ABA IOLTA web resources (*abanet.org/legalservices/iolta*), 31 states have mandatory IOLTA programs and 19 have opt-out programs in which lawyers must participate unless they affirmatively advise the bar that they will not take part in the IOLTA program. Only two jurisdictions, the Virgin Islands and South Dakota, have completely voluntary IOLTA programs. Both the ABA and virtually every state bar retain detailed web sites on IOLTA, which explain the applicable rules and identify participating IOLTA banks. (For a list of state IOLTA offices, see *abanet.org/ legalservices/iolta/ioltadir.html*). For additional guidance, consult these sites as well as the IOLTA office or the bar's LPM advisor.

6. Making the official announcement

Opening a new law firm is one of those rare occasions when you can contact prospective clients without worrying about bar rules on solicitation. That is, as long as the announcement merely conveys information that you've opened a law firm... and doesn't suggest a need for, or ask recipients to use, your services. Otherwise it would run afoul of rules prohibiting direct solicitation. So tell everyone! Announce your new firm to everyone whether you expect them to send you business or not. In a world where everyone seems to be connected by six degrees of separation, you never know who might know someone who knows someone who could use a lawyer. By making an announcement, you're providing recipients a potential referral source.

Potential recipients include:

- School contacts: College and law school classmates and former professors;
- Previous employers: Lawyers and judges with whom you've worked, as well as your previous non-legal employers;
- Family and friends: Close relatives and friends, and friends of your spouse and parents.
- Professional colleagues: Lawyers with whom you've worked and members of bar and professional associations to which you belong.
- Internet colleagues: Lawyers with whom you have contact through listservs or blogging.
- Former and present clients: You may need to check bar rules to ensure that there's no prohibition on making direct contact with former firm clients.

When to make the announcement. Obviously, you can't send announcements until you've left your former law firm. But do have them ready to go the first week you open for business. In particular, you'll want to send your announcements to publications like alumni magazines and bar journals as early as possible as they often have long lead times.

What to say. At a minimum, every announcement—whether a hard copy or e-mail —should contain basic contact information (phone, e-mail, Web and/or blog address), the state bars where you're licensed to practice, and the date your office opens. Space permitting, include additional details such as your intended practice areas, previous places of employment and your educational background.

Making the announcement. You have plenty of options when it comes to law firm announcements. To some, you can send something eye-catching; to others, a formal announcement that describes why you've decided to open your own practice and the practice areas where you plan to focus. Hard copies aren't the only option. The benefit of an e-mail announcement is that recipients can automatically enter your e-mail into their contacts list, making it click on immediately click on your Web link or get in touch later. Incidentally, if you do send an e-mail announcement, consider something a little fancier like a card from *E-vite.com* or an e-mail marketing template at *ConstantContact.com*.

Where to make the announcement. Don't limit your announcements to direct mail. Alert your law school newsletter, local bar journals, legal trade publications, local newspapers, and the regional business press.

7. Setting up your office

Of all of the decisions relating to starting a law practice, the question of where to locate the practice is among the most debated.

Some argue that a conventional, full-time office is critical to the success of a new practice; others (myself included) believe that whether or not you get an office outside the home depends on the nature of one's practice, personality and work habits and, of course, the cost. In my opinion, too many new and potential solos assume they must have Class A space—the highest quality—and jump into a situation without the revenue to support it.

Commercial space

PROS: Even though commercial rents have made a "landlord's market"in the downtown core of some cities (e.g., New York City, Washington DC, Chicago, Los Angeles), the choice of an outside office is still the least complicated option. Because when a client or referral source wants to know where your office is located, it's so much easier to provide a commercial address than explaining a home office, or that you need to meet at Starbucks or the courthouse cafeteria. Commercial space confers credibility, and goes a long way to mute whatever doubts new clients or potential referral sources may have about your new firm. An outside office also offers rich potential for business and networking; the companies with whom you co-locate may seek your advice on legal matters or send you overflow work. And there are less-obvious benefits, too: in an article on solo practice,[1] lawyers Christopher Manning and Melinda Sossaman described how they've used their Washington DC office townhouse as a client magnet. They renovated space on one floor and hosted events—holiday gatherings, political fundraisers, etc. In time, the attendees referred them cases, and those clients generated even more referrals.

For solo Chris Vaughn-Martel, a 2006 law school grad and bar admittee, having a commercial space was also a great business motivator, and he says his decision to lease shared space has been more than repaid in productivity, client satisfaction, business referrals, and contract work. *Having an office helps me stay organized,* he said. *(If I had opened a home office), I probably would have stayed in my pajamas, played with my dog, napped, watched Colbert Report re-runs all day and not gotten anything done. I would have been lonely, probably depressed and unmotivated.*

CONS: As of the 4th Quarter 2007, Class A rents in the strongest markets rose faster than the national average, and were only slightly less expensive in places like Boston and San Francisco. Depending on the region and the address (commercial space in the South is still the least expensive), an outside office can range in the few-hundreds to several thousand dollars a month...and that's without calculating the time and energy to find a suitable office, to negotiate lease terms, and to purchase furnishings, signage, and equipment. Furthermore, depending on the vagaries of the market and local economy, a new solo might have to sign a one- or two-year lease, which would severely limit your flexibility to find less expensive, more appropriate space later. And as if you don't face enough financial pressure, the cost of an outside office space would ratchet up your stress level a few notches—and then there is the commute. Even a half-hour commute in any urban sector is likely to add up to five hours of potentially billable or productive time a week! And if you work part-time and have parental responsibilities besides, you're left with just a few hours to work before you need to turn around to pick up your kids.

The home office

PROS: For many new solos, the greatest single advantage of a home office is lower overhead. If you practice in an urban area (where even a small office starts at $1,000/month), you can expect to save $12,000/year working from home...and that's without calculating a home-office tax deduction. The money you save can be applied to legal research services, marketing materials, and CLE courses. More important, you can select your cases more judiciously instead of feeling compelled to take whatever comes in the door just to make the rent. As for convenience, nothing beats a home office, where the longest commute is from the kitchen to the Aeron chair in your den or spare room. And it goes without saying that a home office works better for parents of young children, allowing them to spend more time with them during the day, and to be there when they return home from school. Note: the IRS has strict requirements about whether your home office qualifies for a tax write-off. To do so, your home office—even a portion of a room—must be used "regularly and exclusively" as your principal place of business.

CONS: For many other solos, the greatest disadvantage of a home office is how it might reflect on their credentials and professional image. But while even that concern has less of a bite these days because of the popularity of tele-commuting and home-based businesses, it doesn't mean you won't confront the occasional insensitivity (e.g, *Must be nice to spend the day in your pajamas*), or lose an occasional project when a client or referring attorney is less confident of your firm's stability or credibility. And there are other considerations:

- Some agencies will not send temps to a home office. If you need someone to work onsite—say, a law clerk to compile an appendix of documents for trial, or a secretary to organize your files—you might need to find other ways to fill your employment needs.
- For some lawyers, the home office environment feels too isolating, and the household distractions and parenting responsibilities interfere with the work flow.
- And for reasons of safety and privacy, it might be helpful to maintain a separate mailing address for some practice areas like criminal defense and family law. A private mail box allows you to receive correspondence and checks without revealing your address, and keeps your home address off court filings that frequently wind up on the Internet. Publication of a home address does not matter as much for lawyers who serve corporate clients or handle contract work for other attorneys. Most of the solos I know who run those types of practices use their home address as their primary contact information.

Most clients will assume you work from a traditional office unless you make a point of saying otherwise. So, unless a client asks where your office is located, or pointedly asks if you work from home, you have no obligation to reveal that you do work from home. Don't ask, don't tell. Sometimes, you may not be able to avoid telling clients or colleagues you have a home office; don't sweat it (note: back when I started my practice from my home in 1993, I always felt I had a huge scarlet H branded across my business suit). These days, tele-commuting is increasingly common, and some clients, particularly those in large corporations or in the high tech industry, may regard a home office as ahead of the curve. Having a standard explanation will make you more comfortable disclosing your home office status. Perhaps, telling clients that you spend

See book updates at author's blog—www.MyShingle.com

so much time at the courthouse that maintaining a physical space was a waste of money and now, you can pass savings on to them. Or, even better, tell them that working from home saves an hour or two on commuting, giving you more time to spend on client matters. In the end, what matters most to clients is the quality of service that you provide and not where your office is located.

The virtual office. Since the 1960s, lawyers have been trimming overhead by sharing office space and infrastructure. But the emergence of a mobile workforce, and the spiraling cost of commercial space, has given birth to a new workplace solution—the "virtual"office.

In the words of Terri Bell, director of virtual office operations for The Regus Group, a major business center provider (*terri.bell@regus.com*), virtual offices can be *a powerful tool for solos and small firm practitioners who want to limit their start-up costs, and to establish themselves alongside larger competitors for a fraction of the cost of setting up a full-time office.*

PROS: If a full-time space isn't in your budget, a home office poses image problems, and you're reluctant to meet clients at Denny's, Starbucks, or the courthouse cafeteria, a virtual office makes a lot of sense. For starters, virtual offices are much less expensive than full-time leased space, typically starting from $75 to $200/month, depending on location, level of service, and the elements of the lease "package". A typical virtual office might include a mail-forwarding service, a shared receptionist to forward your calls, and five hours a month of office or conference room space. Many virtual offices also offer services such as voice-mail, fax, and/or access to hourly secretarial services. One Denver provider even offers free valet parking in a nearby garage—a real perk in a congested city.

According to the Office Business Center Association International (*obcai.com*), there are more than 4,000 shared-office business centers in North America. Many virtual offices operate at prime locations, so you enjoy the benefit of a prestigious address that you could not otherwise afford. Virtual space also solves the problem of where to meet clients, and leases are typically month-to-month and upgradeable to provide more hours of space to meet emergent needs. Virtual space is an attractive option; it gives new solos just the time they need to get their firm up and running so that they can get a better sense of their longer-term space needs.

CONS: Owners of virtual offices tend to nickel-and-dime you, often charging exorbitant rates for such services as faxing…even an extra charge for checking your mail. And if you sign up for a mail-forwarding service, there can be a lag time in getting mail, which could be a problem with a heavy litigation practice in which filings demand a timely response. Many virtual offices typically service hundreds of professionals. As a result, the so-called personal receptionist can come across as brusque or rude (so, you may want to get an Internet fax number and/or a cell phone so clients can call you directly). Note: during your busiest months, the cost of a virtual office could equal the cost of full-time space because you will have to rent more hours of office space. Of course, if you're generating more revenue, you can absorb the additional overhead. In time, your virtual office may cost more than permanent space on a consistent basis, at which time you should start looking for your own office.

The shared office. Shared space is also quite popular. The Wall Street Journal (April 30, 2007) featured one firm that leases shared space in an historic section of Boston. In their lease, they got office furniture, phone lines, Internet access, copy machines, conference rooms and a shared lounge. And, for a few dollars more, virtual locations in the four other cities where the building owner has offices. While the law firm doesn't have an actual physical presence in those other cities, they arranged to have local phone numbers and mailing addresses for each, as well as access by-appointment to office space and support services. Said one of the firm's partners, *It gives us the opportunity to get out there and develop a marketplace without paying for the infrastructure.*

When you share office space, especially with other attorneys, there are several important potential ethics questions to consider:

Does your arrangement adequately protect client confidentiality? You must have a secure place for storing client files that only you or authorized personnel can access. Don't assume that file security only matters when you share space with lawyers who represent clients with conflicting interests. The ability of one of your fellow attorneys to gain advantage in litigation by stealing a look at privileged strategy memos is the least of your worries. The greater danger is the possibility that your suite-mates' employees or guests could take advantage of unsecured files to steal Social Security numbers or other sensitive financial information. If so, you could face disciplinary sanctions or even malpractice liability for exposing your clients to fraud or identity theft by failing to adequately safeguard the financial information in their files.

Other tips for preserving client confidentiality:[4]

- Avoid discussing confidential matters in common outside your office.
- Keep confidential materials in secured and locked cabinets inside the office.
- If you share a receptionist, have your calls forwarded to a private voice mail instead. The message may contain confidential client information which the receptionist might inadvertently share inadvertently with others in the office.
- Don't leave a shared photocopying machine unattended.
- Avoid sharing a fax or printer.
- Shred work drafts.
- Maintain an individual computer; password-protect any shared network.

Does your arrangement give the impression you are part of a law firm? When you lease space in a suite of attorneys, or within a firm, retain your firm's own identity with your own business stationery and name on the door. In some cases, solos share space and the expenses of a receptionist or support staff, and jointly advertise or collectively list

their names on law firm stationery and even a Web site. The appeal of this arrangement is understandable—reduced overhead and the appearance of being part of a
larger group without all of the formalities of an official partnership. Still, such
arrangements could create trouble. There have been several cases where lawyers participating in a collective arrangement have been sued for malpractice committed by an
office mate because the client believed that all of the lawyers operated as part of a single firm. Conflicts of interest may or may not be an area of concern when your
office-sharing arrangement resembles a law firm. According to Jim Calloway, law practice manager for the Oklahoma bar:

> *...As a practical matter, many of the most significant potential conflicts of interest will be recognized*
> *by the clients, or perceived even when they do not in fact appear. If the lawyer down the hall*
> *represents the wife in the divorce case, you are probably not going to convince the husband that you can*
> *adequately and fairly protect his interest. Frankly, you should not even try to convince him and then*
> *represent him.[5]*

If in doubt, consult your state's ethics rules on *conflicts of interest within a law firm* for
guidance.

How much do you know about your future suite-mates? Sadly, there are unscrupulous
lawyers who would take advantage of shared-space arrangements: for example, the ami-
able young lawyer chatting with your prospective client in the lobby, and who may be
trying to steal your business...or the law firm that is renting you space and opens a
specialty practice of its own when they see how busy your practice is...or the solo who
is subletting from a law firm, and steals their client list so he can send out business
solicitation letters. (Note: by the way, this last scenario actually occurred at a firm
where I once worked, and an astute client exposed the solo to a senior partner). I know
of another case where an unscrupulous lawyer subletting space was suspended from
practice for three months. But rather than inform his clients of the suspension and
withdraw from his cases as required, he asked one of the solos subletting from him to
enter an appearance in the cases for the duration of the suspension, even though the
suspended attorney remained involved and retained most of the fees when the cases
settled. What's the message here? When you rent space from other attorneys, you must
engage in the same due diligence as if you were hiring them or referring them a case.
If you don't know the attorneys personally, ask around about their reputations. Check
the bar Web site to make sure the attorneys are in good standing, and haven't had problems with the bar. Sharing space can offer great benefits for new solos, but you need
to find the right arrangement and to avoid the bad apples. Note: if you share space
with a firm and learn that the lawyers are, say, skimming money from client trust
accounts, or practicing with a suspended license, you have an obligation to notify the
bar...or possibly face ethics charges for failing to do so. As an attorney, you don't have
the luxury of turning a blind eye to unethical conduct by other lawyers.

The Office Space FAQ

Q: *For a newbie like myself, office sharing just seems so perfect; maybe too perfect. I wonder if there's any reason to be cautious?*

A: The advantages of subleasing…or office-sharing…are obvious: it's easier on the budget, you have access to a firm library, lunchroom and/or conference room, and there's a good chance of finding mentors and/or referral work. When sharing or subleasing works, it works well for everyone involved. A solo I know rented space from one of her clients (a trade association), and it led to more work simply because they saw her around more frequently. But another solo I know had a very different experience. He sublet space within an existing law firm on the promise that several family law matters would be referred every month. Unfortunately, a few months after he arrived, the firm started its own family law practice. Not only did the referrals evaporate, but the solo found himself in direct competition for clients with the firm from which he rented space. Is there reason to be cautious? Yes. When you explore the shared-space option, don't allow the promise of referrals to dictate your decision.

Q: *I'm worried about overhead, and wonder if the expense of an outside space is likely to be offset by business opportunities of having an office.*

A: I know of a Boston-area solo with an IP practice who, after evaluating her target market, learned that most of her prospective clients and referrals expected her to have permanent office space. So, from Day One she rented commercial space. On the other hand, I work with several established energy regulatory lawyers in the Washington D.C. area who run successful practices from their home. Even though they can afford commercial space, they saw no point in renting an office that would rarely be used. Don't assume that a full-time office is indispensable to success and lock yourself into a lease you can ill-afford. Evaluate your target market before signing anything.

Q: *As a mom with a part-time practice, I want to be available for my kids but not if it keeps me from working on my cases. What shall I do?*

A: If you don't think you'll get your work done because you can't resist the distractions at home, or the isolation depresses you, then the loss of productivity would negate whatever money you save. If your personal work situation or habits preclude you from effectively working from home, renting space makes sense.

Q: *Where's the best place to look for office space?*

A: After searching the usual resources (bar newsletters, local classifieds, law school and courthouse bulletin boards, "for rent" signs), go online. I recommend *craigslist.com*, everyone's favorite online bulletin board. Among other virtues, it's a great source for office space listings in dozens of cities. And don't forget to talk to colleagues about whether anyone they know has space to rent or share. That's how I found a fully furnished office for nearly half the prevailing rates!

Q: *I've decided to get commercial space. I'm just not sure where it ought to be.*

A: In some ways, technology has simplified the question of where to locate your office. After all, the entire federal court system, as well as many state court systems, now have electronic filing systems. And with the exception of filing the original complaint, all other submissions can be made online instead of driving to court. And, of course, you can go online to search court dockets and retrieve files instead of ordering them from a court or agency office. In my opinion, the question of location hinges on what's best for your target clients. If you're starting a general practice, a storefront office or other high visibility space might be just the thing. If you have an immigration practice, you want your office to be closest to the immigrant community. If most of your clients are located out of town, find space near the airport.

Q: *I'm leaving a large firm later this year. I'm accustomed to working in the city, but I'm tempted to get a suburban office. Any suggestions?*

A: Suburban office space usually costs less than in the city, but cost is just one factor among many. Consider:

- *Are you already licensed in the suburban location?* If you work in the city, you may be tempted to move your office to a suburban location to minimize your commute. But that strategy only makes sense if you're licensed in the state where you live. It's not uncommon in large metropolitan areas (e.g., Washington DC/Maryland/Virginia or New York/New Jersey/Connecticut) for a lawyer to work at a firm in Washington D.C. or New York and reside in an adjacent state like Virginia or New Jersey where they've never been admitted to the bar. And many states prohibit lawyers from setting up an office if they're not licensed to practice in the state, even if they specify that their practice is limited to matters outside the jurisdiction. In this situation, you need to consider whether the added cost of gaining admission to another bar will outweigh the potential savings and convenience of a suburban office.

- *What's most convenient for your clients?* Many lawyers assume that a city office is more convenient because of proximity to public transportation and the courthouse. But that's not always the case. If you serve a suburban population, a suburban location is probably easier—and cheaper—on your clients. And if you're located in a suburban area that's served by public transportation, even clients who don't have access to cars can reach your office easily. As for lawyers who run a national practice, most of your clients may be located out of state, so your location won't matter as much because they'll rarely visit your office. And with most courts accepting e-filing now, proximity to the courthouse is less relevant than a decade ago.

- *What's most convenient for you?* Will a suburban office cut down on your commute, or is it closer to your children's daycare or school? If so, that's another major reason to consider the suburbs. And if you're working part time, a short commute will help take less time out of your already overbooked schedule.

- *What's best from a marketing and networking standpoint?* Consider how a suburban location will impact your marketing activities. For some types of practices, networking events and CLE programs are centered around the city. Many bar associations sponsor lunch events, or early evening events at downtown locations which can be a hassle to attend if you work in the suburbs. Also keep in mind that if you've been working in the city before opening your firm, a city location will allow you to meet with regularly with colleagues who would keep you in mind for referrals or contract work assignments.

Q: *I'm concerned what image a home office conveys to prospective clients and other attorneys.*

A: The more thoroughly your home and work space are separate, the more likely you—and others—will think of it as an office. Install a separate phone line, answer the phone with a formal greeting, invest in professional business stationery, and perhaps even establish a separate entrance. Make sure you designate separate spaces for work and home, even it's only screening off a portion of a living room with folding dividers. Most importantly, take care to eliminate from your phone calls any of the background noise associated with home. If you need to meet a client and your home office is not as professional as you would like, offer to come to the client's office or residence as a convenience. For clients visiting from out of town, you can get together for a meal at their hotel or, if they've come to visit an agency or the court, you can meet up at that location.

Q: *I used to think a home office would be ideal because I never socialized much with colleagues at work. Now that my office is at home, I feel isolated.*

A: Your home office is your just primary work location…it's not a cell. For simple human contact

OFFICE SPACE IN EXCHANGE FOR SERVICE

Many new solos look favorably on a work-for-space arrangement. It seems ideal; after all, you get access to office space without adding to your out-of-pocket costs, and it could lead to a relationship that leads to overflow referrals.

Before you sign anything, a cautionary note:

The work-for-space arrangement may not be as beneficial for you as it is for the outsourcing attorney. Do the math: if you put in 30 hours a month—calculated at a modest $100/hour—it comes to $3,000. Now, you may not have $3,000 in billable revenue when you start out. But, if you spent the same amount of time marketing, networking and/or writing articles, you'd probably be able to generate $3,000 in revenues in a couple of months! Now, consider the arrangement from the other side. If the attorney offering space can bill your 30 hours out to clients at $100/hour, he's $3,000 ahead, which is far more revenue than if he simply rented the space! If you have 30 hours a month free, you're better off seeking court-appointed matters for $40 to $50/hour (which will produce $1,500 a month in revenue), or lower paid contract work. If you spent $800 a month on office space, you would still have $700 left over for other business expenses. In short, you would still come out ahead of the work-for-space arrangement. But if it still appeals to you, engage in some due-diligence on the attorney making the offer, and commit the agreement to writing. Sad to say, many attorneys take advantage of work-for-space deals. You may think you're agreeing to a 25 hour-a-month commitment, but then you're given a workload that might take an experienced lawyer 50 hours! Or, you might be pressured to accept dud referrals or difficult clients in addition to your work-for-space duties. Eventually, you find yourself serving as an unpaid associate for the other lawyer rather than as a new, independent solo. If work-for-space sounds too good to be true; it is. Proceed with caution.

…and for marketing purposes…you should be regularly including time for CLE's, business meetings, and client conferences. Such activities are essential; not only do they help build your business, but they also foster personal relationships that can re-energize you. Outside my home office, my favorite work site is the law library, where working alongside frantic law students, and lunching at the cafeteria, reminds me of the camaraderie of my law school days.

Q: *My old law firm let me go, but offered me office space at bargain rates. Should I accept or find my own office?*

A: When you're let go for economic reasons, some law firms make a spare office available at little or no cost to help you launch their own practice. In the short run—six months or so—that can give you some breathing room while you assess your next step. After a few months, though, I suggest making a clean break even if it means sacrificing a free space. The separation will make for a healthier relationship with your former colleagues, and eventually could lead to referrals or references that have far more long-term value than the rent you would have saved.

Before you decide to hang around your old firm, ask yourself:

- Do you really want the firm hanging over your shoulder as you get your practice off the ground? What if one of the firm's clients wants to stay with you or hire you instead of the firm. Imagine how awkward it would be when your client runs into a former attorney in the elevator or hallway.

- By staying in the same office for any length of time, you open yourself up to accusations that you poached one of the firm's clients by conveying the impression that you still worked for the firm.

- What if your new practice is slow to get traction? It's inevitable you would begin resenting those ex-colleagues allowed to stay on.

- Consider, too, how your old firm might benefit. If you have a unique expertise, the firm could give the appearance of an affiliation even though you are no longer formally employed. On the one hand, the firm no longer pays your salary, and yet continues to give the impression it can service matters within your unique expertise. Consider the case of a Connecticut associate: even though he left the firm, the firm retained his photo and bio on the firm Web site.[6] The associate sued.

File a change of address beforehand. Go to the US Post Office website (*usps.gov*), and file a forwarding notice. Solo Amy Kleinpeter suggests, *Submit your request about a month before the move. But remember, if you only submit one request for, say, Law Offices of Amy E. Clark Kleinpeter, the system is not smart enough to recognize variations. For example, if mail is sent to variations such as Law Offices of Amy Clark, or Law Office of Amy E. Klienpeter, etc., the postal system may return it to sender because it isn't an exact match.* To make sure your mail is properly forwarded, submit multiple requests for all possible variations. The online is a dollar per change, and well worth the cost.

Send announcements. To the state bar, to your current and past clients, to all your marketing contacts, to anyone involved in already-filed cases, to the state agency that handles your corporate records, and to whatever alumni and social groups you belong.

Get new stationery. Go online (*vistaprint.com* or *iprint.com*) to get business cards quickly.

Computing. Back up your hard-drive before moving. Change the address on your email signature and on your web site. Also, Google your name to see all the places where your address is located, and update those records, too.

Moving. Avoid moving when there are deadlines looming. But if there are some unavoidable deadlines, pull those files before the move and take them home so you know where they are. Solo Kimberly DeCarrerra also suggests, *Move on a Friday, or long holiday weekend, so your office is up and running on Monday. And plan at least an extra day to get completely unpacked. There's nothing like having to run off to court and can't find the file because you boxed it away for the move.* If you move boxed files into long-term storage, label the boxes carefully and keep a detailed list of what's where.

Telephones. If you are expecting important calls (during the move), have the phone company forward your calls to your cell phone for the day.

Power needs. Check the electric service of your new space, and make sure it is adequate to your needs, and that the plugs are where you need them.

Remodeling. If you intend to do any painting or changing of window treatments or carpet, do it before you move in.

Lighting. Do any of your windows—especially your office windows—face west? If so, you probably will need some sort of window treatment or insulating window film.

Interior design. Measure all the rooms and the dimensions of all your furniture. Make paper icons of the furniture, and move them around a sheet of graph paper until you settle on a layout that works for you. Do the same for the walls, so you know what will hang where especially in the public areas and in your office.

Moving professionals. Use professional movers. Says one solo, *...In one five-year period, I moved four times and remodeled two offices. The only time things went smoothly, was when I wasn't there.*

Sources: Amanda Benedict, Kimberly DeCarrera, Amy Kleinpeter ●

CHAPTER 7

Selecting a Practice Area

"Learning about other legal specialties lets you diversify your practice and engage in cross-selling. There is a direct correlation between substantive competency and revenues." —Carolyn Elefant

For some lawyers, untangling the tax code is challenging, stimulating, and can generate a healthy revenue stream. Is it a good practice area for you? Not if you lack attention to detail or if tax law bores you to tears. Selecting the right practice area is an intensely personal decision, and what seems ideal on paper…or works for others…may not click for you. In fact, it's a lot like choosing a spouse or partner. First, there are such practical considerations as economic stability and general appeal, and—in law as in life—you can't thrive or find fulfillment without compatibility and a healthy dose of passion.

With that in mind, this section presents critical factors that will help you select a practice area, along with some pros and cons for a general or specialized practice. And for those who bring an existing specialty to their new solo practice, we'll suggest ways to expand or add a practice area to your existing repertoire.

What's the Right Practice for You? Eight Important Factors

1. Your passion. No matter what practice area you choose, you're bound to have bad days (like when a client stiffs you on payment or an opposing counsel makes you miserable). It's easy to get past the small stuff, though, when you have a larger vision in mind. How to do it? Identify practice areas that excite or inspire you. For example, if you went to law school because you wanted to make a difference in people's lives and to help them move forward, consider a consumer-oriented practice like consumer credit, bankruptcy, plaintiffs'-oriented employment law, or family law. Do you hunger for the thrill of the courtroom after five years toiling through corporate document reviews? Then make court-appointed criminal work part of your practice portfolio. That way, you're guaranteed court time right from the start. Or perhaps you're frustrated at reading about frivolous lawsuits or the rising cost of litigation. In that case, handle defense-side litigation or develop a practice that delivers quality service to businesses at competitive rates.

2. Your background.

An existing specialty. Perhaps you've come to solo practice with a practice specialty that you developed at your old law firm. In most cases, continuing a practice specialty you enjoy will make the transition easier because you can draw on existing contacts for referrals, and you won't need to spend time learning new skills. So, unless you're seriously unhappy with your existing practice area, or you believe it has no potential in a small firm environment, think twice about leaving it. You can always branch out to another practice area, and phase out the previous one later.

Prior work experience. Prior non-legal work experience in another industry is also a factor in selection. Your experience gives you an edge over your competitors not to mention greater credibility and a list of contacts that you can turn for referrals. Examples:

- Lawyers who worked as insurance adjusters often specialize in personal injury or small business representation where their familiarity with how insurance companies value cases helps them evaluate settlements.
- Lawyers with a high-tech background might do well choosing IP, licensing and Internet law, employment law (such as negotiating non-compete agreements or representing clients in discrimination suits), or even immigration law and offshoring (helping high-tech companies bring foreign workers to the US or to outsource work abroad).
- Many lawyers create practice areas—or niches—out of passions, hobbies, or deep personal interest. For example:

  Lawyer Stephanie Caballero endured eight years of infertility treatment in her quest to have children, finally realizing her dream of parenthood after a cousin carried twins as a surrogate. Ultimately, Cabellero had to adopt her children because the state did not recognize surrogacy. Having experienced infertility and surrogacy first-hand, Caballero (*surrogacylawyer.blogspot.com*) chose to focus her law practice on legal issues related to surrogacy and infertility treatment.

  Throughout law school, Tom Goldstein enjoyed tracking "circuit splits," cases which led to a legal disagreement between federal circuit courts, thus making the case a potential candidate for Supreme Court review. Eventually, Goldstein parlayed his love of Supreme Court statistics into a solo practice specializing exclusively in Supreme Court litigation. See Tony Mauro's *Paper Chase: How a Self Employed Lawyer Became the Best Supreme Court Litigator* (*Washington Monthly* July/August 2004).
- Sam Slaymaker (*slaymakerheritagelaw.com*) specializes in historic preservation law. Having grown up in his family's ancestral home, he developed a passion for preservation, and has served as director of various historic preservation foundations.

3. Your skills.
With enough practice, you can probably master any practice area in time. But face it, some practice areas are more likely than others to complement your natural skills. For example, lawyers who excelled at moot court in law school, or who

now enjoy research and analysis, might find that appellate practice naturally fits their skill set. Lawyers who are detail-oriented will have an easier time in practice areas like corporate transactions, which involve contract drafting or code-based practice areas (like tax or heavily regulated industries), where the placement of a semi-colon can make the difference in the outcome of a case. And, of course, litigation is ideal for lawyers who think well on their feet, and who can organize the large amounts of information generated in discovery.

4. Characteristics of the practice area. With limited time and resources, choose at least one practice area that lets you hit the ground running. New attorneys with little experience, or lawyers looking to change practice areas, should focus on consumer-oriented practice areas like bankruptcy law, simple probate matters, consumer credit and family law, social security and public benefits law, employment law and criminal law. Most bar associations, pro bono organizations and public defenders offer low-priced trainings or seminars in these practice areas, many of which include a "soup-to-nuts" guide to handling a case, relevant forms, case law and even names of practitioners who will answer your questions down the line. The added benefit of many of these practice areas is that you can start small with simple cases (such as undisputed divorces, criminal misdemeanors, a social security appeal), allowing you to learn as you go.

5. Financial considerations. Your financial situation can also impact your choice of practice area. If you want to specialize exclusively in contingency cases, you need to have some way to cover your expenses during the first six months of your practice, or at least be willing to take either contract work or court-appointed work as you wait for your first matters to come to fruition. Other practice areas like medical malpractice (again, on a contingency basis) or class-action litigation involve a substantial financial investment for expert witnesses, deposition costs, and other case-related expenses. Consider, too, that for some practice areas, e.g., IP or corporate securities transactions, malpractice insurance may be prohibitively expensive.

6. Trends. Economic or political trends can often make or break a practice area.

For some lawyers, periods of economic downturn are a good time to enter a new practice area. When one area plays out, the downturn gives you time to get up to speed on a new area without getting overwhelmed. At the same time, some attorneys use a downturn as a time to retire or abandon that practice. Either way, it means less competition…and some of them might even turn over their remaining case files to you. By the time that practice area cycles into another upswing, you could be well-established and ready to handle the influx of new clients.

Political trends can also increase work in some practice areas. Changes, say, in estate-planning, tax or immigration law, can generate work as clients seek advice on how to comply with the new laws. Other practice areas are also susceptible to cycles.

A booming economy can spur growth in such practice areas as real estate or corporate transaction. And, of course, in periods of recession, look for more bankruptcy and consumer credit cases, more fired employees tempted to sue former employers, and more marriages breaking up on the rocks of financial distress.

How to track trends? Keep an eye on the law blogs and online bar magazines. They tend to forecast trends at the beginning of the year, while solo and other legal listservs are a great forum throughout the year for insights on trends and information-swapping on developments in your practice area. And don't forget trade associations, chambers of commerce, and law firms; throughout the year, they all issue studies and reports which sooner or later will show up at Internet news sites.

7. Your schedule. For most practice areas, you can minimize impact to your schedule simply by controlling your workload. If you practice criminal law but your family needs you home every evening, avoid taking night court appointments. But if you want to work part-time, even the best planning won't accommodate certain practice areas. Generally, the most unpredictable practice areas...litigation, family law and criminal law...don't work well for part-time solos. Unless you make arrangements with a dependable back-up attorney, a part-time solo will struggle to cover an emergency appearance that's been scheduled on a moment's notice for your day home with the kids. And while you could hire sitters when you wind up with a matter on your day off, you defeat the purpose of working part-time if it occurs too frequently. As a part-time lawyer, you may also find yourself working from home, in which case court appearances and meetings can disproportionately cut into your workday. Trekking downtown for a 20-minute status conference can take three hours out of a five-or-six-hour workday.

For part-timers, the best practice areas are those where you can make your own deadlines and don't demand frequent face-time either in court or with clients. Suitable part-time practice areas include wills and estate, tax, appellate practice, some types of corporate work and contract lawyering, *i.e.*, handling work on a *per diem* basis for other lawyers.

8. Personality and temperament. Three important questions:

Q: *Would you enjoy working with clients unfamiliar with the legal system?*
A: Such practice areas as personal bankruptcy, personal injury, family law, consumer credit, and employment law require regular contact...and frequent hand-holding ...with clients unfamiliar with the legal system. For some, it's frustrating to explain over and over again the same basic concepts or answer the same procedural questions (*why is this case taking so long...why do I need to fill out all of these interrogatory responses,* etc). Or you may not have the patience to provide the constant personal reassurance and support that many consumer clients require. If you're one of these lawyers, you can

certainly succeed in a consumer-oriented practice. But unless you have competent staff to handle day-to-day interaction with clients, you'll find the demands of a consumer practice enervating. By contrast, some lawyers derive deep satisfaction from working closely with individual clients, helping them put their lives back together and take pride in their ability to make complex concepts accessible. Such lawyers find a consumer-oriented practice highly rewarding.

Q: *Do you thrive on confrontation... or not?*

A: You don't need a confrontational style to succeed in such dispute-oriented practice areas as employment law, family law, criminal law, general litigation or business transactions. Many lawyers in these areas have unassuming or deferential personalities, but enjoy a fierce reputation because of clever strategies and savvy discovery, or persuasive motions and briefs that shred their opponents' arguments. At the same time, when you're involved in a dispute-oriented practice, you do encounter a disproportionate number of aggressive lawyers intent on intimidating opponents (particularly those with less experience), with threats, screaming, insults and generally rude or unprofessional conduct. Some lawyers can shrug off this behavior. If you're not one of them, it can take its toll. But if you still want some litigation experience, or want to take on family law cases, consider these alternatives:

- Federal court practice is generally more mannered than state practice. So if you're interested in litigation, go after cases within a federal court jurisdiction.
- Courts in some jurisdictions are notorious for their more aggressive, rough-and-tumble style litigation. For example, if you're barred in two adjacent states and one favors an aggressive style, you might focus your litigation practice in the other state. Likewise, you might avoid handling disputes in certain courts. Consult with more experienced practitioners for help identifying those courts with more collegial attorneys and judges.
- Take advantage of the trend towards alternatives to litigation. One popular approach in family law is collaborative law, where parties are represented by individual counsel who agree that they will resolve divorce related disputes through negotiation and not litigation. See *en.wikipedia.org/wiki/Collaborativedivorce.* You can also specialize in alternative dispute resolution such as mediation, arbitration and negotiation.

Q: *Do you make others' problems your own?*

A: If you tend to take others' problems personally, you may have difficulty dealing with criminal defense or family law matters, where an adverse ruling can mean devastating consequences for your clients (e.g., jail time or loss of custody of their children). Such cases can take a psychological toll on lawyers who get too close to their clients. Moreover, your inability to keep a healthy distance from your clients' plight could cloud your judgment. For example, you might elicit false testimony from witnesses to defend a sympathetic, criminal client, rationalizing your action with the thought that the client's family will suffer if he's sent to jail. Many unscrupulous clients can sniff out "softies," and may try to take advantage of your empathy with unreasonable or unethical demands. Bottom line: if you can't trust yourself to maintain appropriate professional distance in even the most heart-wrenching cases, I suggest that you steer clear of practice areas like family law or criminal law where those types of cases predominate.

Generalization v. Specialization

For most lawyers, worries about malpractice claims or ethics violations frustrate their desire to develop and maintain a level of competence in several practice areas. At the same time, they worry that "putting all their eggs in one basket" limits their business opportunities especially if their chosen practice area is struck by regulatory reform or economic downturn.

In this section, we'll discuss the major concerns about specialization, and how to expand your practice area:

On specialization—

Q: *How can I decide on a practice area if I'm just starting out?*
A: Even if you have no prior work experience, you probably have a general sense of what types of matters you *don't* want to handle. In my own case, I started my practice with one specialization and wanted to expand. But I knew that family law, with all of its emotional baggage, or trusts and estates (which was incomprehensible to me in law school), weren't right for me. So I turned down cases in those areas from the beginning. By continuing to rule out areas that weren't a fit, I eventually settled on five main practice areas that worked for me (energy regulatory and renewables, court-appointed criminal work, appellate litigation, civil rights/employment law and small business litigation). Eventually, I phased out my court-appointed criminal work, which no longer made sense from a financial perspective, and small-business litigation because I didn't like state court practice. For some lawyers, choosing a practice area is an evolutionary process that involves a good bit of experimentation and trial and error. So if there are several areas of interest, feel free to sample a variety of different client matters. Also, offer to assist an experienced attorney in a particular practice area so that you can learn what's involved without the pressure of handling an unfamiliar area on your own.

Q: *How do I avoid turning away business without spreading myself too thin?*
A: Many lawyers straddle multiple practice areas for fear of turning away business. There's even a name for it: *threshold law.* That is, you take every matter that crosses the *threshold* of your front door. Most new solos are understandably reluctant to turn away business because of concerns about overhead, and anxiety about whether the phone

will ever ring again. But while it's important that a lawyer sample different cases before settling on a specialization, taking too great a variety of cases could, in the long run, stunt your firm's growth. For example, let's say you're juggling a criminal matter, an immigration case, a family law dispute, a bankruptcy filing and a probate matter. You end up researching five distinct practice areas because what you learn for one isn't readily transferable to another. And because different courts and agencies have jurisdiction over each of these matters, you waste time calling four separate court clerks trying to figure out how to file or plead, and then race from court to court to make an appearance. If you're uncomfortable turning away clients, build a referral network. Compile a readily accessible list or spreadsheet with one or two attorneys in different practice areas, so that when a client calls with a matter you don't handle, you can provide the name of other attorneys. Afterward, contact the referring attorney that a case is on the way, and make it clear that you're available for cases in your own area. With a referral system in place, you won't feel as if you're turning away cases... merely exchanging them for cases that suit your practice.

Q: *How can I help my clients if I don't have a general practice?*
A: Many lawyers decline to specialize so they can provide "one-stop shopping" to clients who need help with a variety of legal problems. For example, the lawyer with the transactional practice whose small business clients also have questions about employment matters, IP work, corporate and securities work, litigation, tax law, contract review and negotiation... and even trusts and estate work for company principals. As discussed earlier, you're asking for trouble if you try to handle too many unrelated and relatively complex practice areas. Indeed, even at large firms, companies aren't represented by one lawyer, but by multiple attorneys with different practice specialties. So take some guidance from successful large firms. Establish virtual teams of other solos who specialize in IP, employment, tax and other matters you don't handle, and bring them on board to serve clients with multiple needs. In this way, you'll bring your clients the spectrum of expertise that they demand at a fraction of the cost of a large firm. How might this virtual team work? A family law attorney might pair with a probate attorney to provide seamless service to a newly divorced client who needs to change her will. A personal injury attorney could team up with a tax or finance lawyer for assistance in structuring settlements and advising on the tax consequences of an award. For more information, see *Affiliation, Networks & Project Partnering* (Chapter 11).

Expanding Your Practice Areas. While generalization has its drawbacks, you don't want to narrow the scope of your practice too tightly. In this way, you avoid burnout from handling the same types of cases over and over, you stay fresh by handling different matters, and you create a hedge against economic, political, or regulatory changes. Here are some factors to consider without exposing you to a risk of malpractice:

Look for 'natural' combinations. Peter Roberts, a practice management advisor for the ABA's Law Office Management Assistance Program, advises lawyers to seek out compatible areas that make use of a common skill-set and deal with a common pool of clients. For further details, read Robert's article, *Diversified Practice: Tailor a Good Fit* at *abanet.org/genpractice/magazine/2004/jan-fe/diversified*. Roberts writes that certain practice areas make a natural fit, such as:

- Environment—Real property, and use, environment, mineral right, public utilities, zoning law
- Social work—Family, juvenile, elder law
- Arts—Contracts, copyright, nonprofits, small business
- Science/technology—Patent, health, IP, personal injury, medical malpractice
- Business/ownership—Business and corporate, mergers and acquisitions, startups, contracts
- Personal injury/consumer—Workers compensation, insurance coverage, health provider reimbursement, Consumer Protection Act, and insurance bad faith

Roberts also suggests that you examine how bar associations organize their practice section categories because they frequently group practice areas that go well together or lead to one another. On the flip side, the ABA practice management advisor cautions against combining practice areas that *force you to change gears mentally every time the phone rings.* He also suggests avoiding specialties that lack the potential to transfer clients from one area into another.

Balance stable revenue areas with narrower, or more risky, specialties. Strike a balance between practice areas that generate a steady stream of revenue with riskier contingency or litigation cases that offer higher payouts but may require months or years to collect. For example: combine contingency-based, personal injury matters with court-appointed criminal work. The court-appointed work will pay the bills while you wait for PI settlements, and though civil and criminal procedure are different, both areas will sharpen your litigation skills. Add some spark to such practice areas as corporate transactional work or regulatory law—where you're well compensated by large institutional clients—with one or two civil rights cases in federal court where you recover attorneys fees by statute. You'll learn federal court practice (if you don't know it already), find assistance from groups like the ACLU, and potentially collect fees and publicity for handling public interest work. Consider handling both sides of the same specialty to even out the revenue. For example, some law firms handle both plaintiffs' and defense side employment work. Defense side work typically involves counseling

See book updates at author's blog—www.MyShingle.com

and training companies which generates revenue, while some plaintiffs' matters might be handled on a contingency or reduced fee basis with full recovery of statutory attorneys fees.

Balance narrow high-visibility work with staples. Some narrow niche practices provide enough work to sustain a law firm. Tom Goldstein's Supreme Court practice thrived on an exclusive diet of matters before the Supreme Court, and did not handle any other appellate litigation. But other lawyers have very narrow niches, sub-specialties such as grandparents' visitation, women-owned businesses, or (in my case), ocean-renewable energy. They attract a good deal of attention, but may not account for more than 10 or 15 percent of your business. Rather than give up a beloved or unique niche, pair it with other more general practice areas, such as family law, business law or public utilities law. The "wow" factor of your niche will help draw clients to your other practice areas.

The accidental practice

And then there's the successful accidental practice, the one some solos fall into by being in the right place at the right time. Some examples:

- Donna Newman, a criminal defense attorney, was appointed to represent Jose Padilla as part of a run-of-the-mill, court-appointment program. Shortly thereafter, Padilla was classified by the Bush Administration as an "enemy combatant" and put into military detention, where he was denied access to counsel. Ms. Newman fought her client's case all the way up to the US Supreme Court (*Rumsfeld v. Padilla*, 124 S. Ct. 2711 (2004), setting historic precedent, and in the process becoming a renowned expert on novel areas of constitutional, human rights and military law.
- Baltimore attorney Robin Page West who stumbled into the lucrative area of *qui tam* litigation when she accepted a referral from another attorney too busy to research this area of law. Today, West has litigated many more *qui tam* cases, written a book on the subject, and gained recognition as an expert in the field.
- Sterling DeRamus, an Alabama practitioner, who is now regarded as the local guru on highly specialized technical federal statutes like the Fair Debt Collection Practices Act (FDCPA), COBRA and ERISA, a status which attracts referrals from attorneys in other practice areas. And it's all because when clients happened into DeRamus' office with these types of claims, he took the time to research those statutes—where he had no experience—instead of letting the complex subject matter intimidate him.

Here are a few suggestions on how to discover new practice areas:

Practice serendipity. Set aside that business plan, crumple up that marketing checklist, toss out the how-to guide for building a practice. Instead, venture into unknown territory. Perhaps you sign up for a *pro bono* course in a practice area where you have no experience, or volunteer to organize a presentation for the local bar or a community group on a topic with which you're unfamiliar. In this way, you make contact with different groups that just might provide the lead you're looking for.

Listen more. For example, listen to that small business client who comes to you seeking representation and happens to mention that he's had problems with his insurer. Who knows, you might also find yourself sitting on top of a bad-faith action. Or, spend a little extra time listening to that family law client who comes in for representation in a divorce proceeding and happens to mention that she's just been fired because her boss made a pass after learning of her new single status. Who knows, you might have an employment law matter to pursue. Also, as you spend time with other attorneys, mention that you're eager for new work in a variety of practice areas. Many attorneys may misjudge the value of a case if they're not familiar with all of the potential causes of action, or don't have the time to research an esoteric matter themselves.

Learn, learn, learn. Once you find a potential lead in a new field, learn as much as you can. Run some computerized searches to get the lay of the land, then visit the local law library to search out treatises, law review articles, and trade press publications. Do a Google search to find relevant blogs. If there's a *listserv* devoted to these issues, post a few questions. If a matter puts you before a court or agency where you've never practiced, call up a clerk for assistance with procedural matters, or an agency staffer who might share some of the agency's past experience with the issue. Learn, learn, learn. Most important, find another attorney who's handled similar cases who'd be willing to act as a sounding board or mentor.

Follow up. Once you stumble into a new practice area, make the most of it. Why not write an article for a law review or bar journal? After all, the costs are sunk since the bulk of the research was completed when you investigated the new practice area. It shouldn't take much more time to transform your notes into publishable copy. And if the field is one of sufficient interest—and appears to have lucrative potential—you could launch a blog on the topic.

Some additional thoughts about CLE's:

- To distinguish quality CLE's from the duds, seek out recommendations from lawyers who've taken a particular CLE. Also, check with the local bar. Some will let you access past course materials, which may give you an idea of the CLE's value.
- If you want to learn about a local practice area (e.g., trusts, family law, briefing techniques for your local court, etc), select courses sponsored by state or local bars rather than national CLE providers. Generally, the local presenters are more familiar with the ins and outs of local practice. If you practice in a major urban area, your local bar may also have sections dealing with national practice areas like renewable energy, securities, telecommunications or Internet law. The cost of these courses should be more reasonable than those offered by professional seminar or national CLE providers.

When you run your own firm, there's a direct correlation between substantive competency and revenues. By keeping ahead of the information curve, you can edge out your competitors, and generate billable work advising clients on the implications of new laws. And learning about other legal specialties allows you to diversify your practice and engage in cross-selling. That is, if you're a real estate lawyer and you learn about probate, you can sell clients about your service in both areas. Below are some places to learn about new practice areas:

Pro bono training

Many state and local bar associations or legal aid groups offer free or low-cost *pro bono* training from top lawyers on matters you might use in solo practice, such as public benefits litigation, consumer protection, bankruptcy, trusts and estates or veterans' benefits appeals. Often, the courses include a handbook you can use later in practice. Many of the classes cost less than $100, or merely require a commitment to handle to two *pro bono* cases. Note: so many attorneys usually participate in these programs, there is only a minimal chance that you'll actually be called to take a case.

Court-appointed panel training

When you sign up to handle court-appointed work, (such as criminal defense or abuse and neglect cases), the court or the public defenders' office may also provide extensive training for free or a small cost. Take advantage of this; you'll learn insider tips not ordinarily found in the black-and-white letter law or rules. And as with *pro bono* training, lawyers who teach about handling court-appointed cases are usually willing to help you later on.

Court-watching

Not sure how to argue an appeal or cross-examine a witness? Visit the courthouse and watch other attorneys. And even if you don't know enough about handling the examination of a witness, pay attention to a judge's reactions to see what works. Check the judge's calendar (either at the court Web site, or by contacting the judge's secretary or clerk) to make sure you have a chance to see an actual trial or motion, as opposed to sitting through status hearings. Most judges welcome lawyer/observers in their courtroom. Observing depositions, settlement conferences or negotiations is more difficult because— in contrast to courtroom proceedings; they're generally not open to the public. You might also ask a mentor if you can accompany him/her to a deposition, or volunteer to do some work for an attorney in exchange for observing at a mediation.

Newsletters/magazines/court and agency news

Pay attention to the daily, weekly, national legal trade press. Many large law firms also offer newsletters or action alerts on recent developments that anyone can sign up for at their Web sites. In addition, trade associations and specialty bars also publish electronic newsletters and magazines. They're included in the cost of membership.

Blogs and news feeds

Blogs are invaluable for information in many fields. For example, if you handle appellate matters, Howard Bashman's blog (*appellateblog.com*) keeps you in the loop about dozens of important court cases within an hour or so of their issuance. There are hundreds of blogs on every legal topic you can imagine—from electronic discovery and telecom law, to Maryland personal injury practice or New Jersey family law. To find a blog covering your practice area, seek out *blawg.org, blawgsearch.com,* or abajournal.com/blawgs/.

Continuing legal education

In theory, CLE's help keep your practice skills and substantive knowledge fresh. In practice, though, the cost and quality of these courses varies widely. Some programs will provide you with real substance; others are little more than Power Point presentations by attorneys more interested in generating referrals than sharing information about their practice area. ●

- Taking CLE's isn't just a matter of out-of-pocket costs; the investment of time is often considerable. More and more, though, CLE's come right to your desk via phone or Internet. Such courses are usually less expensive; in fact, many are free. Another increasingly popular option are the CLE podcasts offered by some bar associations. You simply download the podcasts to your iPod or MP3 player, and learn as you commute or work the Stairmaster.

- For lawyers with large firm specialties (e.g., securities law, environmental law), many CLE's are quite expensive. Expect to pay $1,500 in addition to whatever transportation and lodging expenses might be involved. If you can't find a cheaper substitute for these classes, (e.g., a locally sponsored brown bag lunch event or webinar), try this:

- Look for an attorney who would be willing to pay for you to attend the conference in exchange for you sharing the materials and summarizing the conference proceedings. Though you may still have to pay travel and airfare, you can use the conference to network and at least avoid the cost of admission;

- If the conference is local, perhaps you can volunteer to check badges or register participants in exchange for free admission;

- Arrange to purchase the conference proceedings, though sometimes it's several months before the materials are available.

III. The Practice

CHAPTER 8

Dealing With Clients

"My advice to new solos: underestimate your
revenue, overestimate your expenses...and make
sure you get paid up front." —HEIDI BOLONG, SOLO

Now that you've started a firm, your livelihood depends upon your ability to serve clients, because you wouldn't have a law firm without them.

Just about any lawyer who passes the bar can provide competent counsel. But client service—that is, the way you treat and relate to clients—is one of the major factors that will distinguish your practice from others, especially the large law firms. However, serving clients does not make them your boss; clients should not control the way you run your practice. And while clients have important rights that you must respect, those rights do not include keeping you at their beck-and-call around-the-clock, ordering you to discount your services, or forcing you to take a position that violates ethics rules. New solos must learn how to serve clients, without allowing clients to become their master.

This chapter has two sections:

- The first addresses your relationship with clients: how to serve them, how to treat them, how to choose them, and how to deal with the difficult among them. It also deals with your professional obligations under your ethics code, and (b) the personal, intangible ingredients like bedside manner and empathy.
- The second section describes the legal tools necessary to define your relationship with clients; specifically, the retainer or engagement letter, the nonengagement letter, and the termination letter.

The Starting Point: Your Ethics Obligations to Clients

Lawyers often overlook the most basic and essential source of guidance in serving clients: the code of professional responsibility.

The ABA Model Rules of Professional Conduct and your jurisdiction's ethics rules spell out your basic obligations to clients, which include providing competent counsel and zealous representation, guarding client confidences, exercising independent judgment, and charging reasonable rates. Chances are that you haven't cracked open your state code since you studied for the bar exam. If that's the case, take the time to read the code now. The rules and accompanying commentary will give you sound, practical advice on serving clients. Moreover, now that you're actually dealing directly with clients, the words of the code will carry real meaning for you.

Not only do ethics rules guide you in serving clients, they can also shield you from unreasonable client demands. For example, suppose an overbearing client tries to pressure you to mount a frivolous defense that you know will undermine his credibility before the court, or to contact and negotiate with a party whom you know is represented by counsel. You simply state that your state ethics code precludes you from taking the requested action, and if the client persists that you will have no choice but to withdraw to avoid ethics violations. In most cases, once you invoke your professional responsibility, even the bossiest of clients will back off. If they don't, you have reason to terminate them.

Client bill of rights. Some states, including New York, Illinois and Florida, adopt a Client Bill of Rights that attorneys must incorporate in their retainer agreement or post in their office. The document spells out what clients are entitled to expect from their relationship with you. For example, New York's Statement of Client Rights (see below) covers a range of duties that you owe clients, ranging from confidentiality and undivided loyalty to such nitty gritty details as prompt return of phone calls and sending clients copies of papers. Even when not required by the bar, many lawyers choose to develop their own Client Bill of Rights. Putting your commitment to client service in writing demonstrates that you take it seriously, and this will go a long way to ease the distrust many clients have for lawyers as a result of past experience or horror stories from friends.

New York Statement of Client Rights. A. Section 1210.1 of the Joint Rules of the Appellate Division (22NYCRR§1210.1)

1. You are entitled to be treated with courtesy and consideration at all times by your lawyer and the other lawyers and personnel in your lawyer's office.
2. You are entitled to an attorney capable of handling your legal matter competently and diligently, in accordance with the highest standards of the profession. If you are not satisfied with how your matter is being handled, you have the right to withdraw from the attorney-client relationship at any time (court approval may be required in some matters and your attorney may have a claim against you for the value of services rendered to you up to the point of discharge).
3. You are entitled to your lawyer's independent professional judgment and undivided loyalty uncompromised by conflicts of interest.
4. You are entitled to be charged a reasonable fee and to have your lawyer explain at the outset how the fee will be computed and the manner and frequency of billing. You are entitled to request and receive a written itemized bill from your attorney at reasonable intervals. You may refuse to enter into any fee arrangement that you find unsatisfactory. In the event of a fee dispute, you may have the right to seek

arbitration; your attorney will provide you with the necessary information regarding arbitration in the event of a fee dispute, or upon your request.

5. You are entitled to have your questions and concerns addressed in a prompt manner and to have your telephone calls returned promptly.

6. You are entitled to be kept informed as to the status of your matter and to request and receive copies of papers. You are entitled to sufficient information to allow you to participate meaningfully in the development of your matter.

7. You are entitled to have your legitimate objectives respected by your attorney, including whether or not to settle your matter (court approval of a settlement is required in some matters).

8. You have the right to privacy in your dealings with your lawyer and to have your secrets and confidences preserved to the extent permitted by law.

9. You are entitled to have your attorney conduct himself or herself ethically in accordance with the Code of Professional Responsibility.

10. You may not be refused representation on the basis of race, creed, color, religion, sex, sexual orientation, age, national origin or disability.

Beyond the Code: Building a Client-Centered Practice

Client service involves more than honoring your professional responsibilities. It's about taking the time to look at a case from your client's perspective, and then asking what issues matter most to your client. In this way you distinguish yourself from competition. For example:

- How does the legal matter you're handling fit in with the client's overall business strategy or personal goals?
- How is the case affecting your client personally?
- What does your client think about the service you've provided?

Whatever you call this aspect of client service—hospitality, bedside matter, client-centered practice—these skills will set you apart, and leave a lasting impression long after your case has concluded.

The client-centered practice. In a client-centered practice, you try to see a case from the perspective of what's most important to the client. *Sometimes what matters most is not the way the law works, but how a case affects the client or their business.* Understanding this may inform your recommendations or change your strategy. For example, you may believe that as a legal matter, your client has a strong case, but your client prefers to negotiate a settlement to avoid adverse publicity. So, rather than recommend going to trial, you change strategy and negotiate the best deal for your client. Other times, how you communicate with clients is a test of your client-centeredness.

For example, consider two approaches—non-client centric and client-centric—to dealing with a divorce client who has just learned about a spouse's affair. As described by Oklahoma Bar Practice Management expert Jim Calloway, the client is likely to be angry and emotional, and may want revenge or to expose the wrongdoing as a primary goal of the case. The client also may have been told by well-meaning, but misinformed, acquaintances that the affair will have a significant impact on their divorce proceeding in the client's favor. You know that courts used to punish parties for adulterous relationships, but that it isn't as true today. But how would you tell your client that the judge won't consider the affair unless it affects the family finances or a child's well-being?

- In the non-client centric approach, you tell the client: *The judge won't care about the affair; they are so frequent these days that he or she will just disregard it. Affairs don't really matter any more in the eyes of the law. You seem very upset and may need to speak to a counselor. I'm not a counselor; I'm just your lawyer.*

- In the client-centric approach, you tell the client: *I really do understand your pain and anger at your spouse. There's nothing more painful than having a family member lie to you or deceive you. But, there is also nothing any of us can do to undo what has already happened. Your spouse may even regret what was done and feel guilty about it. The court will examine all of the evidence of what has happened previously in your marriage, but when the court reaches a decision it will be looking forward to the future. So, the court might consider the affair when it tells your spouse not to have any overnight visitors of the opposite sex when the children are around. But the court also might order you to abide by those same standards, even though you have done nothing like that in the past. That's because the court is going to be more concerned about the future well being of the children and the impact of certain situations on them than it is concerned about the social life of their parents.*

The first approach brushes aside the adultery issue, the one issue that matters most to the client. The second acknowledges the client's feelings about the adultery but focuses the client on the more important goal of acting in the best interest of the children. For Calloway's complete article, go to *okbar.org/members/map/articles/client*.

Bedside manner. You may think that so long as you serve clients competently bedside manner doesn't matter. But the medical profession, which has examined the relationship between bedside manner and client satisfaction, concludes otherwise. Studies consistently show that patients choose and judge doctors on good bedside manner, which includes honesty, compassion and respect, rather than technical skill. Good bedside manner can increase a doctor's success rate because patients who like and trust their doctors more readily follow their treatment instructions. Most importantly, good bedside manner can increase a doctor's success rate because patients who like and trust their doctors more readily follow their treatment instructions. Most importantly, good bedside manner shields doctors from malpractice actions; patients will not sue doctors they like. Lawyers can enjoy the same benefits by developing a good bedside manner.

Below are six ways to make that happen:

1. Deep listening. We often treat clients more like a law school issue-spotting exam than as human beings with a story to tell. A new client comes into the office, and we reach for a legal pad (or pull out the laptop) and—instead of sitting back and listening to the client's story—we fire off questions to figure out whether the client has a case. Clients want us to fix their problems, but it's just as important that someone hears them out. When we listen to clients we satisfy their need to be heard. Moreover, when we really listen, we get a better sense of what's important to the client and can tailor the appropriate strategy. When you meet new clients, start with an open-ended question. For example, *So, what is it that brought you to my office.?* If they wonder why you're not taking notes, explain that you prefer to listen to the full story first before asking questions.

2. Explain yourself. When clients don't understand why a lawyer takes a particular course of action, they grow suspicious. Consider a simple case where you've agreed to your opposing counsel's request for an extension of time. Many clients will perceive your consent as "rolling over," or compromising your position. From your perspective, though, agreeing to an extension of time reflects professional courtesy and the reality that the judge will probably grant the request even if you object. Most lawyers won't explain a decision to grant an extension of time because they believe, correctly, that they have the final say over procedural matters. Still, having the final say does not excuse lawyers from explaining their reasoning to the client. Letting a client know why you're taking a certain action may be annoying or inconvenient, but it demonstrates that you're acting in their best interest. Moreover, explaining your decisions educates and empowers them.

Here are two sample telephone conversations that show the benefits of a simple explanation:

Situation 1:

Lawyer—*I need to let you know that our summary judgment response is now due on October 1st. The defendant's attorney called me to get a three-week extension for his filing because he has two cases going to trial and he needs the extra time.*

Client—*Why did you agree to a new date? I've been waiting months and months for this case to even get to summary judgment. Their filing was due September 1st. Besides, we would have an advantage if the lawyer doesn't have time to do a good job.*

Lawyer—*Look, that's just how things are done. As your lawyer, this kind of decision is my call and besides, three extra weeks won't make much difference.*

Client—*Yeah, but I've been waiting for over a year to get this far. I need to get my money. And giving the other side more time means that he will file a better brief. Plus, that other lawyer is a jerk, he doesn't even deserve more time. Whose side are you on anyway?*

Situation 2:

Lawyer—*Listen, I thought that I should let you know that the Defendant's attorney called to ask for a three-week extension to file his motion for summary judgment, and I believe that the best course of* action is to agree to the request. I realize that we've been waiting a long, long time to get to this phase, but opposing counsel has two trials before the motion is due, and I'm fairly sure the judge will grant his motion even if I object.

Client—*Yeah, but there's been so much delay already. And why should we give the lawyer more time to file a brief? Won't that help their case? Plus, he doesn't deserve an extension, he was so rude at depositions.*

Lawyer—*I realize the case has taken a long time, and I don't like the delay any more than you do. But the major problem has been that the judge has been very slow to make rulings on some of the issues. And as you know, our case is really complicated, which also explains why the case has taken this long. You have to remember that opposing counsel hasn't asked for any extensions until this one. So because of his past record, along with the size of this case and his schedule conflicts, I'm sure that this judge will grant his request. If I object, I'm going to look unreasonable, and I don't want to jeopardize our good will with the judge on something like this. Also, I realize that you thought the Defendant's lawyer seemed rude at depositions and, personally, I was not a fan of his approach either. But he did not do anything improper. That's just his personality, and personality does not provide a good enough reason to object to his request.*

Client—*Well, OK, now I understand your decision. You're right, it does make sense to just grant the extension. Thanks for taking the time to explain all of that.*

In both situations, the lawyer's decision to agree to the extension is perfectly appropriate. But in the first case, the lawyer does not consult with the client, and then pulls rank rather than explaining his actions. When the client hangs up the phone, he's suspicious of the lawyer's motives. In the second conversation, the client remains confident with the lawyer and also, is grateful because the lawyer took the time to explain the decision.

3. Don't 'nickel and dime' your clients. Good bedside manners encourage clients to call their lawyers with a problem or information about their case. Yet nothing discourages communication more than charging clients for short phone calls or e-mails. When clients receive a bill with a $100 in charges for two ten-minute phone calls (*e.g.,* at $250/hour, .2/hour or 12 minutes = $50), they'll avoid calling you so they don't run up their bill. Some lawyers simply write off short phone calls or charge a higher hourly rate to recover the costs of short phone calls without adding a direct charge to the client's bill. Consider adopting one of these approaches so clients feel that they can call you for a quick conversation without worrying about the meter running.

4. Return calls and e-mails promptly. Many times, you may not want to speak with clients or you simply have nothing new to tell them. Don't ever avoid returning phone calls. More than anything, ignoring phone calls angers clients, making them more likely to turn on you if there's an adverse outcome in the case. If you don't feel up to speaking directly with a client…particularly a problem client…send an e-mail to schedule another time for a phone call. Of course, some clients go overboard, calling several times a week. Even here, don't evade the calls which will heighten the client's persistence.

Instead, talk to the client and assure that you will call whenever a new development arises. Or, if you do not expect changes for some time, invite the client to call you once a month for a brief status update. Beyond that, explain to the client that frequent calls will not move the case any faster. If the persist, you can try charging for the calls and see if that deters them or—if you have a law clerk or secretary—ask them to deal with the client. If these measures don't work and the client's calls begin to impact your productivity, you may need to think about dropping the client.

5. Showing interest in your clients. Simple courtesies go a long way to building relationships with clients. When your clients call, ask how they're doing. This, too, goes to bedside manner. If you know that your clients have a special pastime, be it fishing or spending time with a grandchild, inquire about that. If you represent a company, show an interest in the company's history, its business and mission. Where a case has been particularly stressful for a client, ask how he is holding up. Your client may not say much, but these kinds of questions reinforce that you view him as a human being rather than a case file. Also, empathize with your client when the case isn't going your way. For instance, if you receive a disturbing ruling or motion, why not share that you're also disappointed with the outcome or that you believe it's an incorrect result? Expressing your opinion on the outcome of the case lets clients know that you're involved not just for the fee, but because you truly believe that your client has the stronger position.

6. Saying thanks. Most of us expect our clients to express gratitude for our terrific service. The truth is, we owe our clients our thanks. For us, showing up for court on time (and properly attired) and rehearsing witness testimony for hours are routine. But legal matters are huge burdens on our clients' day-to-day lives. They usually have to take time off from work or arrange for child care to prepare for hearings or attend depositions, and, in some instances, they must buy new clothes to wear to court. They put up with last-minute cancellations and tardy judges. They disclose their life histories to us (near strangers), detail the embarrassing or disappointing events about the nasty employer or the soon-to-be ex-spouse that brought them to our offices. Many cut back on other expenses or make sacrifices just to pay our fees. So, take the time to thank your clients for their cooperation, and let them know how their efforts make you more effective.

Resources for a client-centric service

With so many practice-management advisors blogging, there is a proliferation of online resources on how to build a client-centric practice. You can find good advice at a variety of blogs, including *whataboutclients.com, patrickjlamb.com, legaleaseconsulting.com, legal sanity.com, goldenmarketing.typepad.com,* and *davidmaister.com.* Many of these blogs offer tips for building relationships with more sophisticated business clients, thus allowing solos to gain an edge over large firm counterparts. These blogs also share lessons of exceptional client service from other service industries, such as real estate, high-tech, the medical profession, and the hospitality industry. For a more extensive list of client-service blogs, visit *abanet.org/lpm/lpt/articles/slc05061*.

Empowering and Involving Clients

Involving clients in their case can change the outcome for the better. If you're skeptical, consider the case of Sheila Kahanek, one of five Enron executives indicted for a Nigerian barge scandal that was discovered around the time of Enron's collapse. Of the five, only Kahanek was acquitted, in part because of the active role she played in her defense. Kahanek (who is the *only* Enron executive ever acquitted, though some convictions have been reversed on appeal) organized and analyzed the thousands of documents designated as evidence by the prosecution, and shared valuable insights about the inner workings of Enron that helped her lawyers at trial. According to her attorney, Dan Codgell, *There's no way I would have won the trial without Sheila working her ass off. She literally had this trial indexed, highlighted, organized...she knows every document in the case—cold.*[11]

Not every client will be as sophisticated or motivated (then again, not every case is as complicated as Enron). Here are some tips for making clients active participants in their case, no matter the size or type of client:

Write a synopsis. Before clients come in for a consultation (particularly, where you offer a free consultation), ask clients to prepare a brief summary or time-line of the events that lead up to their case. (Don't have clients send the summary in advance because they may get the impression that you will start working on the matter when in fact, you have not yet agreed to represent them). You can even prepare simple intake sheet that will give you some of the facts needed to help you evaluate the case. Skim over the case summary when the client arrives. The case summary/intake exercise forces clients to focus on the facts of the case and helps them understand that any legal matter, from a lawsuit to preparation of an estate plan or corporate documents, requires their active involvement. More importantly, a survey collects the facts you need from the client on paper and helps you identify those potentially problematic clients who won't cooperate or can't follow instructions. Think about it; if clients are unwilling to invest a half-hour to fill out an intake form, are they going to spend the time required to gather documents or prepare for depositions?

Set up a client folder. Former Florida Bar practice-management advisor and management consultant Rjon Roberts, author of *How to Make It Rain*, advises lawyers to teach clients to organize materials by giving them a folder with your business card clipped to the front. When clients leave the office after the first meeting, include copies of any materials...an intake form, a retainer agreement and (if you're lucky), a copy of the client's check. Instruct the client to use the folder to file any information that you send to them and to bring it to all subsequent meetings and court proceedings. For higher tech or more sophisticated clients, consider creating an *extranet* from which

Q: What sort of information should I get from the client at our first meeting?

A: First, assure clients that the attorney-client privilege applies, even if they have not formally retained you. Clients, particularly those who are less educated or involved in such sensitive matters as domestic violence or bankruptcy often need these reassurance before they divulge any personal information. In the course of the meeting, collect as much contact information as possible, including current mailing and e-mailing address, and home, work and cell phone numbers. Ask the client to specify the preferred point of contact. You also want to gather information on the names of other relevant parties in the case so you can run a conflicts check. Where a business client is involved, ask for information about subsidiary, parent and affiliate companies to rule out any conflicts. As for substantive information, what you need depends primarily on the types of cases your handling. In Appendix 4 (Creating a Sample Forms Library), you'll find a variety of client intake forms for different types of consumer practice, including family law, criminal, bankruptcy and probate. Some of these forms are general enough to adapt to other practice areas.

Q: A prospective client wants me to assist with a litigation matter in federal court. I've never appeared in federal court before. Do I tell the client it's my first time?

A: As a general rule, you should avoid telling prospective clients that you've never handled a particular matter if you believe that you can competently handle it. You may think that you're merely being honest in admitting to clients that you're a first timer, but clients will view your disclosure as an explanation for potentially inadequate performance and will immediately lose confidence in your abilities. Of course, where a client asks point-blank whether you've appeared in federal court, you must answer honestly...but not without a little damage control. Explain that you've gained more litigation in state court than many federal court practitioners, and that it is common for experienced litigators to practice in new courts all the time. ●

you can upload files and encourage clients to download or print documents if they want to keep hard copies. A folder or *extranet* system makes clients (particularly less sophisticated clients) feel important because you trust them enough to give them responsibility. And of course, these systems save you time by cutting down on client requests for documents or status updates. See Appendix 2 (Running a Practice) for more information.

Help your clients know what to expect. With clogged dockets and understaffed agencies, most proceedings just plod along, often taking six months to several years to resolve. Often, there's little that you can do to expedite the process except to make sure that you adhere to all of your deadlines. But most clients (especially business people accustomed to closing deals in a matter of hours) simply don't realize how slowly grind the wheels of justice. Frustrated, they may blame you for the delays. That's why you should take the time at the beginning of case to describe to your clients how a particular proceeding will work. You might draw a time-line that identifies each phase of the proceeding, with a low and high estimate of its duration. (In fact, as discussed in the next section, your client fee estimate should include an outline of the process and estimated cost). Explaining the process lowers clients' expectation about the time involved, which will minimize their frustration. Clients also worry that a long process will cost more. Assure them that a lengthy process does not necessarily translate into excessive legal fees. Many times, cases go into dormancy for periods of three months or more while you await a ruling, during which time, the client won't incur additional charges.

Encourage clients to gather information on the case. As a lawyer, you're the expert on the law in each case, but your clients are the source of facts. So use your clients as a tour guide to lead you to facts that will help you build a strong case. What kinds of facts can clients provide? Here are some ideas:

- Clients can help put a case into context by describing the customs and practice in their particular industry, a company's process for retaining documents or training employees, or a spouse's Internet habits. Understanding the context of the case can help you prepare discovery requests or assess the potential strength of your clients' arguments or settlement position.

- Clients can use their inside knowledge to identify potentially helpful witnesses or ferret out intelligence from friendly insiders. (Bear in mind, however, that once a case is in suit, some jurisdictions prohibit represented parties from communicating directly and transmitting the information on to their lawyers). Many lawyers overlook their clients as a resource, assuming that their clients will either convey irrelevant information or worse, lie or exaggerate facts. You should always verify a clients' description through another source where possible. But don't rule out clients as a source of information unless and until they give you reason to distrust them.

- You don't have to send clients a copy of every minor filing before it leaves your office, but do let clients review drafts of important documents, especially contracts, summary judgment motions, or responses in administrative proceedings. At a minimum, clients may catch factual errors that are either inadvertent or result from your misunderstanding of what the client originally told you. And you'd be surprised; some clients may even have decent suggestions about a potential strategy or contract provision, or feedback on points that deserve more (or less) emphasis. Too many lawyers let ego keep them from showing clients their work product, because they don't want to be challenged or corrected, or because they're afraid of looking as if they are less than omniscient. But clients will appreciate that you've solicited their input, and they'll respect you even more when you show respect for their ideas. Plus, it never hurts to have a second set of eyes review a document, even if those eyes belong to your clients.

Dealing With Difficult Clients

Ah, the clients from hell...that assorted collection ranging from the high-maintenance and nutty to the downright nasty or insulting. They call too much, they bounce checks, they denigrate lawyers (and by association, you), they ignore your advice to their detriment, they refuse to pay bills, and they repeatedly threaten to grieve you. As one management expert describes: *Your worst clients are destroying your business. They demand 80 percent of your time and energy and produce only 20 percent of your profits.*[22] Sooner or later (hopefully, sooner) you will reach a point where you must fire these clients lest they ruin your practice or even your life.

Here are some tips for dealing with difficult clients:

Stay cool. Dealing with a troublesome client is a rite of passage. You're not a bonafide solo practitioner until you can share at least one war story about an outrageously horrible client.

Share your misery. You may think your client's antics are unique, but at least one of your colleagues has dealt with similar behavior... or worse. Seek out other solos for advice on how to deal with your troublesome client. But even if they don't have any productive ideas, the mere sharing of your misery will relieve your stress and help put the situation in perspective.

Put everything in writing. There's always a chance a problem client may eventually file a grievance against you. So, as much as you may want to avoid dealing with this client, it's important all communications with them are put into writing. Here is where e-mail can make a difference. When the problem client calls, respond by e-mail. This way you have a written record of your communications, and it rebuts any potential claims that you were not sufficiently responsive.

Raise your rates. Let the relationship run its course by finishing up any remaining work and avoiding new matters. When you complete the final piece of work, send a termination letter (details later in this chapter) along with a final invoice, stating that your representation has ended. If the client calls to retain you later, politely explain that you are not accepting new matters. Or, raise your rates significantly if you think that will make your dealings with the client any more palatable. If the client balks, you're rid of him; if he agrees, well, at least you'll earn more for your troubles.

Withdrawal in active matters. When clients act up during a matter that promises to last awhile, take stronger steps to fire the client. Author's note: I believe you should broach the topic of withdrawal through personal communication, such as a phone call or office visit (followed up by written confirmation) unless your relationship has deteriorated so badly that you cannot engage in a civil conversation or you fear for your personal safety. But even when you advise your client by letter of your intent to withdraw, invite the client to call with questions. Otherwise, they may complain to the bar that you suddenly pulled out of the case without any discussion.

Some additional thoughts:

Let them down easy. Explain that you cannot provide the level of service that the client deserves or that you don't feel that your style fits your client's needs.

Be candid about payment. If you withdraw for nonpayment, remind the client that, like any professional service provider, you're entitled to payment when you render service. If you're dealing with clients who have the means to pay but choose not to, no further discussion is warranted; you're better off rid of them. As for the client who truly can't afford to pay you, explore payment by credit card, family loan, or having the client continue the case *pro se.* You might also suggest the client contact a bar referral service, a less expensive attorney, or refer them to *pro bono* or legal aid clinics. Stand firm in your decision to withdraw. You may feel sorry for clients who lack resources, but if you routinely write off fees, you'll find yourself just as impoverished as your clients.

Cite your retainer agreement. Where a client lies about a material aspect of a case or engages in conduct that's hurting his case and wasting your time, remind the client of his obligations under your retainer agreement. Stress that the retainer agreement is a two-way street, and that you can't effectively serve a client who ignores your advice. Realize that sometimes, you may not find relief from an overbearing client. When a case is a few months from trial and your client won't let you pull out, the court probably won't grant a withdrawal either. Moreover, in some jurisdictions, particularly criminal cases, courts hold little sympathy for lawyers who haven't collected enough money up front from the client to carry them through the duration of the case.[33] In a worst case scenario, ride out a difficult client as best you can. And vow to choose more carefully next time.

Send a termination letter and files. Once you withdraw from representing a client, send a short, polite letter acknowledging the end of your representation. For ongoing matters where the client will need to retain new counsel, include a copy of the client's file.

Don't get cynical. Don't let the client from hell sour your experience of solo practice. For every problem client, you will find dozens of model clients who pay their bills on time (with checks that don't bounce!), express gratitude for your service, refer you cases, treat you to fancy lunches, and even send you gifts at holiday time. Serving clients like these makes solo practice a rewarding experience, one you should not sacrifice because of a few bad apples.

Choosing Your Clients With Care: Due Diligence & Deal-Breakers

There's no foolproof method to avoiding clients from hell. But by choosing carefully and putting measures in place, you can minimize your risk of winding up with them. Some experts advise that you walk away from these clients entirely. That's nice advice if you have multiple clients beating down the door. But you don't usually have the luxury of turning away cases when you're starting out.

In the following section, I've outlined various risk-factors, and identified whether some clients only require additional "due diligence", or if they are "deal breakers":

Prior representation (due diligence). Has the client been represented by other attorneys in this matter? Personality differences or true lawyer incompetence can explain one unsuccessful attorney-client relationship. But rather than reject a client who has

S̲ee book updates at author's blog—www.MyShingle.com

already worked with one attorney, engage in due diligence; review the files or speak with the previous attorney to assess what went wrong the first time around.

Serial relationships (deal-breaker). Serial changes in representation indicate one of two things: a chronically dissatisfied client who in time will probably complain about your service, or a client who lacks the ability to pay the bills. Neither trait makes for a desirable client. In short, several prior unsuccessful dealings with lawyers is a deal-breaker.

Client with nothing to lose (due diligence). The most unreasonable clients are those with a contingency matter in which they don't pay any fees up-front. They're playing with other people's money, in this case yours (or if not your money, your time). Consequently, contingency clients often feel that they have nothing to lose by turning down an acceptable settlement or pushing for risky and more costly strategies. If you're handling contingency matters, you can't avoid non-paying clients. But you can mitigate the likelihood of unreasonable conduct by forcing non-paying clients to take a stake in their case. You can have these clients pay the filing fee and cost of serving a complaint or ask them help out on the case, for example, by collecting documents or organizing their case file. This investment might only amount to a few hundred dollars or a couple of hours of time, but at least the client will have something at risk.

Selective listener (due diligence). Pay close attention to any questions or comments that a prospective client raises during the initial consultation. Let's say that you've told Selective Listener that most cases of his type settle for $5,000, but you're aware of one case in another jurisdiction that settled for $15,000. If the Selective Listener says, *So, you're pretty sure I can get at least $15,000?*, you need to undertake some due diligence. If you plan to accept this client, you must meticulously document all oral communications and provide a detailed, written budget for the case (otherwise, Selective Listener will claim that he thought you said the matter would take five hours, not 25 hours). By planning ahead, you can avoid misunderstandings or unrealistic expectations that would otherwise result from a Selective Listener as a client.

Work for an interest in the case (due diligence). Sometimes a client will offer you an interest in their company in exchange for representing them at no charge. Though many experts classify this arrangement as a deal-breaker, you might discover an opportunity if you apply due diligence. Find out more about the company. Is it an industry leader in an up-and-coming field? Have you seen write-ups about the company online or in your local business journals? If so, you might consider handling a small piece of work; perhaps an incorporation or a short administrative filing to get your foot in the door of a potentially lucrative market. Of course, you could just as easily assume that you will never see any return from this type of arrangement. All things considered, check your local disciplinary rules to ensure that rendering legal service in exchange for stock options or an equity interest in a company does not run afoul of any ethics rules governing business transaction with a client. Author's note: my recommendation is to forego a work-for-equity arrangement in situations where a company requires extensive work, such as arranging a financing or preparing a legal opinion letter, where you face significant liability exposure. Definitely a deal-breaker.

Client who balks about fees (due diligence). Conventional wisdom suggests that you reject clients who haggle over fees because they'll always balk about paying bills. The trouble is, many resources—including some bar associations, and some books published by Nolo Press, a self-help, legal publisher—advise clients to negotiate fees with attorneys.[4] Be warned: if you automatically reject everyone looking to bargain, you may find yourself without clients. With some due diligence, however, you may salvage some hagglers without compromising your ability to get paid. For example, try to get a sense of what the client can afford and propose a strategy within that budget. Or adopt some of the alternate billing structures discussed in the next section. Most important, accept a large retainer up front, that's enough to fairly compensate you for your work even if you never see another dime from the client. If the client won't pay the retainer, that's your deal-breaker.

Clients with unreasonable expectations (deal-breaker). Fortunately, many clients with an axe to grind can't afford to hire an attorney, making them deal-breakers from the start. But even when Axe Grinders can afford to pay, think long and hard before taking them on. Clients willing to spend money to extract revenge or make a point often possess uncompromising, "blame the world" personalities. If don't achieve the results they want, Axe Grinders can afford to sue you for a full refund or even malpractice. Bottom line: when well-off clients have no other goal but a bone to pick or a score to settle, it's a deal-breaker.

Gut reaction (deal-breaker). When you meet a client for the first time, you form quick, visceral impressions based on the client's appearance and conduct:

- Is the client dressed like a slob or neatly attired? Slovenly dress may be typical attire for your client's work, or it could reflect a lack of respect for lawyers or the legal process.
- Does the client look you in the eye or stare up at the ceiling or down at their shoes? Lack of eye contact might be shyness or lack of confidence...or avoidance or lack of candor.
- Does the client tell you only his side of the story with a running narrative of how they were wronged by each and every action? Or do they try to provide you with a fact-based account? A self-absorbed client obsessed with how every event impacted them may have more difficulty accepting your advice than the client who can examine their case more objectively.
- If the client brings a spouse or family remember, does she treat him with respect or in an insulting or deprecating manner? How clients treat family members can shed light on how they may interact with you.

These seemingly insignificant factors may add up to nothing...or they might be subtle clues that give you some small insight into the client. Don't disregard your initial impressions or gut reaction. If the client makes sexual innuendos or asks you to engage in illegal or shady conduct...or simply gives you the creeps...that's a deal-breaker. Many lawyers who wind up with the client from hell say later that they always felt that there was something "off" about the client but they ignored their first impression.

Should I Represent a Client With a Matter Outside My Area of Expertise?

Most ethics codes prohibit lawyers from accepting matters that they are not competent to handle. It's a classic Catch 22, because how can you achieve competence in new areas if you're precluded from handling them for lack of expertise? Below are a series of questions to consider before taking a case where you don't have prior experience:

Do you have any related experience? The skills you learn in one field transfer to another practice area. If you've only handled litigation matters in state court, you can certainly manage federal court litigation because many of the skills and processes are similar. Yet if you've only handled corporate transactional work, you may have trouble taking on a complicated custody matter unless you obtain a little more experience in family law.

Can you readily learn the skills you need? Many bar associations publish practice guides and hold frequent CLE's on basic matters like will and trust preparation, bankruptcy or criminal defense. These materials are all available at reasonable prices. If a client with a simple bankruptcy matter comes into your office, chances are you can figure out what to do by signing up for a crash CLE class or purchasing a guide to practicing bankruptcy law. By contrast, if you choose to represent a client in a complicated and obscure regulatory matter, you may need more time to master the subject matter, and you won't find as many inexpensive resources available to guide you.

Can you find a partner or second chair? Let's say you attract a lucrative matter that you've never handled, like a serious medical malpractice action or an employment discrimination case. You should not handle the case on your own, if only because you will face stratospheric malpractice liability if you make a mistake. But you don't have to refer the case out if it interests you. See if you can find an attorney to come on board as a partner or mentor, and work the case in exchange for a portion of the fee. In this way, you have an opportunity to learn more about a new practice area and perhaps even get paid for it. Take note: unless the case really has high, monetary potential, most attorneys won't have much incentive to participate in this kind of arrangement.

Is the case worthwhile financially? When you take a case outside of your expertise, you may face a steep learning curve and not be able to charge the client for the extra hours needed to come up to speed on applicable law. Consider whether the benefit of learning a new area of law is worth the trade off of reduced fees, or whether you are better off referring the case to an attorney with more experience in that field.

What is your malpractice exposure? When you take a case outside of your practice area, consider your potential malpractice exposure. A case outside your area of expertie that doesn't involve much money poses little risk, but a case with significant dollars at stake may open you up to a serious malpractice claim.

Defining the Terms of Client Service: Retainer, Nonengagement & Termination Letters

Your relationship with clients begins and ends with a written letter. The *retainer* letter defines the terms of your relationship with your client; the *disenagement* letter defines the reasons for, and the terms by which you conclude, your relationship; and the *non-engagement* letter declines representation of a client. This section will discuss some of the basic elements for drafting these letters. Note: most state bars have online versions of these letters (see Appendix 4 for links to sample state forms). You may decide to modify the state forms, but they will include whatever language you need to comply with your state bar requirements.

HANDLING CALLS FROM PROSPECTIVE CLIENTS

Q: I get several calls a week from prospective clients who want legal advice over the phone. Often, they have a simple questions that I could answer in a few minutes. Other times, they have a complex problem which I can't address without knowing all the facts. But when I tell them that, they think that I'm non-responsive and will help only so long as the meter is running. What can I do? I don't want to drive away a potential client.

A: Some lawyers have an assistant or answering service take calls to weed out prospective clients who only want free advice. Rather than take these calls by phone, you could instruct your assistant or answering service to schedule an appointment for the client.

Develop a system for responding to simple requests that you can easily answer without wasting your valuable time. The best approach is to add to your Web site a Frequently Asked Questions (FAQ) section that explains the basic concepts and procedures in your practice areas. Putting together a FAQ section does require an investment of time, especially if you provide detailed or state-specific information. In the long run, though, a FAQ section saves you time, because you (or whoever answers your phones) can invite callers to consult the FAQs and call back to schedule an appointment if they still can't find the information they need. If you don't want to draft FAQs yourself, you can license content from sites like *Nolo.com.*, or assemble materials from various blogs so consumers can easily find information on a topic. (For examples of attorney Web sites that use FAQs, see the Keyt Law Firm's Web site (*keytlaw.com/azprobat/probatefaq.htm*, or Grant Griffiths' blog (*kansasfamilylawblog.lexblog.com*).

Just as doctors or auto mechanics cannot diagnose a problem over the phone, you can't be expected to render advice on legal problems without a detailed examination of facts and related documents. Offer to schedule a meeting at your office. If the caller persists in getting a question answered or declines the meeting, wrap up the call quickly. The caller has made it clear that they're only seeking free advice. ●

Retainer agreement (engagement letter)

This is the contract that, along with the Rules of Professional Conduct, governs your relationship with your client.

A well-drafted engagement letter sets out the specific responsibilities the lawyer undertakes, as well as the client's obligations.[5] From the bars' perspective, a retainer agreement safeguards clients from unscrupulous attorneys who take advantage of their clients by trying to extract more money midway through a case, or to cheat clients out of the rightful cut of a settlement. Grievance committees and courts stringently enforce written retainer requirements, going so far as to bar lawyers from recovering fees for work performed in the absence of a written retainer.[66] Most lawyers realize that retainer agreements protect clients, but tend to overlook that retainer agreements protect lawyers as well. In fact, no tool (besides malpractice insurance) more effectively immunizes lawyers from overreaching clients, malpractice claims, or fee disputes than a well-formulated retainer agreement.

A well-drafted retainer agreement detailing the services that you will…and, more importantly, *will not* provide during the course of representation…can ward off subsequent claims that you failed to undertake a task or meet your professional obligations. For example, in New Jersey, a tight retainer letter making clear that the attorney would not review a previously negotiated Property Settlement Agreement (PSA) that was incorporated by reference in the terms of a divorce, spared a divorce attorney from a malpractice claim when it turned out that the PSA had inaccurately valued the property subject to distribution.[77]

A retainer letter is particularly critical for lawyers offering unbundled legal services (details later in this chapter).

A retainer agreement eliminates any confusion about your right to payment where a client switches to another attorney mid-course or fires you right before the case is settled. Consider a contingency matter in which you don't collect fees until a judgment or settlement is secured. Let's say you spend dozens of hours investigating a case and drafting a settlement demand, only to have your client switch to another lawyer a few weeks before the case ultimately settles. Even though your efforts helped produce the client's settlement award, you may not collect a dime of it in some jurisdictions because you no longer represent the client, and the terms of your retainer no longer apply. You can avoid this result with a well-drafted retainer that obligates your client to compensate you for time spent on a contingency matter (either *quantum meruit, ie.*, based on hours spent, or some *pro rata* percentage of fees obtained) where the client severs the relationship before an award is recovered.

When you're just starting out without any clients, it's hard to foresee the day you may actually want to get rid of some of them. But as your practice takes off, you'll encounter clients who don't pay their bills, balk at providing vital documents, or hog so much of your time your service to other clients suffers. Because the day that you need to "fire a client" will come sooner than you think (and it's a rite of passage, so look forward to it!), you might as well prepare yourself for it by drafting some standard terms for your retainer agreement. Specifically, your retainer agreement should contain a section that reserves your right to withdraw where your clients fail to live up to their obligations under the retainer (such as failing to pay bills or cooperate with you). But even where your retainer agreement establishes grounds for withdrawal, in pending matters where you've already entered an appearance, the judge or hearing officer must approve your exit from the case. Some judges will honor the terms of your retainer, and will permit withdrawal where permitted by the retainer agreement. Other judges are less sympathetic—particularly when it comes to withdrawal for nonpayment—and have refused to allow lawyers to withdraw for non-payment where they failed to collect enough money up front to ensure payment throughout the case.

The well-drafted retainer. Check your bar association's Web site or Appendix 4 (*Creating a Sample Forms Library*); either or both may have model engagement letters that you can use as a starting point. Below are some steps to drafting a retainer letter:

Scope of work. The introduction of your retainer letter should describe the expected scope of work. First, summarize your understanding of the scope of work based on your discussion with the client. Memorializing the scope of work that you were asked to perform will help eliminate any misunderstanding later. Here's an example: your client asks you to research and recommend a potential corporate form and jurisdiction for incorporation. You draft a form retainer stating, *You have retained me to assist with incorporation of your business.* Later, you invoice the client as follows:

1/07/07	2.5 hrs	Research LLC, C-Corporation and partnership structures in Delaware and Pennsylvania
1/08/07	1.0	Review client's business plan to determine client's priorities and business goals as relevant to formation
1/08/07	1.7	Draft memo recommending Pennsylvania LLC for client, with supporting case law and analysis
1/08/07	2.5	Draft Pennsylvania LLC for client

| Total | 7.7 | Rate: $200/hour | Total | $1,540.00 |

Immediately upon receipt of invoice, the client calls and the following conversation ensues:

Client (voice rising)—*Hey, what's going on? I thought you said it would cost $500 or $600 to prepare an LLC. So, why is my bill $1,500?*

You (calmly)—*As you remember, we were not sure what structure would best suit your needs because of the unique work you plan to do. So we discussed my doing some research on various structures in different jurisdictions to come up with an optimal business form…*

Client (interrupting)—*I don't remember you saying this extra work was involved. I hired you to incorporate me, not for any other fancy lawyer stuff. And the agreement I signed just says that you're going to incorporate my business. Why did you need all that research anyway? You're a lawyer; aren't you supposed to know the law?*

With your vague retainer agreement, you're on the losing end of this argument. See if you can split the difference and move on. As for the future, here's a preferred approach:

Dear (name):

I enjoyed meeting with you yesterday afternoon. Your plans for your venture sound exciting and I am glad that I can play a role in getting your company off the ground. As I understand from our meeting, you would like to retain me to recommend an appropriate corporate structure for your company. To this end, I propose to research benefits of the LLC, partnership arrangement and C-corporation in Delaware, a common jurisdiction for incorporation, as well as in Pennsylvania where you plan to do business. I will provide a recommendation to you, supported by a summary memo or letter evaluating each option. Thereafter, I will draft the necessary papers to establish the structure that we will use.

Explain the different stages of the case. Sometimes, a client retains you for a matter that will continue over a course of months or even years. Detailing the process in your retainer letter lets your client know what's ahead so your invoices don't induce sticker-shock. Also, dividing your representation into separate phases gives you an opportunity to pull out at a natural point if you find that your case is not as strong as you had initially assessed. Finally, clarity about different phases of a proceeding means that you avoid gaps in representation that invariably lead to malpractice claims. One common situation is where you agree to represent a client in a personal injury or other type of trial matter. The court dismisses the case on summary judgment and you lose at trial, so you inform the client of the decision and close out the file. Meanwhile, the client may not recognize that a specific phase of the case has come to an end and assumes you will appeal. By the time you realize that the client expects you to file an appeal, the deadline has passed, and you have a malpractice action or grievance on your hands. Use the retainer to specify at what point your representation ends to protect yourself from this all-too-common outcome in the future.

Here's some sample language from a retainer agreement involving employment claims:

I have been retained to assist you with your claims arising out of your wrongful termination by Employer. As you explained during our initial meeting, you believe that your termination resulted from unlawful, racially discriminatory conduct by your Employer. The scope of my representation will include investigating your claims through review of your personnel file and the Employee handbook that you will provide to me, as well as interviews with individuals who you identify as having knowledge of these events. I will also research and identify the various federal and state causes of action which you have against these entities, prepare any necessary notices of claim, file a complaint with the EEOC or state human rights organization and/or a complaint in federal district court, and pursue the case to the conclusion of a trial or until a satisfactory settlement has been reached, whichever comes first. I reserve the right to withdraw from the case, and terminate this Retainer Agreement upon the conclusion of the proceedings before the EEOC or state human rights commission.

The scope of work under this Retainer Agreement does not include appeals of adverse, or final decisions. In the event that you receive an adverse decision at the conclusion of a proceeding before the EEOC state human rights commission or at trial... or if the case is dismissed on a Motion to Dismiss or a Motion for Summary Judgment before trial... any subsequent appeals will be handled pursuant to a new Retainer Agreement to be negotiated at that time.

Detailing the scope of work for unbundling. A growing number of lawyers now offer unbundled service as a less-costly alternative to full-service representation. Unbundling allows clients to purchase discrete services from lawyers, such as researching a legal issue or drafting a pleading rather than a full-service representation. Lawyers offering unbundled practice run the risk of malpractice claims unless they clearly delineate each party's responsibilities. As professionals, lawyers must comply with applicable standards of care in representing clients, which generally means handling all aspects of the case, rather than just select pieces. Unless lawyers clearly state that they will not perform certain tasks, they remain responsible for them and will be liable for malpractice for non-performance. You can avoid this outcome by drafting a retainer provision that describes those tasks that you will perform and those you will not. Also, take the time to explain the limited scope of representation to clients and have them initial these portions of the Retainer Agreement to memorialize their understanding of the arrangement.

A sample provision appears below:

The rules of professional responsibility for the state of _____ allow me to offer unbundled legal services. As we discussed, I propose to draft a complaint for violations of civil rights associated with your termination from your position as an administrative assistant with the State Department of Public Education. I will charge a flat fee of $500 to draft the complaint. I will provide you with an electronic and hard copy of the complaint. My obligations under this agreement are limited to the following: I will draft the complaint described above for filing in the _____ State Superior Court and advise you in writing of the deadline under the applicable statute of limitations by which you must file the complaint. My responsibilities do not include filing the complaint, serving the defendants or any other further involvement in this matter. As we discussed, you will be responsible for filing the complaint at _____ State Superior Court and effecting service on the defendants in the matter. Should you decide to retain me for further work related to this matter, I will draft a supplemental Retainer Agreement.

_____ (client's initial) My lawyer has explained the foregoing provisions to me. I fully understand and agree that I am responsible for filing the complaint and serving the defendants in this matter._

You can find other sample retainers for unbundled legal services at *unbundledlaw. org/retainer_agreements/sample_retainer.htm.*

Be clear about fees. A retainer agreement should describe your billing methodology (*e.g.*, flat-fee, contingency) for a particular matter. Many lawyers include a fee estimate or budget either in the retainer agreement itself or as an addendum, an approach that I strongly endorse (for details, see Chapter 9). A contingency agreement must make clear that clients do not pay if you do not collect an award, and specify the percentage of fees that you will retain. State whether the client or the attorney will pay costs associated with litigation, such as payment for deposition transcripts and expert witnesses. Some state bars, such as Florida, have explicit language about fees that you must include in your retainer agreement.

Discuss your billing and office policies. Do you charge for expenses like phone calls, photocopies or legal research fees? Do you require an *evergreen retainer, i.e.,* a retainer amount that the client must replenish whenever it reaches a certain minimum level of funds? Will you notify clients when you withdraw funds from a trust account (some bars require attorneys to provide notice)? Can clients call on Saturdays? Your retainer agreement should detail all of your office policies in plain language that clients can readily understand. Before your practice gets too busy, take the time to draw up a standard Billing and Office Policies section to include in all of your retainer agreements.

Discuss basis for withdrawal from case. As described earlier, you can also use a retainer agreement to lay a foundation for letting you out of representation. Below is some sample language that might serve as grounds for withdrawal:

The following events will be grounds for my withdrawal from this case at my discretion following a written Notice of Intent to Withdraw:

- *Failure to pay the agreed upon Retainer Fee or to keep current with payment of case costs as required under the terms of this Agreement;*
- *A misrepresentation about the facts or events in the case, whether intentional or negligent, or an intentional omission or concealment of facts or events, and whether or not the misrepresentation or omission have a material bearing on the case;*
- *A refusal to provide me with documents or other information in your possession that are necessary for the successful prosecution or defense of your claims;*
- *Client conduct such as failure to cooperate or other conduct that makes it unreasonably difficult for me to carry out the representation effectively or efficiently; or*
- *A request that I undertake actions which either violate the law or the [state] Code of Professional Responsibility.*

Include 'sunset provisions'. Sometimes, clients may receive a retainer letter and sit on it for six months before returning it. By that time, the statute of limitations may have run, or you may be occupied with other matters and can no longer handle the case. Thus, your retainer letter should establish a date by which the provisions will expire due to client inaction.

Example:

Please return a signed copy of this retainer letter and return it with the agreed upon retainer fee of $5,000 [within 2 weeks of receipt of this letter/by X date]. If I do not receive a signed copy of this letter and the retainer fee by the date specified, I will not commence the work described, and the proposed terms of representation described in this letter are [hereby revoked/no longer valid].

If you don't hear from the client by the anticipated date (and it's a client that you'd like to represent), contact the client for an explanation. If the client still doesn't comply, as added protection, follow up with a brief non-engagement letter (discussed, *infra*) to clarify that you are not representing the client because of his failure to abide by the terms of the retainer agreement. If the client responds, you can consider extending the terms of the retainer agreement or negotiating a new arrangement at that time.

Comply with state bar rules. Check your state bar rules to ensure that your retainer letter requires certain provisions. Some states may require you to give notice of intent to withdraw from a case in writing, other bars may require you to disclose whether you have legal malpractice insurance. Other states may have specific rules that apply when you ghostwrite pleadings or provide unbundled legal services. Make sure that your policies and fee schedules comply with bar rules and applicable state law. For example, where state law limits your recovery in workers compensation matters to 20 percent of an award, make sure that your retainer agreement doesn't give you a 30 percent cut. A court will not allow you to collect the higher fee and in fact, might declare the entire agreement void, and bar you from collecting any payment.

Sample forms. See Appendix 4 (*Creating a Sample Forms Library*) for online links that provide sample retainer letters available.

Declining a Case: The Non-Engagement Letter

Once you've interviewed a client, you may decide immediately that you don't want to accept the case. Perhaps you suspect a potential "client from hell", or perhaps the case lacks merit. If so, don't string the client along; let him know right away that you're not interested. You can offer a vague reason, such as scheduling problems or lack of expertise. If you decide to share your view of the merits of the case, be sure to let clients know that other lawyers might differ and encourage them to seek a second opinion. Of course, even when you turn a case down at the end of your initial meeting, you still must follow up with a letter. But at least clients will know where they stand and can begin to explore other options. Sometimes, clients have a legitimate claim, but the cost of hiring a lawyer outweighs the amount at stake. Or, the clients' complaint involves poor customer service rather than conduct that would give rise to a lawsuit. In these circumstances, direct the client to self-help options, such as writing a letter to customer service, filing suit in small claims court or, if available in your jurisdiction, a court-sponsored *pro se* program. In some instances, you may want more time, either to evaluate the case more closely or to find a referral for the client if you don't feel qualified to take the case yourself. Whatever your reason for holding on to a case, set a date for getting back to the client with your decision and stick to it. When clients don't hear back, they may incorrectly assume that you've decided to accept the case…and they can sue for malpractice if your inaction results in loss of their claims.

Do's and don'ts of non-engagement letters.
When you decline representation, you must send a *non-engagement* or *declination* letter that makes clear that you will not take the case. Non-engagement letters are particularly important where a client has provided you with information about the case or paid a consultation fee (many times, clients will believe that payment of a fee or your review of documents secures representation). Many malpractice insurance providers require you to send non-engagement letters as a condition of coverage. Less is more when it comes to drafting engagement letters. The more you say—about when the statute of limitations runs or why you're turning down a client— the more you increase your liability exposure. Below, some do's and don'ts for drafting the non-engagement letter.

DO make clear that you are not taking the case. After an opening sentence thanking the client for coming to meet with you, you must state that you will not accept the client's case. Use firm language and avoid hedging (e.g., asking the client to call you with further questions, which could suggest to the client that you're still thinking about taking the case).

DO NOT express an opinion on the merits without telling the client to seek a second opinion. Let's say that you advise the client that you don't believe her discrimination claim against her employer has merit. The client drops the matter, only to discover after the deadline from bring suit has passed that her coworker, won $25,000 for a similar claim. The client could blame you, claiming that she would have gone forward with her case but for your opinion that it wasn't worthwhile. To avoid this outcome, qualify any opinion on the merits with a caveat that other lawyers may have differing views and the client should seek a second opinion. Or you could simply avoid any discussion of the merits of the case at all, and turn it down without explanation.

DO tell the client to seek a second counsel as soon as possible. Advise clients to find another attorney if they remain interested in pursuing the case. Provide the client with contact information for your bar's referral service or, where applicable, a legal assistance bureau. Giving the client additional information preempts a follow-up phone call from the client asking for other referrals.

DO NOT offer any advice on statute of limitations. Specifying a statute of limitations for the client's claims is a recipe for disaster. If you make a mistake about the applicable statute of limitations, you can face a malpractice action, as one Chicago firm did when it told a client she had two years—rather than one—to file a wrongful death action. Relying on the firm's advice, the client did not visit a second attorney until after the one-year statute of limitations had passed, too late to file the claim. The client successfully sued the first firm for its inaccurate advice on the statutory deadline. You often cannot calculate a statute of limitations until you are aware of all of the facts involved in a case.

Consider the following scenario, as posted by solo and law blogger Jon Stein at *thepracticeblog.com/2005/12/sending_ding_le.html*:

> When a client comes to you for a consultation, how accurate is their information? They may tell you something as benign as, 'I was rear-ended by John Smith.' They may leave out the part that Mr. Smith was working for the state of California at the time of the accident. They may do it intentionally; they may do it unintentionally, or they may not have investigated and may not know. The problem is that Mr. Smith, a private citizen, can be sued up to two years after the accident. But the fact that Mr. Smith is a state employee means that you have to file a claim within six months of the accident, and then your lawsuit six months after the claim has been denied.

In this example, if you do not know that Mr. Smith was working for the state, and you give the two-year statute, you may end up committing malpractice. Sure, you could have a defense that you did not know all of the facts, but then you still have to pay to put on a defense. Why not avoid it in the first place by not putting down any specific date?

DO *decline politely and graciously.* No one likes rejection, particularly a client who may have already unsuccessfully shopped her case to three or four attorneys. Even where a client is a pest, there's no need to antagonize him. A law professor at a state-funded law school clinic learned this lesson the hard way, when she rejected a potential client with these remarks:

> Our independent professional judgment is that your persistent and antagonistic actions. . . would adversely affect our ability to establish an effective attorney-client relationship with you and would consequently impair our ability to [represent] you.[88]

Angered by the insults in the lawyer's kiss-off letter, the client sued, arguing that the clinic discriminated against him in declining representation because of his political views. It doesn't cost you anything to treat with respect a client you're rejecting. In fact, the client may bring you other matters in the future. Find ways to decline a case graciously to ease the pain of rejection for a disappointed client.

DO *send the letter in a manner that acknowledges receipt.* Most bar practice managers advise that you send a letter by US Certified Mail with a return receipt. If a trip to the post office will detain you in getting the letter out, send e-mail or fax, both of which will also give you a record of transmittal.

Below is a sample disengagement letter that applies all of these do's and don'ts.

Sample Non-Engagement Letter:
Via Facsimile and Certified Mail, Return Receipt

Date

Dear Mrs. Jones,

Thank you for taking the time to meet and share the details of your case. I am sorry but I will not be able to represent you in your defamation action against the Mayor. As I indicated during our initial meeting, defamation actions fall outside my area of expertise, so I could not give your matter the level of service that it deserves.

You should be aware that any action in this matter must be filed within the applicable statute of limitations. I have not investigated the applicable statute of limitations, so I cannot advise on any applicable deadlines. If you remain interested in pursuing this matter, I recommend that you immediately consult with another lawyer concerning your rights in this matter so that you do not compromise any potential claims. If you cannot find another attorney, contact the State Bar Lawyer Referral Service at [phone number and e-mail].

I am returning the documents that you provided to me at our initial meeting. Again, I do not plan to take any further action in this matter.

Best of luck.

Resources when breaking the news. Below is a list of resources for clients who you can't represent for whatever reason. Supplement the list with resources that you're aware of and keep some copies handy. When you turn a case down on the spot, you can give clients a copy of the list, highlighting those resources that may be useful or you could include the information along with a non-engagement letter.

Bar referral service. Almost every state and local jurisdiction has a bar-referral service that will provide prospective clients with names of attorneys who might take their case. Some referral services are free for clients; others require a client to pay a *de minims* fee of $25 or $50 to the Bar to defray the cost of administering the program.

Law school clinics. Some local law schools run specialty clinics that handle family law, immigration, First Amendment, or even environmental or international issues. Some local universities also sponsor incubator programs for start up high-tech companies or small businesses and may be able to help fledgling entrepreneurs draft a contract or identify sources of funding. Familiarize yourself with law school and university offerings in your area, since they might be able to handle cases that many practitioners are not qualified to handle or are unwilling to handle for free or reduced cost.

Lawhelp.org. This Web site helps low and moderate income people find free legal aid programs in their communities, and answers questions about their legal rights.

Nolo Press. The nation's leading provider of do-it-yourself legal solutions for consumers and small businesses (*nolopress.com*). Best known for its publications that help individuals and companies handle legal matters without a lawyer, the Nolo site also offers extensive substantive legal information.

Small claims court materials. In some jurisdictions, small claims courts provide extensive resources on their Web site, including forms for filing a complaint and how-to guides on the appropriate procedures. Other jurisdictions are not as user-friendly. Direct clients with minor matters to the small claims site or to the court clerk's office where they can obtain information on small claims procedures.

Local **pro se** *clinics.* Courts in some jurisdictions have *pro se* clinics or advisory lawyers who will help unrepresented litigants. Some clients may feel more comfortable as a *pro se* knowing that the court can provide assistance.

Better Business Bureau. Helps customers and companies resolve complaints through various types of non-judicial dispute resolution. The BBB process could provide customers with small complaints an alternative to hiring a lawyer.

Consumercomplaints.org. For clients whose matters are more customer-service oriented (for example, a customer orders a toy that doesn't work and the company won't issue a refund or rude service at a fast food restaurant), *consumercomplaints.org* is an option. Consumer Complaints retains a database of complaints about businesses nationwide and consumers seeking relief can search the database and see if other consumers have faced similar problems. The ability to access to complaints against companies gives consumers more leverage to achieve a favorable result.

RULES FOR REFERRALS

If you intend to refer a case to another attorney, ask yourself these questions:

Is the case worth referring? Don't pass off a dog of a case to another lawyer because you're too afraid to say no to a client. You won't generate any good will by consistently referring lousy cases to other lawyers; to the contrary, they'll stop referring cases to you.

Are you referring the case to generate a fee? Some jurisdictions permit referral fees where lawyers can earn a tidy sum off the referral of profitable cases. But most jurisdictions do not allow lawyers to collect referral fees unless they contribute substantially to the case. So if you practice in a jurisdiction that bars referral fees, don't expect any more value from referrals beyond a nice lunch or gift from the receiving attorney. There are many reasons besides a fee to refer cases. In doing so, you can still help clients even if they've brought a matter beyond your expertise, making them more likely to return to you with other cases in the future. More importantly, referring cases generates good will; other lawyers will reciprocate and drive business to your firm.

Do you know the referral? Try to limit referrals to attorneys with whom you've worked personally, or who come highly endorsed by close colleagues. Though it's unlikely that a client will sue you for negligent referral (though some jurisdictions recognize negligent referral as a cause of action), you'll feel embarrassed if the lawyer you recommended botches the case.

Did you check out the basics? Engage in additional due diligence before referring cases. Check your bar's Web site to determine whether the lawyer you want to refer is in good standing or has been the subject or disciplinary complaints. You might also ask the lawyer whether he has malpractice insurance. Though most jurisdictions do not require lawyers to disclose their own past bar complaints or lack of malpractice insurance unless directly asked, you should tell clients about the referral's disciplinary record and malpractice status.. ●

Government agencies. Some types of cases are initiated by filing administrative claims, a procedure that clients can handle on their own. Many of the agencies that process these claims, such as the EEOC, human rights agencies, consumer affairs departments or public utility commissions frequently work with non-lawyers and have user-friendly forms as well as staff who may interview your client to gather information.

The Termination (Disengagement) Letter

A termination letter documents the end of the attorney-client relationship. The precise contents of the termination letter will vary based on the reasons for ending the relationship, but all letters should include the following information:

Describe the reason for the termination. Your termination letter should discuss the reason that you are no longer representing the client. Perhaps you have completed the matter for which you were retained, or perhaps you are withdrawing because the client refuses to pay. Or maybe the client grew dissatisfied with your service and decided to hire another lawyer and discharge you. During the course of representation you may also discover a conflict of interest which will compel your withdrawal.

Description of how to obtain files and file retention policy. Ideally, you should transmit a copy of the client's file along with the termination letter. If files are voluminous, offer to make copies at the client's expense or retain the files at your office for inspection. You should also describe your own document retention file, *i.e.,* how many years you will hold the files. Check with your bar association to determine how long you must hold files. Some jurisdictions do not require lawyers to grant access to files unless the client has paid his bills, and where withholding files will not prejudice the client in an ongoing matter. Consult the bar to determine when you can ethically retain a client's file.

Document your position. If you fire a client or withdraw from a case for non-payment or lack of client cooperation, or any other reason stated in the retainer agreement, identify the client's obligation under the agreement. In addition, document all prior attempts to notify the client of non-compliance. For example:

> *Section 4.1 of the Retainer Agreement that you signed (copy enclosed for your convenience) states that Client's failure to provide attorney with required documents shall be grounds for withdrawal. According to my records, on June 1st, 2007, I called you and asked you to provide your income tax returns for the past three years. As you know, we are required to produce these documents in discovery in order to sustain your claim for damages. During our call, you agreed that you would send the returns. I followed up with a reminder by e-mail on June 15th, 2007. At that time you stated that you would retrieve the returns from storage. Two weeks later, I notified you of my intent to withdraw from representation if you did not provide these income tax returns. A month has passed and I have not heard from you. As I explained, I cannot move forward with your case until I have copies of your tax returns. Therefore, with this letter, I am notifying you of my withdrawal from representation and termination of our Retainer Agreement.*

Where a client discharges you, your letter should express acceptance of the decision, but at the same time, document your reason for taking the approach that you did. For example:

Dear Mrs. Jones,

I am sorry to hear that you have decided to retain another attorney to represent you in this contract dispute. I realize that you are eager to litigate this matter in state court, but I stand by my original opinion that the terms of the contract mandate arbitration. I believe that any a court would regard any action to resolve this in a judicial forum as frivolous and would dismiss the case. Accordingly, as we have already discussed, I remain unwilling to file suit.

I wish you the best of luck going forward. Please have your new counsel contact me to arrange for transfer of the files.

Settling up fees. Your termination letter should describe the client's fee obligation at the time the relationship is severed. Where you withdraw from a case for non-payment, restate the amount that the client owes, even though it is unlikely that the client will ever pay (unless you sue for fees) once you withdraw. When you are discharged by a client in a contingency matter that you worked on for many hours, remind clients that they remain responsible on an hourly basis for time spent on the case once it is settled (include an invoice detailing the time spent and amount owed).

Closing information. When you end your relationship with a client because a matter has run its course, close your termination letter with a thank-you, and an invitation for the client to contact you on other matters. Enclose a business card so that the client can get in touch with you in the future. Some lawyers may include a client satisfaction surveys that clients can complete and return. For involuntarily terminations or withdrawals, you can't do much more than wish the client the best and leave it at that.

CHAPTER 9

Billing & Fees

"The biggest goof happened in my second month as a solo. I did some work very quickly, and I completed it before the bank notified me that the client's check had bounced! I'm a quick learner. Now I wait for checks to clear."—TRACI ELLIS, SOLO

It may come as a surprise, but many solos don't give as much thought as they should to the method by which they charge for services. Instead, they adopt the practices of their former firm or other lawyers, which means: (a) they bill by the hour at market rates for ongoing matters like litigation, appeals or corporate negotiations; (b) they charge flat fees for commodity type services such as wills, trusts or incorporations, and (c) they take a 33 to 40 percent cut of proceeds received in contingency cases. Now, as you think about starting your own firm, you have an opportunity to re-examine the traditional ways of pricing and to take an approach that both delivers value to your clients and maximizes your revenues.

In this section, I'll review traditional and alternative billing methodologies.

The Billable Hour

Black's Law Dictionary defines a billable hour as a unit of time used by an attorney to account for work performed and chargeable to a client. Most often, time is recorded in increments of a tenth-of-an-hour (some use quarter-hour), and clients are billed for the hours worked multiplied by the lawyer's hourly rate.

Many lawyers believe the billable hour has been a staple of the legal profession since the dawn of time. In truth, the practice came of age as recently as the 1960s. According to a legal journal article by Karen Dean (*The Billable Hour's Staying Power*, Fulton County Daily Report, June 20, 2006), the billable hour gained traction in part because it forced law firms to keep accurate time records, which in turn allowed them to set income projections and performance goals.

The relative simplicity and accuracy of the billable hour explains why it remains the "predominant method of billing for legal services."

In recent years, though, as the cost of legal services surged and associate morale declined under pressure to meet billable quotas, the billable hour has come under attack. Among other things, it rewards inefficiency, since the longer lawyers spend on a task the more they get paid. Some even contend that the billable hour encourages fraudulent overcharging because the system pressures lawyers to inflate their hours to meet quotas or increase revenues.

In a preface to the 2002 *ABA Commission Report on the Billable Hour*, then-ABA President Robert Hirshon wrote: *The billable hour is fundamentally about quantity over quality, repetition over creativity. With no gauge for intangibles such as productivity, creativity, knowledge or technological advancements, the billable hours model is a counter-intuitive measure of value.* Five years later, the ABA Journal dedicated its August, 2007, cover issue to the billable hour with a dramatic cover headline: *The Billable Hour Must Die.* In the article, lawyer/novelist Scott Turow wrote, ... *Dollars times hours sounds like a formula for fairness. What could be more equitable than basing a fee on how and hard a litigator worked to resolve a matter? But as a system, (the billable hour) is a prison. When you are selling your time, there are only three ways to make more money—higher rates, longer hours, and more leverage... if I had only one wish for our profession, I would want us to move toward something better than dollars times hours. We have created a zero-sum game in which we are selling our lives not just our time.*

One mistake solos make is to assume they should adopt the billable hour because large firms do. But it is the large firms that benefit to a greater degree, and the reason is "associate leverage": the firm's partners accrue profits not just from their own billables but from those generated by their associates. For a hypothetical firm with a 1:3 partner/associate ratio and an annual associate profit margin of $150,000, the partner earns $450,000 simply off the associates' work alone. By contrast, solos who adopt the billable hour are limited by the amount of time they work. If they bill 1,000 hours a year at $250 an hour, they gross $250,000; if they bill 2,000 hours, they gross $500,000, but they're also back to working law firm hours.

Some clients fear the billable hour because it does not give any certainty over potential fees, leaving them feeling vulnerable to bills that never seem to end. Sometimes, though, you will have no choice but to bill by the hour, depending upon the types of matters you handle. In fact, many court-appointed criminal programs pay participating lawyers a set rate for hours worked. Likewise, if you handle cases for an insurance company or a government agency, they may also limit you to hourly billing. Thus, if you rule out use of billable hours entirely, you may have to sacrifice certain types of work.

How Much Should I Charge? Every discussion about legal fees ultimately returns to one of two questions—*how much should I charge*, and *how do I make sure to get paid?* This is true whether it's a debate over the billable hour versus alternative fee structure... the wisdom of competing for clients on price... whether to charge for an initial consultation... the level of detail you should include on your bills... or whether to sue a client to collect an unpaid bill. Most lawyers make the mistake of addressing these two questions independently without realizing their interrelationship. Ultimately, your firm's profitability hinges on how you resolve both of these issues.

Consider three examples:

- In an extreme case, John Smith decides to charge clients $2,500 (five times the going rate) to prepare a simple will on the theory that a well-drafted will saves money by minimizing the possibility of an expensive and protracted will contest by a disgruntled heir. Though reasonable in theory, he's unlikely to find clients when they can have their pick of lawyers who provide the same service at a fraction of the price.

   Bottom line: Smith has given thought to *how much should I charge*, but ignored the question of *how can I ensure that I get paid* because he can't get paid without any clients.

- Jane Short is retained to represent a client in a possible age-discrimination action. She explains to the client that she bills $200/hour, and that she requires a $10,000 retainer to cover her first 50 hours of work. Without inquiring about the client's overall budget, Ms. Short recommends and embarks on an aggressive litigation strategy. Even before discovery has concluded, she exhausts the retainer, and puts in an additional $10,000 worth of time for which she has not been compensated. When she bills the client for unpaid fees, and asks the client to replenish the retainer amount, the client says she's out of money.

   Bottom line: Jane knew how much to charge, but she gave no thought to whether her strategy fit her client's budget, and how to get paid if it didn't.

- Just a few weeks after starting his practice, Ralph Young receives a referral to represent a large apartment complex in eviction proceedings. The landlord agrees to pay Ralph $1,500/month to appear in landlord-tenant court four days a month. Each court appearance would last no more than three hours, for a total of 12 hours per month or a rate of $125/hour (not bad for a new attorney). Like clockwork, the landlord pays Young his fee at the beginning of each month. After a few months, Young's practice picks up and he finds that he's working late at the office to compensate for the time spent in landlord-tenant court. Moreover, with the half-hour of prep required for each appearance...and the hour-long commute to and from court...he's spending closer to 18 hours a month on the matter, reducing his fee to $83/hour.

   Bottom line: Young has no problem getting paid. But he neglected to take to calculate the true cost of his time, *i.e, what to charge*, for the arrangement.

Setting hourly rates. If you decide to bill by the hour, how do you decide your hourly rate? Sometimes you won't have a choice. If you handle court-appointed work

---

See book updates at author's blog—www.MyShingle.com

or defense cases for an insurance company, the court or the company will establish your rate of pay and you can take it or leave it.

In most other cases, you have the flexibility to set your own hourly rate, you can take one of two approaches: (a) determine the going or market rate and adjust accordingly for various factors, as I discuss below, or (b) calculate a rate that reflects your overhead costs and the hours you want to work. Don't obsess over whether you've selected an appropriate rate. Ultimately, clients care far more about the reasonableness of your bill, rather than your hourly charge. Clients would rather pay $300/hour for an experienced attorney to resolve a matter in five hours than $100/hour for a rookie who burns through 20 hours. And clients also want an estimate of how long a case will take, so they have some certainty regarding the potential total amount. Thus, even as you try to figure out an hourly rate, keep the bigger picture—your overall fee—in mind.

What follows are several sources for calculating applicable attorney rates:

Legal journals. If you intend to compete with large firms, you may already be privy to their billing rates. But the legal trade press often publishes the billable rates for associates and partners at large firms in you area.

Court files. The federal courts maintain a schedule of fees called the Laffey Matrix that apply in reimbursing prevailing parties for attorneys fees under fee-shifting statutes such as the Civil Rights Attorney's Fees Award Act. See *en.wikipedia.org/ wiki/Laffey_Matrix* (lists current fees). Court opinions awarding attorneys fees provides another source of billable rates that the courts regard as reasonable.

The Internet. Some attorney Web sites list their billing rates. Though these rates are often accompanied by various caveats, they offer a benchmark for what others charge. A new attorney directory (*avvo.com*) lists lawyer profiles online, and includes an entry where lawyers can specify their fees.

Colleagues. Attorneys don't like to flaunt their hourly rates, but most attorneys will share their rates, as well as those of colleagues, if you ask for guidance. Naturally, you'll gather the best information on rates from colleagues in a similar geographic location who practice the same area of law. Note: even in same practice areas, rates may vary depending upon clients. In energy regulatory work, one of my practice specialties, firms that represent large utilities tend to charge 20 to 30 percent more than those that represent government entities and consumer interests.

Adjustments. Once you have a sense of the appropriate hourly rate, you can adjust it as needed. Here are some reasons you might wish to do so:

The experience factor. Your experience may warrant an upward or downward rate adjustment. Adjust down if you're new to a field or practice to give clients more incentive to hire you, and adjust upwards if experience allows you to handle a task in half the time so that even at higher rates your clients receive enhanced value.

Type of client. You're not required to charge the same rate to all clients (which is one reason that you may not want to list your hourly rates on your Web site). Many times, municipalities or other public entities cap the fees that lawyers can charge. Or, a client may be able to guarantee you a certain number of hours of work, provided you cut 20 percent off your hourly rate. Be flexible with rates for clients with a promising matter but who can't afford your hourly rate. Alternatively, you can use some of the other billing approaches to accommodate clients with tight budgets.

Matter handled. If you're a true solo, you'll handle all aspects of a case, from organizing files, reviewing documents, responding to discovery and researching and drafting briefs. Should clients pay your $200/hour rate just to handle administrative tasks? If your case involves a large amount of non-legal or paralegal-related work, you might consider trimming your rates for those tasks, particularly if you can't outsource them.

Overhead-based system.

Overhead-based system. Another way to calculate your billing rate is to base it on such factors as how much you want to earn and how many hours you're likely to bill (or, if you already have a steady cash flow, how many hours you want to work).

Let's say you want to earn $60,000 (before taxes) in your first year of practice, and your overhead (e.g., office, insurance, computer system—but not salary) comes to $2,000/month. You would need to gross $84,000 to hit your target. And assuming that you would bill at least 10 hours a week to start, working 48 weeks a year, you can calculate your rate as follows: $84,000/(48 x 10) = $175/hour. You can play with this number, bumping it by 20 percent (or $210) to account for potential non-collection or seeing how it compares to the market rate. At a minimum, you should apply the overhead-based method of calculation to ensure that you're billing enough to cover your costs and to turn a profit.

Contingency fees: pros & cons.

Contingency fees: pros & cons. As you know, in a *true contingency* case, lawyers do not charge clients for representation, and advance the costs of the case (*e.g.,* deposition transcripts, expert witness fees), in exchange for a percentage of the amount recovered at trial or during a settlement. Where you fail to obtain a judgment or settlement, you don't get paid at all, irrespective of the amount of work you did. Related to the true contingency case are *hybrid contingency* arrangements, where the client rather than the attorney pays the costs, or where the lawyer works for a significantly reduced fee (*e.g.,* $75 an hour or a flat retainer amount) in exchange for a percentage of the final award. Traditionally, contingency fee arrangements have been reserved for personal injury work, medical malpractice, large class actions and collections, though some lawyers will also work on a contingency basis in civil rights matters, such as employment discrimination or police brutality. Ethics rules prohibit working for a contingent fee in family law or criminal cases, as made clear in Rule 1.5(d) of the Model Rules of Professional Conduct of the American Bar Association.

PRO and CON. Contingency fee cases may offer an opportunity for substantial financial gain. Depending upon the matter you handle, you may be able to recover the equivalent of double your hourly rate... or more. And contingency rates afford personal satisfaction by creating a mechanism that enables you to serve clients who might otherwise lack the resources to gain access to our justice system. On the other hand, contingency fees come with significant risk; a 100 percent contingency practice won't provide a steady source of revenue. In addition, if you're new to your practice area, you may have difficulty evaluating the worth of cases, causing you to take a disproportionate number of cases where you wind up with small settlements or even no money at all. Moreover, many of the really high-revenue contingency matters often involve a significant investment, such as payment for medical or economic experts, investigators, subpoenas and deposition transcripts. If you're just starting out, you may not have the resources.

Setting contingency pricing. Most contingency fees range from 25 to 40 percent of an award. Lawyers often offer stepped rates, taking 25 to 33 percent for pre-complaint settlement; 33 to 35 percent for post-complaint settlement and 35 to 40 percent of an award following trial. As Foonberg describes in *How to Start and Build a Law Practice*, lawyers may charge between 45 and 50 percent in slip-and-fall cases due to the difficulty of establishing liability, while the standard for collection matters ranges from 25 to 30 percent. Consider deviating from the so-called standard contingency fees to distinguish yourself from competitors. And as mentioned above, consider a variety of hybrid approaches. For example, for cases of questionable merit, you could require the client to advance the costs, or pay a discounted fee as you go, plus a percentage of the amount eventually recovered. More than any other type of pricing mechanism, the Bars impose restrictions on contingency-pricing arrangements. Failure to adhere to applicable ethics rules may cost you your fee if your client raises a challenge. Most jurisdictions adopt some version of ABA Model Rule 1.5, which requires that lawyers put contingency fee agreements in writing and explain how the fee is calculated. Specifically, Model Rule 1.5 states:

> *A contingent fee agreement shall be in a writing signed by the client and shall state the method by which the fee is to be determined, including the percentage or percentages that shall accrue to the lawyer in the event of settlement, trial or appeal; litigation and other expenses to be deducted from the recovery; and whether such expenses are to be deducted before or after the contingent fee is calculated. The agreement must clearly notify the client of any expenses for which the client will be liable whether or not the client is the prevailing party. Upon conclusion of a contingent fee matter, the lawyer shall provide the client with a written statement stating the outcome of the matter and, if there is a recovery, showing the remittance to the client and the method of its determination.*

In addition, some jurisdictions cap percentage of recovery that lawyers can collect in certain types of matters. Make sure your fee agreement complies with any cap mandated by statute or your ethics rules.

Flat-fees per task.

Many lawyers charge a flat, *per task* fee for routine, finite matters like real estate closings, wills and trusts, incorporations, simple bankruptcy filings, uncontested divorces, and certain types of regulatory and permit applications. Often, these tasks are referred to as *commodities* services because they do not involve significant individualized attention, and they are capable of automated production through use of forms and computer programs. Some lawyers use flat-fees for appellate matters or criminal cases. So long as you can reliably predict the amount of time involved, a flat fee can work.

PROS. Per task billing makes sense in cases where lawyers can predict with some precision the time required. And because lawyers automate preparation of some of these types of documents, thus enabling them to charge relatively low flat fees to clients. Finally, flat-fees give clients certainty so they can budget for paying fees and also eliminate the need for regular invoices.

CONS. A new lawyer will almost certainly lose money on flat-fee tasks. While a practicing lawyer can churn out a basic will in an hour or two, a new attorney may need a day for each of the first few wills he or she prepares. Even where you're experienced, you may find it difficult to compete in the legal commodities market and still turn a profit. That's because many lawyers use wills, incorporations and similar matters as loss leaders to attract more profitable business. And other lawyers try to compensate for low rates for commodities through high volume, often relying on paralegals or staff to draft the documents initially. Unless you adopt one of these business models, you may not find flat-fees for commodities work worthwhile. Many lawyers advertise flat fees for commodities work on web sites or in ads, so it shouldn't be difficult for you to figure out the going rate. When you handle a matter for a flat-fee, your retainer agreement should state the fee. More importantly, the retainer must also specify that the fee does not include any matters beyond the particular deliverable, *e.g.,* will or bankruptcy petition.

Service packages. Many lawyers who represent corporate or business clients develop service plans, or packages, entitling the company to some monthly amount of phone calls or hours of representation. Under such plans, clients usually receive a discounted hourly rate. Extra services such as litigation matters are handled outside the service plan, under separate retainer.

PROS. Service packages benefit clients by giving them access to a lawyer without worrying about the meter running every time the phone rings. From your perspective, the relationship established could give you an inside track for future business.

CONS. Service packages can be a tough sell. Companies that have own in-house counsel may not have an interest in a service plan unless it addresses a niche topic. And even though you may deeply discount your rates, they may never be low enough to attract companies that prefer do-it-yourself form contracts and online incorporations. Finally, service plans accustom clients to your reduced rate, and they may balk at paying your regular rate for matters outside the service plan. A number of firms offer service packages, so a search on the Internet will give you an idea of some of the possible pricing options. Generally, a service plan should include the following features:

- A set fee for a certain number of hours of tasks, such as counseling either by phone or e-mail, simple contract review or drafting at a discounted rate;
- A description of matters where the client might retain you, but which fall outside the scope of the service plan

Value-billing. One criticism of the billable hour is that it focuses on time spent, rather than value to the client. By contrast, *value-billing* attempts to quantify the value of the services that you provide to clients. Here's a description of value billing from a *Law Practice Today* article by Wendy Werner (September 2004):

> *It always makes sense to talk about fees in terms of value. What separates you from your competitor is not simply that you will each do quality legal work, but that you provide a unique understanding of the value this service provides your client. Hourly billing can be the antithesis of value-based services. What is it worth to your client to avoid expensive litigation? What is it worth to your client to operate a business free from worry about meeting legal deadlines and having compliance issues handled in a timely and accurate manner? By providing a value-added service you become a trusted advisor focused on your client's business success, rather than a service provider sending monthly invoices. It is hard to quantify the value of prevention. But any client who has been through costly litigation should have an understanding of the value that a strong partnership with a legal advisor can bring.*

Some types of billing described above, like flat-fees, are a rudimentary form of value-billing. Other value-billing methods include:

- Providing for recovery of success fees, where you collect a percentage of revenues that you recover or save for a client;
- Voluntarily adjusting a bill downward to reflect a disappointing outcome;
- Money-back service guarantee where you allow clients to obtain a full or partial refunds of charges that they don't believe were justified
- Development of flat fees that reflect the value that your service provides.

With growing dissatisfaction over the billable hour, value-billing represents the trend of the future. At the same time, the question of quantifying one's value to clients will require far more thought and analysis than simply choosing an hourly rate (which goes a long way to explain why the billable hour is so entrenched). Value pricing also presents a different dilemma for lawyers. Because while other professions may wish to engage in arbitrary pricing, lawyers have an ethical obligation to ensure that our rates are reasonable. For additional information on figuring out how much to charge, including resources on value billing, go to *thebillablehour.com/resources.*

Q: What is alternative billing, and what are the advantages over the billable hour?

A: Alternative billing refers to billing arrangements other than the traditional billable hour. There are several different alternatives. Here are a few examples:

- Contingency: The lawyer gets paid a percentage of the client's recovery at the end of the case. The fee can be a fixed percentage or a sliding scale.

- Flat fee: The lawyer charges one fee for the entire engagement—usually in predictable or repetitive matters.

- Blended or hybrid: Blended fees combine different billing methods. (e.g., flat fee for litigation up to the time of trial, and hourly billing for the trial itself; or a flat fee with a performance bonus based upon achieving the client's stated goals).

- Staged: The fee is set in stages (e.g., $500 for written discovery, $1,000 for depositions, $5,000 for trial, etc.). Staged billing can also be used to set the fee based upon the level of difficulty or complexity as the matter evolves.

- Value-billing: A term used for any billing arrangement that is based upon the value of the engagement to the client, rather than on the costs or inputs (including hours) involved in the representation. Sometimes the outcome or value isn't a financial result, but some other intangible result, such as peace of mind, etc. The fee is then set based upon what the client wants or thinks is significant. It is only after ascertaining the client's desires and priorities that the fee can be determined. With alternative billing, lawyers often collect more of their fees. There is little (or no) concern about writing down, writing off, or otherwise negotiating fees after the service has been rendered. Fees are more likely to be paid up front. Administrative work for billing and collections is reduced or eliminated. This can result in less staff costs and/or more time for revenue-generating work. Cash flow is more consistent. Alternative billing arrangements often require detailed conversations with clients at the outset of the matter, which help lawyers pre-qualify clients better, alert them to potential problems earlier, and weed out "nightmare" clients before they become a headache.

Q: *I'd like to try a flat-fee arrangement, but I can't get away from basing my fees on estimated hours. What are your suggestions?*

A: In order to price effectively, you must be able to articulate the value your firm brings to its clients, such as what benefits will the client receive, and how important are those benefits to the client?

Many factors can influence the fee, just as many factors influence a lawyer's hourly rate, including: experience, results, training, practice area, geographic area, understanding of the client's situation and ability to solve the client's problems, among others. But the only reason that any of these factors affects the ability to charge a particular fee is because the client believes that they add value to the engagement. The key is to have a detailed conversation with the client about expectations and the manner in which success and fees are measured. One of the main components of a value-based fee system is that the fee is set at the beginning of the engagement. But that doesn't have to mean that you quote one fee for the entire engagement if you don't have complete information. You can use a system of *change orders* which would adjust the fee in the event that the client's objectives or the scope of the matter change from what was originally agreed.

You might consider providing an estimate or price range, giving a high and low based on your experience (make sure the client understands that this is just an estimate). Give yourself some wiggle room on the low end... and be mindful that some clients will assume that the low is what they are going to pay. Or price the project in stages, with ranges for each stage set as the matter progresses and you have more information.

Provide your potential clients with examples of the kinds of variables that are likely to result in a change order or increase in the fee. Ensure that your fee agreement clearly sets out the details of the fee structure and that a change order will result in a change in the fee. Articulate the changes in your fees in terms of the benefits to the client and what the client thinks is important.

Q: *Alternative billing sounds good to me, but how will my clients react?*
A: Most clients prefer alternative billing to hourly billing. Alternative billing allows the client to make an informed decision about whether legal services are affordable before those services are rendered. There are fewer surprises for the client, and they can budget for legal fees in advance. Even if the fee must be altered from the original estimate, if the lawyer has articulated the factors that would affect the fee and communicated them to the client, there will be less resistance to the increase. Alternative billing also eliminates many conflicts between lawyers and clients, and clients are less likely to question a bill they've agreed to ahead of time. They're also less likely to question whether a lawyer should perform a certain task if they don't perceive that they're paying 'extra' for it. And clients will be more likely to cooperate and communicate with their attorney and provide them with necessary information if they aren't worried that every contact with the lawyer costs more money.

Q: *Are there any ethical considerations that I should take into account with alternative billing?*
A: Each state's individual ethical rules vary, and lawyers must read the individual rules carefully. Issues to be aware of include: duress (which may arise if the fee-arrangement is changed on the eve of trial), fee-splitting, doing business with clients, acquiring an interest in litigation, and of course, the state's rules on managing client's funds and use of trust accounts. Courts look at the reasonableness of an attorney's fee. Although many lawyers see the time-sheet as the proof of the reasonableness of the fee, the amount of time that was spent on the case isn't the real proof of reasonableness (and often courts discount the time-sheets and substitute their own determination of whether the time spent was reasonable). Time is only one factor.

The factors which most courts consider in determining whether a fee is reasonable or ethical include (among others):

- Time and labor required;
- Novelty and difficulty of questions involved;
- Skill necessary to properly perform the legal services involved;
- Time limitations imposed by the client or the circumstances;
- Amount in controversy and results obtained

But the courts only get involved in establishing the reasonableness of a fee if there is a dispute with the client (or in rare cases in which the courts set the attorney's fee). A client who agrees to a fee and scope of work up front is less likely to challenge the fee later.

Ethical alternative billing includes ascertaining the client's expectations, agreeing to the scope of work and setting the fee up front, using change orders when the scope of work changes, and confirming the details with the client in writing. Establishing and documenting value up front with the client (i.e. what the client wants to accomplish and/or the cost of doing nothing or of not obtaining the desired result) will be much better "proof" of reasonableness than a time-sheet.

Q: *Where can I learn more about alternative billing?*
A: Check out these resource blogs:.

- Legal Ease Blog—*legaleaseconsulting.com*
- Vera Sage Institute—*verasage.com*
- Golden Practices—*goldenmarketing.typepad.com/weblog*
- Examplar Law Partners' Inside the Firm of the Future—*chrismarston.blogspot.com/index.html*
- ABA Commission on Billable Hours Report (2002)—*abanet.org/careercounsel/billable/toolkit/bhcomplete.pdf*
- Also look for "value billing" or "alternative billing" titles by Ron Baker, Alan Weiss.

  —Allison Shields (*Allison@LegalEaseConsulting.com*) is a New York-based lawyer and practice management consultant

Should I Charge For Initial Consultations? Lawyers fall into two distinct camps on this question.

Some say an initial consultation fee eliminates the *tire-kickers*—those individuals seeking free advice. Others justify the fee by saying that, without it, they lose too much time and revenue otherwise. And it should be noted, that many lawyers experience high cancellation rates when clients aren't obligated to pay for the first meeting.

On the other side of the argument, some lawyers find that a free initial consultation is an effective marketing tool, helping increase the odds of signing a new client. Others use free consultations as a competitive necessity, to avoid losing prospective clients to lawyers who don't charge. For example, most personal injury firms offer free consultations, as do mega law firms, which court prospective business clients with elaborate full-day meetings and expense account lunches (all on the firm's dime, of course). Note: if you plan on a personal injury practice or competing for clients with large firms, don't even think about charging for an initial consultation.

Personally, I favor free consultations. In my opinion, they encourage clients to size up the rates, personalities and proposed strategies of different lawyers, and choose the

On the question of whether to compete on price, most lawyers and practice experts react sharply. They argue that it undercuts competitors on a race to the bottom, or that it attracts clients who care only about cost, and who will forever haggle over rates instead of appreciating the quality of your service. Both opinions have merit.

Many lawyers who do offer bargain basement prices, or who accept clients at severely reduced rates, believe they compensate for lost revenue by increasing the number of clients served. In the end, though, they wind up juggling too many files, giving cases short-shrift, and eventually get hit with grievances. Once caught in the cycle of low-paying, high-volume work, it's difficult to escape: the lawyer's jammed schedule leaves little time for marketing efforts that would attract more lucrative work, while the low margins leaves little available revenue to outsource a portion of their work. Note: lawyers who accept court-appointed work seem most vulnerable to the low-fee, high-volume cycle; they accept lower rates because the court guarantees payment and then, instead of trying to wean themselves from low-fee cases to find more profitable work, they take on even more court-appointed cases because they've grown dependent on the regular payments).

In some instances, though, competing on price may help you attract clients who couldn't otherwise afford an attorney, or to give clients an incentive to hire you over a more established or experienced firm. Here are some factors to consider:

Does a lower price make you more appealing?
If you're a new lawyer, charging less-than prevailing rates may help you attract business. Say you opened a practice six months ago and want to handle family law cases. If you charge the same $250/hour fee as the colleague down the street who's been practicing for five or more years, why should a client hire you? Naturally, you tell clients you're hard-working and can offer better service than your more established competitors. But every lawyer says that, and there's no way to make good on the claim unless you get the client in the door. So, in this case, charging $175 or $200/hour—a 20 to 30 percent discount—may persuade clients to throw you the business. Competitive rates also give an edge to lawyers who compete against larger firms. Charging lower rates often enables lawyers to attract clients who can't afford BigLaw prices...and even some who can. A growing number of large, corporate outfits able to pay top-dollar are opting for smaller firms in mid-sized cities because they charge less than the mega-firms. To learn more about this trend, read Larry Bodine's blog at *legalmarketing.typepad.com/blog/2005/11/convergance_is_.html*. Bodine gives several examples of 2–3 person firms handling work for Fortune 500 companies.

Will cutting costs create a market?
Sometimes, charging below-market rates allows you to capture clients who would not otherwise hire an attorney. For example, many small businesses do without legal advice because they assume they don't have room in their budget to hire a lawyer. But if you can develop some kind of service for this target market—perhaps a flat, monthly fee that entitles the business to call you up to a certain number of hours each month, or a special "help line," where you charge $50 or $75 for a half-hour call—they may decide to use you. And as these businesses grow, you'll have an inside track for future work at your regular rates.

Are your competitors charging lower rates?
In some cases, you may have to cut your rates to keep in line with competitors. Though not widely known, many large firms will substantially cut their rates, by as much as 50 percent, to reel in clients with the potential to grow. For example, a large firm might offer discount rates to handle regulatory affairs for a small telecommunications provider, but require the company to commit to using the large firm for future big-ticket items such as venture deals, IPOs, and merger work. If you want to compete against the large firm, you'd better be prepared to make sure your rates match, or you can kiss your prospective client goodbye.

Can you compete on cost and still turn a profit?
There's no greater mistake than trying to make up reduced costs through volume. Don't offer significantly discounted prices unless you can preserve a decent revenue stream by maintaining low overhead, outsourcing some of the tasks that don't involve your expertise, or using technology to increase your efficiency in delivering the service. Of course, most solos already incorporate these cost-conscious measures in place, which is why we are able to compete on price to begin with.

How low will you go?
When it comes to competing on rates, don't go too low. Discounting rates 20, 30, even 40 percent below those of your competitors, will certainly help generate business...and raise eyebrows of other lawyers. If you're handling uncontested divorces for a flat fee of $75, where other lawyers typically charge $375 or more; or your hourly rate for telecommunications regulatory work is $100 when standard rates start at $200/hour or $300/hour, clients will conclude that you're desperate or grossly inexperienced. Remember: when you charge too little, you're more likely to attract clients who won't sufficiently value your legal service, no matter how inexpensive it is.

best fit. I believe this lays the groundwork for a smooth working relationship.

By contrast, when clients must pay for a consultation, the cost deters them from shopping around; or, having paid for a consultation, the client feels pressured to retain the attorney. When a client feels that he's stuck with you because he had no other choice, he's more likely to resent you when the case goes badly, or he may start looking for another lawyer when you present him with advice that he doesn't want to hear. Though I advocate free consultation, I realize that too many freebies can interfere with one's profitability, or wreak havoc with your schedule if clients aren't showing up for appointments.

Here are some ways to experiment with free consultations without letting them encroach on your billable work:

Schedule consultations after hours or during down time. Studies suggest that for every five-minute interruption, people require at least the same amount of time or more to fully resume their original task. So if you schedule consultations for periods of the day when you're likely to be researching a legal matter or writing an article, you won't just lose the half-hour for the consultation, but another half-hour or more to refocus. To avoid added time loss, schedule consultations for a time of day when they cause the least interruption—either first thing in the morning, or at the end of your workday, when you're too tired to concentrate on more substantive work. You'll find that prospective clients usually prefer these time slots anyway, because it minimizes conflicts with their work schedule.

Limit the amount of time for a consultation. If you don't put a limit on the length of a free consultation, you may find yourself spending the entire day talking to clients for free. So allocate a limited time frame; say, 30 to 45 minutes—long enough to gain a decent understanding of the client's problem, but not so long that clients can talk your ear off. At the same time, don't place ridiculous limits on the length of a consultation such that they don't have any value. For example, many lawyers limit free consultations to 20 minutes. In my view, that's a waste of time. After preliminary introductions are out of the way, you're left with only 15 minutes to get at the substance, which doesn't give the client enough time to explain the facts of their case, or for you to ask the necessary questions to properly evaluate the matter. Even worse, some lawyers who advertise free consultation offer only the first 30 minutes gratis, after which the meter starts running. To me, that borders on a bait-and-switch. Clients—who have no idea how long an intake interview ought to take—come in expecting a free meeting, only to wind up paying because the 30 minutes didn't allow enough time to accomplish anything.

Require clients to fill out an intake form. To weed out the tire-kickers, try sending an intake form when you make your appointment. Require clients to return it at least 24 hours before the consultation. And if they don't return the form, cancel the appointment. Those clients who can't be bothered to complete the form are probably not serious about hiring a lawyer.

Charge an administrative fee for consultation. If you find that a large percentage of your appointments for free consults result in "no shows," consider asking clients to secure appointments with a small fee of $50 or $75. You can always refund the money when they show up for the meeting, or apply it to your first invoice if they hire you, or you can charge a reduced hourly fee for the initial consultation.

Billing For Expenses

Imagine going to your dentist to get some work done, and he mails you an invoice that itemizes his fee and a supplemental charge for the Novacaine and disposable gloves. Or you go for lunch one day, and the waitress hands you the check for the food *and* the napkins *and* those little packets of catsup and mustard. Irritating, isn't it? Well, most lawyer see nothing wrong in adding onto a $750 invoice the $2.20 it cost to photo-copy a pleading or the 90 cents it cost to mail it out. What do clients think about this? It goes something like this: *I paid $750 for this business incorporation, and my lawyer can't afford the $3.10 to mail me a copy of the paperwork! You* may believe that listing every individual charge shows precision or attention to detail, but to clients it sends a message that you intend to squeeze out every cent you can. Does that mean that you shouldn't try to recoup the cost of phone calls or photocopies? Not at all. Instead, treat these expenses as you would other overhead costs, like office rent or malpractice, and recover them in your fees.

For example, assume that you incur the following expenses for all of your clients (and your own needs) on a monthly basis:

Cell phone (used as primary phone)	$200/month for unlimited minutes
Computerized research account	$250/month
Electronic fax service	$15/month
Average postage	$30/month
Photocopying	$50/month (toner cartridge cost)
Total	$345/month (or $4,140 annually)

Assuming that you bill 1,000 hours a year, and you want to assign these costs to paying clients (even though in practice, you also use your fax, your phone and such for non-billable or administrative work), you'd only need to add $4.10 to your hourly billing rate to recover these costs. In other words, instead of charging $175/hour and list the cost of faxes and legal research for each individual case, simply charge $180 an hour with no add-ons. Not only do you not antagonize your client, you save time otherwise spent tracking and allocating these costs to individual clients. Of course, a client matter sometimes entails an extraordinary charge, *e.g.*, several hundred dollars in pho-tocopying expenses associated with a court filing. In this case, assigning the cost directly to the clients makes sense and won't raise their ire. Finally, avoid marking-up expenses; for example, charging 25 cents per photocopy when your true cost is

10 cents. Clients resent mark-ups because they produce added profit for the lawyer without yielding any benefit for the client. Even large corporate clients, which once willingly paid the mark-ups charged by their mega-firm attorneys no longer tolerate paying above cost.

How to Get Paid

Nearly every lawyer has been stiffed at least once by a client.

Sometimes, an adversarial opposing counsel or *pro se* litigants may drive up costs well beyond what you budgeted, and the client simply runs out of money. Or a client decides he doesn't feel like paying more than the initial retainer. Or a client may complain about your work quality, or results, and balks at paying and you decide to write it off any remaining balance rather than invite a grievance. As you continue your practice, you'll learn there are precautionary measures to help minimize your chances of non-payment. Some of the measures…like collecting a retainer or accepting credit card payment…are obvious. Others, like sending regular invoices, providing a comprehensive case budget, or identifying sources of payment other than your client, are less intuitive, but do increase your odds of getting paid for your services.

Retainer fees. The best insurance against non-payment is to collect what you can up front. Of course, just because you receive it doesn't mean you can spend it; in most jurisdictions, where you receive payment in the form of a retainer for work that you have not performed, you must deposit it in your trust account, and release the amounts earned after you invoice the client. Moreover, be aware that most jurisdictions will require you to return any unearned retainer balance to the client even if the retainer is designated as "non refundable."

In a recent Michigan case, the Attorney Grievance Board sanctioned a family law attorney who collected a $4,000 "nonrefundable" retainer fee, and then refused to return the unearned balance of $2,500 after her client changed her mind about getting a divorce. The Board explained that even though the client had paid an advance retainer, the money was intended for services to be rendered in the future. Since the lawyer did not provide this service, she was obligated to return the unearned retainer balance even though she had termed the retainer "non refundable." The Board went on to describe that a non refundable retainer is only appropriate in situations where it intended to preserve a lawyer's availability to handle a matter, and not where it will be used for payment of fees. Moreover, the attorney's fee agreement clearly stated that a non refundable fee is being made to commit the attorney to represent the client. For a discussion of differences between a "retainers for advance payment" and non refundable retainers, as well as case law from multiple jurisdictions, read Michigan Attorney Grievance Board v. Patricia Cooper, Case No. 06-36-GA, at *admich.org/coveo/opinions/ 2007-09-17-060.36.pdf.*

Bottom line: consult this Michigan decision as well as your bar's rules on non-refundable retainers before you spend money paid as a retainer that you have not yet earned and may be liable to return.

But what if a client can't fund a large retainer? You have two options—an *evergreen* retainer, or a credit card payment:

The evergreen retainer. When it happens that large legal matters may run tens or hundreds of thousands of dollars, clients may not have the ability to pay your estimated fee up-front. In such cases, you can use an *evergreen retainer* which the client must replenish when it reaches a certain level, specified in your fee agreement. For example, an evergreen provision might read: *You must provide a $5,000 retainer, which I will deposit in a client trust account and apply to my fees as they are incurred. Prior to disbursing any money from the trust account, I will invoice you for services rendered through that date and notify you of withdrawal. When the balance in the trust account reaches $2,500 or less, you must replenish the account to restore it to the initial $5,000 starting balance. I will notify you when the account reaches the $2,500 level and provide you with fourteen days (14) to replenish the account.*

Credit cards. Credit cards are the preferred form of payment for doctors and accountants. Many lawyers, though, are still uncomfortable accepting them for payment. Some argue that keeping track of credit card merchant fees present too many problems from a trust account perspective; others resent paying the three or four percent merchant fee each time a client pays some or all of their bill. While these arguments carry some validity, the legal profession can't deny credit cards are an attractive solution (especially if clients get air miles for every dollar charged).

Some credit card payment basics:

How do I set myself up to accept credit card payments? You can sign up for a merchant account with your bank or an account through such online services as *Paypal.com* or *authorize.net.* Another newly available service is Accept by Phone (*accept-by-phone.com/attorneys*). With most of these services, you pay for a set-up fee and/or a monthly charge, as well as a percentage per transaction charge that typically ranges from three to four percent. Shop around (even Google is getting into merchant accounts), and evaluate different services, focusing on what will prove most convenient to clients.

Who pays the transaction charge? Some jurisdictions do not allow attorneys to pass on credit card transaction fees to customers. Even if your jurisdiction allows the practice, don't do it; clients will most likely resent it—and you—if you charge them extra to use plastic. And let's be honest: while the cards are a client convenience, they benefit lawyers even more by locking in payment for services. You may gripe about paying a $30 charge each time you take a $1,000 retainer, but consider it insurance; without the credit card, there might be occasions when the retainer was unrecoverable.

Do credit card payments go to my trust account or operating account? Treat payments by credit card as you would cash payments. Credit card payments for work already performed can go directly to your law firm account; credit card payments for future work go to the trust account. Once you put the money in the trust account, you can immediately disburse amounts associated with work already performed. Some practice advisors believe that sending electronic transactions directly to the trust account, before you can review them, can create problems. Jim Calloway, law practice management advisor for the Oklahoma bar, recommends you set up a special trust account reserved for processing credit card transactions, as described in this online article (*okbar.org/members/map/articles/cards*).

What should I do to reimburse clients for credit card fees that are deducted before the funds are deposited into my trust account? Because of transaction charges, the $1,000 payment your client makes by credit card will show up as $970 when deposited in your trust account. You can handle this matter in a few different ways: some jurisdictions may allow you to retain extra money in the trust account to cover credit card fees without running afoul of prohibitions on commingling personal and client funds. Other jurisdictions recommend that you credit clients for the amount taken from the retainer payment or reduce your final bill by that amount. Consult the trust account guidelines for your jurisdiction to determine how you to properly reimburse clients for fees associated with credit card transactions.

How do I handle charge-backs? One reason we all prefer payment by credit card is that if we're dissatisfied with service we can complain to the credit card company and ask them to reverse the charges or hold them in a suspended account pending resolution of any disputes. This poses a problem. If the client obtains a charge-back, and you've already disbursed funds from your trust account to pay your fees, any refund to the client will be made from an unrelated client's trust monies, which would constitute a misuse of funds. Practice expert Ed Poll suggests that you can avoid the charge-back problem through an advance agreement with your client not to seek a refund.

Says Poll, *You can prevent (charge-backs) if you get the client to agree that no dispute with the law firm will be raised with, or adjudicated by, the credit card company. In other words, the client agrees that the charge is non-refundable! The credit card company, when shown the client's agreement, will not credit the client nor debit the law firm. Any dispute between the client and the law firm, then, will be adjudicated in the right forum: the State Bar disciplinary system or the court for a malpractice/negligence action.*

For details, go to Poll's blog: *lawbizblog.com/cash-flow-finances-using-credit-cards-to-pay-legal-fees.html#discussion.* Another option suggested by a Massachusetts bar ethics advisor (see *mass.gov/obcco/credit*) is to ask the bank to process charge-backs to a separate account, rather than to your trust account. In this way, law firm money, rather than client funds, will be applied to the charge back.

A tight retainer agreement. Sometimes in the middle of a case, a client may stop paying their bills, or stop replenishing their retainer account. In this situation, you might find yourself bound to finish up representation unless your retainer agreement expressly reserves your right to withdraw upon non-payment. See *Defining the Terms of Client Service* (Chapter 8), where I discuss how to draft a retainer agreement that lays the groundwork for terminating representation when a client fails to pay.

Identifying other sources of revenue. A client may have the means to pay for a case, but not know it. In some matters where clients are sued, a business or home owners' insurance policy may cover the cost of legal expenses to defend the suit. In most jurisdictions, an insurance company's duty to defend is broader than its duty to indemnify, which means that the insurance company may be obligated to pay defense fees even where it takes the position that there's no coverage for liability. Take the time to review your client's insurance policy to see whether you can argue for coverage for defense costs. Insurance companies often allow policy holders to choose their own attorney. Even if you aren't on the company's list of attorneys, that won't necessarily disqualify the client from hiring you on its insurance company's dime. In some types of actions, clients may be entitled to recover attorneys fees if they prevail in a lawsuit. For example, most federal and state civil rights statutes provide for recovery of attorneys fees. And often, leases or contracts allow the prevailing party to collect legal fees as well. The availability of attorneys fees sometimes give clients incentive to bring a suit that they otherwise would not have pursued.

Invoices

Prompt invoices to clients showing the time that you devoted to a particular matter increase your chances of getting paid promptly.

Some guidelines:

Accuracy and detail. Make sure your invoices are both accurate and sufficiently detailed. Clients may not know whether 3.2 hours or 10.3 hours is a reasonable amount of time to draft a memo. But they will certainly recognize "red flags," like an entry where you billed 32 hours in a single day, or where you billed for three meetings with the client and only held one. More importantly, realize that your invoices may be scrutinized by others than your client. If a client disputes your bill, your invoices will serve as Exhibit A, and will need to include enough detail to stand on its own. In a contentious, multi-million dollar dispute over a fee petition submitted by prominent NYU professor Burt Neuborne for his representation of Holocaust survivors, Neuborne was publicly criticized for "slip-shod" records (*e.g.,* New York Times *tinyurl.com/odcpl*).

Bottom line: when you draft invoices, assume that at some point, they will find their way into a judicial proceeding. If you've never seen an invoice, and aren't sure how much detail to include, look at the guidelines set by the court for submission of time records in reimbursable fee cases. If your court has accessible electronic dockets (the federal courts all do, through PACER), you can download fee requests submitted by attorneys, which will give you an idea of the level of detail that your bills ought to contain to satisfy clients and survive judicial scrutiny. One caveat on including excessive detail in invoices that arise when you represent municipal or public bodies subject to public information act and open meeting laws: generally, members of the public can access a municipality's or state's invoices, and where the invoices contain extensive detail, they may allow people to learn about internal strategies or decision-making. Be sure to clarify that the detailed invoices fall within the scope of attorney-client privilege, and that only the total amounts of time spent are subject to disclosure.

Timeliness. Send your invoices promptly, when your good work is still clear in the client's mind. Clients are busy, and even if they raved about your work they may have forgotten all about it if they don't get your bill until three months later. Of course, if you don't invoice at regular intervals, and continue to work, you risk non-payment for larger amounts of work. Pick at least one day each month to invoice clients, and if you can't get the bills out yourself, outsource the task.

Are you billing for something tangible? Clients are more likely to pay bills and not question them if they see tangible activity in a case. For instance, if you draft a contract for a client and send a bill, the client associates your fee with a product (the contract), and realizes that he owes you for it. By contrast, if you're working on an extensive research project or ongoing proceeding and you bill your client monthly, he may wonder what he's paying for. You have two options: if the matter overlaps two billing periods, but is finite, you can simply wait until you complete the project to bill for it. In a matter that continues with no end, you should prepare a monthly status report, describing the work you've done to date. You can also reconcile the amounts billed to date with your estimate, to assure your client that the case is proceeding on budget.

Flexibility. If possible, be flexible with clients who run short on funds midway through litigation, particularly where the fees exceed any estimate you may have provided. For instance, if a client begins to run short on money, but the case has potential, you could renegotiate the fee agreement, shifting from hourly fees to a contingency arrangement. Where a case promises benefits like publicity or an entre to a hot new field, consider reducing your fee or allowing your client to spread payments out over time.

In my opinion, the benefits of a fee estimate outweigh the drawbacks in their ability to weed out clients who can't... or won't pay.

Let's say you draw up a detailed estimate that shows a range of fees from $15,000 to $75,000, based on a variety of scenarios (*e.g.*, adverse rulings, bothersome opposing counsel, proceeding to litigation if administrative process fails). Your estimate may trigger a useful discussion over how much the client can realistically spend, and whether you can develop a strategy that fits their budget. Of course, there's always the chance your client could go to a competitor, who tells the client *"the case shouldn't be much trouble,"* and calculates a fee of only $20,000. If that happens, your competitor may have done you an inadvertent favor: the client may only have had $20,000 to spend... and, if the case takes a turn for the worse, your competitor will have to put in many uncompensated matters.

In this section, we'll discuss how to arrive at a fee estimate, both for cases where

See book updates at author's blog—www.MyShingle.com

you charge by the hour and those where you plan to apply value billing. We'll also discuss who ought to bear the risk of an underestimate—the lawyer or the client.

The hourly estimate. Estimating potential case costs is like playing chess; you need to think ahead and consider all the possible angles and moves that the case may take. Draw from your experience in other similar matters that you've handled at your firm, or at a prior job. If you don't have an experience base, talk with a colleague to get some idea of how long similar cases can take, and what types of issues might arise that would increase the budget. Some matters on your estimate may be covered by a separate fee agreement.

The flat estimate. What if you underestimate the cost of a case? Who pays the extra…you or your client? Some lawyers, myself included, believe that you are bound by your estimate and are responsible for bearing any costs above your original estimate, subject to a few caveats. In contract law, risks are generally allocated to the party best able to control and plan for them. As an attorney, you have more expertise than your client in figuring out how much a case will cost and in controlling the costs as litigation proceeds. Thus, where a case goes beyond your estimate, generally, you ought to absorb the additional costs. In my own case, I believe that the accuracy of my estimates speaks to my credibility. As my law firm Web site states:

> We are one of few law firms that will set a realistic budget for our clients and stick to it. If we exceed our estimate, our firm—not the client—assumes the cost. After all, if a law firm lacks the expertise to develop a realistic budget, will it have the expertise to handle your complicated matter? And if your lawyer cannot be trusted to keep her word on fees, is she worth entrusting with your case?

THE FEE ESTIMATE

The relationship between a fee estimate and the issue of how to get paid makes sense if you consider the two main reasons clients don't pay: they run out of money, or they come to believe that additional payment is not justified in light of high fees with no apparent results. You can avoid either outcome by providing your client with a fee estimate up front. A fee estimate won't eliminate the potentially high costs of legal service but at least, they won't take your clients by surprise. A fee estimate is also important because it puts hourly billable rates in context. Telling clients that you charge $150 or $300 an hour won't mean anything unless they know how it fits with the overall bill. And developing a fee estimate forces lawyers to plan their cases strategy up front and adopt a proactive approach, instead of simply reacting to opponents. Given the benefits of such estimates, why do so few lawyers take the time to prepare them?

John Toothman, founder of Devil's Advocate, a legal fee management consulting firm, explains:

One reason lawyers are reluctant to give clients a brutally frank estimate at the threshold is that it may scare the client away, with the honest lawyer losing out to lawyers willing to bait the hook with something more palatable to land the client. Another drawback is the expectation that a step-by-step plan gives clients about the path the matter should take, not just its cost. For example, even if legal fees are on budget, the client may become perplexed if the lawyer's predictions about the matter's likely path turn out to be misguided. If the lawyer predicted that the court would block discovery on the XYZ issue, which the court then declines to do, not only is the lawyer going to have to explain the new discovery expense, but seeds of doubt about the lawyer's judgment have been planted.

Legal Fees: A Primer for Law Firms, 10(11) Accounting for Law Firms (Leader Publ. Nov.1997). See online at devilsadvocate.com.

At the same time, sometimes a client's own actions—perhaps failure to cooperate or some deception about material facts—can lead to unexpected delays and added work. For example, if you're handling an employment termination matter where the client fails to tell you that she lied about her experience on her job application, you may have to perform additional research to determine whether her claims remain viable. In these cases, binding estimates don't apply; the client should bear the added costs resulting from his actions. Moreover, you should encourage client candor and cooperation when they realize that failure to do so will cost them extra. Of course, the unexpected could happen—for example, a court's decision to reverse 50 years of precedent—that could add to your original estimate. In these unpredictable situations, you may want to submit the contractor's equivalent of a *change order*, in which you would explain the unexpected new development and ask the client to authorize additional work. Limit use of *change orders* to very unique situations that could not have been predicted through diligence.

SHOULD YOU SUE FOR NON-PAYMENT?

Suppose you withdraw from a case for non-payment, or you conclude a case but the client fails to pay for the last installment of work (most likely because with the case over, he or she no longer needs your service). Should you sue for non-payment of the unpaid balance? Some lawyers believe suing for fees isn't worthwhile because it exposes you to a malpractice claim or grievance. Others argue that unless you go after all money owed, you'll gain a reputation as a push-over and other clients will also try to stiff you. Both arguments have some merit depending upon the circumstances. Any suit for legal fees ought to be a last resort. So, before you even seriously consider a suit, evaluate whether you've exhausted all other possibilities for collection. Here are some criteria to evaluate in deciding whether to sue for fees:

- While delegating collection to staff makes sense, you ought to make one effort to contact the client about overdue fees. During your phone conversation, ask the client whether nonpayment has resulted from dissatisfaction with your service. If the client's complaints have any merit at all, you should reduce the bill.

- If your client has simply run short on cash, perhaps you can offer some payment options. Can the client pay by credit card? Is he willing to make monthly payments? Are there ways that clients can offer something else of value…perhaps an equity interest in the company, or in-kind services to reimburse you, at least in part, for unpaid fees?

- In the fourth edition of the ABA's *Solo's Guide to Collecting Fees*, attorney/contributor Linda Ravdin suggests proposing fee-arbitration to the client. She writes, *Probably the number one advantage [of arbitration] is that the client cannot use a malpractice counterclaim as a defensive maneuver, because you do not have to agree to arbitrate malpractice claims unless a local rule or your fee agreement requires it.* Arbitration is also faster and less expensive than a court proceeding.

If you've ruled out these options and still have no alternative but to file suit to recover the fee, consider these issues:

- You more than anyone know about the time and expense of a legal proceeding. If not much money is at stake, ask yourself whether the costs associated with a lawsuit are worth it. And when you calculate the cost of a suit, assume that you will hire someone to represent you. Though seemingly benign on the surface, a fee dispute can become emotionally charged, with your former client questioning your competence and efficiency, and perhaps filing a grievance against you for good measure. Unless you're represented in a fee action, your emotions may get the best of you and cloud your judgment.

- When you sue for a fee, the quality of your service becomes fair game. Can you document that you performed in accordance with applicable standards of care? Are your time records accurate, and do they fairly reflect time worked? Is the amount that you're seeking to collect reasonable? A time sheet that shows that you billed 30 hours in a single day or that you billed for a court appearance on a Sunday when the court was closed will sink your claim for recovering your fees.

Q: What do you remember about your first day as a solo?

- Walter James III (class of 1987)—"I remember having a conference call that took about four hours. When I finished, I realized I had almost paid my entire overhead for the month."

- Grant Griffiths (class of 1997)—"I remember being scared to death! I looked in the mirror and wondered where I was going to get the money to put food on the table and pay my office overhead."

Q: How did you establish a revenue stream in the beginning?

- Sergio Benavides (class of 2005)—"…Flat-fee investigations."

- Spencer Young (class of 1995)—"…Contract lawyering."

- Denny Esford (class of 2003)—"…Document reviews for large-scale litigation."

- David Abeshouse (class of 1982)—"Clients who came with me from my former firm, and I also jumped head-first into business and legal networking which helped me grow my practice."

- Grant Griffiths (class of 1997)—"I took every court-appointed criminal case I could get. I also took the minor divorce cases that the large firms in my area didn't want to mess with."

- Sarah Meil (class of 2003)—"With the help of savings, some estate-planning work, and a few appearances for a local solo attorney, I was able to pay my rent from the start."

- Traci Ellis (class of 1990)—"I wouldn't say I had a revenue 'stream'…it was more like a revenue 'drip'."

Q: What do you remember of your first few months of solo practice?

- Walter James III (class of 1987)—"I remember thinking, 'Why didn't I do this five years ago?'"

- Spencer Young (class of 1995)—"I remember feeling just about as alive as I've ever felt."

- Sergio Benavides (class of 2005)—"There was a lot of frustration those first few months. I went through tons of bad intake consultations, and dealt with free-loaders who wanted free legal advice. I also recall having clients agree to representation, only to back out at the last minute."

- Varand Gourjian (class of 1999)—"I remember having a lot of free time and smoking a lot of cigars."

- Denny Esford (class of 2003)—"I remember worrying that my contract assignments would suddenly end with no replacement in sight. But a week after my first assignment, I had another…and I have been working continuously ever since."

- Scott Wolfe (class of 2005)—"That first month or so was very challenging. I remember feeling scared and self-conscious. Luckily, I kept my expenses low and tried to take as many fixed-fee and retainer cases as possible. I also started practicing in post-Katrina New Orleans, and this was actually very fortunate. During that period, many attorneys there were still displaced, and there was a lot of business coming into the city to help with the rebuilding process. I took a few insurance dispute cases on contingency, and used that client base to find other clients who needed LLCs, contracts, and the like. I also had two quick settlements that put some breath into my firm's lungs, and from there I consciously grew my non-contingency work load as I grew the contingency end."

To read the complete interviews, go to Appendix 6.

CHAPTER 10

Generating Cash Flow

"I wouldn't say I had a revenue stream right away, it was more like a revenue drip. But every time one of my articles ran in a real estate investment magazine, I got three or four calls that resulted in a few new clients."—TRACI ELLIS, SOLO

Just starting out, you may have to go at least a month or two (or more) before finding a paying client let alone to complete the work and to collect your fee.

How do you generate revenue in the meantime?

In this section, I'll discuss how to generate what I call "fast-cash", including the ever-popular contract (*per diem*) work, placement agency assignments, lawyer-to-lawyer networking, court-appointed criminal work, adjunct faculty positions, online ad assignments, writing gigs, bar referrals and more.

In defense of fast-cash, it does alleviate some of the financial pressure so you don't feel compelled to accept marginal cases or difficult clients just to pay your bills. But it's worth noting that fast-cash assignments can be addictive, a temptation for new solos that might lead to neglect the marketing so critical to attracting their own, more lucrative clients. You could, for example, open your new firm by accepting a document-review assignment at $35/hour plus overtime (for a total of 50 hours). Good money, especially if the assignment lasts a few weeks. But what if it goes three months? Ten-hour days, 50-hour weeks, don't give you much time for client-development. Yes, you would have more income, but you wouldn't have advanced your goal of getting your new practice off the ground.

That caution aside, here are some time-tested ways to generate revenue:

Contract (*per diem*) work

Temporary placement agencies. Lawyers have always shifted temporary assignments through office-sharing or other arrangements, but the first placement agencies didn't appear until the 1980's; two decades later, contract lawyer placement is flourishing. Now every major legal market in the country supports competing agencies. Most of them work with in-house legal departments and law firms, although placements are also made with government agencies and with other solos.

Here's how it works: lawyers (or law office administrators) call the agency—

usually at the last minute—to request a temporary placement when they need help. The agency reviews the hiring lawyer's requirements, and searches its database (the "pool") for appropriate candidates. The hiring lawyer makes the final choice. Most law firm placements are litigation-related (depositions, legal research/writing, and other pre-trial preparation); corporate work is usually run-of-the-mill aspects of major transactions—due diligence review, drafting purchase agreements, routine counsel within the corporation. When I started my firm, an agency hired me to serve as local counsel for a major corporation headquartered in another state that wanted to dismiss a personal injury matter filed in federal court in my jurisdiction.

In recent years, law graduates and new admittees have found more agency assignments involving project-management, and the review, analysis, and coding of documents in complex lawsuits.

To receive payment, the solo submits time-records approved by the hiring lawyer. Some agencies pay solos as independent contractors, others pay them as employees (note: solos paid as independent contractors often must wait to get their money until the agency is paid by the hiring lawyer). Agencies charge $40 to $125/hour to the hiring lawyer, and pay you $30 to $50/hour or occasionally as much as $70-$100/hour for a unique expertise or foreign language skill.

Direct sources of contract work. Whether you're a new admittee, an experienced lawyer, or a specialist, define your market and the nature of your offer. Contract lawyers often make the mistake of not specifying what they bring to the table, assuming they'll attract more business if they say they can handle any problem. But if your offer is unclear, you won't be able to convince other lawyers to pay for your services. *Narrow your focus and you broaden your appeal.* It may go against logic, but this advice is proven time and again.

Before you make contact, consider:

- Find out if a market exists for lawyers with your expertise.
- Identify the kind of projects you would like to handle, and which hiring lawyers are most likely to offer that kind of work (busy solos are more likely candidates than firms with an army of associates for legal research and writing, and litigation assistance). If you would rather focus on transactional work, your best bet may be vacation- or leave-coverage for boutique firms with that specialty.
- Approach small companies not targeted by the contract placement agencies; for example, companies with only one in-house lawyer.
- Decide whether or not to limit the geographic area in which you offer your services. If you're willing to travel—whether to the next country or out of the country—you increase your chances of finding work.
- Your former law firm—that is, if you left, or are leaving, on good terms—may be a good source of contract work. Your firm may agree to retain you on a contract basis to finish up projects while it looks for a new attorney.

- For a complete discussion on rate-setting strategies and alternative billing arrangements, see *The Complete Guide to Contract Lawyering* (3rd edition, 2003).
- *The classifieds.* Ads for contract positions can be found in your law school alumni office, the back pages of the local bar journal, and online at *craigslist.com*. Because Craigslist doesn't charge for ads (or just a modest amount in some cities), it attracts all types of classifieds, including those from attorneys who could not afford to involve a placement agency. Sift carefully through the postings; there are many interesting opportunities, some of which don't pay very well. Also, when you deal with an attorney through Craigslist, you should…at a minimum…visit the lawyer's Web site and check their disciplinary record.

  Note: even where an ad is seeking a full-time attorney, consider submitting a resume and offering your services part time where the position involves a unique, hard-to-find expertise. Years ago, I responded to an ad for an energy regulatory associate. In my cover letter, I described that I had started my practice but wanted to work on issues that I couldn't handle on my own. As it turned out, the hiring lawyer preferred my flexibility because he could avoid committing to a full-time hire. He retained me on a contract basis. After a few years, the arrangement turned into an *of counsel* relationship which lasted 10 years. It never hurts to send your resume; the hiring firm may find that your resume is so superior that it may prefer to use your services part-time rather than hiring a less experienced associate.
- Networking: The most efficient way to find contract work from other attorneys is by networking (either in person or by participating in online listservs), and cold-calling, For more information on networking, see chapters 14 and 16.

Below are some Do's and Don'ts when networking for contract work:

DO tell lawyers that you're looking for contract work. It sounds obvious, but when you meet other lawyers, be explicit about your willingness to perform contract work. Many attorneys just starting out will tell other lawyers all about their practice expertise and that they are looking for referrals. But often they don't take the next step…demonstrating their willingness to help with overflow work on a contract basis. I guess they figure it makes them look desperate for work. Trouble is, most attorneys assume that new solos would be insulted by an offer of contract work at lower rates, so even if they have a need to outsource, they won't mention it. Remember: if you want contract work, you have to ask for it.

DO suggest ways you might help. Some lawyers have never considered using contract attorneys, assuming that they are only suitable for major document-review assignments or brief writing. Be creative: suggest ways that you might help another lawyer, such as ghostwriting an article, writing blog entries, or attending meetings, standing in *at status* hearings, or defending depositions where the lawyer's presence is not required.

DON'T oversell yourself. If you're looking to perform contract work, don't oversell your skills. In the long run, it's counter-productive. Most lawyers are very, very busy (which is why they need help to begin with), and they don't have time or budget to provide on-the-job training. They want someone who can come on board and assume responsibility for a matter. So, if you do accept an assignment to draft a motion, be prepared to deliver a good product, or to figure out how to draft it on your own... off the clock. If you perform poorly, not only won't you get the lawyer's repeat business but they're unlikely to refer you business either. In short, even if you really, really need the money, don't accept a contract assignment unless you're confident you can make a good impression.

DON'T send mass mailings. You may think that reaching out to every attorney in your local bar association increases your chances of finding contract work. In truth, mass communications—electronic or paper—usually wind up deleted or recycled. Frankly, five targeted calls to attorneys you know—or even cold calls—will give you better results than mass mailings. You make a far better impression when attorneys see that you've taken the initiative to call them by phone.

DO make it easy for lawyers to hire you. You increase your chances of getting contract work by having both electronic and hard copies of an updated resume—and your best writing samples (one short, one long)—ready to send. If you're marketing to local attorneys, offer to stop by their office if they wish to meet. And draft a basic retainer agreement for contract services so they don't have to take the time to create their own. Make it easy for them to hire you.

DO take precautions to ensure that you get paid. Many contract lawyers mistakenly believe that they needn't worry about getting paid because they're dealing with attorneys. Unfortunately, some attorneys may try to squirm out of paying contract attorneys, particularly when they're unable to recover the cost from their clients. When providing contract services to attorneys, prepare a contract that memorializes the terms of your arrangement. Your agreement should make clear that your payment is *not* contingent upon the attorney collecting payment from his client, and also that the attorney must pay upon completion of your work, *not* when he collects from the client. As a contract attorney, you have no control over selection of the client, nor are you paid enough to assume the risk of non-collection. So if an attorney balks at these terms, your course is clear: turn down the assignment.

Resource—*The Complete Guide to Contract Lawyering: What Every Lawyer & Law Firm Needs to Know About Temporary Legal Services* (3rd edition, 2003).

Legal services plans.

Legal services plans are purchased by employers to provide employees with coverage for minor matters; e.g., divorce, trust and estate, bankruptcy. When you join a legal service plan, you're listed in the plan's network in the way health insurance companies maintain a network of physicians. Clients can contact you directly for an appointment, after which (depending on the plan) either the client or you can apply for reimbursement for those matters covered by the plan. Most plans do not require attorneys to join the network, nor are attorneys limited to one plan

When it comes to contract work, price matters. If I have a well-paying client with a discrete project that I can outsource and receive client-ready work in return, I will pay top rates. But if I just need general research or help with discovery or writing projects, I'm not going to pay more than $75/hour…if that much. Why? Because in my area (around Washington DC), there are dozens of well-qualified people willing to accept the work for $50–$75/hour. I once posted a Craigslist classified to get help on a Summary Judgement motion. I received more than two dozen responses, ranging from lawyers with 40 years of experience to former BigLaw, Ivy attorneys who had relocated to the area for a spouse, and all of them were willing to take the project for a $50/hour rate just to build a resume. So why would anyone take contract work if it's a lower rate? Easy cash (most attorneys pay on time; at least I do), and a chance to build a relationship with a lawyer who might refer cases in the future. So, as someone who has purchased contract services, here is what is useful to me as the hiring lawyer:

- **Make life easy for me:** Call me, and follow up. Describe how you will keep in touch with me if I hire you. I have hired way too many clerks who took an assignment and I never heard back for 2 weeks.

- **Tell me what you can do for me:** I know that you want work from me, but I'm also interested in hearing how you think you can help me. If someone approached me with an offer to help upgrade one of my blogs or market my trade association and had specific ideas, I'd hire them. I have so much on my plate that I often can't even find the time to devise an assignment to delegate, so if a contract attorney were to do that for me, it would be great.

- **Be flexible on rates:** Look at the going rates in your area and with your expertise before establishing your rates. As I said, I am the beneficiary of lots of first-rate lawyers in my area because so many of them wind up relocating with spouses who are in the military or work in administrative or congressional offices, have fellowships, etc. So, I don't pay top-dollar unless absolutely necessary.

- **Make sure you have the credentials:** If you are going to hold yourself out as a legal researcher or writer, make sure you have the credentials to match. When I posted on Craigslist, I could not believe all the writing samples that had typos, conclusory statements, and over-the-top language (e.g., "clearly this…clearly that"). Using "clearly" drives me crazy; if it's so clear, you don't have to keep saying so. On the other hand, some samples were really first-rate.

- **Don't be a job snob:** If you sign up with a temp agency, don't be too quick to pass up low-paying assignments. When I started my firm, I signed up with a contract agency that needed local counsel to file a motion to dismiss on behalf of a national casino chain. I only received $40/hour (1994 rates), but it was an interesting and easy assignment, it helped pay expenses, and it impressed other lawyers that I was representing a national corporation. And, because I did a great job, the temp agency called me a few months later for a really interesting assignment at the US Postal Service, representing the agency in administrative proceedings arising out of a defective restructuring that was reversed by the court. Again, I only made $35/hour, but I did the work part-time (15-20 hours a week), and wrote dozens of motions, took a bunch of depositions and had a few administrative hearings. It was easy, low-pressure work, and it enabled me to pay the rent for my first office space. After 6 months at this gig, I had too much high-paying work to make it worthwhile anymore, so I left. But it was one of the most interesting legal jobs I'd ever had. ●

network. You can learn more about legal service plans by speaking with attorneys who participate in such networks, or by visiting (and registering) at the plan's Web sites. Prepaid work offers a predictable income stream as well as a chance to build a relationship with plan members, who may hire you for more profitable matters outside the plan (such as personal injury cases), or refer you to their friends. While prepaid work doesn't pay much, many solos have discovered the benefits outweigh the lower margins, as described in a National Law Journal article by Sheri Quarles (*Solo, Small-Firm Use of Prepapid Plan Grows;* April 26, 2007). The article is available online at *law.com/ jsp/article.jsp?id=1177491865520*).

Appointments & publicly funded projects

Almost every state has a court-appointed criminal panel, from which attorneys are assigned to represent indigent criminal defendants, and are compensated by the court. Rates for legal services and eligibility for criminal appointments differ from state to state, and between state and federal court. Most state court programs allow inexperienced attorneys to accept criminal cases and to provide free or low-cost training through the public defender's office or local law school. In some states, lawyers are compensated hourly at rates ranging from $35/hour to $85/hour; other states pay a flat fee per case, such as $1,500 for misdemeanor, or $3,000 for felony matters. Federal appointments usually pay more but are harder to get, and may be reserved for more experienced attorneys.

When it comes to court-appointed work, the key word is "lead time"; allow yourself as much as possible. In jurisdictions where court-appointed pay is high (and competition stiff), you might not receive an assignment for two or three months. And while you can count on payment from court-appointed work (every once in a while, a system may temporarily run out of funding, and lawyers must wait until a new appropriation issues), the court may take six to eight weeks to process your invoices. Some jurisdictions do not permit you to apply for payment until a case concludes, which means that in more complicated matters you may wait several months before you can submit your invoice. So, if you're hoping to rely on court-appointed payments early on in your practice, sign up for such programs as early as you can. Other court-appointed work includes juvenile criminal matters, and child abuse and neglect cases which are handled similarly to court-appointed criminal cases. Courts can also appoint attorneys as executors of estates.

Writing positions

If you enjoy writing, or have a practice specialty, you may be able to generate additional revenue with law-related writing assignments. One long-established legal publisher— BNABooks (*BNABooks.com*)—occasionally needs attorneys to summarize case law, or to write book chapters, in the areas of labor and employment law, labor relations, health law, employee benefits law, arbitration and ADR, IP law, and occupational safety and health law. In the case of other publications, they often advertise in legal newspapers or at *lawjobs.com*.

Adjunct faculty positions

Recent trends in legal education have opened still other fast-cash opportunities for new solos. Facing tight budgets, many law schools are trimming expenses by hiring part-time adjunct professors. In fact, adjuncts comprise 50 percent of the faculty at some law schools. And in response to student demand for more practical skills training, law schools have also started to hire practicing attorneys rather than traditional academics (nor are law schools the only source for teaching jobs; paralegal programs and business schools also need lawyers to teach classes). Adjunct professor positions don't pay much—$2,500 to $7,500 per semester—but enough to pay some bills or bankroll your marketing efforts.

The time-commitment for teaching positions varies. Your first class will require a significant investment of time to develop the curriculum. Once completed, you shouldn't need more than a few hours to tweak your syllabus for subsequent classes. Grading papers can also be time-consuming, though the amount depends upon class size, and program requirements (e.g., some programs will allow you to get by with one final exam, others may require you to create a mid-term and written papers).

Adjunct positions offer several benefits: a) an adjunct professorship looks impressive on a resume (particularly if you're teaching in an area of expertise you hope to market to clients), b) most classes meet at night or for an hour or so once or twice a week and won't cramp your day job, and c) adjunct status often provides access to law libraries that might not otherwise be open to the public, and, in some instances, will enable you to use computerized research and other research resources at no charge from an academic account at your school.

RFP services

Government agencies and municipalities sometimes post ads or issue Requests for Proposals (RFPs) for a wide range of legal services, among which might be a position to serve 15 hours a week as a municipal attorney, or serving as a hearing officer in administrative adjudications. As with contract work, government and municipalities offer lower rates than private clients. But working for a public entity provides an excellent networking opportunity and access to future work.

Bar referral

Bar referral services won't necessarily generate fast-cash, but they are another source for generating clients. In some jurisdictions, bar-referral services yield paying clients, while in others you won't get as a much as a phone call. Bar-referral programs generally do not charge lawyers much to participate, so you have nothing to lose by signing up.

CHAPTER 11

Growing Your Practice

"If you want to grow your practice, don't work 100 percent of the time. Work 80 percent and market yourself 20 percent."—ED SHARKEY, SOLO

When bankruptcy attorney Jay Fleischman started his firm, he was working a 15-hour day—every day!—self-managing three lawyers and a dozen staffers. Examining his records, Fleischman realized that administration was occupying over half his time, and overhead and staff salaries were consuming a large percentage of gross revenues. So, Jay downsized. He split off from his partner, and took the firm's bankruptcy practice and one assistant. Today, he is entirely on his own, using technology to increase efficiency. And because his overhead sharply decreased, his take-home pay is much greater. (Source: *ABA Journal*, April 2007)

Like Jay, many lawyers remain solo for the long haul, leveraging technology to carry a larger caseload, and to handle more complicated cases as their practice grows. In this way, they remain independent, and have the potential of making big money by keeping overhead low.

While this works for some, other lawyers choose to grow their practice by partnering up, teaming with other lawyers, hiring associates, outsourcing, or hiring part-timers. In this chapter, I'll discuss why and how you might want to think about some of these options.

Four Reasons to Grow Your Practice

To leverage more profitable work. Most solos first consider adding staff when their burgeoning workload has them overwhelmed. But "overwhelmed" doesn't mean the occasional 70- or 80-hour week offset by long dry spells. The time to seriously consider growing your practice is when you regularly spend more time working than you would like, or when you are so busy you are turning away profitable matters because you're unable to handle any more work.

To compete with larger firms. Sometimes, in order to compete for large, institutional clients, a solo must have a team in place to mitigate concerns about reliability and manpower.

To offer broader range of legal services. Some solos choose to grow their practice because they want to provide one-stop shopping to clients who have wide-ranging legal needs. For example, a small business client might need help with employment matters, tax, securities and corporate formation and litigation. Since many solos typically specialize in just two or three practice areas, partnering with another lawyer makes possible a broader array of services.

To share the burdens of solo practice. Not everyone wants to work alone. Some lawyers grow their practice because in addition to the camaraderie, they can share the burdens of a solo practice with one or more others. In this way, they can spread out the cost of overhead and technology, and have back-up when one of them takes vacation.

A Whole New World of Staffing Options

Historically, solos have addressed their needs for expansion by partnering up or hiring associates. Today, there's a whole range of in-between solutions. Consider:

Outsourcing. Outsourcing lets you remain flexible in addressing your staffing needs, and makes available better-quality lawyers or staff than you could afford on a full-time basis. Outsourcing is a low-risk way to sample how additional staff might help your firm. Outsourcing is typically used to handle sporadic, finite projects, such as document-review in a large litigation, the brief you don't have time to write, or the court appearances where you have a conflict. When you outsource, you pay only for the work performed. But flexibility cuts both ways; most outsourcing occurs on a project-by-project basis, and means that when you get busy, your preferred contract lawyer or freelancer may not have time to handle your work. For details, see Chapter 12 (Outsourcing).

Part-time workers. At some point, you will have routine administrative tasks or recurring research that demands more than sporadic assistance. For this, consider a steady part-time arrangement involving a set number of hours per week. For part-time secretarial or administrative work, consider *virtual assistants*, though this can be quite costly, especially for low-level work like sending out invoices, confirming appointments, or assembling mailings. By shopping around, you should be able to find a student or a stay-home mom eager for the work. Sometimes, too, you can find experienced legal secretaries who wish to moonlight. Altogether, these workers can be hired for $10 to $20 per hour, as compared to the $30 or $40 per hour for professional virtual assistants.

For paralegal or associate work, law students should be able to handle low-level tasks like legal research for a fraction of the cost of a full-time associate or paralegal.

One of my colleagues hires 2nd or 3rd year law students at $20/hour for 10-15 hours a week (roughly $200-$300 per student). So that he can oversee their work, he has them work onsite for the first few weeks, but then they're free to work from home. Even when he doesn't have enough billable work to pass along, he still pays their weekly salary but assigns them marketing tasks or other non-billable work. For additional reading, lawyer Enrico Schaefer's law.com article, *Virtual Workers Cut Overhead at Law Firm*. In the article, Schaefer describes how his firm regularly employs part-time, virtual attorneys.

The 'mommy pool'. With so many female lawyers taking the "off-ramp" in search of work/life balance, solos in most markets have unlimited access to a deep pool of talented, hardworking, highly-credentialed lawyers. Several solos have capitalized on this trend, using "mommy lawyers" to build quality practices. One such solo is Joanne Sternleib, herself a lawyer/mom who left a top firm to start a trusts and estates practice. Today, she runs a virtual firm comprised of four other lawyers—an assistant and two law clerks—who, like herself, are moms who need a flexible schedule. As Joanne describes:

> … They [attorneys and staff] work out of their own homes, on their own schedules, and whenever they want. It doesn't matter to me when they do the work as long as it gets done. They are independent contractors and work-flexible schedules. There are no set hours, no billable hour requirements, no guaranteed hours, and no guaranteed pay. I generally pay my associates a pre-set fee for each project they do, and I generally charge clients the same way except for estate administration or court proceedings, which work better as hourly billing. I keep track of everything with a super-notebook system that tracks matters and due dates, and I rely heavily on electronic technology which is essential for my practice to operate as it does.
>
> Source: jdblissblog.com/2006/07/joanne_sternlie.html.

Nor is it just lawyer/moms employing other lawyer/moms. Other solos also recognize the value of this under-utilized pool of professionals.

Kassra Nassiri, a Harvard-educated lawyer who partnered up with a colleague to start a firm, hires stay-at-home moms to help litigate his plaintiffs' firm's multi-million dollar matters. Featured in San Francisco Magazine (*Who Says Being A Lawyer Has to Suck?* Feb., 2007), Nassiri says, *These women appreciate the opportunity to use their hard-earned skills in a way that doesn't interfere with raising a family.*

Full-time hires.
If outsourcing or part-time options won't work for you , perhaps it's time to consider a full-time hire. Some factors to consider:

• Are you at or beyond capacity? Are you regularly turning down large matters that you can't staff through outsourcing or contract attorneys? A full-time hire makes sense if it allows you capture business opportunities that you'd lose due to inadequate staffing.

- Are you willing to train your staff? When you outsource, you can typically bring someone on board who already has solid experience. But when you fire a full-time employee, chances are that you can only afford a less-experienced junior-hire. For some lawyers, that works well, because they enjoy training young attorneys and new graduates. Consider Mark Zimmett, a former BigLaw attorney who started his firm in 1990 and depends on young associates to help him manage multimillion-dollar cases. In an article in American Lawyer (*Lessons from a Large Firm Partner Who Set Up His Own Shop*, April 2007), Zimmett writes: [*My*] *associates have been relatively young, generally two to four years out of school. Smart as they are, they are inexperienced... I enjoy teaching them, and I believe they enjoy their work and value their training. They stay for three or four years, then move on with their careers, often with my help.*

- Will the new-hire free you up so you can bill additional hours? Law practice management consultant Ed Poll recommends, "Hire when you're at the point that you can produce enough billable work to justify hiring that persons, or when they can take work off your desk so you can do more billable work. Can you churn out enough billable work to match the new staff person's $30,000 or $40,000 salary? Your break-even point is when the additional revenue generated or reduced strain on you equals the increased cost of hiring someone. Anything above that is gravy."—Source: Ed Poll (as quoted in *Hiring and Working with Support Staff: A Guide for Solo and Small Firm Lawyers*, at *cba.org/cba/PracticeLink/WWP/supportstaff.aspx*).

- Are you capable of delegating work? This question may sound odd, but let's face it—some lawyers don't like to relinquish control of even the most seemingly insignificant details. David Leffler writes in his *Being Solo* column (GP Solo Magazine, May 2004) that some lawyers believe they alone can do things the "right way", and experience so much anxiety letting go of tasks that they prefer to handle everything themselves. *If you don't truly understand the benefits of employees,* Leffler writes, *You will never make any hires, or the hires you do make will be doomed to failure. This will prevent you from changing your law practice from one where you feel overwhelmed and without any time for the rest of your life, to one which* [allows for more balance].

Bottom line: if you can't trust yourself to delegate work, don't bother hiring anyone. You will just waste your time and theirs.

Affiliations, Networks & Project-Partnering.

Some solos, particularly those in metropolitan areas, may be competing for larger clients who either have wider ranging legal needs or who buy into the stereotype that solos can't provide quality work for corporate clients. If you've encountered this during your first year of practice, you may want to consider teaming up with another lawyer, or a group of lawyers, to form a partnership.

Joel Bennett, a Washington D.C. lawyer, explores the benefits and drawbacks of partnership or merger in *Expanding Through Merger—and the Sequel* (*Flying Solo*, 4th ed., 2005).

DON'T BE AFRAID TO HIRE   *By Ed Sharkey, Esq.*

I started my law firm in May 2003. At the time, I had been practicing for 10 years, first with a mid-size firm in Baltimore, then with a large firm in Washington, DC. My practice was business, securities, and pension litigation. To open my new firm, I leased space from an established solo. I had a portfolio of clients that moved to my new firm, so I was busy from the outset, handling all of the legal and administrative work with the help of the other solo's legal secretary. There were three considerations motivating me to hire:

First, I could do no more work. I had exceeded my capacity after about six-months...second, I wanted to grow the firm (there were marketing initiatives I wanted to undertake but could not because I was overloaded)...and third, I knew some of the work I was doing could be delegated without undue risk. So, I went to law school listservs, and posted a paragraph seeking a law clerk for research and writing. In the post, I described the practice and emphasized the flexibility of the schedule.

I solicited a commitment of between 10 and 15 hours per week, and guessed at an appropriate hourly rate. The market validated my guess...I received multiple resumes.

I hired one law clerk, then two, etc. The capacity was scalable. During weeks when the work was less, I did not have an idle associate sitting at a desk. When it was busier, I had multiple clerks from which to seek extra time. In addition, I was able to task them with some marketing projects, which was more cost-effective than doing them myself. Finally, the cost was modest, and I did not need to add space, computers, health care, or bar fees. When I reached the point where I had five law clerks at the two-year mark, I concluded that it would be better to hire a full-time associate. The law-clerk model made it easier to transition to a full-time associate than it would have been starting from scratch. The flow of work was proven. In addition, I had experience with multiple prospective associates who had clerked for me. I searched the National Association for Law Placement (NALP) Web site to survey associate salaries in Baltimore. I used that as a metric for the salary. In addition, I offered health insurance under my PPO and participation in a 401k profit sharing plan. The firm pays a non-discretionary three percent of salary into the retirement plan. In addition, the firm pays discretionary bonuses twice a year based upon firm profitability and associate performance and productivity. I made an offer to my best clerk, and she accepted.

I have always hired for attitude. Prospects must demonstrate a minimum level of competence (for law clerks, I look at grades and writing sample), but attitude is most important. I look for people who will take personal responsibility for their matters. People who see their duties as a personal obligation important to the goals of the firm rather than as a job. Such people look for ways to contribute to the goals of the firm. They also address unforeseen contingencies that arise in performing their work, rather than just doing what they were told. Finally, they assume greater responsibility over time, increasing the firm's ability to delegate more to them. The model has worked especially well. I aggressively seek to delegate in order to maintain my target level of marketing. If our team reaches capacity and work encroaches on the marketing, I add scale by hiring again. In this way, I have grown from one lawyer in 2003 to two lawyers, a full-time paralegal, a part-time administrative assistant, and three law clerks in 2007. ?If you want to grow your own practice... Don't work 100% of the time. Work 80% and market 20%. Aggressively look for ways to delegate. Hire for attitude. Get people who are interested in learning and taking on greater responsibility. Don't be afraid to hire. If you make a mistake, you can always adjust.

Ed Sharkey (esharkey@SharkeyLaw.com) practices business law and litigation in Bethesda, Maryland.. ●

Those PROS include:
- Providing additional backup to other lawyers,
- A decrease in pro rata overhead,
- An ability to generate better quality business referrals to and from partners.
- Better quality institutional clients,
- An ability to hire associates and staff, and to generate income from their work.

And the CONS:
- A loss of independence related to working hours, spending decisions and personnel, and possibly added start-up costs and moving expenses.

When entering a partnership, you need to hash out the details of the arrangement in a partnership agreement. Partnerships usually fail because the partners never made their goals clear at the outset, or they failed to discuss or reach agreement on such critical issues as the sharing of profits and costs. Bennett notes that he and his potential partner spent a considerable amount of time developing a formula for capitalizing start-up costs, sharing operating expenses, and splitting profits, all of which were contained in the partnership agreement or other written documents.

Creating a formal partnership can offer practice benefits, but it is also a complicated process. Take the time to get to know your potential partner and candidly discuss your goals. If you're not ready to invest the time, or take the risk, in creating a formal partnership, you can still capture the benefits of size and scope of expertise through more flexible arrangements like affiliations with other lawyers or project-partnership teams. Consider:

Alliances or networks. Some solo or small firms join forces without a formal merger by means of shared space, network or affiliate arrangements. Such alliances generally market their services jointly, relying on each other for cross-referrals. In this way, the firms maintain their own identity without having to squabble over profit-sharing or workload. These customized arrangements suit many solos because they open up additional resources while enabling a solo to maximize his or her autonomy and flexibility. The variety of alliances and networks is limited only by your imagination…and bar ethics rules. Generally speaking, you must make clear to clients that even though you share space, or that you team up with your colleagues, each of you operates independently. You can reinforce the appearance of independence by creating your own stationery, business cards and Web sites, and by entering into separate retainer agreement with clients when teaming on a project. For example, Red Mountain Law describes itself as *independent law firms for business and business people.* Its lawyers all have their own Web sites, a fact which is clearly delineated on the group Web site (*redmountain law.com*). At the time of its creation, the lawyers of Red Mountain Law made clear in a press release that they were joining forces but not merging, and that each would continue to serve clients independently. *See Small Firms Establish Networks to Broaden Service Offerings* (Birmingham Business Journal, September 25, 2006).

Below are a few examples of alliances, networks and shared space arrangements:

Space share. The option calling for the fewest formalities has lawyers with different practice areas sharing space and referring cases back and forth. J. Cheney Mason, one of the solos profiled in the ABA Journal, sublets space to other attorneys he handpicks for integrity and/or practice expertise. As a group, the lawyers trade ideas and referrals while maintaining independent practices. This arrangement gives the participating lawyers a little camaraderie…as well as lowering their overhead and providing a resource for referring clients. Source: Meg Tebo, *When It's About More Than Money*; ABA Journal, April 2007; *ABAjournal.com/magazine/the_secrets_of_million_dollar_solos.*

Virtual law firm. Patrick Begos, a Connecticut attorney in the three-man firm of Begos & Horgan, took a slightly different approach. As Begos describes in a GP Solo article (*The Virtual Law Firm,* July/August 2003), he leased space for his own firm and discovered that lawyers with complementary practices in other suites were bouncing questions back and forth, referring clients to one another, and teaming up on projects. In time, the group decided to create a virtual firm; a collective in which they would cross-market one another's practices so that clients would have full-service representation. For additional discussion, read Enrico Schaefer's blogcast on virtual law clerks and attorneys at *tcattorney.typepad.com/virtuallawclerk.*

Alliance. The Red Mountain Law Group is an example of an alliance of firms providing complementary expertise in a variety of practice areas. One firm handles wills and trusts, a second handles commercial and residential real estate, and a third oversees securities work. At the same time, the attorneys in each firm continue to serve their business and individual clients in other practice areas.

Alliances also work for smaller firms that can offer expertise or other unique services to large firms. Some large firms seeking to service corporate clients that demand diversity team up with smaller women- or minority-owned firms to compensate for lack of diversity in their ranks. The large firm gets the benefit of diversity, while the smaller firm can leverage off the large firms' resources and marketing measures (source: *Day Pitney Forges Alliance With Minority Owned Firm,* D. Malan, Connecticut Law Tribune, April 24, 2007).

Project-partnering. Let's say a potential client comes to you with an issue outside your expertise, or it involves matters in multiple jurisdictions, or it exceeds your existing capacity. Ordinarily, you would probably turn the case down, or the client would ask for a BigLaw referral. That doesn't have to be the case now: with project-partnering, you can transform your one-man band into a full-service firm. Jeffrey Berger, principal attorney in the Berger Law Firm in Washington DC, and who was profiled in Legal Times (*The Virtual Law Firm,* Feb. 23, 2004), likens project-partnership to free-agency in professional sports: lawyers can put together the best team based on a lawyer's expertise and costs. For example, suppose you're a corporate lawyer representing a company that plans to acquire another company. Your client asks your help handling a downsizing and how to structure the new entity to take advantage of tax benefits. While you feel capable of handling the buy-out, you recognize that the employment and tax issues are outside your expertise. Now, through project-partnering, you can team with an employment and tax lawyer to service the client. The advantages are three-fold:

- You can create a team of experts while still remaining involved in the project.
- The agreements are flexible and last only for the duration of a particular project (so if you weren't fully satisfied by another team member's work, you're not obligated to use them for future projects).
- It's a convenient and non-threatening way to network and build relationships with other lawyers who may also bring you on board for their own projects.

What better way to introduce yourself to other lawyers than to offer them potential business opportunities to work on matters for your clients. Of course, the success of project-partnering depends on the quality of attorneys involved. Since good lawyers tend to be busy lawyers, you may have some difficulty in securing lawyers for your partnership teams. Or, you may discover that some members of the partnership don't share your standards (perhaps they don't return phone calls promptly, or they produce sloppy work), which may reflect badly on you.

Here are some project-partnering tips:

- *Seek out potential team-members.* Identify a list of go-to lawyers in different practice areas who might assist on client matters. When you attend networking events, learn about other lawyers' practices and the type of cases they handle. Get together for coffee or a meal, and gauge their level of expertise with a couple of substantive questions. Listservs are another source of potential project partners. In my own practice, I have asked other lawyers to team up on projects, and have been asked by others to team up based on impressions formed as a result of discussions online.
- *Billing rates.* Get a sense of what your partners generally charge, and what types of billing arrangements they're willing to accept. If you work with lawyers located in other parts of the country, you may find a disparity of as much as $100/hour in rates. Will the lower-billng lawyer agree to continue these rates, or will he want to raise them when he learns others on the project are charge more? And the reverse—if you work for a client with a limited budget, will a costlier team member be willing to reduce their fees, perhaps in exchange for the opportunity to work on a unique case? And...will your team consider alternative billing arrangements?
- *Billing preferences.* Determine your client's preference for billing. Some may want to include bill from each of the lawyers involved, while others may prefer one bill from the original lawyer that includes all of the fees. Consult bar rules to ensure

that your billing arrangement complies with your jurisdiction's rules on fee-splitting.

- *Retainer letters.* Team members should have their own retainer letters in place with the client, as well as adequate malpractice coverage for the matters they're handling.
- *Watch out for overlap.* Naturally, if you're working with other lawyers on the same matter, you'll want to coordinate to avoid duplication of effort where issues overlap, and to ensure that your contemplated approaches don't conflict. At the same time, you don't want to bill the client for every little communication with team members, or for glancing at every document that you're cc'd on by the other attorney. The purpose of a project partnership agreement is to increase efficiencies for clients, not to double- or triple-bill.

Of Counsel Relationships

ABA Formal Opinion 90-357 describes an *of counsel* relationship as one characterized by "a close, regular personal relationship" between an attorney and a law firm. There are numerous variants, ranging from an arrangement which resembles part-time employment where the *of counsel* is on the payroll and commits to providing a guaranteed number of hours each week or month, to an arrangement one where an *of counsel* offers expertise on an as-needed basis. An *of counsel* can share physical space with a law firm, or a firm may pay for a portion of counsel's overhead if he or she retains outside space.

An *of counsel* relationship can offer various benefits to a solo. Obviously, an *of counsel* arrangement that guarantees a fixed level of income at or near your usual billable rates can help smooth out cash flow problems. In addition, an *of counsel* relationship can enhance your credibility; clients may be impressed that larger firms want to take advantage of your expertise. And remember: an *of counsel* relationship works both ways. Just as the firm will feed you work and bring you into cases, you can also refer cases to the firm as well. Of course, when you enter into an *of counsel* relationship, your affiliation with the firm could potentially conflict you out of certain projects.

You can also use *of counsel* relationships to take advantage of other attorneys' talents whom you can't afford to hire. Perhaps there's a superstar associate from your former firm whom you'd love to bring on board, but you don't have enough work to pay a full-time salary. You could offer an *of counsel* relationship, with guaranteed payment for a fixed number of hours. The associate could spend the rest of her time building her practice, and could either service new clients on her own or divert them to the firm. One example of an *of counsel* relationship comes from Florida litigation and IP lawyer, Elio Martinez, in *Of Counsel: An Alternative to Solo and Firm Practice* (GP Solo Magazine, July/August 2006). Martinez writes:

> . . . My of counsel arrangement is simple. I maintain a separate and independent practice while occupying an office at my friend's firm. I keep my own schedule, develop my own clients, and run my own firm. In exchange for office space and a percentage of fees collected for my work on my friend's cases, I guarantee that I will work a certain number of hours per month on those cases. This

arrangement is beneficial to us both: he has some of the burdens of the practice lifted from his shoulders by someone he knows and trusts, and I have guaranteed work and income every month, as well as an office where I can grow my practice. The of counsel arrangement also provides me the added benefit of always having someone with whom to discuss issues and ideas, as well as assurance that in my absence someone will be there to step in and handle emergencies on my cases.

Where to find *of counsel* arrangements. Most of counsel arrangements arise out of already existing professional relationships, so target those contacts first in looking for an *of counsel* relationship. Here are some suggestions:

Look to former relationships. If you worked for the government or in-house at a corporation, you may have worked closely with a small firm that represented clients in matters that you handled. Or, you may have worked on *pro bono* or bar projects with other firms and built a solid relationship. Contact those lawyers when you begin your firm because it could be that they, too, formed a favorable impression, and they would welcome an opportunity to work with you in an *of counsel* capacity.

Sell your capacity to draw business. If you formerly worked at a government agency, or as a prosecutor, or at a BigLaw firm, your background can help a firm draw clients. A firm that represents criminal defendants can enhance its reputation and distinguish itself from the competition with a former prosecutor on board. Likewise, if you're a former BigLaw attorney, you can build the image of a small local litigation shop that wants to attract Fortune 500 companies as clients.

Blogging. If you have a unique practice area, be sure to demonstrate your expertise by starting a blog. In this way, other firms may be impressed by your analysis of issues and view your practice as a natural complement to their own.

Networking. Good old networking—coffee meetings, bar events, and other activities where you meet other lawyers—only increases your chances of finding *of counsel* arrangements. Get to know other lawyers, their practices and needs, and an *of counsel* opportunity may present itself.

Sample forms or contracts. Since many *of counsel* arrangements arise out of close relationships, lawyers often don't formalize them with much more than a handshake. If you're not comfortable with that informality, several bar associations offer sample agreements you can modify to suit your specific needs. The Georgia Bar's Law Practice Management Office has a sample agreement at *gabar.org/public/pdf/lpm/oca.pdf.* St. Louis solo and tech guru Dennis Kennedy has compiled an exhaustive list of of counsel resources, including sample agreements, ethics considerations and other materials. Go to *denniskennedy.com/archives/001036.html.*

Leaving Your Practice for Another Firm

After practicing on your own awhile, you may find that you've created opportunities for yourself that didn't previously exist. Perhaps you started a law firm because no one wanted to hire you, or because you craved hands-on experience, or more flexibility that

Like many lawyers, I took the first job offered after law school. I joined a boutique firm representing a major union client in a civil litigation practice. It was immensely boring. I had no client contact or freedom to explore the areas of law I was most passionate about...estate planning and probate. It was because my parents died young, and I was thrust into a probate proceeding. Even as a third-year law student, I knew enough to hire an attorney rather than handle it myself. But after the ordeal, I knew what I wanted to do in law: help clients with estate planning, and to support them as someone who had been there. So, after two years in civil litigation (and a baby along the way), I quit and went on my own.

Two years later, I had built a thriving estate planning and probate practice, embracing all forms of marketing and networking. Blogging was especially effective. As a result of my blog, I was contacted to speak at a CLE seminar with two others, one of whom was a partner at an established firm near my home. After the last seminar, he asked if I was interested in working at his firm. I was intrigued. After three interviews in as many days, I received an offer. This at a time when my own practice was booming and was a lucrative source of income.

What persuaded me to move my practice under the wing of the firm? Immediate health insurance for me and my family; instant secretarial and paralegal support for my clients; and the promise that I could continue to blog, network, and generally run my practice as I had as a solo...but this time with instant staffing in legal, administrative and human resources areas.

I enjoy working for my firm, and I'm proud to be working alongside a group of esteemed colleagues. And I am more valuable as a lateral hire because I was a solo. I know what it is like to watch the bottom line, to hustle to get clients, to keep clients satisfied, and to deal with staffing issues. When I reflect on it, my solo journey was leading me into a firm setting where I could practice in the areas I was most passionate about.

Here are some things to think about if you're transitioning or returning to a law firm:

- When analyzing your offer, factor in costs of health insurance, retirement plan contributions, vacation/sick pay as part of your compensation package. Also factor in the costs of not having to pay for malpractice insurance and annual bar dues among other costs for which you were previously responsible.

- Be up-front with your clients about the transition. Obtain their consent to take their matters to your new firm. Put in writing which cases you'll bring over and any fee-split arrangements.

- Tell your new firm that your first month of work will be a transition period, and that you will be burning the candle at both ends working at your new firm and dissolving your former practice. Your billables may be low in the first month or two because winding down a practice takes time.

- Send a welcome letter to your contacts with your new business card. Your transition is a reason to reconnect with your contacts and former clients for business development.

Jennifer Sawday (tldlaw.com) practices in Southern California with the firm of Tredway, Lumsdaine & Doyle, LLP.

your employer couldn't provide. Now, a year or two later, you have a portfolio of business, several trials under your belt or a go-to blog. Now, the law firms that once spurned you, or refused to accommodate your career goals or lifestyle, have come knocking at your door. Naturally, you're flattered at the attention…but don't let it cloud your judgment. Getting hired by a firm may boost your ego, but you need to consider whether moving to a firm is right for you. Ask yourself the following:

What's my motivation for wanting to move to a firm? What makes you think this firm is different from other places you worked? If you once felt stifled by layers of bureaucracy, you may never be satisfied working for someone else. By contrast, if you left your former firm simply to satisfy your curiosity about solo practice, or to gain some courtroom experience, you might find satisfaction returning to a firm now that you've achieved those goals.

Are my existing clients compatible with the firm? You may have built an attractive slate of clients, but can you continue to serve them at a larger firm? Will the new firm raise your rates outside of your client's price range? How will the firm handle potential conflicts between your clients and existing firm business? When conflicts arise, most firms retain the client that generates more revenue, which means that your smaller clients might get the boot. And how do your clients feel about you moving to another practice? Are they concerned that they'll be serviced by low level associates or lawyers with whom they have no relationship? Your client portfolio is one of your main sources of leverage to negotiate for compensation and other benefits.

Are my lifestyle and practices compatible with the firm? As a solo, you've set your own hours, often leaving the office by 5 pm to make it home for dinner. Will the firm tolerate your early departure when everyone else stays until 7 pm? And you're probably accustomed to implementing marketing strategies or submitting articles for publication without approval from anyone else. How much autonomy will you have at the firm, and can you deal with the restrictions on your decision-making?

CHAPTER 12

Outsourcing

"Whether you choose to charge your client more than what you pay for (outsourced) services, outsourcing is still cost-effective for your client, since even a rate that includes a reasonable profit to you will generally be less than your own hourly rate."

—LISA SOLOMON, SOLO

In recent years, outsourcing has gained real traction among large law firms. Solo practitioners, though, have been slow to embrace contract lawyering and enjoy its cost-efficiencies. For one thing, many solos are unaware of the robust and reasonably-priced freelance market, and, for another, they miss the benefits by holding on to the all-too-common reluctance to ask for or accept help—or even to admit that they need any. *Lawyers aren't used to asking for help*, says the former owner of a West Coast contract lawyer placement agency. *They just work harder.*

Do you need contract help?

To see if you might be a candidate for help from a contract lawyer, check as many of the statements below as applied to you in the last year:

- Your billable hours increased enough to make you feel overworked, but not enough to justify hiring another associate.
- You turned down revenue-generating work because you didn't have sufficient staff or expertise to handle the matter.
- A client complained about your delay in attending to his problem, or you had to make excuses for not doing what you promised.
- You took on a matter that made such extraordinary demands on your time for several months that you felt you were neglecting other matters.
- An issue outside your area of expertise arose in the middle of a case, and you didn't have time to explore it adequately.
- The court set an accelerate trial date in one of your cases, and it conflicted with a series of depositions you had scheduled in another case.
- You needed someone to assist you as "second chair" during a complicated trial.
- The external demands of your practice—phone calls, court appearances, client conferences, settlement negotiations—took so much time and attention that you

didn't have the opportunity to concentrate on the legal issues and strategies of your cases.

- You wanted to take parental leave, vacation (even a sabbatical), but didn't because you wouldn't have had adequate coverage during the absence.
- You dreamed about scaling back your practice so you could devote more time to your family, a side business, or a hobby.
- You took on a case in which opposing counsel appeared to have six or seven lawyers to your one.

The best cure for procrastination is not to see it as a personal failing, but a sign you need to offload parts of your practice. If you checked even one of these statements, you have good reason to develop a relationship with a contract lawyer. If you checked *more* than one statement, you should start developing that relationship now.

What to Expect From Outsourcing

Profitability. Outsourcing projects can increase your firm's profitability. It allows you to take on new cases you might otherwise turn down because you're overwhelmed with other matters. Just as important, outsourcing can rescue you from the consequences of uneconomic cases that you may have accepted out of desperation. For instance, suppose you agree to represent a client on appeal for a flat-fee of $2,500 but the case takes double the 25 hours you originally estimated. Your effective billing rate is reduced to $50/hour. If you're beginning to attract more work at your rate of 150/hour, you're better off outsourcing the lower-paying work to a contract attorney for $50/hour and clearing it off your plate. In fact, some solos leverage outsourced work to generate extra profit for their practice.

Consider the advice of Lisa Solomon (*QuestionOfLaw.net*), a New York-based legal research and writing consultant:

> *. . . Outsourcing legal research and writing projects can enhance your bottom line. With one exception (Maryland), all the bar associations—including the ABA—have determined that an attorney may charge the client a premium, or reasonable measure of profit, in excess of the research and writing provider's cost to the attorney as long as the total charges to the client are reasonable. Regardless of whether or not you choose to charge your client more than you pay for legal research and writing services, outsourcing is still cost-effective for your client, since even a rate that includes a reasonable profit to you will generally be less than your own hourly rate.*

Increased flexibility. Hiring lawyers have found contract lawyers to be one of the most efficient ways to manage scheduling conflicts. Once you've been practicing awhile, you'll get a better sense of the ebb and flow of your workload to determine whether to invest in a full-time associate or staff. In the meantime, outsourcing legal research and writing on a project basis lets you ramp up when your caseload is heavy and cut back when it isn't. But if you hire a full-time associate or paralegal in anticipation of several long-term proceedings, and those cases settle a few months later with no other billable work in sight, you're left with a salary to pay and no revenue to cover it.

Improving client service. One of the most valuable but least noted benefits of using contract lawyers is in the area of client relations. Because contract lawyer rates have not kept pace with direct-to-client rates, the hiring lawyer can make a profit and offer the client a lower-than-usual rate. For example, a hiring lawyer who bills out her own time at $200/hour can hire a senior-level contract lawyer at $80/hour, charge the client only $150/hour, and still realize a small profit. Inexpensive trial assistance is another client benefit. Former solo Daniel Edwards says, *The first time I hired a contract lawyer was to assist me during trial. I made a checklist of points I wanted to be sure to cover. The contract lawyer's task was to watch the testimony, and check off each I covered. As I went through the examination, I'd occasionally swing by the desk and get reminded of the issues I hadn't yet raised. It worked so well, I've continued to hire assistants whenever I'm in trial.*

Reducing the risk of malpractice. When you juggle a caseload, there is a greater likelihood that some matters may get overlooked or given less attention than required resulting in missed deadlines. In fact, the majority of bar grievances arise out of cases neglected by solo and small firm lawyers who couldn't find the time to work on them. Outsourcing now and then to catch up on your files might save you from a malpractice complaint.

Increasing career satisfaction. Think about how pleasant your practice would be if you could take a break from boring and routine work and not sacrifice income. Contract lawyers let hiring lawyers focus on the aspects of practice they enjoy most without losing profit. And for those lawyers who relish oral presentations and attorney-client interaction, legal research and writing is drudgery at best. Or, as one solo put it, *A day in the library is a day in hell for me.* Contract lawyers also provide an opportunity for solo and small firm practitioners to juggle part-time or flexible schedules. Two Seattle bankruptcy lawyers wanted to maintain an alternative practice. They both worked four days a week, and one of them would leave in mid-afternoon so she should be home with her children. They hired an experienced bankruptcy lawyer to come in two days a week on a contract basis to create the equivalent of two full-time practices.

Stress reduction. Solos are often reluctant to outsource because of the need to squeeze every nickel from every case. It's understandable, but wearing all the hats takes a heavy toll. Outsourcing helps relieve the stress that comes from long hours, relentless deadlines, difficult clients, contentious adversaries, and the lack of vacation. Just one example: instead of avoiding your problem cases, consider outsourcing these matters to a contract attorney who can act as an intermediary and deal directly with problem clients or attorneys. BigLaw partners frequently delegate the task of communicating with annoying clients to associates. By outsourcing, you achieve the same result.

HOW THE HIRING LAWYER BENEFITS

Hiring lawyers control costs and enhance profits by:
Avoiding the higher cost of adding a new permanent lawyer to the staff; Charging more per hour to the client than the contract lawyer costs; Reducing outside legal fees paid by in-house legal departments and government agencies; Taking on cases they would have declined because of staffing shortages.

They manage growth by:
Hiring contract lawyers to handle extraordinary workloads; Avoiding the need to lay off or downsize if their workload should later decrease; Determining whether there is enough work on a long-term basis to warrant a permanent hire; Avoiding the hasty hire of a new associate or partner when another suddenly leaves the firm.

Hiring lawyers increase flexibility by:
Covering normal fluctuations in workload without increasing fixed overhead; Temporarily broadening the scope of their practices; Filling in a service gap with a contract lawyer rather than moving an associate without adequate experience into that slot; Using contract lawyers to cover scheduling conflicts.

They improve client service by:
Passing cost savings for routine work on to the client; Making partner experience and oversight more cost-effective; Broadening their ability to provide technical expertise; Providing a sophisticated product for a client in a cost-effective way.

They reduce the risk of malpractice by:
Hiring contract lawyers to do a thorough job on something they do not have time for; Freeing up time to respond quickly to client calls and concerns; Filling a service gap with a contract lawyer rather than moving an associate without adequate into that slot.

And they increase career satisfaction by:
Focusing on aspects of practice they most enjoy without losing profit; Billing the necessary hours without exhausting their permanent staff; Making part-time or flexible schedules feasible.

The Complete Guide to Contract Lawyering (3rd ed., *Arron/Guyol*) ⬤

Tasks Suitable for Outsourcing.

Almost any legal matter can be outsourced, so long as your client does not expect that you will personally handle the matter, or the matter does not involve an obscure expertise that you are uniquely competent to handle. Matters suitable for outsourcing include:

Legal research and writing.

Legal research on specific questions raised by your client during the course of a case, or to evaluate the strength of a new client matter. Besides memos, you can outsource cite-checking and editing to a law student who has worked on a journal, or to a junior attorney who is generally capable of performing these tasks.

Litigation practice

Briefs and motions. Many attorneys outsource appellate brief writing because they lack appellate expertise, or are too close to the case to objectively identify the strongest arguments. Appellate work is also readily severable from the underlying matter. You can also outsource drafting motions.

Court appearances. Rather than spend three hours waiting for the judge to convene a status hearing, outsource your court appearances to a contract attorney. If you do, provide the attorney with the case file and your phone number in the event the judge decides to inquire about substantive issues.

Depositions. Defending depositions does not require extensive familiarity with the facts of the case and lends itself well to outsourcing. By contrast, the task of taking depositions is less cost-effective to delegate because your hire will need time to learn the case or may miss an opportunity to ask important questions because of lack of conversancy with all of the details.

Document review. For years now, large firms have been successfully using contract attorneys for document-review, and many now offshore document-review projects to India. With most documents now in electronic format, a contract attorney can handle your document-review offsite.

Discovery requests and responses. For simple litigation matters, a contract attorney with a litigation background can review your complaint and prepare discovery requests, work with a client to provide responses, or identify which requests are objectionable.

Practice management

Administrative. A virtual assistant can perform a wide range of administrative and secretarial tasks such as billing, bookkeeping, and marketing support.

Secretarial/document preparation. A secretary or transcription service can convert dictation into written work, or format and finalize your already-typed drafts.

Answering service. A service can handle incoming calls and assist in scheduling.

Creating, ordering, scanning client files. Contact document-scanning professionals if you want to run a "paperless" operations. You'll still have plenty of files that require organization, and when they get out of control, hire a student, administrative assistant, or professional organizer to put things in order.

Marketing

Market research and analysis. Interested in expanding your practice into a new area of law but don't know much about the economic potential? Outsource the task of market research to a law student with a business background.

Branding. Increasingly, lawyers are recognizing the power of branding—that is, the package of images, concepts and slogans—to distinguish their firm from others. Outsource this task to a professional marketer.

Public relations. At the outset, you probably won't be handling cases of public interest or matters of high media visibility that would warrant having a PR consultant. Still, as your caseload grows, or if you suddenly find yourself handling a sensitive, high-profile matter, it would be wise to seek the guidance of a PR professional. For state-specific consultants, seek out the long-established Public Relations Society of America at *prsa.org.*

Back-office management. If you have employees or a high-volume practice, you would benefit from outsourcing the following accounting responsibilities:

Accounting. To balance the books, reconcile client payments, and manage documents for tax preparation

Payroll. Many lawyers use payroll companies to cut employee checks and send them to direct-deposit accounts.

Invoicing. If you can't find the time to invoice clients regularly, outsource the preparation of invoices to someone who can spend a few hours each week or month converting your time records into invoices, transmitting them to clients, and following up on collection.

THE RANGE OF CONTRACT ASSIGNMENTS

Legal Research
- Discrete issuesComprehensive analysis and overview; Arcane areas of law

Persuasive writing
- Memoranda in support of or in opposition to motions, Trial briefs, Appellate briefs, Settlement conference, arbitration or mediation submissions

Preparation of other litigation documents
- Complaint, amended complaint, Answer, affirmative defenses, counterclaims, Interrogatories, requests for admission, document requests, Jury instructions, Orders and judgements

Document review and analysis
- Your client's; to produce in response to adversary's request
- Your adversary's; produced in request to your request
- Your own, to prepare a chronology or overview of key events

Appearances
- Take or defend depositions
- Judgement debtor exams
- Routine motions, status conferences
- Substantive motions
- Administrative hearings
- Arbitration, mediation, settlement conference
- Trial
- Appellate argument

Preparation or review of non-litigation documents
- Corporate articles, by-laws, minutes, resolutions
- Partnership agreements
- Deeds, mortgages, trust deeds
- Loan documents
- Wills and trusts
- Prenuptial agreements
- Securities filings
- Plan and disclosure statement for Chapter 11 bankruptcy

General assistance
- Organize a file in preparation for trial
- Interview witnesses
- Take a second seat at trial
- Help out on transactional work
- Prepare an initial draft of the article, book, or CLE materials

Expert assistance
- Brainstorm or give strategy advice on complex or unusual problems
- Fill in for vacation, sabbatical, family leave, hiring gaps
- Handle the specialized aspects (e.g., tax, environmental) of a matter
- Make use of a non-law professional background (e.g., medicine, accounting, engineering, computing) to assist in technical areas
- Carry a business purchase and sale or real estate deal through to closing.

The Complete Guide to Contract Lawyering (3rd edition) ●

Technical needs

Computer networking set-up. You can probably set up your own computer. But outsource more technical needs, such as networking multiple office computers, integrating computer and phone systems, or installing additional memory and back-up.

Practice-management systems. Some attorneys prefer to set up and learn for themselves how to use a practice-management system. If you're short on time, or you want to customize your system for special applications, hire a consultant.

Web design. At *craigslist.com, Guru.com, Elance.com,* and *Sologig.com,* you can find many competent Web designers and developers in your area. For basic Web templates (and domain registration), go to *godaddy.com, dotser.com, register.com,* among others.

Selecting and Working With Contract Lawyers

If you've never worked with contract lawyers, or if you worked with them but had unhappy results, you need to think through the search process. It's a mistake to regard contract lawyers as fungible commodities. Their skills, personalities, and work styles are as diverse as any other group of lawyers, and investing time in the selection process is one of the best ways to assure a match with your needs.

A phone conversation should suffice if you're interviewing candidates in different locations. But a face-to-face meeting is best. Evaluate the candidate's listening skills and note their nonverbal clues. Guarded or inconsistent answers could signal problems with the candidate's representations about credentials and/or experience. Non-responsive answers, or responses that indicate the candidate did not understand your concerns, may presage problems following instructions or understanding the nature of an assignment. A few questions worth your consideration:

What's the ideal candidate? Do you need an introverted researcher, or a charismatic personality to charm a difficult client or tame a contentious opponent? Do you prefer a "take-the-ball-and-run-with-it lawyer, or one who does precisely what you ask? Do you want someone who is detail-oriented or big-picture? Match the credentials to the need. Is the ideal candidate an experienced or entry-level lawyer, a paralegal, legal research service or litigation management assistance? If you have a low-key personality and pride yourself on your reasonableness and courtesy, the last person you'll want standing in for you is a mad-dog litigator (and the reverse is true). Style may be less of an issue for behind-the-scenes projects, but even there it should not be ignored.

Is the candidate self-sustaining? Some solos have office space for a contract worker, others prefer to make virtual arrangements. If you're outsourcing offsite, make sure the candidate has reliable computer equipment and standard word processing and software. And any candidate offering legal research services should also have access to a law library and online legal research system, or—at a minimum—the ability to use

See book updates at author's blog—www.MyShingle.com

whatever reference resources you use. Outsourcing a short-term project generally isn't worthwhile if you need to teach an applicant how to use a research tool or a piece of software. Find someone who has the skills to start right away.

What is the candidate's work experience? Review with care the candidate's portfolio. For legal research, evaluate the candidate's writing style, and analytical and proofreading skills. Many lawyers believe their law school class in legal writing qualifies them as a specialist. In truth, few lawyers have superior legal research and writing skills. Make sure you check the candidate's work product to verify any claims of expertise. In the final analysis, would you be proud to sign your name to the work they've done?

What are the candidate's references? Among the qualities you're looking for are reliability, honesty, punctuality, cooperativeness. Unless you know the candidate personally, or they were sent by an agency, you'll want to confirm they have the credentials and expertise represented. Verify law school graduation and admission to the bar. Check at least two employer (or contract work) references. And if you intend to rely upon the special expertise of a contract lawyer, pay attention to coverage for professional negligence. Ordinarily, your supervision of the lawyer places liability on your shoulders. Your reliance upon the advice of the contract lawyer specialist could shift the burden. In either case, though, if the contract lawyer is uninsured, you face possibleexposure.

How do the candidates present themselves? The impressions given by candidates—on their resume and on their Web site—are often revealing. For example, some contract attorneys boast of writing skills but maintain Web sites riddled with grammatical and spelling errors. Verify that the person you hire can talk the talk...and walk the walk.

Does the candidate have the right attitude? More than anything, a successful outsourcing candidate is one committed to freelancing. There are those who handle outsourcing assignments who are biding their time until a better offer or permanent employment comes along. For this reason, they may be less motivated to satisfy you because they're not interested in repeat business. Other candidates have an employee mentality, and may nag you for extra work or more permanent hours. If you want a satisfying outsourcing experience, find a candidate as devoted as you to being a successful free agent.

WHICH CRITERIA MATTER MOST TO YOU?

Credentials

- Years of experience
- Prestigious institutions (law school, firm, corporation)
- Honors and awards
- Outstanding references

Areas of experience or expertise

- Substantive law
- Particular court (e.g., bankruptcy, appellate)
- Drafting skills (negotiated or form agreements)
- Writing ability
- Oral skills
- Aptitude for dealing with technical issues
- Attention to detail

Personal qualities

- Responsible, reliable, punctual
- Compatible with your personal style
- Truly stimulated by the law, and how it works
- Able to communicate well
- Able to work under pressure
- Able to absorb information quickly
- Creative
- Abel to think fast on their feet
- Able to work independently
- Able to follow instructions.

The Complete Guide to Contract Lawyering
(3rd edition) ●

Checking each applicant's credentials and conducting personal interviews may sound like a lot of work. But it's worth it when you consider the cost of project poorly done, a client who's unhappy with the result, or your own loss of time as you repair the damage. Once you've made a tentative selection, assign the lawyer a small project not critical to the success of the matter and has no immediate deadline. This way you can judge their work and compatibility with your practice style with a minimum of risk.

Working with contractors.

Hiring lawyers and contract lawyers alike recognize that agreeing on the contract lawyer's rate is a key step in striking a deal. Other factors play an important role as well—the nature of the assignment, the economics of your law practice, and your relationship with clients.

Be precise. Many lawyers give only a vague description of research projects they want to outsource, and then blame the contract attorney for an unsatisfactory result. When you outsource work, be precise; describe exactly what you want. For legal research projects, prepare a memo describing the matters you want researched, or identify the issues for inclusion in an appellate brief. And be clear about what you expect. In some cases, a hiring lawyer wants a contract lawyer to just list cases and summarize them rather than prepare a memo. If that's what you want, say so before the contract attorney runs up a huge bill for drafting a full memo.

What to pay. Contract rates depend on location and experience. To determine the going rate, ask colleagues what they pay for comparable work, and call a temp agency to find out what they would charge for someone with so many years of experience. More experienced lawyers usually complete the project faster and more competently… and have the judgement to handle unexpected situations that could prejudice the client. If the contract lawyer works in your office, using your equipment, the rate paid should be lower than for assignments they complete without using your facilities. The lower rate accounts for the portion of your overhead attributable to the contract lawyer's work.

Establish reasonable deadlines. Establish deadlines for deliverables as well as a timetable for certain goals. Remember, your contract hire may be juggling projects for other clients, and will need to prioritize matters with firm deadlines over those without deadlines. Request status reports, but be reasonable. Don't insist on a three-day turnaround on a project you know would take at least a week to complete.

Set a budget. When you work with a freelancer, ask for a budget or an estimate. Freelancers have different billing policies; some (like graphic designers or Web developers) charge flat fees and will spend as much time as necessary to develop a logo or site that satisfies you. Others bill by the hour. Where your freelancer cannot estimate the time involved, either ask for progress reports at designated intervals or cap the hours you want the provider to spend.

The etiquette of payment. Just as you don't like working for free, neither does your temp. Don't balk if you're required to put down a retainer or a deposit. And, when the work is done, pay on time...and don't make payment contingent on your ability to bill their time to, and collect from, the client. Contract attorneys don't earn enough to bear to risk of non-payment.

Finding qualified contractors & consultants

Referrals. The best way to find competent outsourcing candidates is through good old-fashioned referrals. If a colleague raves about a contract attorney, get the individual's name and contact information. In this way, the hiring lawyer reduces the risk that a candidate is unqualified or irresponsible.

Go online. Many outsourcing candidates maintain Web sites or blogs with online portfolios. A contract attorney or other outsourcing candidate who takes the initiative to set up a dedicated Web site is likely to offer solid professional service, and a well-designed site will provide writing samples, past work experience, and endorsements. Caution: some online entities use the Internet as a front. They advertise that they handle legal research but send the work overseas. Check to make sure that they're providing the services they claim. Other online sources for legal freelancers—listservs and online mailing groups.

Local universities. Law students are eager for hands-on experience and the chance to earn some extra money. Virtual clerkships and project work are especially appealing. To find willing law students, post ads with the law school's career placement office, or e-mail one of the professors teaching a course on your practice area and ask him to announce job openings at the end of class. A college's general placement office is also a good source of administrative support and other non-legal assistance. Note: college placement offices may take several days to run your posting through various levels of approval. And don't expect a timely response during exam time.

Craigslist. As a pool of talent for outsourced project work, *craigslist.com* is an extraordinary resource that reaches into all 50 states and 14 world capitols. For some cities, Craigslist does not charge for ads while in others the cost is minimal—around $25 per posting. And because the site draws from such a wide audience, you're likely to receive multiple responses within a few hours of placing the ad. It goes without saying that because Craigslist operates only online, you can count on the candidates being computer-savvy and capable of handling online assignments. If you're offering a decent salary or interesting work, Craigslist will probably generate more responses than you can reasonably review.

Blogs. Posting a job on a popular law student blog, or a blog in your practice area, is another option. Posting ads on blogs is inexpensive, but if a blog doesn't get much traffic your ad will be slow to attract prospects.

Bar association newsletters. Bar publications don't charge much to place ads, but there's usually a long lag time between submission of the ad and publication. Bar newsletters make sense only when you don't have an immediate need for a short-term project.

IV. Marketing

CHAPTER 13

Lawyer Marketing Overview

"Keep marketing, and never... ever... rest on your laurels."—Walter James III, solo

Historically, the legal profession turned up its nose at marketing, regarding it as unprofessional or undignified. In fact, until 1977, most bar associations did not allow lawyers to advertise. But in *Bates v. Arizona*, the Supreme Court overruled bar association restrictions on lawyer advertising, finding that they violated the First Amendment. *Bates* opened the door for much of the consumer-directed lawyer ads we see today in the Yellow Pages and on TV. And, as the legal profession has grown increasingly competitive, even large firms with corporate and business clients have been forced to market to survive and expand. In fact, many large firms employ a marketing staff headed by a chief marketing officer who may earn as much as $400,000 a year (*San Francisco Business Times*, Nov. 26, 2004).

With so many lawyers marketing 24/7, today's solos need to set aside whatever discomfort, dislike, or fear they have for the marketing process, and find cost-effective (but dignified) ways to stand out from the crowd. In this section, I'll provide a marketing overview along with specific techniques.

Learning to love marketing

We all know that marketing attracts clients and generates more revenue. You'd think this alone would motivate us to engage in marketing on a consistent basis. Not so. What usually happens is that once we reel in a couple of revenue-generating clients marketing takes a back seat while we take care of business. When our active matters conclude, we're right back where we started... hungry. To be effective, marketing needs to be done in ways that bring personal fulfillment not just a means to an end. In a way, it's not so different than the argument for exercise: you're more likely to stay with it when you enjoy it. So, find ways to enjoy marketing... and not just because it helps the bottom line.

Marketing makes you a better lawyer. Much as we think of the practice of law as a noble profession or a lofty intellectual pursuit, lawyering—when you get down to it—is all about advocacy, or selling your client's case. Every day, trial lawyers *sell* juries on why their clients are entitled to a favorable judgment... appellate lawyers *sell* judges on why a lower court erred... corporate lawyers *sell* their clients' preferred deals during negotiations. When you are engaged in marketing, you're selling something just as important; you're selling yourself. You may disdain marketing, or you may feel uncomfortable doing it, but if you don't value your services enough to sell them to others, how can you effectively advocate for your clients?

Marketing gives you more control over your practice. How you market your firm influences the types of clients you attract. For example, running an ad in a local paper that offers *Bargain Rates For All Legal Matters. Free Initial Consultation,* is likely to pull clients without the ability to pay even modest fees or who seek free advice. By contrast, writing an article for a business publication on creating charitable trusts could put you on the radar of high-earning clients with lots of assets. Simply put, a little strategic marketing can rescue you from the clients-from-hell. Think about the message your current marketing sends, and how you can tailor it to attract the clients you want, not the ones you don't need.

Marketing builds name recognition. Tired of toiling in obscurity in the corner office, grinding out memos and briefs for others to sign? That's probably one reason why you've started your own law firm to begin with. But why stop there? With your own practice, you can market yourself into a position of expertise and acclaim in your field. Consider attorney Howard Bashman, who launched a blog called *How Appealing* (*appellateblog.com*). Though Bashman was already well known locally, his blog soon catapulted him onto the national stage with a following of journalists, federal judges, and law students. Two years later, he left a partnership at a large Philadelphia firm and started his own now-successful appellate boutique practice with clients from all over the country. But you don't need a nationally-recognized blog to brand yourself. Back in 2004, Molly Gaussa, a new Pittsburgh-area solo, was struggling to pay rent…that is, until she decided to follow her passion and brand herself as The Pet Lawyer (*thepetlawyer.com*). As described in the Aug. 25, 2006 issue of the Puget Sound Business Journal, Gaussa handles all types of animal-related matters, from estate-planning for pets and dog bite cases to drafting breeder contracts. Plus, she's a regular on local radio stations and widely quoted in the media. What's your niche, and are you making the most of it?

Marketing calls upon your creativity. You don't need to spend thousands of dollars on the Yellow Pages or a listing for Martindale-Hubbell (now Lexis-Nexis/Martindale-Hubbell). If you allow it, marketing gives you a chance to apply your ingenuity to find low-cost ways to communicate your message. In fact, some of the most effective lawyer-marketers I know have found business through inexpensive campaigns such as running a blog or sponsoring a seminar or a local sports team.

Marketing is an adventure. Working for yourself is isolating, making it easy to forget you're part of a larger universe. When you get involved in the marketing process, you inhabit a larger, more interactive space and you open yourself up to amazing possibilities. I've had occasions where some assistance I provided *gratis* to other attorneys yielded referrals several years down the road. Or one of my blogs, or a bar magazine article about my practice, generated a phone call or e-mail from someone I knew in college or at a former job. In avoiding marketing, you miss making connections that pay unexpected dividends. So, think of marketing not as a job…or as the key to your firm's survival…but as a way to find opportunities that bring more success and fulfillment than you ever imagined. In a phrase, stay open to *connection.*

The Balancing Act

When you start your firm, it may be difficult to imagine that you'll grow so busy someday that you won't have the time to market yourself. Until that day arrives, though, you must find a balance between marketing and the practice of law. Here are some practical tips to keep those efforts on track and to make them more efficient:

Work in batches. Instead of setting aside an hour or two to write *one* article, dedicate a single morning or weekend afternoon and write two or three at a sitting. Once in the writing mode, you produce content more efficiently (if you also remember to ignore phone calls and e-mail). This technique also applies to blog posts. At the start of each week, draft four or five posts and set your software to automatically post them over a period of days. You'll save time and create the impression that you're blogging regularly, which will help keep your readers. This advice works equally well for cold-calls. Once you've gathered your contact information, it's as easy to make 20 calls as it is 10. See Chapter 15 for a discussion of cold-calling.

Make use of down-time. Figure out creative ways to use down-time. Some lawyers use time in the carpool line to jot down marketing ideas, others use commutes to call contacts and set up meetings. One solo blogger we know likes dictates blog posts en route to work on a small digital recorder, and has them transcribed by an assistant.

Engage in passive marketing. You can market even when you're working. If you have a matter scheduled at the court, arrive a few minutes early to chat with other lawyers who waiting around and get a sense of whether they may have work to refer. Or, if you attend a conference or a public hearing—especially one that will be transcribed or broadcast on the web—volunteer a comment and preface your remarks with your name and information about your practice. Your remarks may impress someone in the audience who might approach you afterwards with follow-up questions.

What can you outsource? Marketing is one area where large firms hold a significant advantage. At the trade conferences I attend, I often see a marketer staffing a booth for one of the BigLaw firms, or setting up prospective client meetings for one of their attorneys. But just because solos and small firms don't have a BigLaw marketing budget, there's no reason you can't do a little strategic outsourcing. Hire a law student or university marketing student to help schedule meetings, identify future speaking opportunities, or follow up with people you meet at conferences. A freelance marketer can also prepare informal reports identifying trends or unfilled niches within a practice area. For example, suppose you wanted to develop a practice specialty of representing women who choose single motherhood by choice. Your freelancer could surf the web to determine the demographics of this category, what types of legal issues they encounter, and whether any existing services currently cater to this population. If your freelancer is also a law student or young attorney, you might also ask them to compile recent case law that deals with legal issues relevant to single parenting. For a few hundred dollars, outsourced marketing can jump-start you into a field (or spare you from wasting more money on a losing idea) at the same time you're generating billable revenue.

Team up with a marketing buddy. If you find yourself procrastinating, establish a marketing "buddy group". It might consist of a couple of lawyers...either in complementary practice areas in your city or those with the same practice area in different locations...where there's no possibility of competition. Your group might meet for a finite period; say the time it takes for each of you to create a marketing plan and follow one's goals. Or you can agree to meet or hold a conference call weekly, exchanging ideas, sharing successes, and getting feedback on new ideas to sell your service or improving your campaign. Some lawyers also gather to avail themselves of group marketing and coaching services or classes.

Set aside time for marketing calls. Schedule marketing time with the same discipline you schedule client meetings and calls. For example, block out Tuesday mornings between 9 and 11 to engage in some type of marketing...to either set up meetings, make cold calls, or to follow up with people you met at a conference. Note: while Friday afternoons would seem like a good time for marketing follow-ups, remember that some people leave early for the weekend. Admittedly, marketing with a disciplined schedule is difficult, and, yes, things will slide when you're truly swamped. Do your best. But if you're just starting out, go the extra mile; do carve out some time just for marketing...and stick to it.

The one-a-day principle. Just as you take multi-vitamins, make some marketing effort...no matter how small...a part of your daily routine. Post to your blog (you *do* have a blog, don't you?), send a helpful link to a potential client, respond to an RFP, or call a possible referral source. On their own, these activities might not seem significant, but collectively your efforts will add up when you jot down each activity on a calendar or spreadsheet and look back at the end of a month.

Just because the Supreme Court (Bates v. Arizona) opened the door to lawyer advertising, doesn't mean bar associations embrace advertising with open arms. Because while the bars do regulate advertising in the name of protecting consumers, the truth is that most bar associations either distrust—or do not understand yet—the new wave of lawyer marketing efforts like Web sites and blogs that educate the public about the law.

As recently as 2006, the New York bar proposed regulations that would require lawyers to seek approval for all advertising…including Web sites and blogs…and to retain a hard copy of all ads for up to three years. As dozens of lawyers pointed out, the proposal would mean the death-knell for blogs, which might be updated several times a day, and which would make prior approval of each change unfeasible.

Other bar associations require lawyers to include lengthy disclaimers on Web sites, clarifying that the sites do not constitute legal advice…that e-mailing the lawyer for information does not rise to an attorney-client relationship…and that prospects should not include confidential or proprietary information. Such disclaimers do make sense, particularly where your Web site targets a consumer-oriented or less sophisticated population. A disclaimer can protect you from situations such as (a) a conflict where a prospect, who doesn't know you've been retained by her adversary, sends you confidential information in an e-mail seeking representation or (b) liability for suits asserting that your failure to respond to e-mails for three months caused a client to miss the statute of limitations for filing suit.

Every jurisdiction has its owns peculiar rules related to advertising, which are too varied to summarize here. Instead, I offer the following tips for addressing ethics issues related to advertising:

- **Rules are rules.** Technology provides additional tools for advertising, but doesn't change the basic rules. If the bar precludes you from running print ads proclaiming *World's Greatest Lawyers*, chances are the bar won't allow a similar ad if it's posted on a Web site.

- **Deception and superlatives.** In some ways, restrictions on lawyer marketing aren't all that different from fair practices governing ordinary advertising. Just as the FTC and consumer laws prohibit deceptive practices, the bar is no different. So, misleading techniques like dressing up as a doctor to gain access to an accident victim in a hospital to pitch your services won't pass scrutiny. Nor will running a bait-and-switch ad offering $350 uncontested divorces when you subsequently charge $2,500. Of course, the bar frequently perceives deception where no ordinary, rational human would detect it. The Florida Bar prohibited a law firm from using a pit bull in its logo, finding that such advertising was deceptive *because there is no way to measure whether the attorneys in fact conduct themselves like pit bulls so as to ascertain whether this logo…conveys accurate information.* Read more about this decision, at *myshingle.com/my_shingle/2005/11/an_ethics_decis.html.* Likewise, the Nevada bar would not allow an attorney to call himself a "Heavy Hitter", fearing the public might believe he was the *only* Heavy Hitter. For more on this, go to *myshingle.com/my_shingle/2006/03/more_bar_sillin.html.*

  Superlatives are another big no-no because the bar believes consumers are incapable of determining if lawyers are truly the greatest or super. Not too long ago, the New Jersey Bar issued a ruling prohibiting lawyers and firms chosen for listings in publications like Super Lawyers and Best Lawyers from touting that designation in their advertising (a ruling challenged by the publishers of Super Lawyers). For more on this, go online to read Alyson Palmer's account in the Fulton County Daily Report(). The article points out that Georgia's bar, and others, have not adopted New Jersey's position, and permits lawyers to proclaim their selection as Super Lawyers. Consult your bar about what's allowed in your jurisdiction.

- **Testimonials may be a red flag.** Testimonials from other attorneys, but especially from clients, add marketing value to a Web site or brochure. But many bars prohibit testimonials because of the potential for deception and inability to verify information (since most clients will want to provide testimonials anonymously if you've handled a sensitive matter for them). Even if your bar association does not allow client testimonials, determine whether you are similarly precluded from including in marketing materials endorsements or recommendations from other attorneys.

- **Professional referral networks.** Most bars run lucrative referral services, where attorneys pay a fee in exchange for referrals. Naturally, those bar services take a financial hit if you choose to get referrals from competing sources. So watch out when you join groups like BNI, or similar professional referral services, where you pay a fee to join and you agree to engage in reciprocal referrals. Such arrangements violate ethics rules that prohibit payment of a fee in exchange for referrals (bar-referral services are exempt from these rules). Likewise, some bars are wary of for-fee referral services, in which lawyers pay for a listing with a service that subsequently refers them to clients. The New York Bar's Opinion 799 sets forth considerations for lawyers considering registering for these services. Allison Shields, a New York attorney and law practice expert, posted a summary of Opinion 799 at *legalease.blogs.com/legal_ease_blog/2006/12/ethics_and_inte.html*. In her post, Shields said New York lawyers should refrain from using referral services if:

  …The directory 'recommends' the lawyers that subscribe [the opinion also explains that a service 'recommends' a lawyer, when it provides names of attorneys who specialize in "slip and falls" to a client who writes in with a slip and fall problem], or otherwise 'makes claims about the competence or character' of the participating lawyers; the service 'analyzes' the prospect's legal problem in order to find a suitable lawyers; or the service does not specify the means of communication lawyers may employ when responding to prospective clients who post on the site.

- **Read the bar rules yourself.** You'd be surprised how frequently lawyers exaggerate the constraints of the bar rules on advertising. I once attended a bar event where an attorney insisted that a particular state required lawyers to use their name or their law firm name in the URL for their Web site. (In other words, a lawyer could not call a site *MarylandFamily Lawyer.com*, but would have to call it *MarylandFamilyLawyerJoeSmith.com*. The opinion didn't sound right to me, so I researched the matter. The attorney was wrong; using superlatives in a URL (e.g., *GreatestMarylandFamilyLaywer.com*) was not allowed, just as it wasn't allowed for print ads, but a generic URL could be used so long as the Web site itself provided the full name of the law firm. Don't take anyone's word for what you can and can't do when it comes to advertising until you read both the rules and any related ethics opinions yourself. You may be surprised to learn that an activity that others believe is prohibited, is in fact, allowed. If, after reading the bar rules, you're still not sure whether your ad passes muster, contact ethics counsel. You can also seek guidance from ethics counsel on what to do where one of the jurisdictions where you're licensed allows a particular form of advertising while another prohibits it.

- **The court of public opinion.** Even where the bar allows certain advertising techniques, that doesn't mean that you shouldn't employ them. Ads depicting you as an aggressive, hard-nosed lawyer will attract litigious clients who expect results, and who won't be afraid to sue you if they don't get them, while ads that emphasize your low costs will generate penny-pinching clients who may not pay their bills. Other tactics may draw ire from the public or other lawyers, and result in what legal ethics blogger David Giacalone calls "e-shaming." In a blog post entitled, *E-shaming and Lawyer Conduct*, he warns that the effects of questionable conduct—if it is cited in the media or makes it way online—can linger on search engines long after the original event:

  …Were I a law professor, I'd be warning my students that Big Blogger is watching and will catch you, should you make gaffs or violations that find their way online. Were I a law firm manager, I'd be warning my colleagues that cyber-shaming is to be avoided at all costs. (And) if I were a lawyer prone to professional missteps, I'd be trying very hard to be on my very best behavior and to perform competently and diligently at all times. Your 'mistakes' will be available online for all time.

  —David Giacalone *(blogs.law.harvard.edu/ethicalesq/e-shaming-and-lawyer-conduct)*

Before you take a certain advertising approach, consider how it will play in the most important court in the land: the court of public opinion.

Additional resources. The ABA has compiled online links to state rules on lawyer advertising. Go to *that* reports on emerging developments in lawyer advertising. For ethics rules specific to online advertising, visit Kevin O'Keefe's *LexBlog at compilation of articles from the Corante Between Lawyers blog at betweenlawyers.corante.com/archives/legalethicsandadvertising.* ⬤

CHAPTER 14

Traditional Marketing

"Putting up a billboard won't make you rich, and doing direct mail or buying a Yellow Page ad won't do you much good. Your first goal should be to create a brand." —Scott Wolfe, solo

Today, with all of us immersed in the Web, so many traditional marketing techniques have a quaint, even old-fashioned feel. Yet, some clients—particularly older clients or established, institutional-type businesses—may prefer a more conventional approach. For best results, diversify your marketing, and use techniques that play to your strength. For example, if you're an introvert who dislikes crowds, do your networking at small gatherings; if you're a busy parent working part time, arrange coffee meetings instead of long lunches; if you're targeting large international clients, skips the Yellow Pages ads or seminars at your local library. In short, tailor your marketing process to your personality and the needs of your practice.

In the sections that follow, you'll find pros and cons of different marketing techniques, and their appropriateness for specific practice areas.

Yellow book ads

If your client base is mostly consumers, it's logical to assume you would advertise in the Yellow Pages. After all, isn't that why phone books in every major city have 100 pages or more of "attorney" listings, including full-page ads, four-color inserts, refrigerator magnets, and slick back covers? Some of the biggest, splashiest of these Yellow Pages ads cost thousands…even tens of thousands of dollars…well beyond the reach of most solos. But before you sign a year-long Yellow Pages contract, ask yourself four questions:

- *Do your target clients use the Yellow Pages?* If you specialize in employment law and want to defend companies in employment disputes, you won't find much business with phone book ads. Even if you want to handle plaintiff's side employment cases 10 or 20 percent of the time, such listings are simply too costly to build a small piece of your business.
- *How frequently do your target clients use the Yellow Pages?* Even if you're aiming for a total consumer-oriented practice, many of your prospective clients may now be using the Internet to find legal representation. A 2006 study by an online

marketing firm discovered that Yellow Pages use has dropped by at least 50 percent because of online searches (read Kevin O'Keefe's blog at *kevin.lexblog.com/2006/11/law-firm-internet-marketing/local-internet-search-rules-yellow-page-use-drops-by-at-least-half*).

- *Are the Yellow Pages your most effective marketing channel?* Many lawyers justify a $5,000 annual expense for Yellow Pages ads, calculating that the ads will pay for themselves if they yield just one $5,000 matter. The real question isn't whether you'll recover your investment, but whether that same money might be better spent on other marketing channels such as blogs, Google ads, or even hosted seminars that might generate $10,000 or more in business.

- *Are there less costly alternatives?* Many communities publish local versions of the traditional Yellow Pages with far less costly ad rates. If Yellow Pages ads are appropriate for your practice, why not experiment with the smaller circulation books before signing an expensive contract?

Martindale-Hubbell

First published in 1868, Martindale-Hubbell is one of the oldest and most familiar lawyer directories in the country. In addition to lawyer profiles, it includes a peer-review rating system by which lawyers are assigned a grade of CV, BV or AV (the highest), based on peer-assessment of one's legal ability and ethics. Martindale-Hubbell is also available online (*martindale.com*). The cost of listings vary with the space and amount of information provided (e.g., your Web site, firm profile, a list of representative clients). On average, expect to pay several hundred dollars a year for a listing (though there is no charge to add your name, location, and practice area to the online version). Most large law firms do have listings, and many corporate clients and large firm attorneys rely on them in search of counsel or possible referrals, and regard a full listing or an AV rating as more prestigious. If you have a consumer-oriented practice, a listing may be of little use. If you serve corporations or compete with large firms, it may confer added credibility and may help clients find you although these days corporate counsel are just as likely to check a referral's credentials on Google as they are through Martindale-Hubbell.

The Importance of Branding

Branding creates for a law firm a consistent image and message.

According to marketing consultant Mark Merenda, the goal of branding is to create or manipulate a perception in the mind of a consumer so that he or she is favorably disposed toward your firm before they ever get into a sales situation with you. The methods of achieving this are corporate identity (e.g., logo, business cards, stationery), Web sites, blogs, collateral material, e-newsletters, and such traditional marketing methods as advertising and signage.

"Branding is crucial yet frustrating for lawyers," says Merenda (*smartmarketingnow.com*).

"It costs money but shows no measurable return on investment. After all, no one ever says they hired you because of your snazzy brochure." Branding and image, he says, are especially important when the product—e.g., legal advice—is "invisible", and when clients lack a rational basis for the hiring decision. Under those circumstances, added weight is given to more emotional factors.

Logos

For lawyers, more than other business people, it's one's firm's name that matters most. It's how clients identify you; it's how lawyers and judges recognize you. For that reason, your name is the best possible logo. Think of some of the most recognizable online logos—*Google* with its basic font style and primary colors, *Yahoo* with its bold red capital letters, *Paypal* with its simple, blue-outlined white letters. Text-only logos, they are void of any superfluous shapes or distracting squiggles. For these world-recognized companies, and many others, the name is the brand. Dan Hull, founder of the national law firm *Hull McGuire*, makes the best argument for your name as your logo in a blog post at *whataboutclients.com/archives/2006/01/firm_logos_are.html*). In it, Hull writes:

> *. . . And I would add that if you already have a logo, don't change it. But if you don't have a logo, don't bother to develop one. Logos are really about your 'look'. Whether you know it or not, your firm already has this 'look'. Your 'look' is on your stationery/letterhead, envelopes and (if they match), your business cards. These all have your firm's name on it. Hopefully, these same patterns, lettering, and colors are reproduced on your marketing materials—Web site, brochure, blog. When people see Hull McGuire PC, usually underlined in burgundy with black Gothic lettering on pastel-colored stationery or business cards, that's us; our trade dress and our 'look'. Clients, agencies, courts, and contacts have been seeing it for 12 years. The repetition does it, and it likely has value. We wouldn't change that look even if we decided we didn't like it . . .*

Some final thoughts here: refrain from vague or artsy logos, and you would do well to also avoid legal cliches such as gavels, architectural columns, and the scales of justice. And if you're thinking about using an animal graphic in your logo, make sure you consult your local bar rules first. Some jurisdictions prohibit use of animals like sharks or pit bulls as law firm "mascots," finding their use deceptive or undignified. For extensive coverage of the Florida court's decision to ban use of certain animals in advertising, go online to read Florida Court Puts Down Pape & Chandler's Pit Bull, an article posted at *blogs.law.harvard.edu/ethicalsq/2005/11/17/fla-high-court-puts-down-pape-chandlers-pit-bull/*.

Tag lines

Tag lines, those catchy, 10 words-or-less mottos that strive to define the essence of one's firm, fall into one of three categories:

A. Tag lines that highlight the type of law you practice. One of the most provocative tag lines I know belongs to David Kaufman, a Washington D.C. solo who represents individuals and companies in the rough-and-tumble litigation arising out of business deals-gone-bad. David's tag line reads, *We do business brawls* (sm). His Web site, of course, is *businessbrawls.com.* In Maryland, attorney Mark Spellman has a wills and trusts practice with a tag line that calls attention to his willingness to visit clients where they will be the most at ease. The tag line—*Legal House Calls: Legal Services in the Comfort of Your Home.* And in southern California, solo sports lawyer Howard Jacobs has a niche practice of defending athletes accused of using illicit substances. His tag line: *Keeping You In The Game.*

Finding a fitting tag line for the type of law you practice can be tricky, particularly where you practice in more than one area. Thus, more lawyers tend to use tag lines that convey the type of service they provide. A few other examples:

Hire the attorneys you need, not the firm you don't (sm), from The Klein Law Group (*klein lawpllc.com*), a three-person firm in Washington D.C. Their tag line implies that clients won't have to deal with the bureaucracy and added costs of a large firm if they're merely seeking representation for telecommunications matters.

Big firm expertise, small firm attention (sm) from New York attorney Alex Simpson (*alexsimpsonlaw.com*), who focuses on corporate, transactional and securities matters, typically handled by large firms. Simpson's example suggests he can bring clients the skills of a large firm lawyer, but with more personalized service of a smaller firm.

Changing the way law is practiced, from the law firm of Enrico Schaefer (*traverselegal.com*). In this way, Schaefer wishes to make clear that with innovative practices his firm can provide more efficient and cost-effective service than traditional firms.

B. Tag lines that describe the service you provide. When it comes to tag lines that focus on the type of service you provide, avoid use of "expert" and similar superlatives. Most bars prohibit phrases suggesting that your service is superior to other lawyers (e.g., *Houston's Best Family Law Attorneys*) on the theory that consumers can't judge the accuracy of these claims. Likewise, most jurisdictions forbid use of terms like *expert* or *specialist* (e.g., *NJ DUI Experts*) unless you've received bar-approved certification.

C. Tag lines that are geographically focused. Some law firms use location as a selling point. For example, a Delaware firm that aims to serve as corporate counsel for out-of-state firms might tout itself simply as, *Your local Delaware counsel* or, *In-state counsel for out-of-state law firms.* Many firms located in Washington D.C. use their close proximity to Congress and federal agencies to draw clients with such (hypothetical) tag lines as, *A national OSHA practice in the heart of the nation's capital.*

What makes your firm most attractive to potential clients? Your location, your unique practice area, or perhaps your devotion to client-service or low rates? As you struggle to find just the right phrase, focus on your firm's core strengths...in 10 words or less. When you think you've nailed it, put the tag line through a Google search. As original as you may be, you might very well discover two dozen other law firms using the same tag line...or a variation thereof. As a legal matter, you can adopt a tag line similar to one used by others because most are not unique enough to qualify as service marks or trade marks. But what's the point? Your firm deserves its very own tag line. For a list of the top 100 law firms' taglines, check out *lawmarketing.com/pages/articles.asp? Action=Article&ArticleCategoryID=6&ArticleID=173).*

Law firm swag

Swag is a term used for branded promotional items—pens, calendars, magnets, notepads, tote bags, coffee mugs, etc.—all screened with your firm's name/logo and contact information. Effective marketing tools or just more junk? Some lawyers believe swag—especially pens, calendars, and notepads—keep your name in front of clients. You be the judge. An appellate lawyer I know listed the rules of appellate practice on bookmarks and distributed them to trial attorneys he considered potential referral sources. The bookmarks served as a quick reference for relevant deadlines in appellate cases as well as a reminder of the appellate lawyer's services. My vote for the most useful promotional gadget? Computer flash drives. At $10 or $15 each, they're not exactly a cheap giveaway. But they do make impressive and useful gifts for corporate and business clients. Moreover, you can load them with relevant cases or articles that you've authored. And each time you post new articles to your Web site, you can contact your client and remind him to plug in his flash drive and download your new materials.

The elevator speech

You're at a party with a roomful of strangers, and someone extends a hand and says, "*So, what you do?*" If you ever struggled to find just the right few words, you understand the concept of "elevator speech"—a description of professional services so succinct it can be delivered riding up to the second or third floor. Whether or not you have an "elevator speech," most legal marketing experts are in agreement: you do need to have ready a brief summary of your practice. But whether it's something snappy, with the feel of a sound-bite, or something simple and direct, is up to you.

Some suggestions:

Avoid vague legal terms. Most non-lawyers won't have a clue what sort of work you do if you say you're a litigator or a transactional or regulatory lawyer. Instead, use the simplest terms. If you say, *I'm a lawyer who helps clients resolve disputes in court,* it's more descriptive than, *I'm a litigator.*

Use plain English. Imagine you've been asked to speak at a sixth grade career day. Now, how would you explain the nature of your work, and—even more challenging—to make them care about it? Use plain English; it has the highest retention value. What follows are a collection of short, descriptive 'elevator speeches' collected by attorney

Sarah Holz (*womenrainmakers.com*), and posted at Tom Kane's Legal Marketing Blog, *legalmarketingblog.com/marketing-tips-what-message-does-your-elevator-speech-convey.html*):

> *I'm a bond lawyer. I help hospitals and nursing homes raise cheap, long-term money for projects. Over the last 15 years, I have helped hundreds of institutions raise billions of dollars.*
>
> *I'm a corporate lawyer. I help companies of all sizes, both public and private, buy and sell businesses, and come out of it still liking each other.*
>
> *I'm an employment lawyer. I help employers do what they really want to do, run their businesses, without being side-tracked by discrimination claims, strikes or other employee problems.*
>
> *I'm an insurance coverage litigator. When my clients get sued, I make sure that their insurance companies, and not my clients, pay the claims.*

If you get stuck generating your own 'elevator speech', go online. Two online tools... *15secondpitch.com/new* and *elevatorspeech.com*... can get you started.

Sponsorships

Sponsorships are a time-honored marketing practice in which a law firm goes to the expense of hosting extracurricular bar conference activities—a golf tournament, a lunch, a cocktail hour—in exchange for having the firm's name branded on conference materials. Needless to say, this level of marketing is well beyond the budgets of solo practitioners. Anyway, few people attending these conferences realize who sponsored the activity, and those who do probably don't care. If you want, sponsor an event to raise money for a good cause, or to give back to the community. Many lawyers sponsor kids' sports leagues or local charitable events because they're personally committed to the event. Even if your sponsorship doesn't generate clients, you'll get personal satisfaction from your contribution.

Print & Electronic Media: Making the Most of Both

While blog readership is soaring, some of your prospective clients may attach more credibility to entire articles than blog posts. I'm not suggesting you stop blogging; just diversify your communications. Solo appellate attorney Howard Bashman (*hjbashman.com*) is a good example. He's got a wildly popular blog—How Appealing—at *appellateblog.com*, and still takes the time to write a monthly column on appellate practice for *Law.com*.

Here are some other, more traditional communications options:

Old media. Online articles attract more readers all the time. Thankfully, though, we are still a nation of readers of traditionally published content (otherwise the *New York Times, Wall Street Journal, BusinessWeek*, the *ABA Journal*, etc., are in big trouble). Despite downsizing and greater dependence on syndicated material, the dailies and specialty magazines still welcome op ed articles and other think-pieces by subject-matter experts on such topics of consumer and business interest as real estate investment, home remodeling, estate planning or long-term care insurance. Regional publications, especially small dailies and weeklies, represent an even greater marketing opportunity. Send a note to a section editor proposing an idea. If accepted, the finished piece—anywhere from 750 to 1,500 words—can be used for mailed reprints or digitized for your Web site. You can also provide copies to prospective clients dealing with similar issues.

Law review articles. Law review or scholarly articles require a great investment of time and energy, but they can establish you as an expert in your field and make a solid impression as you market your services. If you want to get your writing into a respected publication, or use an article to leverage your way into a new practice area, seek out a more experienced attorney as your co-author—an idea suggested by Ari Kaplan (*Summer Associates Can Write Their Way to Success*, National Law Journal, June 19, 2007).

Because of the time demands of a scholarly article, I don't suggest attempting it unless you can piggyback the article on research that you've done for other matters. And try to offload additional research and cite-checking to a law student. Once your article appears in print (usually six to eight months after submission), send copies to existing and potential clients, and alert the media and bloggers interested in the topic.

Pamphlets and books. There may be times when you want to provide existing and prospective clients with something more substantial than an article. For instance, if you represent employers, you're probably asked the same questions, such as, *Am I subject to federal employment* law? ... *Can I fire an employee who just had a baby and never shows up for work?* ... or, *What is a reasonable accommodation under the Americans with Disabilities Act?* For marketing purposes, consider assembling a short booklet to give to prospective clients. One company, Tips Products International (*tipsbooklets.com*) can produce a professional looking pamphlet and market it on their site. Another increasingly popular option for lawyers and others is an e-book, a virtual book "published" online that requires readers to download it for themselves. You can find e-book vendors by searching the web. If you prefer, you can also self-publish materials in a more traditional book format. Attorney Ben Glass, a medical malpractice expert and marketing guru has authored five such books and sells them from his Web site (*vamedmal.com*). Among the titles, *Five Deadly Sins That Can Wreck Your Virginia Accident Case...* or, *Why Most Medical Malpractice Victims Never Recover a Dime: Medical Malpractice Crisis in Virginia?* And now you can also convert your blog posts into printed form by using a service at *Blurb.com*.

Public relations.
Any time you do something related to your practice... giving testimony on a piece of proposed legislation, winning an important case, or publishing an article... issue a media release. You can send your press release to traditional media outlets, or try one of the free press release distribution services online, such as *24-7pressrelease.com* or *24-7pressrelease.com/PR.com/press-releases*. And don't forget to send your press release to relevant blogs, since bloggers are always eager for new stories. Law marketing consultant Nader Anise (*naderanise.com*) is a huge proponent of media

releases as a legal marketing tool. In an article for GP Solo (*abanet.org/genpractice/solo/2000/summer/summer2000advice.html*), Anise writes:

> ... *The fastest and easiest way to gain attention is through a press release. A successful strategy is to refer to yourself as an 'expert' in the first sentence. It's not unusual for a reporter or editor to condense and copy the contents verbatim. Even a small write-up employing this tactic gets your name out there. And it costs nothing. The benefits can expand if other reporters see your name and contact you for future articles or comments. Readers will think of you when they need a lawyer. And your colleagues may call with referrals...*

Client reminders. If you practice in areas like trusts and estates or corporate law, your clients' circumstances may change following your completion of an initial matter. For example, you might prepare an estate plan that names your client's wife as the beneficiary, but the client has since divorced. Or the corporation you formed three years back may have disbanded, but the members never formally dissolved it. In practices like this, you might send out annual mailings to clients, asking whether any events require an update of previously prepared documents. In your mailing, invite clients to call you at no cost, or to set up a complimentary appointment to determine whether any updates are required. Or offer a discount for any changes.

Client alerts. Direct-mail alerts are similar to e-mail alerts. Essentially, the alert informs clients of recent changes in the law or new precedent which might impact their business, or require updates to work that you've prepared. Invite clients to contact you for a brief consultation for additional information on new developments.

Incident-specific mailings. An incident-specific mailing is one which responds to an incident involving a client. One example is where lawyers purchase names of drivers arrested for DUI and send letters introducing their firm. Or, a lawyer might learn from the public record that a federal agency has taken an enforcement action against several companies, and might contact those companies with information about the firm. Please note: depending upon the specifics, you may run afoul of ethics rules that prohibit direct solicitation. Also, prospective clients are often offended to learn that lawyers can access their names when they've been arrested for DUI, and might not welcome the mailing.

Targeted mailings to other attorneys. Most unsolicited mail to other attorneys about your services—whether you're seeking referrals or contract work—will wind up in a recycling bin. The one possible exception is if your mailing offers some tip or advice valuable enough to pique a busy attorney's interest. For example, a tax attorney seeking to work on personal injury deals with structured settlements might write to PI attorneys, explaining current tax law related to settlements. The tax attorney might even suggest proposed language that PI attorneys might include to minimize their clients' tax liability. This kind of direct mail works because it *shows* rather than tells what the tax attorney can do to solve problems. In this way, targeted mailings are more likely to generate a response than a generalized letter about a firm's tax expertise.

Newsletters. These days, law firm newsletters are sent almost exclusively by e-mail. Between printing and postage, mailing newsletters is just plain expensive. And even if clients prefer a printed newsletter, they can always print a copy offline. Expense aside, traditional newsletters require additional production time, which means your articles won't be as fresh as in an e-mail version. Printed newsletters won't generate any more information than electronic newsletters, though you may want to keep a stash of newsletters to distribute at a trade show or to leave in your office.

Brochures/flyers. As more firms create an online presence, they're moving away from the glossy collateral material that once dominated the profession. Brochures are a static medium, and costly to update, especially if you've ordered a large supply from your printer. At the same time, some lawyers do find that it's useful to have some printed marketing materials for distribution. Some options:

Online printing companies. A quick online search yields many popular printing companies (*iprint.com* and *vistaprint.com* are just two that come to mind), who for a reasonable price can print four-color, coated-stock brochures and flyers in even the smallest quantities. Working with online printers is preferable if what you want is an inexpensive brochure or flyer for a seminar or conference table.

Create your own brochures. If you're handy with desk-top publishing programs, create your own brochure and print them on quality paper on your own printer. This way, you can update as needed. But don't do it yourself if your desktop skills aren't great, otherwise you end up with an amateur-looking product that reflects badly on your firm.

Create a marketing packet. A "marketing packet" eliminates the need for a brochure entirely. And it's as simple as purchasing some quality folders from an office supply store, and stuffing them with your resume, a business card, and printed content relevant to your target audience (*e.g.,* published articles, media write-ups, and/or a list of services and fees). For the cover, I suggest you have one of the online printing companies print you a roll of self-sticking labels with your firm's name/logo.

Building Relationships Over Time: Person-to-Person Marketing

P2P, or *person-to-person marketing*, requires direct, face-to-face contact with prospective clients or referral sources.

PROS: Immediate feedback. Your prospects will let you know if they want to retain you or speak to you further about your services. P2P marketing also helps you gather first impressions about a prospect's needs. Then, based on their response...and their body language...you can tailor your sales pitch mid-conversation. Some P2P marketing, like participating in bar association events, lets you build relationships over time. For example, you might wind up coordinating a bar event with a large firm partner and impress him with your organization skills or creative ideas for discussion topics. As a result, you gain a contact who you can approach for work, referrals or a references. And while Internet marketing is a terrific way to find some clients, sometimes only a personal connection will do.

CONS: P2P marketing tends to cut into your prime work time…and budget… because it takes place at lunch, early evenings or at out-of-town seminars or speaking events. And while treating a prospect to a $50 lunch at a good restaurant now and then won't hurt, the costs can mount. Even accepting an out-of-town speaking gig may end up costing as much as $700 (including airfare, hotel and conference fee). On the other hand, you can control the costs of P2P marketing: attend less costly conferences or decline invitations to speak where the sponsors won't waive the conference fee or pay your way. Or consider visiting prospects in their office instead of inviting them to a meal. You'll make their life easier and save yourself the cost of lunch.

Referrals

According to law marketing consultant Stephen Fairley, law firm referrals are the Holy Grail of business development (*thecompletelawyer.com/volume3/issue5/article.php?ppaid =4421*). Says Fairley, referrals almost always convert into actual clients because (a) they have an active need for legal service (otherwise they would not have sought a referral), and (b) they trust, and are more willing to accept, the advice of the friend or colleague from whom they sought the referral. Frankly, though, there are no "secret shortcuts" to generating referrals. Clients and colleagues most often refer business to lawyers they know, respect and trust—and such relationships take time to cultivate.

Below you'll find some additional tips to help find referrals:

- Potential referral sources may not know you're actively looking for additional business until you take the time to remind them—sometimes repeatedly.
- Seek out some type of marketing activity—*pro bono*, bar, or trade association work—serving as a resource hub or listserv participant so your initiative and legal skills are more visible.
- Target referral inquiries to those with whom you have an existing relationships— former law firm colleagues or a judge for whom you clerked. If you've just completed a matter for a satisfied client, ask the client to recommend you to others. Don't forget family and friends as potential referral sources.
- Soliciting referrals from lawyers in the same practice allows you to capture "conflict" clients, while lawyers who have a different specialty may send you cases that they don't handle themselves. Suggest you target referrals within and outside your own practice area.
- Build relationships with lawyers whose practices are complementary. Some practice areas raise the same crossover issues regularly; e.g., a just-divorced family law client who will likely want to change a will or who may need to file for bankruptcy to escape a spouse's debt.

- Take the time to educate lawyers who may not see the practice area connection. For example, a transaction attorney's business clients may have concerns about the impact of a merger or acquisition on employees. If you're an employment attorney, suggest ways that you can assist these types of clients. Or, at least assist the attorney who's handling the business transaction.

- Be generous with *gratis* advice when other lawyers call with basic questions that involve your area of expertise. After discussing the matter, the lawyer might decide it's too complicated to handle and may either refer the case to you or bring you on as special counsel. If you find yourself repeatedly dispensing advice to the same lawyer without any return, feel free to cut the conversation short…or to quote your rates.

- Let potential referral sources, such as clients or other lawyers, know that you're actively seeking business otherwise they may not think you want it. As lawyer Dan Hull points out at his blog, What About Clients *(whataboutclients.com/archives/2005/10/asking_targeted.html)* lawyers are notorious for failing to ask prospective clients what they can do to earn their business.

- Ask your clients for introductions. Says Matt Homann at *nonbillablehour.com*, clients might feel pressured if you pump them for more business, but they may be willing to put you in touch with other leads.

- Make it easy for people to pass your name around. For example, when you close out a client file, include several business cards that the client can distribute to friends in need of a lawyer.

- Avoid *quid pro quo* referral arrangements where you agree to refer business to another attorney or business in exchange for their referrals. Such arrangements violate ethics rules in many jurisdictions that prohibit lawyers from offering something of value (a cross-referral, in this case) in exchange for referrals. In addition, *quid pro quo* arrangements put pressure on you to refer business to someone who may not be right for the job.

- Don't forget to thank your referral source. Where a referral converts into a piece of business, send a gracious "thank you" and, if appropriate, a small gift (unnecessary if you pay a referral fee). Even where the referral doesn't become a client, thank the referrer. This simple gesture is the best guarantee of continued referrals.

- Be prepared to address some of the nuisances of a referral-based business. In some practices, lawyers find themselves plagued by lunch invitations from real estate agents or financial planners eager to discuss the potential of cross-referrals. If you're pressed for time, but you want to keep the door open to future referrals, meet for coffee instead, or extend an invitation to drop by your office with materials. Or request information that explains how a referral arrangement might benefit your practice (for example, a financial planner might explain that she's prepared to refer divorced clients who need to change their wills).

- And then there's the matter of "dud referrals." Many times, experienced lawyers—perhaps believing they're doing a good deed—will pass off loser cases on a younger attorney. Give the referrer the benefit of the doubt...the first two or three times...with your thanks, of course. If you receive more than three duds, explain to the referrer that you're grateful for their interest but that you aren't interested in handling cases of marginal merit or representing clients who cannot pay. Your call will put the referrer on notice to pre-screen cases before passing them on.

Trade groups & associations

Joining a trade group or bar association is an opportunity to meet prospective referral sources and clients at sponsored lunches, happy hours, speaking events and conferences. Opportunities for conversation are limited, though, and often you find yourself competing with others trolling for business. When it comes to networking events, they can be just as demoralizing as the singles dating scene if you happen to be abandoned mid-conversation for "someone more important".

The real value of trade groups or bar associations comes from personal participation. Getting personally involved, lets you work with other lawyers or experts in the industry. It's these interactions that build long-term relationships with prospective clients and referral sources. Most trade groups—particularly the smaller local or regional groups—are desperate for help. So even if you're a new law grad, you shouldn't have any trouble finding a role. From a networking perspective, the best committee job involves arranging a speakers' panel. It allows you to help develop an event agenda and—even better—to help contact potential speakers (which gives you a convenient excuse to introduce yourself to some of the prominent names in your industry). Writing the committee newsletter—which involves attending group events and interviewing group speakers—offers additional visibility.

There are dozens of bar associations, trade and local groups (*e.g.*, chambers of commerce, neighborhood advisory committees) you can join. I suggest mixing it up: (a) join a specialty bar association or mentoring group that provides you with substantive information and access to experts in your field; (b) a trade or business group that serves professionals and businesses within one industry rather than just lawyers, and (c) a local bar association or networking group so you can build relationships with lawyers in your immediate community.

If you can't find a trade group or association to suit your interests, form your own. Or, create a subgroup within an existing organization. One attorney I know started a solo and small firm networking group within her local women's bar association. In my own case after years of representing ocean energy developers, I co-founded the Ocean

See book updates at author's blog—www.MyShingle.com

Renewable Energy Coalition (*oceanrenewable.com*) to give ocean energy start-ups access to legal and lobbying resources they otherwise couldn't afford on their own. For more information on starting your own group, go to Chapter 16 (*Becoming a Resource Hub*).

Bar associations. Most jurisdictions have city, county and statewide bar associations. In my own experience, I find that in large urban areas, e.g., outside of New York, District of Columbia or Boston, the city and county bar associations offer the best "bang for the buck." Often, they are quite active, and sponsor dozens of events each month. With close proximity to large firms and universities, the city and county bar-sponsored panels and seminars are stocked with leading speakers. Moreover, many of the city bars offer seminars and panels on traditionally BigLaw issues like Sarbanes Oxley, securities or re-insurance law, at a fraction of the cost of the ABA or professional CLE companies. And because city bar events are located so close to many law firms and offer quality panels, they often attract a large turnout so you can meet more people.

Specialty bars. You can find a bar association devoted to virtually every practice area, ranging from the National Association of Elder Care Lawyers to the Defense Research Institute (a professional group for insurance and civil defense attorneys). Most specialty bars publish have newsletters, journals, blogs, and listservs, and even member-only databases that make available a steady stream of information relevant to your practice. Specialty bars also produce quality forms and practice guides that can help you learn new skills. Whether you already have a specialty, or you're interested in developing expertise in a new practice area, specialty bar membership is vital to keeping abreast of developments and making contacts with experts in the area. Specialty bars will cost more than state or city bars, typically ranging between $150 (for more recent law grads) to $400. They're a good value, and many will grant a no-cost trial membership. Also, if you ask, some groups may be willing to waive or discount fees for new practitioners.

Constituency bars. Just as you'll find a bar association for any practice area, you'll also find a bar association for many different constituencies of lawyers—women, African -, Hispanic-, and Asian-Americans, religious groups, and even lawyers of certain political affiliations, such as the conservative-oriented lawyers division of the Federalist Society. All these special-interest groups sponsor events that address issues of interest to their constituency. For example, a woman's bar association may have events on part-time and contract lawyering or returning to work, while a Muslim Lawyers' association might sponsor events on profiling or immigration issues.

Inns of Court/law school consortiums. Some groups focus on mentoring and skills, creating valuable networking opportunities. If you prefer working closely with others and building relationships rather than meeting large numbers of new people, this type of organization may work best. Law school consortium programs—*lawschoolconsortium.net* and *lowbono.org*—provide training, mentors and support to new solos who establish firms to serve low-income communities. Though the programs focus on training through participation, you may meet mentors and other lawyers who have contract work or cases to refer. Inns of Court (*innsofcourt.org*) is another type training/mentoring group with a goal of "improving the skills, professionalism, and ethics of the legal profession." It specializes in civil and criminal litigation practice, and gives younger attorneys an opportunity for mentoring from more experienced advocates and judges.

Alumni groups and law firms. Your law school and undergraduate university probably sponsor alumni activities. Not only do they provide a way to re-connect with your past, and support your alma mater, but to develop new contacts as well. These days, many large firms are creating alumni networks of their own, attempting to stay in contact with attorneys who departed for in-house positions or other law firms, and who might be in a position to refer business back to their former firm. The Aug. 4, 2005 issue of New York Lawyer described some of these programs (*Law Firms Leverage Alumni to Drum Up Business*). The article said in part ...

> ... *New York's Paul, Weiss, Rifkind, Wharton & Garrison sends out its annual Alumni News, which includes stories about the firm, alumni notes, and three or four alumni profiles per issue. The 500-lawyer firm also invites alumni to attend its annual outing at the Big Apple Circus. At Silicon Valley's 545-lawyer Cooley Godward, the alumni Web site includes proprietary legal publications and polls on subjects like the most important attributes for outside counsel. Alumni networking vehicles include alumni web pages, newsletters and even 'mentoring committees'...*

These alumni programs benefit the departing lawyers as well, providing another way to find potential sources of business. In fact, they may even give you an edge in getting work. For example, suppose you want to take cases too small for large firms to handle. You could call Partner Smith at the ABC firm to ask that he send cases your way, but he would probably dismiss your request or, at best, launch into a lengthy check of your references. By contrast, if—like you—Partner Smith once worked at XYZ firm, and you found his name through their alumni network, he might be more receptive to your call. He may not have immediate work, but at least you won't have to overcome the credentials hurdle because your previous employment at XYZ would give Smith confidence in your abilities. Granted, this all seems very superficial. But in a credential-obsessed profession, you must grab the edge where you find it.

Chambers of commerce and advisory groups. If you want to use your law degree to serve your local community, join local business groups. Keep in mind that chambers of commerce often draw very, very small businesses that cannot afford to hire a lawyer. On the other hand, many of these new businesses often don't know other lawyers; so, if you introduce yourself, or avail yourself of their products, they may call you eventually. Local advisory groups are another way to use your expertise to the community's benefit, and to market your service at the same time. Many communities and local government now have citizen-advisory committees, which advise local government on a wide variety of issues like healthcare, air quality, zoning and ethics. The committees are typically populated by non-lawyers who specialize in the subject matter within the committee's jurisdiction (for example a healthcare committee might have a scientist from a pharmaceutical company, a nurse and a healthcare policy analyst), thus providing a chance to make contacts with others in your area of expertise. And since advisory groups are often called upon to brief county and local government, you may have a chance to meet government officials who might consider retaining you for other matters. Or you might have a chance to testify at a local hearing, which will earn you some media visibility.

PRO BONO PUBLICO: THE BUSINESS OF DOING GOOD

Most lawyers overlook *pro bono* work as a potential networking technique…and it's a huge mistake. Getting involved in a *pro bono* program, particularly those sponsored by prominent community organizations (e.g., the ACLU or Washington Lawyers Committee for Civil Rights), gives you a chance to let other attorneys with whom you're working to see first-hand the quality of your work. And it's worth noting that lawyers who are familiar with your work *are more likely to refer you cases or to call you for contract work*. Moreover, if you do a really good job, your name is likely to come to the attention of other lawyers who sit on the organization's board.

That's what happened to me when I started my practice. When I worked at a firm, I was heavily involved with the Washington Legal Clinic for the Homeless, a local *pro bono* organization. I continued my *pro bono* work even after starting my practice and, eventually, was honored for my service. At an awards reception, I spotted a prominent energy attorney who served on the board of the clinic. I introduced myself, and we chatted about our respective energy practices. A few weeks later, he started inviting me to some of firm's educational events, and later his firm retained me to handle several projects on a contract basis. You may think that marketing through *pro bono* is crass. But let's face it…everyone does it. Large law firms use *pro bono* programs to provide hands-on experience to associates, and to generate positive publicity for the firm. What's important is that you take *pro bono* work seriously for its own sake, and represent your clients in a professional, high-quality manner. If you do, your motives for getting involved are beside the point. Remember, there's nothing wrong with doing well by doing good. According to *The American Lawyer* magazine (September, 2005), the five areas where a *pro bono* lawyer can make the greatest difference are in family law, consumer law, elder law, employment law, and national security. ●

What You Don't Know About Networking

There are many generalized business networking groups that provide networking opportunities for all types of local businesses. Some provide informal networking opportunities along the lines of a chamber of commerce group. Others, like the BNI, a business-referral network, create structured environments that encourage members to actively refer business to each others (e.g., members commit to refer business to a suitable person within their group before sending it to someone outside the network). Many state bars prohibit lawyers from joining BNI or similar groups, finding that their practice of encouraging cross-referrals violates ethics rules that prohibit lawyers from *giving something of value* in exchange for receiving a referral. In the bars' view, the *something of value* would be the lawyer's promise to make referrals to other group members in exchange for referrals to the lawyer. In addition, the bars believe that membership in the group compromises a lawyer's independent judgment because lawyers would make referrals not based on the merits of another service provider, but rather, because the group allegedly obligated lawyers to make the referral. (For commentary on the utter irrationality of these rules, see my May 1st, 2005 blog post, *Maryland Bar Ruling Banning NonLawyer/Lawyer Referral Groups Discriminates Against Solo and Small Firms* (at *myshingle.com/my_shingle/2005/05/maryland_bar_ru.html* and my June 22, 2005 blog post on rational ethics at *myshingle.com/my_shingle/2005/06/rational_ethics.html*). Many lawyers who practice in jurisdictions that allow lawyers to participate in referral groups swear by their value. At the same time, even where the bar allows you to join, you may find that the composition of the groups—primarily, small local businesses—aren't a great source of referrals anyway. So whether or not your bar allows you to join a professional networking and referral organization, do consider forming your own group.

Networking events. If you're like me, you're inundated with invitations to networking events—lunches, breakfasts, happy hours, speaker events, holiday parties and more. Some are sponsored by some of the previously mentioned groups, others by college and law school alumni associations, or your former law firm. Invariably, these events find you standing awkwardly in a room full of strangers, or sitting alone at an empty lunch table, or trying to extricate yourself from a conversation about widgets. Here's the scoop on networking events: they're not the best way to meet potential clients. At best, you make a decent contact for every 10 events you attend. And yet...and yet...just because you shudder at the use of 'network' as a verb, you shouldn't give up on networking events. You need to attend them every so often if only to show your face within the industry or the group. Because that one contact you do make might turn into a major client. So, here are a couple of ways to make the best of (and even enjoy) networking events:

Choose high-value events. With so many networking events, opt for those that offer some value beyond a meal or happy hour. Attend lunch events whose speaker is prominent in your practice area, or there is a panel on emerging issues. This way, even if you don't meet anyone worthwhile, at least you'll have learned something new. Plus, a topic-focused event will give you meat for conversations with other participants.

Bring business cards.. Bring a few dozen business cards to every networking event you attend. Offer a card at the outset of a conversation or before you depart. When you're attending a lunch or dinner event, circulate your card around the table. If you've forgotten your cards, collect as many as you can from others. Or, if you have a PDA, you may be able to beam or e-mail your information to others. (For more tips on what to do if you left your cards back at the office, check out my blog post (*Help, I Forgot My Business Cards*) at *myshingle.com/my_shingle/2006/07/helpiforgotm.html*.

Approach groups carefully. If you notice people clustered in groups, approach casually and stand by, listening to the conversation. At some point, there'll be a pause when you can interject a comment. For many years, I made the mistake of barging into such conversations, thinking that my nerve would impress others. In reality, it was a turn-off.

Don't sit at an empty table. Seek out tables that are partly full. Ask whether you can join a table, and, if granted permission, introduce yourself to others before you take your seat and distribute your business card.

Don't stay too long or get too deep. When you engage in a conversation, don't talk too long or get into too much detail. Your prospect probably isn't interested in the nitty gritty of how a particular agency works or why a contract should be worded in a particular way. Ask questions about what the other person does, rather than focusing on what you do. Be sure to exchange business cards, and jot down information about the other person (*e.g.,* manager for public relations at HR company) if you don't have a good memory. Likewise, even if you run into people you know well, keep the discussion short and arrange to call for a get-together at another time.

Cut your losses. When I started my law firm, I trudged to numerous networking events. In fact, that's how I found my first client. I wasn't always so fortunate. There were times when the person with whom I was talking would gaze over my head, scanning the room for someone "more important." And there was many a bar event, where I would hear patronizing remarks like, *It's so nice that you started a little law firm.* One lawyer congratulated me on my "gumption," and actually patted me on the head. So, cut your losses; learn to recognize when an event is a dud and leave…or head to the bar and observe the scene for that novel you're working on.

Host your own networking event. Instead of waiting for an invitation, hold your own event. If you have office space or a conference room, invite people to drop by for a happy hour. Home-office lawyers might rent out space at the bar association or reserve a private room at a local bar or restaurant. Or organize regular lunch or breakfast meetings for lawyers or other contacts you've met through listservs. Lawyers from the Boston and Washington D.C. contingents of the ABA's *solosez* listserv organize monthly lunches or dinners, while groups of "solosezzers" in other cities plan get-togethers around visits by out-of-town members. Meetings that evolve from listservs or other online interaction are enjoyable because you've already established relationships online. And the meetings often produce more referrals or marketing leads because you've had more of a chance to explore possibilities in direct conversation.

What Comes After Networking

While you may make some decent contacts at networking events, a group setting doesn't lend itself to closing a deal or delving into specifics about the services that you provide. For that, you need a personal meeting with your prospect. Here are some tips to make one-on-one meetings more productive:

Why not breakfast? You'd be surprised how many lawyers and business people welcome a pre-work meeting as early as 7 a.m. It's an excuse to get out of the house early, and doesn't interfere with their day's business. Moreover, breakfast is way less expensive.

Don't do lunch. Whatever you do, avoid inviting lawyers or prospective clients to lunch. For one thing, if you work part-time or from home, lunch takes an enormous chunk out of your day. Second, a lunch atmosphere is too relaxing, making it awkward to take notes or make an assertive pitch for business. And, let's face it, lunch can be costly, particularly if you visit a decent restaurant. Of course, where a prospect invites you to lunch, or is visiting from out of town and doesn't have any other openings except lunch, you should accept.

Offer to stop by. Make life convenient for your prospect, and offer to come by their office. Even people who are short on time can generally spare a half-hour for a quick meeting.

Come prepared. If you're after contract work, your packet should include a resume, at least two writing samples (an article or two, and some sort of formal legal writing like a brief or memo); contact information, and a few references with current contact information. You might also include a sample contract that the attorney would sign to retain your service, and excerpts from bar opinions on the ethics of marking up rates paid to contract attorneys. If you're meeting with a prospective client, include a resume, a list of similar projects or matters that you've handled for other clients, and copies of relevant articles or speeches that you have given on the client's matter of interest.

Listen, listen, listen. When meeting with a prospective client or

NETWORKING FOR SHY PEOPLE

For someone who isn't naturally outgoing, networking and other such events can be especially daunting; even painful. This is particularly true when you're new to a group or you're attending an event for the first time and everyone else seems to know each other. They're greeting one another like old friends, and perhaps sharing jokes or stories that an outsider can't relate to. How do you break the ice?

Allison Shields (*allison@LegalEaseConsulting.com*), a New York solo and practice/marketing consultant, offers the following tips on what shy people can do to market themselves at networking events:

- **Arrive early.** When you arrive early, you're not as likely to be intimidated by a room full of people who are already talking, laughing and sharing inside stories. If you're one of the first to arrive, chances are that you'll have an easier time striking up a conversation with the other early-birds. Don't be afraid to tell them you're new to the group and that you're looking forward to meeting other people.

- **Seek out the host or group leader.** Introduce yourself to the host or group leader. Tell them that this is your first time attending, and that you don't know anyone. Ask them if they can introduce you to a few people in the group.

- **Bring a friend.** If you're uncomfortable talking about yourself or introducing yourself to others, bringing a friend can help ease the pain. Let your friend introduce you and you introduce her. It's often easier to talk about someone else and what they do than it is to talk about yourself. But be careful; avoid the trap of talking only to your friend and ignoring the rest of the group. That defeats the purpose of attending the event.

- **Look for other outsiders.** Scan the room for other people standing alone or looking as lost as you are. It's usually more comfortable to approach someone standing alone than it is to try to break in to a group that's already engaged in conversation. Chances are that you aren't the only one who is shy or uncomfortable, and teaming up with someone else can make things easier. Work the room together and introduce one another.

- **Head for the bar or the food table.** This suggestion isn't meant to hide out; it's meant as a conversation-starter. Again, for shy people, approaching one person is usually easier than approaching a group. Standing in line at the bar or the food table is a perfect opportunity to strike up a conversation with the person in front of or behind you. ●

referral source, don't brag. Put the focus elsewhere, and ask lots of questions. Find out what they do and what challenges they face. Only then should you describe your services in a way that responds to their needs. Here's an example of two approaches in a meeting with the CEO of a small technology company:

The wrong approach:

CEO: *I'm glad we could follow up after that seminar. I have a couple of questions for you.*

Lawyer: *Well, first let me tell you about myself. I graduated from Duke Law School, and started my legal career at a Top 10 firm. I worked on dozens of IPOs and really learned the ins and outs of the tech industry. I worked on several matters for Bill Gates a couple of times since Microsoft was our client. Oh that Bill, he's quite an innovator. In fact, I think that my own approach to the law has a lot in common with Bill Gates; we both have a long term view of the industry. That's the approach I always took advising clients at my old law firm. I'd tell them that they always needed to keep their ducks in a row, because you want to be prepared for that IPO.*

CEO: *Well, as you know, we're not Microsoft, and we're not thinking IPO at this point. In fact, we're making an effort to keep our company small. Now, we've had some interest in either outsourcing to another country or bringing talent here from overseas. But we're not just clear what approach would work best for us.*

Lawyer: *Look, I should tell you that an IPO is really the way to go. Big bucks. And then you sell the business and move on to something new. I really recommend an IPO. It's real complex stuff. You know, I'm one of the few attorneys around here who can really make deals like that.*

CEO: *I know that other companies like that approach, but it's not what I'm after at this point. I'm far more interested in finding other options... like outsourcing, as I said before.*

Lawyer: *Oh yes, well, outsourcing. That's really the wave of the future. India is just making a killing off that. Hey, have you ever been to India? I went there on my honeymoon. Great country, smart people. Do you like Indian food? After my trip to India, my wife took up Indian cooking as a hobby. Of course, maybe we should have outsourced that! Ha! Ha!*

CEO: [long pause] *Look, it's been interesting chatting with you, but I just realized that I've got a conference call coming through in a few minutes.*

The Right Approach:

CEO: *I'm glad we could follow up after that seminar. I have a couple of questions for you.*

Lawyer: *Great. I also have some questions for you. I was really intrigued by your remark about the need for small companies to engage in measured growth. Is that something that your company is struggling with?*

CEO: *Yes, it's one of our greatest challenges. For example, we don't want to invest in hiring new employees, so we're looking to outsource markets. Going overseas is less expensive, but we're concerned about keeping control over the product and confidentiality issues. On the other hand, we'll pay more if we have to hire here.*

Lawyer: *I'm familiar with this issue. In fact, I just completed an analysis for another client facing similar issues. We identified some confidentiality concerns, but managed to develop contract language to mitigate potential problems. I also took a team approach to evaluate other options. For example, I consulted with a colleague of mine who runs an immigration practice for advice on the process for bringing temporary workers from overseas to work on site as another option. And I spoke with the company's insurance providers regarding their concerns about liability. Would this kind of analysis be useful for your company?*

CEO: *That sounds very interesting. It would be good to have some sound information instead of relying on speculation. But with so many people working on the project, it sounds like it could get costly.*

Lawyer: *I understand that costs are a concern. And I can address that in one of two ways. I can prepare a project budget with a capped limit, or I can come up with a flat rate that will reflect my time as well the potential cost savings that you might recognize from the solutions that I develop. In any event, I would head the team, so I'd be the point person for billing. You wouldn't need to send separate checks to other people who I might collaborate with on this project.*

CEO: *Great, let's move ahead with that.*

Obviously, the first example demonstrates what not to do: the lawyer focused on himself, name-dropped, and boasted deal-making credentials that may not have been relevant or accurate. Worse, he delved into personal matters, indulged in inappropriate humor, and failed to take the hint about the CEO's real concerns. In contrast, the second lawyer initiated a substantive conversation about the CEO's problem and volunteered ways that he might help fix the problem.

How to Get Conference Speaking Gigs

You have two options for speaking engagements: speak at an event sponsored by another group (e.g., bar association, chamber of commerce or trade group), or market your own seminar. Below, we discuss the pros and cons of each, followed by some important how to's:

PROS & CONS. Sponsored conferences offer several important advantages. Conference organizers handle all the details, and your presence on the program confers prestige, and brings you into contact with prominent figures in your field. Naturally, the competition for conference presentations is intense. And, if you practice in a traditionally BigLaw area, you will discover...if you haven't already...that the large firms can skew the selection of presenters in its favor by sponsoring conference events in exchange for speaker slots. And it's not uncommon for conference organizers to pack panels with five or six speakers to attract more sponsorships. So, even if you do get invited, you may have just a few minutes to make your presentation. *A cautionary note*: some conferences are populated by other lawyers who may swipe your information, and use it for their own presentations.

Sponsoring your own seminar puts you in the driver's seat. You can feature yourself as the sole speaker, and perhaps even charge an entry fee to recover costs. Of course, you're responsible for such mundane (and time-intensive) details as selecting the venue and promotion. As a general rule, a do-it-yourself seminar works best for practices that serve individuals or small businesses. Your audience is less likely to pay attention to your reputation, and more likely to regard you as an expert simply because you're a licensed attorney. And they will appreciate the chance for some free information on issues that affect them, their family, or their business.

Choosing a conference. Do you want to target clients directly? Then, select conferences or trade shows populated with potential clients…not lawyers. Or, do you want an audience of lawyers? A colleague of mine specializing in legal research and writing services for lawyers speaks a few times a year at bar events and CLE seminars. Other solos find that by speaking at bar events—even on topics that don't relate directly to their practice expertise—can give them exposure and plant the seeds for future referrals. See Joan Rigdon's article, *Going Solo*, in the January 2006 issue of *Washington Lawyer*. It describes the speaking experiences of former DC solos Linda Ravdin and Joel Bennett, who continue to get referrals from other lawyers on the basis of their presentations. Incidentally, lawyers who practice in consumer-oriented areas (e.g., estate planning, real estate, small business) should think about offering an adult education course sponsored by a local community college or adult ed provider.

Start small. As a marketing channel, conference presentations rank high among law firms. Competition for speaking gigs is intense. In fact, some of the top conferences in my industry attracts *hundreds* of proposals for just a few dozen speaking slots. If that's also true in your field, don't just limit your efforts to large, prestigious events; focus on the smaller regional events and trade associations overlooked by most large firms. Smaller events, or even adult/continuing ed courses, can be preferable: after all, you're more likely to be a featured speaker than being one of a panel of lawyers who each have just a few minutes to speak. Furthermore, because smaller events are generally more collegial and intimate, you have a greater chance to talk with attendees afterward.

Identifying conferences. You're probably already familiar with the handful of conferences where you might want to speak. Go online to locate industry newsletters and blogs, and to identify trade associations where speakers are needed for annual conferences, lunch meetings, and other events. Some large conferences or adult education programs have a formal process for submitting a proposal. For those that don't, send an e-mail introducing yourself, along with your resume and a list of previous talks (if any).

Choosing a topic. Visit a conference's Web site for any clues to prior presentations. This will tell you what issues the group regards as important, and help you guard against submitting a proposal on a topic covered earlier. Unless the conference is geared towards less sophisticated clients or novices, avoid the basics (e.g., *Steps to Getting A Patent*). Instead, think of specific problems, such as, *Protecting Your Company from*

Employee Harassment Actions After the Landmark Jones v. Smith decision.

What's always popular are presentations based on "tips" and lessons-learned, such as *Don't Become the Next Jeffrey Skilling: Lessons Learned from Enron, and How to Avoid a Similar Scandal* or, *Top 10 Tips for Tending To Tricky Tenants: A Landlord's Guide*. Cross-over talks—applying knowledge from one industry to another—also do well. For example, a presentation on how banks can protect themselves against liability for identity theft could be modified for Internet providers with similar concerns. Note: cross-over talks offer a good entre into a related industry.

Should I ask for payment? Whether you get paid for your talk depends upon the industry. Keynoters, authors, and subject-matter gurus can demand... and get... thousands of dollars for their presentation. But lawyers rarely have the same bargaining power. In fact, competition among lawyer/presenters is so intense that if you require compensation the conference may simply find another speaker. Whether or not you do get paid, some groups will pay travel expenses or waive conference fees. And some programs will even share a portion of the proceeds collected with speakers. Bottom line: your speaking practice is unlikely to earn much if any revenue... except whatever new business the talk might generate.

Presentation pointers. Most of the larger conferences have strict guidelines about your presentation, and may require you to use PowerPoint or submit a paper in a specific format. Requirements for small conferences vary; many will not have any requirements, giving you discretion over form and content. If you choose to use PowerPoint, be prepared to bring your own projector if the sponsor doesn't have one. And if you are presenting on a screen, always distribute a handout of your talk, or e-mail it to attendees afterwards. Include a decent amount of real substance in the presentation. You want your presentation to have staying power beyond the presentation, to serve as a document that people will keep on hand and reference and call you about in the future. Even if your audience is comprised of novices, they'll be impressed if you provide cites to actual laws or regulations rather then simply paraphrasing them.

Make the most of your presentation. In the weeks before your talk, do a little extra-curricular PR, distribute a short media release as well as sending an e-mail alert to colleagues who might attend... ask permission of the conference organizers to have your presentation recorded or videotaped for posting to your Web site later... and, before your presentation ends, let the audience know you will be available afterward to take questions.

Conducting your own seminar

The venue. Pick a location convenient for the intended audience. Public libraries work well; they attract retirees and senior citizens interested in estate-planning issues. Libraries are also a convenient location for parents, who can drop older children off in the reading room while they attend your seminar. If you're targeting other attorneys, rent a bar association meeting room or office conference room.

Incentives. It doesn't cost much to provide drinks and snacks, or bagels and coffee, for 20 or 30 attendees. Also, consider a raffle to maximize attendance. The prize might be an iPod, a magazine subscription, or a gift certificate to a local restaurant. Raffles are an incentive to attend, and provide a means to collect business cards or contact information so that you can hold a drawing for the prize. Finally, send participants home with helpful information, stamped with your law firm logo or name. Even if attendees don't express immediate interest in your services, a handout gives them information so they can contact you later.

Advertising. Many newspapers, even major publications (for example, *The Washington Post*) have events sections which will publish events at no charge. Post flyers in areas that will attract your target audience; for example, if you plan to talk about legal issues related to remodeling, leave a stack of materials at local hardware and home-improvement stores. Use your blog or Web site to post information about your seminar. Contact other bloggers and ask if they can write a post about your seminar. And e-mail your contacts and clients about your seminar as well.

The Follow-Up. No matter what combination of marketing tools you use—direct mail, blogs, articles, speeches, networking—you won't achieve the results you want without follow-up.

Consider:

The 48-hour Rule. After every networking event that you collect a bunch of business cards, then send some kind of *enjoyed meeting you* e-mail within 48 hours of the event.

Call every few months. After you've met with a prospect, call every few months to see how they're doing. Sometimes, your call will catch a lawyer in the midst of a busy period and your call reminds him to outsource work to you.

Keep in contact with clients. When you think an issue like a new statute or recent case might impact a client, send a brief e-mail attaching a copy of the statute or case along with a brief description of the implications. If you've helped a client avoid a lawsuit, call a few months later to make sure that the problem hasn't reemerged. You might discover the client has other problems requiring your assistance.

Other marketing resources. Check out this Findlaw portal with numerous links to marketing articles: *lawyermarketing.com/CM/Marketing/Marketing36.asp*. Also see a collection of marketing posts at my blog—*myshingle.com/my_shingle/marketing_making_money/index.html*.

Evaluating Marketing Techniques

Marketing effectiveness isn't static; what's good one year may not be worth the time or expense the next. You should constantly analyze your marketing initiatives to ensure that you're making the most of your time and investment:

Re-evaluate. As your practice changes and grows, a once-inexpensive marketing investment may now cost more. For example, perhaps those bar-planning committees you joined when you had time on your hands are eating into your billable hours now. If so, maybe it's time to rethink, at least cut back, on your participation and put your marketing resources towards efforts that don't require as much legwork.

What's your client-conversion rate? When prospects inquire about your services, take a moment to ask how they learned about your firm. The number of inquiries is an important metric to your public visibility. More important is your "client-conversion rate"; that is, how many inquiries and leads a month do you convert into sales? Suppose a popular law blogger who generates 30 free consultation appointments a month, captures only a single, thousand-dollar client per month. If the lawyer is blogging 10 hours a month, and spending 15 more hours a month on free consultations, his conversion rate is…dismal. If your own blog is generating a disproportionate number of people interested in free consultations, it's time to charge for consultations, or seek out other techniques that give you access to individuals willing to pay for your services.

What's your marketing ROI? Simply put, ROI (return on investment) is a measure of how much money is generated by a particular form of marketing. For example, if you spend $5,000 a year on Yellow Pages ads that generate $10,000, your ROI is 200 percent and you earn $2 dollars for every dollar you spend. ROI is important because it helps you compare the effectiveness of different marketing tools, and figure out how to allocate limited marketing dollars. Let's consider the Yellow Pages: at a glance, spending $5,000 to earn $10,000 in fees seems reasonable; after all, you're doubling your investment. But what if half that $5,000 was spent on search engine optimization (SEO) to boost your online visibility, and the balance to create a "top tips" pamphlet that you distribute through your Web site. And what if these two marketing initiatives generated $25,000 worth of clients…an ROI of 500 percent? You would have earned $5 for every dollar you spent. In this context, that Yellow Pages ad doesn't seem like such an attractive investment.

Q: What marketing advice do you have for new solos?

- Brian Rabal (class of 2005)—"Join civil, social and fraternal organization, and shake hands with as many people as you can."

- Jill Pugh (class of 1994)—"Cultivate relationships. At least once a week, I have lunch (or coffee) with a colleague, a former client, or a potential referral source. I track personal and professional information for everyone I come into contact with, so that if I run across something that might be helpful or of interest I can forward it to them. And volunteering to chair the employment law section of my state's trial lawyer association has been a wonderful opportunity to meet more experienced employment law attorneys and to raise my profile."

- Sergio Benavides (class of 2005)—"Make friends with lawyers in all practice areas. Take them to coffee, to lunch. If you take them out and give them a nice lunch, even attorneys making $200, $300 an hour will be willing to chat about your legal work from time to time. Think of it as an investment. You want to get on their radar, so they take your phone calls, answer your questions, and refer you work. Also, make thank-you calls and send thank-you notes. During the holidays, I send Starbucks gift cards. What lawyer doesn't love coffee?"

- Heidi Bolong (class of 1987)—"Think about what you have to offer your clients that no one else can…and get paid up front."

- Mark Del Bianco (class of 1984)—"Getting good clients is all about networks; hometown, college, law school, government, firm, etc. So, unless you have two or three good, separate networks, making it as a solo is very difficult. Which means that unless you spend a lot on advertising, you may have to spend a decade or more building up your networks before going out on your own."

- Varand Gourjian (class of 1999)—"Target one area of the law and sell yourself as the best in that area."

- Walter James III (class of 1987)—"Keep marketing, and never ever rest on your laurels."

- Traci Ellis (class of 1990)—"The best marketing I've ever done has been to write articles for a publication read by my target clients. It's free publicity, and I always get calls. I suggest that solos find those publications (relevant to their practice) and get published. It's free marketing…and it works."

- Spencer Young (class of 1995)—"Use the Internet, be nice to everyone, hang around courthouses, and constantly assess the effectiveness of your own strategy."

- Scott Wolfe (class of 2005)—"My advice (for new solos) is to read those business and marketing books at the bookstores. Not the books for attorneys and attorney marketing (although those are also helpful), but the general business advertising books. Second, billboard ads will not make you rich, and direct mail and Yellow Pages ads also do little good. Advertising won't be successful unless you have a broad strategy; it only works when many mediums are combined, and the message is consistent. The only way your ads will be remembered is if they are everywhere."

To read the complete interviews, go to Appendix 6. ●

CHAPTER 15

Marketing 2.0

"In my own solo law practice, blogging is the only
marketing I do at this time." —Grant Griffiths, solo

Nowadays, you simply can't run a solo practice without Internet access. It's essential for everything from legal research and court and government documents, to court filings, blogging, and client communication. In this section, we'll discuss some of the new marketing options available to you.

To begin with, you can establish an online presence for as little as a few hundred dollars, or—what's more typical for small law firms—pay $1,000 to $3,000 for modest customization. Of course, depending on a site's complexity and sophistication, design and development budgets can easily spiral $5,000, $10,000...and up. But if you are short on cash, and have the time and the aptitude, you can create your own site. Many Web hosting companies offer fairly simple "website-in-a-night" packages that let you customize a variety of templates (to find them, Google the phrase "Web site templates" and take your pick). Even the blogging services (e.g., *Wordpress.org* and *Type pad.com*) are getting into the act, making it possible for you to create both Web and blog sites. Below are some additional suggestions to get you started.

Web Basics

Most likely, your domain name—that is, your Web address—will designate your firm (e.g., *joneslaw.com, johnlewis.com*), or describe your practice (e.g., *marylandprobatelawyer.com*). There are arguments for adopting one or the other. For example, domains that highlight a firm's name are usually easier for clients to remember although descriptive names seem to increase one's search engine visibility. For this reason, many lawyers register two Web addresses—one with a descriptive name and another promoting their firm's name—and they make sure their sites are designed to automatically redirect visitors from one site to the other. Note: be aware that some bars impose limitations on permissible descriptive domain names, so consult your local ethics rules. A few additional considerations:

- Don't use the name of the host server in your web address, as in *aol.com/johnlewislaw*. Such domains are difficult to remember and look unprofessional.
- Avoid any disputes over domain ownership; make sure you—and not your Web designer or someone else—has the rights to the name.

- Register the domain yourself so you can see if the name you select resembles any existing domain (for example, *NYTrustsandEstateslaw.com* and *NewYorkTrustsand Estateslaw.com*). If there's any likelihood of confusion, start over. Domain registration is inexpensive (under $10 per name), and there are dozens of reliable registration sites (among them, *Godaddy.com*, *Verio.com*, *Register.com*).

At a minimum, your site should include a resume, contact information, a section featuring the philosophy of your firm, copies of articles you authored or where you were interviewed or featured, some writing samples (e.g., briefs, motions or contracts with confidential information redacted), a list of representative clients, and—if permitted by your bar association—client testimonials. And make sure to include the jurisdictions where you're licensed to practice, and a description of all of your practice areas. Below are some additional suggestions to get you started:

Focus on your client. Instead of boasting about awards or a precedent you created, describe any accomplishments in way that prospective clients see how you might help them. For example, you could say, *I received a favorable ruling from the State Supreme Court in the historic case of Homeowner v. Zoning Board*. It would be better if you said, *I rescued a family from forced demolition of their home. The Zoning Board had declared the house in violation of height restrictions, but I successfully convinced the state Supreme Court to overturn the Board's decision. It was the first time the court ever reversed a Zoning Board decision on appeal. Read the decision here* (and you offer a link to the decision). I also recommend that your site have sections that describe you ("About Our Firm") and the types of clients you typically serve ("About You"). For example, a personal injury attorney specializing in family law with an emphasis on collaborative process might have an "About You" section that reads, *You are considering divorce but want to avoid a lengthy litigation procedure and the recrimination and expense that inevitably accompany a protracted process.*

Include a photo. A professional photograph not only adds personality to your site, it also helps clients and other lawyers recognize you if your first meeting is outside the office.

Keep your site current. Update your site as frequently as you need to reflect changes in your firm, such as the addition of an associate, a move to a new location, or if you're going to post news relevant to your clients.

Frequently asked questions. An FAQ section serves two purposes: it demonstrates the range of your knowledge and educates visitors at the same time. For example, if you handle consumer bankruptcy cases and get a lot of *If-I-file-for-bankruptcy-will-I-lose-my-house?* sort of calls, you can simultaneously educate clients and promote your practice by directing them to the FAQ section on your site.

The fee-posting dilemma. Should you post your fee or not? The minority view is that you *should* post your fees to satisfy client curiosity, and to filter out those unwilling or unable to pay your rates. The majority view is that you *should not* post your fees because some clients will assume they can't afford you and won't bother to call. Of course, if your site says that you charge $250 an hour, a client might expect a $2,500 bill, when in reality the task might just require four hours of work and cost less than $1,000). Also, once you post your fees, they must be made available to all. This limits your flexibility to develop the rate packages that some clients prefer over an hourly rate.

Disclaimers. If your Web site targets consumer clients and includes an e-mail address or form, you should include disclaimers, that information sent will not be kept confidential and that sending information does not create an attorney client relationship. Such disclaimers prevent site visitors from later claiming they thought you were representing them because they sent an e-mail with all their court papers. To avoid claims of unauthorized practice in jurisdictions where you're not licensed, you should also specify that the site is informational and does not constitute legal advice.

Comply with bar rules. Some bars have restrictions on what you can use for a domain name. Others require you to identify the jurisdictions where you practice or include a statement that your site constitutes advertising. In some jurisdictions, lawyers must even submit a copy of the Web site to the bar for review. Chances are that the bar will never discover a non-compliant Web site. But other lawyers, particularly your competitors, might.

Search engine optimization. A Web site is worthless if prospective clients can't find it. That's why, Web experts recommend you invest in some level of search engine optimization (SEO), to improve your site's online visibility. SEO can get expensive, but there are several simple things you can do on your own:

- List your Web site with multiple search engines to improve to its ranking.
- Seek out opportunities to link your Web site (or blog) to others to raise its visibility among the search engines whose rankings are based on the number of a site's links.
- Include your Web and blog addresses in your e-mail signature to help drive more traffic to your site and to increase visibility.
- Add a blog to your Web site, or create a stand-along blog. There's nothing as cost-effective as blogging to improve search engine rankings. Each blog post—even a simple, three-line post every few days—will increase your visibility among the search engines.
- Submit blog posts or Web sites of interest to "social bookmarking sites". Social bookmarking (e.g., *Digg.com*, *Stumbleupon.com*) lets users share favorite blog posts or Web sites with others. A high ranking on a social bookmarking site can drive significant traffic to your own site. For more social bookmarking sites, go to *en.wikipedia.org/wiki/List_of_social_software#Social_bookmarking.*
- Volunteer to host BlawgReview (*blawgreview.com*). BlawgReview is a weekly round-up of highlights from lawyer blogs that is hosted at a different site each week. Any blogger can sign up to be a host. Hundreds of visitors read BlawgReview each week, making it a great opportunity to introduce others to your blog.

Author's note: In some niche-oriented practice fields, you won't find much competition from other sites, so SEO is not as important. For many years, I was one of only a handful of attorneys specializing in ocean-renewable energy, so any online search relating to these terms would put my firm up in the top five results. By contrast, if you're one of 50 New York lawyers handling personal injury cases, you may want to consult with an search engine optimization consultant on how to improve your site's ranking.

Blogging

It's been some 10 years since the blog was born. And love them or hate them, they've given everyman (and everywoman) a global soapbox. But even if you're not inclined to start your own blog, reading them should be part of any legal marketing strategy for their ability to identify new practice areas and impress clients with your wider field of view. Of course, with hundreds of legal blogs (and more online every week), the question is, "how does anyone keep up with them all?" You can't, so you do the next best thing: you rely on Web sites called "news aggregators" or "newsreaders" to zip through your favorite blogs, sorting and scanning posts at regular intervals and alerts you when your favorites have been updated. Some newsreaders are even accessible via phone and other mobile devices Popular newsreaders are *Google.com/reader*, *bloglines.com*, *feedburner.com*, *Netvibes.com*.

For additional resources:

- Go to *commoncraft.com/rss_plain_english*, a great online video on how newsreaders distribute blog content through RSS feeds, and to *schwabe.com/library/rss_tutorials.htm*, an online audio tutorial on setting up your own newsreader.
- To find law blogs to, go to *Justia.com, Blawg.org*, or the ABA's Journal Online (*abajournal.com/blawgs*), each of which maintains a comprehensive list of law-related blogs. You can also add feeds from newspapers and some courts and federal agencies to keep abreast of new decisions and current events.
- Or perhaps you're looking for insights from bloggers on a new court decision or legal trend. Run your search through a blog search engine like *blogsearch.google.com* or *Technorati.com*, both of which have the capacity to search more than eight million blogs! If you want to search just law-related blogs, go to *Blawgsearch.com*.
- Even if you don't have the patience to sit at your computer reading blog posts, you can download many of them in audio form to an iPod or other MP3 player. Lawyer Denise Howell of *Bagandbaggage.com* offers a fairly regular and substantive podcast on IP matters, as does Craig Williams of *mayitpleasethecourt.com*. You can find a list of law-related podcasts at *blawgcast.com*.

Not only will writing a blog keep you current in your field, but it can also help establish you as an authority in your practice area. And if you don't want to establish your own blog, you can always contribute "guest posts" to some of the most popular legal blogs, and in that way increase your visibility online. All together, blogging provides unparalleled marketing benefits. And, sometimes, even revenue. Many popular law bloggers have leveraged their experience into paid gigs for other blogs or legal news

TOP 10 TIPS FOR SUCCESSFUL BLOGS *Grant D. Griffiths, Esq.*

In my own solo law practice, blogging is the only marketing I do at this time. I no longer place ads in the Yellow Pages, and I get more new business from blogging than I ever did with any previous marketing efforts. When I'm asked how I turned a blog into a successful marketing tool, I offer these tips:

- **Title selection.** Choose with care the name for your blog. In my opinion, this is the single most important item in starting a blog which will help it be successful. My own blog is called the Kansas Family & Divorce Lawyer. In deciding on the title, I wanted to give the search engines and those doing the search the terms they are looking for. First is the location, *Kansas*. Next is what they need, *family & divorce lawyer*. That's it. Do not call your blog by your firm name. People will not be searching for you or their problem by your firm name. But do put your firm name somewhere in the blog.

- **Search engine optimization.** The title of the post you place in your blog is also important for successful search engine results. Your post should include terms for which your target readers are looking. In my own blog, I try to use in every post such key terms as *divorce, child custody, visitation, retirement division, property division,* to name just a few. You need to decide for your own practice what terms people might use in search of help with their problem.

- **The frequency factor.** The frequency of placing post on your blog is another factor in its success. In the beginning, you may want to post often. I posted to my blog daily for the first two months. The fact a blog can be easily updated, and are updated, is just one reason why search engines tend to pick up a blog before they will pick a static Web site. Once your blog is established, daily posting is unnecessary. I tend to post to my family law blog weekly instead of daily.

- **Successful topics.** Topic selection is another important factor in a blog's success. I suggest start by posting the basic law to your practice area. Usually the basic law includes the questions you're getting from your clients, and the questions people are looking for on the Internet. Next, post about what people are actually searching for. One way to determine that is by using a service which provides you with blog statistics. Most blog service providers provide information on the various search terms people are using to get to your blog. If you adopt those terms and then do a post to answer their questions, you will see your blog move up in the search results rather quickly.

- **Pay attention to readers.** Provide a means for your readers to subscribe to your blog (most of the popular blog packages like Blogger or Typepad will automatically include a subscription link for RSS feed on the site). You can use RSS (Really Simple Syndication), a format for delivering regularly changing web content. Or you can offer a means for your readers to subscribe to your blog and receive notice via e-mail.

- **Writing style.** Your prose style should match that of your readers. If you are writing to the general public, write in plain English not legalese.

- **Keep things simple.** If you are writing a practice area blog, I suggest you not use it as a political soapbox. Create another blog to express your personal and political views. The readers of your practice area blog don't care about politics. They have a problem and they are looking for answers to that problem.

- **Stay tuned in.** You should read other blogs which are about the same area of law you want to blog about or are blogging about.

- **Link, link, link.** You should link to as many blogs that cover the same practice area as you. If you link to them, you will get noticed and others will want to link to you."

Grant D. Griffiths (kansasfamilylawblog.lexblog.com) practices family law in Kansas.

journals. To set up a blog, check out two free blog-creation sites…*Blogger.com* or *Word press.com*…or *Typepad*, whose basic package costs under $100 a year. Once you're ready to commit to a blog, you can stay with one of these services or upgrade to a more professional blog, such as those created at *Lexblog.com,* (a blog design service dedicated to lawyer blogs).

Do you need both a blog and Web site? Consider:

Do you have one main practice area, or several? Kevin O'Keefe, founder of *Lexblog* (a company that creates blogs for lawyers) says that a blog alone will work provided that a lawyer specializes in one area. So long as the blog "publisher" (e.g., a lawyer or law firm) is doing work in primarily one practice area, a blog alone works well. Where a conventional Web site is also needed is if the lawyer or law firm does different kinds of work, i.e., estate planning and family law. A blog covering both areas of law cannot be used to enter into a niche discussion and network on the net. The blog will then need to be on one topic and a Web site used to showcase what the lawyer or law firm does in these two areas. Source: Kevin O'Keefe *(kevin.lexblog.com/2007/06/law-blog basics/do-you-need-a-conventional-website-if-you-have-a-blog/.*

Will you commit to blogging? If you're leaning towards a blog-only solution, are you willing to commit to keeping the site updated? A Web site is "timeless" in the sense that the material posted generally isn't date stamped. By contrast, blog posts include a date, and if visitors see that your most recent blog post is six months old, they may assume the site is no longer active.

Listservs, Social Networking & Other Online Marketing Options

Online directories. The cost and effectiveness of online directories vary greatly. With free directories, you have nothing to lose except the time it takes to register. If you're considering a fee-based directory, factor in (a) whether a listing in the site will make you more "findable" on the Web, and (b) whether can determine its effectiveness by getting listed for a trial period. Some, like *Lawyers.com and Nolo.com*, lists lawyers by practice area, while *LawGuru.com* is skewed towards lawyers with consumer-oriented practices. Online directories feature different levels of interactivity. For example, at *LawGuru* you have an opportunity to respond to questions from prospective clients, and to post the responses for all users to view. *Avvo.com*, launched in mid-2007, is another online directory, and was created to help consumers find and select legal representation. It also allows lawyers to create—at no charge—a profile that includes a photo, resume, and testimonials from colleagues and clients. Avvo has generated some controversy, though, because it ranks lawyers on a 1–10 scale based on experience, professional achievements, and disciplinary sanctions, and lets clients post comments about lawyers. Note: *At the time of this writing, Avvo is the subject of a class-action suit by a group of lawyers who allege that the ratings are inaccurate and misleading to consumers.*

Online referral services. Lawyer referral services (among them *casepost.com*, *legal match.com*, *legalfish.com*), operate a little differently from online directories. They use questionnaires to gather extensive case information from prospective clients, and then forward to lawyers in a given region and practice area to respond if they wish. In this way, attorneys are only sent clients with matters specific to their practice area. Note: some referral services are expensive ($3,000 to $4,000/year), and some of their sales people can be aggressive... even deceptive. For example, it's not unusual to get a voice-mail message that a referral company has a referral for you. When you return the call, you might get pitched that ... *if you were really committed to building your firm, you'd be willing to risk $3,000* or, ... *We don't want to do business with the types of law firms that consider $3,000 to be a lot of money.* Some referral services offer a money-back guarantee, and/or an extra six months free if you don't get any clients. Those promises may not be meaningful, because if the service didn't bear fruit during early on, another six months might be irrelevant. As for the money-back guarantee, make sure you understand when it kicks in—if you haven't had any referrals, or if you had some but they turned out to be unsuitable. Make sure the guarantee covers both situations. And before you put down your money, do a little digging:

- Search the web and *solosez* archives (*mail.abanet.org/archives/solosez.html*) to see what other lawyers think about specific online referral services.
- Consult with lawyers whom you trust, as well as bar practice advisors, for their advice on the value of certain services
- Ask if a service will allow you to sign up for a short, three-month trial so you can limit your exposure.

Online advertising. At this time, the most popular online ad program is Google's AdWords (*adwords.google.com*). It adds "sponsored links" to the world's most popular search engine, and works like this: you create a small, boxed, three-line ad that makes use of "keywords" that describe your practice area(s). For example, you might use keywords like *Toledo Ohio civil rights lawyer*, or *Oakland personal injury*, or *mesothelioma attorney Texas*. When someone searches for those or a combination of similar keywords, your ad appears to the right of the search results. And this is where things get can get expensive: if someone clicks on your ad for whatever reason, Google charges you the cost of the keyword (a process known as "pay per click"). According to a Web site that tracks keyword prices (*cwire.org*), some keywords are relatively inexpensive (*bankruptcy lawyer* is $9 per click, *patent lawyer* is $5 per click), while *tax lawyer* can cost $35 per click, *Oakland personal injury lawyer* can cost $58 per click, and *mesothelioma attorney Texas* can cost more than $65 per click! Depending on the keywords you select, and the frequency with which your ad appears, pay-per-click could put a big dent in your marketing budget. Here's what Google says about its online ad program:

. . . Google AdWords shows your ad as often as possible within the budget you set. You're charged a small portion of the budget each time a user clicks your ad, so the higher your budget, the more ad impressions and clicks you may receive. You won't be charged more than this amount each month (though in some cases you may be charged less).

You can also place ads on blogs at *blogads.com*. These ads range in price from as little as $10 per week to several thousand dollars weekly, depending upon the site.

Social networking. For business professionals, the social networking landscape includes a growing number of fast-growing Web sites.

Not so long ago, *Facebook* and *Myspace were* regarded as social networking sites for partying college kids. That hasn't changed much, but the 35-and-older crowd—including a growing number of lawyers—are discovering *Facebook's* potential as a business tool. In fact, according to BusinessWeek Magazine, the number of thirtysomething visitors to *Facebook* have more than doubled, and they account for nearly half of the site's visitors. For more on its potential for lawyers, read solo Ernie Svenson's blog post at *ernietheattorney.net/ernie_the_attorney/2007/07/keeping-up-appe.html.*

By far, the Internet's largest social networking site today is *MySpace.com*, which has been adopted by the under-30 crowd and attracts more than a third of the entire social networking audience. As of this writing, *MySpace* isn't yet on the radar of many lawyers, which was a PR coup for Pittsburgh solo Anicia Ogonsky, whose *MySpace* profile links to her firm's Web site. This one-woman exercise in Web 2.0 marketing got her a radio interview and an article in the Pittsburgh media. Some lawyers may question the professionalism of *MySpace* as a marketing channel. But for young attorneys—Anicia is 28—it makes sense, and as her initial feedback suggests, it works.

For business professionals, the largest social networking site is *LinkIn.com*. Of more than nine million users using it to recruit staff, and pursue job or business opportunities, some 212,000 are registered in the "law practice industry", among them some 90,000 attorneys. *LinkIn* works like this: once you're registered, you create a Web profile linking you to colleagues, friends, and professional acquaintances. Once your network is built, you can access the contacts of others. . . and the contacts of *their* contacts. In addition, *LinkedIn* will post endorsements for your service, which will give you more credibility with potential contacts. A basic *Linkedin* account is free; upgrades that allow you to connect with a wider range of people and view their resumes cost extra. You can use *LinkedIn* to help establish yourself as a "resource hub", a technique described in the next chapter.

In late 2007, the ABA Journal reported two new social networking sites for lawyers. The first—*LawLink.com*—is a lawyer-only site intended to serve as a general forum for referrals, information-sharing, and discussion of professional issues. The other site—still on the drawing board at this time—is *LegalOnRamp.com*, which will be a members-only community of corporate in-house counsel and the law firm attorneys that represent them.

Listservs. As discussed earlier, listservs are a great way to get answers to practice-management questions, and to develop a sense of community to stave off the isolation of solo practice. Listservs are also a terrific marketing tool. Members often post messages in search of attorney referrals for friends or other clients. Other times, list members may have overflow work to outsource, and use the list to find lawyers willing to handle the work on a contract basis. In addition, lawyers on the list—for example, a real estate attorney and a probate attorney—might team up to serve a client whose problems involve both areas of expertise. Of course, with some listservs (like *solosez.net*, whose roster now approaches 3,000), you won't generate much business unless you stand out in a positive way.

Here are some tips to generating business through a listserv:

- Try to respond at least once a week to questions you're competent to answer. If, for example, you practice employment law in New York and there's a question on employment law in California, you might analyze the problem from a general perspective and share some insight on how New York law works. Even if you're a new practitioner, or you practice in an obscure field of law, you can still contribute. Likewise, if someone is looking for a case or a sample complaint or an article on a legal topic, run a quick Internet search and see if you can come up with something responsive.

- As you begin contributing, your skills and knowledge will come to the attention of other lawyers, and they in turn may wish to refer cases or retain you when they're familiar with the quality of your work. If, however, you don't know the answer to a highly technical post, don't respond. In one stroke, you could lead the questioner astray and embarrass yourself at the same time. Likewise, be mindful of the tone, grammar and spelling of posts. Listservs are a highly visible forum, and you will find yourself the subject of a swift (and public) reprimand for any nasty or rude missives, especially if your target is one of the more eminent members of a list.

- If some of your listmates have practice areas that complement one another, contact them off-list and continue the conversation about potential work opportunities.

- Set up a signature line for your e-mail that indicates where you're located and licensed to practice. In this way, other listserv members can learn more about you, and, if your post finds its way to other lists, your contact information will become even more important.

Teleseminars and webinars. Teleseminars and webinars let you share your knowledge without ever leaving your office.

In a teleseminar, you deliver your material by phone while participants listen in on a conference call phone line; in a webinar, your message—both audio and visual—is delivered online. They're a win-win for everyone involved. For you, they're inexpensive to produce and more convenient than crossing the country to speak on a panel; for your audience, the technology allows them to participate from home...even via cell phone in their car! If you have a national practice, teleseminars and webinars are a great way to address "attendees" all over the country simultaneously. And if you practice in an area of immediate interest to corporate clients, you may even be able to convert a teleseminar or webinar into a revenue-generator. With many conference fees costing upwards of $1,000, not to mention travel expenses, a teleseminar or webinar offering the same material for $99 is a bargain. Think of it: if 20 people call in for an hour, you will have made 20 contacts who could potentially convert to clients—and earn $2,000 besides.

Teleseminars and webinars combine the best of both worlds, and they let you to get paid for marketing. And they're neither costly nor difficult to set up.

For teleseminars, it begins by selecting a conference call vendor online, and reserving a call-in line and phone number. Services vary by vendor, but the event can be enriched by emailed materials, Power Point presentations, and a transcription that can be sold or given away to participants. For webinars, conference registration vendors (among them, *eventbrite.com* and *acteva.com*) generate a list of registrants and collect payment for the event. There's no long-term commitment, and for most you pay either a minimal fee and/or a small percentage of each transaction. One webinar provider—*gotowebinar*.com—even offers do-it-yourself software and a free trial.

Teleseminars and webinars aren't just for corporate and business clients. They're a convenient way for your clients to learn more about such matters as setting up a trust, legal/tax issues related to college savings plans, or caring for an elderly parent.

Matt Homann's Marketing With Technology presentation at a recent ABA Techshow is available online—*thenonbillablehour.typepad.com/nonbillable_hour/files/homann marketing_with_technology.pdf*. Homann offers a list of 50 great marketing tips as well as links to 50 blogs with marketing ideas.

GUARDING YOUR REPUTATION ONLINE

As the Internet makes information more accessible, it is imperative you stay vigilant about guarding your reputation online. Because at the same time that your colleagues and prospective clients can see what is positive about you—your work, your writings, your pro bono awards—they can also find embarrassing photos, any disciplinary record, and any best-left-unseen comments posted on listservs and elsewhere.

Here are some suggestions to keeping your reputation intact in the Internet era:

- **Know what's out there.** Regularly run your name or your law firm name through search engines to see if any negative information is in circulation. If you discover negative comments about your services, see if the site owners have a policy that allows for the removal of comments. In extreme cases, where information posted is easily discoverable (e.g., appears at the top of your search results) and damaging (e.g., prospective clients question you about those comments and then decline to hire you), you may need to consult an attorney who specializes in Internet defamation to evaluate your options.

- **Watch what you say and where you say it.** Bear in mind that a search engine like Google often indexes listservs or mailing groups that you may have believed were private. So if you post about a personal problem on a listserv, or lob posts riddled with profanity, those messages may pop up when someone searches your name. To avoid such embarrassment, keep your messages tame (something you should be doing anyway) and post sensitive questions anonymously.

- **Think twice about the advice you give at seminars.** A Pittsburgh-based immigration law firm learned a hard lesson when its lawyers advised seminar participants they could bypass federal immigration laws on hiring foreign workers by creating recruiting campaigns designed "not to find qualified US workers" (therefore opening the doors to hiring overseas). A video of the event found its way to a computer programmer who inserted his own editorial subtitles about how the firm was advising companies to break the laws, and then he uploaded the video to YouTube! More than 120,000 viewers downloaded the video, including two US Senators, who sent a letter to the firm asking it to explain its advice. For the full story, visit *legalblogwatch.typepad.com/legal_blog_watch/2007/06/watch-what-you-.html.*

- **Take preemptive action.** Tell clients about readily discoverable, negative information that they may find themselves. For example, if you've got a grievance on your record, disclose it and explain it to clients. Chances are they'll appreciate your honesty and won't hold the infraction against you. If, however, clients discover your grievance through an Internet search, they may suspect you of holding back information. If preemptive action is required, don't come down too hard. For example, when someone passed a copy of Nixon Peabody's awful law firm theme song—*Everyone's a winner*—to a legal gossip Web site, the firm threatened a cease-and-desist action if the song wasn't removed (for details, visit *legalblogwatch. typepad.com/legal_blog_watch/2007/08/is-nixon-peabod.html.* The firm's heavy-handed action only drew more attention to the song (eventually, YouTube removed it from the site), and generated negative commentary about the firm's lack of humor around the blogosphere. Bottom line: if something embarrassing makes its way out on the Internet, try to diffuse the situation with humor or find a way to make the attention work to your benefit.

- **Optimize the visibility of your positive accomplishments.** Add attorney and client testimonials to your Web site (if allowed in your jurisdiction), update your blog more regularly (which will move your blog posts to the top of search results), and invite bloggers to comment on your blog posts (many of them may have complimentary remarks which will also show up in search engines). As you generate new and positive information about yourself, the negative comments will sink to the bottom of search engine results where, hopefully, they'll go unnoticed. ●

CHAPTER 16

High-Impact Marketing

"Marketing is easier when you reach out to a niche audience instead of to 'everyone' in your general practice area." —David Leffler, author of *Niche Marketing: The Inside Track to Client Development*

Ask lawyers how they feel about cold-calling, and you hear things like... *tacky... cheesy... an act of desperation.* Which is unfortunate, because lawyer-to-lawyer cold calling happens to be one of the most effective, inexpensive, least time-consuming ways of making new contacts and finding work. After all, in a competitive market, lawyers get business by seeking it out... not waiting for the phone to ring. And if you're just starting out, and you want to start making court appearances for other lawyers on a contract basis, cold calling is an excellent way to begin. Open up your bar association directory and call 10 lawyers... as many as 30 if you devote a half-hour to the exercise three mornings that week. Of the 30 lawyers, maybe only one may have work, but—who knows?—maybe two other lawyers will ask you for follow-up information. Not a bad return for a 90-minute investment.

As with other forms of P2P (person-to-person) networking, cold calling gives you an immediate response: *yes, I have an immediate need,* or '*no thanks*'. And because cold-calling allows for direct interaction, you might discover that even if your prospect doesn't need you to make a court appearance, they might have a small matter suitable for referral. One young attorney I know finally mustered the nerve to try cold calling. The payoff: one of her prospects praised her initiative and referred her some contract work. Here are some tips to get started:

Compile a list of prospects. It might include attorneys from whom you seek referrals or contract work; old clients to whom you haven't spoken in years; businesses you'd like to introduce to your firm. Note: avoid direct calls to consumer clients that might be construed as impermissible solicitation under ethics rules.

- *Set aside a block of time.* Cold calling is best from 10 to 11 am and 3 to 4 pm.
- *Expect rejection, but put a smile in your voice.* Your armor will toughen as you work through the list.
- *Follow up.* Be sure to follow up... that day if possible... with writing samples or other materials that you promised to send.

- *Leverage technology.* Use one of the many contact-management software tools (Excel, Act!, GoldMine) to track your efforts, making note of the your prospect's name, response, and any necessary follow-up.
- *Work from a script.* Identify yourself and your firm, and describe how you know the prospect and why you're calling. For example:

Hi, this is Jane Jones. I'm an attorney, and I just opened a practice here in Cooksville. I've gotten your phone number from the county bar directory. Is this is a good time to talk?

[If yes, continue]

Sample 1 (seeking referrals)...
I'm calling to introduce myself to the other lawyers in town, and let you know that I'm available for referrals in bankruptcy cases. I recently handled a couple of matters for some of the Jones Law Firms' clients, and they were happy with the results. And because Jones Law doesn't practice bankruptcy law, they are glad to have a reliable source to refer clients.

Sample 2 (seeking per diem work)...
I'm calling to ask if you have a need for a lawyer to draft motions or briefs on a contract basis. I recently started providing research and writing services on a contract basis to other lawyers, and I really enjoy this aspect of practice. Right now, I am actively pursuing more of this type of work.

—Adapted from the author's chapter in *How to Capture and Keep Clients* (ABA, 2006).

Why You Should Be A Resource Hub

A decade ago, few of us were involved in organized networking.

Now, of course, networking is a verb, an accepted (and dreaded) component of a practitioner's life. Why? In a word...rejection. The lack of control can demoralize even the most hard-charging extrovert. But what if you could gain control of the marketing dynamic by making yourself the go-to person to whom others gravitate? You can, by becoming a "resource hub", a concept outlined by New York solo David Abeshouse in his article, *The Power of Networking* (New York Law Journal, Nov. 7, 2005; available at *law.com/jsp/law/sfb/lawArticleSFB.jsp?id=1131098715777*).

In a few words, resource hubs are individuals called "connectors", who bring individuals or groups together, getting them to communicate, interact, and ultimately do business together. Introduced in Malcolm Gladwell's best-selling book, *The Tipping Point*, hubs are the next stage in networking. As a connector, you become infinitely more valuable to prospective clients and existing clients, as well as to a network of contacts and resources. It's a great concept for marketing, rainmaking, and client retention and acquisition. In short, a win-win-win, benefitting you, your clients or prospects, and all the other contacts or resources you bring into the equation.

Here's how it can work: say you have a client who needs a tax lawyer, but it's outside of your area of expertise. You refer him to two or three contacts in your network, and suddenly the client regards you as his go-to lawyer—his resource hub—even if your firm can't always handle all of his needs. As a hub, you also have access to attorneys with whom you can collaborate on client matters, thereby avoiding the need for the client to leave and hire a large full-service firm.

Though you can become a hub by meeting people through other networking events, starting your own group offers the best way to put yourself at the center.

Here are a couple of different ideas for possible networking groups:

- Become a resource hub for other parents at your child's daycare or school. Many parents who work would like to get to know other parents, but they lack the time for PTA and other similar activities. However, they might be able to justify a business development event where they could get to know other parents while you build your business at the same time.
- Set up a monthly lunch or breakfast for local listserv or local bloggers. Meeting in person, you may discover other business opportunities. As the hub, people will constantly have your name in front of them and at the top of their list for referrals.
- Be a resource hub for a group of attorneys who aren't direct competitors. Members of the group would be in a position to outsource work to each other if one of their projects proved too large.

For more information on resource hubs, see David Abeshouse's article, *The Power of Networking* (New York Law Journal, Nov. 7, 2005, and available online at *law.com/jsp/law/sfb/lawArticleSFB.jsp?id=1131098715777.*

The Key to Niche Marketing

Niche marketing targets a narrow group of customers whose needs are not directly or adequately served by other providers.

What's your niche? It might target a certain populations; say, postal employees, same-sex couples, high-income professionals seeking divorces, Hispanic business owners…or maybe certain topic areas; say, pet law, alcohol beverage law or special education law. (For advice on selecting a niche, see Chapter 7). Why have a niche? It's the easiest way to distinguish your practice from other lawyers. Think about it: if you go to a dinner meeting with a dozen other lawyers, who will you remember? The other real estate and zoning lawyers…or the one historic preservation attorney? Even if your niche accounts for only 10 or 20 percent of your revenues, the exposure it buys will generate a substantial amount of business.

Here are some ways to do well with a niche:

A niche reflects your talents and interest. A colleague, David Kaufman, is an experienced martial artist who has a niche practice in karate law. Avid cyclist Amanda Benedict includes bicycle accident litigation as one of her specialties. Boston-area solo

Andrea Goldman (*andreagoldman.blogspot.com*) uses her business litigation background to carve out a niche in disputes between homeowners and contractors.

The ethnic/diversity markets. Attorneys who serve ethnic markets, particularly the nation's growing Hispanic population, are in heavy demand. Even as society grows more integrated, there's a greater demand for minority-owned firms, or for lawyers who specifically serve certain ethnic populations.

Know what to expect from your niche. Niche practices may confer attention and acclaim, but are not necessarily cash cows...nor do they have to be. A unique niche can bring exposure and contacts which can lead to billable work in related practice areas. For example, a niche in representing couples in foreign adoptions is likely to attract more general adoption cases.

Niches are narrow in focus, but demand more skills. A niche practice sounds tempting because you can focus on a narrow area. But there's a catch: a niche practice may encompass a specific topic (e.g., historic preservation law, animal law, billboard litigation, veterans' law). But beneath the surface, these practice areas encompass a variety of skills. For example, someone specializing in animal law might need to be familiar with family law (to handle pet custody cases), tort law (for dog bite cases), or estate planning (to ensure that owners can provide for a pet after their death). If you enter a niche practice, be prepared to handle all of the issues it may generate, or affiliate with other lawyers who can take on the issues for you.

Don't niche too narrowly. Don't rely on your niche for more than 75 percent of your practice, and far less if your niche is especially narrow. And when you market your niche, be sure to mention your related practice areas. For example, introduce yourself as, *I handle all kinds of elder law matters, with a special focus on issues related to long-term care insurance.* In this way, you can capture those prospects with a more general need for an elder law attorney that doesn't necessarily involve long term care insurance.

Marketing your niche. As David Leffler writes in *Niche Marketing: the Inside Track to Client Development*, marketing is the part of a niche practice that's the most fun. It's fun, he says, because things tend to go easier marketing to a niche audience than to "everyone" as part of your general practice. And because you're identified as an expert in your niche, potential clients will feel more inclined to hire you because of your recognized expertise.

So how do you gain recognition as an expert and market your niche? Here are several ideas:

- Blogs are an ideal medium to advertise a niche practice. Unlike an ordinary web site, you can use a blog to provide a stream of news and information relative to your niche, thus demonstrating your expertise. If you have several niches to market, you set up a corresponding number of blogs. In addition to two other blogs, Lawyer Grant Griffiths also runs a Grandparents Visitation blog (*grandparent visitation.blog.com*).

- Look for groups interested in your area of expertise so that you can give talks or write articles for their newsletter. Participating in these events may lead to calls but more importantly, helps build your reputation.
- Tom Goldstein, a young attorney who established a Supreme Court litigation boutique, Goldstein & Howe (now Howe and Russell) was quoted in an interview, *...Once you define yourself as the only person who does something, you've automatically defined yourself as the people who know the most about it. We [Goldstein & Howe] are a thousand times more effective when we say we are the only law firm that focuses principally on the Supreme Court.*

Opening Up Your Practice to Nontraditional Consultations

New lawyers often wonder how to distinguish themselves from established competitors without competing solely on price. One way is through nontraditional consultations—house calls, client visits, and off-hour consultations.

Let's face it, most people—whether they punch a time clock, or are busy executives—are unable to take time out of a busy work day to visit a lawyer. So why not accommodate them? Accept appointments two nights a week from 6 until 9 pm, or mornings between 7 and 9 am...or even open your doors for several hours on the weekend. Advertising this off-hour availability is likely to attract prospects, who, because they couldn't take off from work, may have been putting off their estate planning or help on an employment discrimination matter.

On-site visits are another way to set yourself apart, and certainly endear yourself to homebound individuals—the elderly, parents of young children, and the sick or injured. Corporate clients would also appreciate an on-site visit. Site visits also give you an edge, because they let you learn your clients' business, and to identify other issues that might need to be addressed. Let's say, for example, that the president of a small company retains you to draft a non-compete agreement. Rather than draft and e-mail the agreement, you volunteer to drop it off. While waiting for the client, you notice a group of employees making inappropriate remarks to an attractive young assistant. When you speak with the company president, you can tactfully bring the incident to his attention, and inquire whether the company has any policies on sensitivity training, or a procedure for bringing complaints about harassment internally. From a single visit, you might get hired to help draft an employment practices handbook. Note: if you visit clients' homes, be sure your Web site has a photo so clients recognize you at the door.

Online Video Podcasting

Law firm Web sites have been around for at least 10 years. But lawyers have barely started to scratch the surface with podcasts, and even more recently, online videos. In particular, YouTube, with its simple system for uploading videos and embedding them in Web sites and blogs, makes it easier than ever for lawyers to implement video technology for marketing. And though podcasts have their place, videos are—in my opinon—more captivating than one-dimensional podcasts, and tell clients more about you and your effectiveness as an advocate.

- Allison Margolin, a Los Angeles criminal defense lawyer specializing in drug crimes, has an online video commercial. The three-minute video gives prospective clients a chance to see Margolin at the courthouse, where she discusses with her client the motion that she plans to file, and she shares her philosophical objections to criminalizing marijuana. Her video even subtly gets across Ms. Margolin's impressive educational credentials—a BA from Columbia and a Harvard Law degree. The video is interesting, compelling, and it gives clients a glimpse of what Margolin's practice is about even before a client steps into her office.
- In New York, lawyer Nicole Black produces *The New York Minute*, a series of short, bi-weekly video commentaries in which she offers her opinion on newsworthy New York court cases (see *nylawblog.typepad.com/suigeneris/ny_minute/index.html*).
- And in Los Angeles, solo Kelly Chang has positioned herself as an expert on family law matters through a series of online videos (available at *videojug.com/user/USEX0093*).

It used to be that video (in the form of TV commercials) was a medium reserved for PI attorneys and deep-pocket law firms. But that is so 20th Century. Now, just imagine the possibilities of online video, from promotional videos like Margolin's to informational videos on writing wills or explaining the landlord tenant court system. Video is a medium that represents the wave of the future for lawyers, one which not only lets you display your competence, but lets your passion and enthusiasm shine through.

V. Frequently Asked Questions

CHAPTER 17

FAQ for New Solos

From Law School to Solo *by David A. Swanner, Esq.*

Q: *Where should a new solo begin looking for work?*

A: Two areas of law where there is always more work than money is family law and criminal. Of course, charging $1,500 for doing $2,500 of divorce work isn't good business, but it could be a lifesaver if you're just starting out. Also, remember that clients with small cases do shop for price. In the long run these are not the clients who will make you happy or profitable... but they will help you get started.

Here are other paths to consider:

- Established lawyers often require a minimum retainer of $5,000 before talking to clients regarding a divorce situation. As a result, they turn away quite a few people who can't afford the retainer. As a new lawyer, you probably won't have the same overhead, so call established attorneys about sending you clients who can't afford their fees. At the same time, inquire if they're interested in handing off cases too small for them to take on. As a start-up, you will be able to profit from some of these cases while an established lawyer might not. It will be your job to screen these cases to see which ones you can help with profitability.

- Every attorney has a certain number of appointed family court or criminal cases. In larger firms, the appointed cases get pushed to the youngest associate. In smaller firms, the attorneys handle the appointed work themselves. Talk to those attorneys, and tell them you will handle their appointed cases for a flat rate. If you price it right, they'll be delighted to have someone take it over for them. Also, if you get some experience in handling certain kinds of cases, you can price the cases attractively, help your client, and still make a profit.

- Talk to the Clerk of Court and let her know that you are looking for cases, and would be happy if your name comes up more often than it should in the rotation. Often times the court is looking for someone who actually wants the cases.

- Rent a spare office from an established attorney and see if they have overflow work you can perform. Or, find a more experienced attorney and tell them you will do all of the work and give them the fee if they will give you the forms and tell you what to do.

Q: *Will clients trust, or even hire, a new solo?*

A: Yes, because most people don't know how little one is taught in law school. When I opened my practice, I always candid with prospective clients. I'd tell them, *'I've been practicing four months and haven't handled a case like this before, but this is the approach I would take.'* And then I would describe how I proposed handling their matter. When I finished, I'd say something like, *'I just want to let you know up front that because I'm new I won't immediately know all the answers to your questions but I will get the answers for you.'* And, then, depending on the size of the case, I might add: *'... And if it looks like it's going to be a difficult situation, I won't be shy about asking a more experienced lawyer for help, or to call someone to take over the case if it's appropriate. I won't let pride get in the way. Handling your case correctly is the most important thing to me.'* I used a variation of this, and it worked like a charm. People would say, 'Okay. We'll go with you.' I was often sort of stunned, thinking, 'Really? You will? Holy Cow!' It is my opinion that people want lawyers who will talk to them without talking down to them, who will work hard on their case, give them straight answers, and not charge too much.

Q: *How can a new lawyer compete with experienced lawyers and established firms?*

A: By 'out-hustling' the more established firms... by giving faster service... by being more responsive... by just plain being nice. Talk to the clients, find out about their business, find out what they want... and then do it. What's great about being your own boss is that you can spend whatever time and effort a case needs *even if the amount of work is grossly out of proportion to the fees that you will earn.* I did that on purpose when I started out. Of course, I tried not to do that twice. But if you want to compete with experienced lawyers and established firms, it's important that once you get involved in a case that you do whatever is necessary to handle the case properly. Even if it means taking a beating in the fees on a case. There's plenty of time to analyze later what you did, and what you can do better next time.

Q: *How can I finance a new practice just out of law school?*

A: A practice can be started on a shoestring if necessary. I know because I did it. I started a practice in a small Southern town on $1,500. I was young, stubborn, and single. I had an old (but paid for) car, a computer, printer, and most of the other things needed to generate legal paperwork. Back then, my overhead was $350 a month. And even with a little legal work, it wasn't that hard to pay the bills. Where can you get the money to open your own practice? Credit cards, home equity loans, parents, friends. Even a traditional loan if you already have established credit and a history with a bank.

Q: *I know how to research a legal issue, but what about practical things like filing a complaint?*

A: Just ask court personnel or other lawyers. It's amazing how far a little humility goes. Say something like, *'This is the first time I've ever filed one of these things. Do I have everything I need or is there something else I have to do on this?'* Most court personnel will be glad to help only because it makes life easier when filings are done properly. And believe me, you won't be the first young lawyer they've had to help out…and there are many experienced lawyers who do things wrong and never learn the right way things to do things.

Q: *What are the most important quality to succeeding right out of law school?*
A: An entrepreneurial spirit. Skills can be learned, attitude can't. And then there's all the other ingredients to a lawyer's success that have nothing to do with the practice of law…like setting up and running an office. As the person in charge, you'll have to deal with the copier repair guy, the phone guy, the computer guy. You'll have to handle money issues, staff issues, upset or nonpaying clients, and make sure you reconcile your trust account on a monthly basis so it meets state reporting requirements. If you're thinking, *I don't want to deal with all that junk, I just want to be a lawyer,* you may not be solo material. If, however, you're thinking, *I can provide clients better service at a lower cost, and put more money in my pocket,* maybe you are cut out to be a sole practitioner.

Q: *Do you know anyone who solo'ed right out of law school?*
A: Yes, me. And, for what's worth, here's how I got my start: I went to law school in Ohio in the 1990s, and moved to South Carolina, where I took the Bar and opened my practice. My father had a business there, so I was able to work out of his office. That way I didn't need a copier, receptionist, conference room, or other office amenities. In the beginning, I did commercial leases, incorporation, real estate closings. I didn't have that much work (a good thing, too, because I didn't know what I was doing, and it took a long time to do even basic legal tasks). And after awhile, I learned I could handle most any matter as long as I was willing to spend three times as much time and effort as it would normally take with an experienced lawyer. As part of my education, I talked to, and lunched with, older lawyers. They threw me their scraps and cast-offs. Some of them were worthwhile and some weren't. In time, I learned what to look for. After six months, I hired a paralegal; within a year, I had two employees. We did a lot of real estate closings, and a fair number of car wreck cases. In time, my real estate and trial practice were clashing. So, I decided to stop doing real estate and focus on litigation. I started attending ATLA Colleges, got involved with our state's trial lawyer association, started attending and speaking at conferences, and—in time—found myself becoming a better lawyer. Right now, my practice is just trial work. We do worker's compensation and personal injury. My clients have received a number of decent jury awards. In 10 years, I've built a solid practice doing the kind of law that I want to practice. It's taken time, being nice to people, working hard, focusing on truly helping my clients, working on getting better at what I do, and taking a few wrong turns along the way. But back to the original question: yes, you can start your own practice straight out of law school. It's tough but not impossible.

—David Swanner (*info@davidvsgoliath*) practices in Myrtle Beach SC.

From BigLaw to Solo *By Carolyn Elefant, Esq.*

Q: *My partners say going solo is career suicide. How do I respond?*

A: Going solo was never career suicide. In fact, in today's topsy-turvy law firm environment starting your own practice is less risky than ever. Clients are tired of associates with little experience handling their cases. As a result, they're leaving large firms in search of more reasonable rates, and better, more personalized service, elsewhere. And, as I point out below, those clients who don't leave voluntarily may find themselves bumped by a conflict of interest. Career-suicide? Just the opposite. As the rate of associate-attrition rises, law firms are having difficulty retaining attorneys who can provide quality service to clients. Thus, they're reaching out to former firm lawyers, either those who went in-house or to women who took off time to raise children, to convince them to come back to the fold. As a result, more large firm attorneys who decide to leave have a safety net. If they've done well at the firm, they can return later. So, if one your firm's partners tries to dissuade you from solo'ing, explain your decision this way: that you're grateful for all the firm has provided, but that you're eager for court time and to have full responsibility for client matters. That developing hands-on experience will benefit your career in the long run, and make you more valuable if you ever decide to return to large firm practice.

Q: *I specialize in a BigLaw practice, e.g., corporate securities, antitrust, management side labor and employment, etc. Is that enough to sustain my own firm?*

A: Yes, absolutely. Consider…

- As firms continue to grow, they often don't provide the same level of service, and may also be resistant to keeping rates down or to implement flat-fee or alternative-billing arrangements. For these reasons alone, corporate clients are reporting greater dissatisfaction with the service provided by their existing attorneys. One study showed that 70 percent of the Fortune 1000 were dissatisfied with their existing law firm (see *In House Counsel Axing Law Firms*, Sept. 8, 2006, by Sandra Pruferat at abanet.org/journal/ereport/s8inhouse.html) My advice is to target disgruntled clients and any who have been priced out of the BigLaw market. To attract clients looking for a high-quality alternative to standard big firm practice, use your web site and/or blog to let people know you offer flat-fee or value-billing, client newsletters and personal service.
- Bring your BigLaw expertise to areas where it's more in demand. For example, a city like Washington D.C., has scores of firms specializing in areas like communications or utility regulation. But in outlying jurisdictions, like Maryland and Virginia, far fewer firms handle these matters, though there's still a demand for these specialties. If you previously practiced in a large-city firm that is adjacent to other jurisdictions, think about targeting opportunities in those areas.

- If you're located in a secondary market, tout yourself as a local specialist to take advantage of what law marketing consultant Larry Bodine calls "pinpoint marketing". As Bodine wrote in his blog:

... The new trend is 'pinpointing' or 'cherry-picking'. It's where big corporations keep detailed lists of 'approved counsel' all over the country and hire them for specific purposes. I know this is happening because I'm seeing it happen now. I get into many law firms, advising them on business development, and find that no one in the firm is concerned about convergence. Instead, they're all trying to get onto those approved counsel lists. For example, I talked to a partner from a three-attorney firm in a mid-sized East Coast city, and their two big clients were major US auto makers. They only did one particular area of law for the mammoth auto companies. But note: this is a three-lawyer firm working for two Fortune 10 companies! In 2005, corporations began seeking out litigation boutiques in Buffalo, rather than fly their megafirm lawyer up from New York City. (Elsewhere) big companies began hiring local specialists, who charged local rates, to handle local problems in Baton Rouge. After a while, I began to notice that lots of little firms everywhere are getting work from Titanic publicly-held companies. A general counsel can save a lot of money with 'pinpointing', and get nice personal service to boot. These little firms give the big companies the red carpet treatment.
From Larry Bodine's blog (legalmarketing.typepad.com/blog/2005/11/convergance_is_.html).

Q: *How do I compete with BigLaw's marketing department and connections?*
A: Solos are nimble in ways BigLaw isn't, and solos can do what BigLaw can't; experiment with different marketing messages and marketing channels without having to run through bureaucratic levels of approval. Make sure you cover the basics; invest your time and marketing activities in ways that give you broad exposure, such as publishing articles, speaking at high-profile conferences, and developing a robust blog that ranks well in Google searches. When you get busy, make sure you leverage your time by outsourcing to freelancers some marketing activities, such as follow-up, production of marketing packets, or identifying new business areas.

Q: *My Ivy League law degree got me my BigLaw job, but do clients really care?*
A: Some do, some don't. Some clients don't ask or care where you went to law school as long as you get the job done. In fact, guys like Gerry Spence or the late Johnny Cochran didn't attend top-tier law schools. They built their reputations on fierce trial skills. For some clients, your education and legal credentials may be an added draw, particularly for younger attorneys who don't yet have extensive experience. And if you specialize in an area not typical for a top-tier law grad, your credentials will also help you stand out. Allison Margolin, a criminal defense attorney specializing in drug-related crimes, has an online video (*youtube.com/watch?v=bD9yfvu31Bs*) that prominently displays her Harvard Law degree which distinguishes her from other criminal defense attorneys. Why not give your own law degree more marketing prominence? Example: the tag line of a personal injury attorney might read, *Insurance Companies Have Ivy League Lawyers. Why Shouldn't You?*

Q: *How can I leverage my BigLaw background and judicial clerkship to get more referrals?*
A: If you previously had a clerkship, let your former judge know you've gone out on your own. Judges are often asked to recommend attorneys, and if your judge was happy with your work, he or she is sure to pass along your name. Also, consider working with a law school's adjunct faculty. With a top-tier degree and tenure at BigLaw, you would be an attractive hire. As discussed earlier, an adjunct position will help build your resume, provide some additional revenue as you start out, and can lead to business from your students and other faculty members.

Q: *After five years at BigLaw, I've taken only a handful of depositions and have never been to trial. Without this experience, how do I get anyone to hire me?*
A: As discussed earlier, opportunities for training and hands-on experience abound, through CLE's, pro bono work, and simply observing others in court. If you're still at your firm and haven't yet left, consider signing up for some practical CLE courses or getting more involved in the firm's pro bono program so that you can hit the ground running when you go out on your own.

Q: *My previous firm had expense accounts around town, big listings in Martindale Hubbell, and an expensive office in a Class A building. Even if I could afford all that, do I really need it to succeed?*
A: Most clients don't want to waste time in your office if they can avoid it. Besides, if you have a modest office, or even if you work from your home, you can always visit your clients on site, making the issue moot. And if you have clients outside your area, the interior design of your office won't matter if you've done a good job. But if you are sensitive about your work setting, seek out some of the newer shared office spaces. Even if they are luxurious, they're affordable on an as-needed basis. As for expense-account clubs, forget it; identify a few regular restaurants that provide good service and a quiet atmosphere, and meet your clients there. Incidentally, time-conscious business clients prefer breakfast meetings over lunch...a savings for you. As for listings in Martindale-Hubbell, that's your call. But like the rest of us, more and more corporate clients are turning to online search engines to check an attorneys' credentials.

Q: *The experts say not to compete on price. So how do I compete with BigLaw?*
A: Never pitch a client on price alone. Corporate clients may be cost-conscious, but they're not destitute. And they won't choose a firm just for a bargain price. Does price matter? Of course it does; it's just not primary. Many corporate clients who choose small firms over their large firm counterparts do so both because of quality of service and cost considerations. In many cases, lower rates—in the form of reduced-hour fee or flat-fee and alternative-billing arrangements—can make the difference between a client using your firm or going with a BigLaw competitor. More than anything else, client dissatisfaction with large law firms is associated with poor quality service and

lack of personal attention. So, make your pitch based on value. Make clear your rates derive from passing on overhead savings and increased efficiencies. Also make clear that you guarantee personal responsibility for every aspect of a case, from drafting contracts and writing briefs to the accuracy of their invoice, and that you employ the latest technology—from e-mail and electronic filing to extranets and wikis—to resolve your cases and communicate with clients.

From Government to Solo By Carolyn Elefant, Esq.

Q: *I'm leaving government to start a firm, but I don't have any business and I'm not sure how to build it.*

A: As a former government attorney myself, your inside knowledge of how your agency works gives you an edge in several ways:

First, having worked at an agency, you'll be more adept in keeping abreast of newly issued decisions which you can report and analyze on a blog or in an electronic newsletter. Establishing a reputation as the go-to source for the latest information will help attract clients.

Second, most agencies now maintain online dockets with documents filed by companies and trade groups with business before the agency. The documents will generally indicate whether the entities are represented by inside counsel or an outside firm. You can use your familiarity with your former agency's docket system to identify unrepresented entities with business before the agency, after which you can determine through your networking relationships, whether you have a contacts at any of these companies. Moreover, by following the docket, you can anticipate situations where a firm representing two clients in a single proceeding may run into a conflict of interest, either because the clients' interests grow adverse, or the firm merges with another firm that also represents clients. Track these development so that you can position yourself to bid for the client if its law firm is conflicted out of the case.

Third, look for speaking opportunities where you can showcase your expertise. For example, offer to speak to an industry group on topics like, *Filing a complaint under Agency X's New Rules, or, Ten Ways to Stay Out of Trouble With Agency Y.*

Finally, keep in touch with former colleagues at your agency. When you finally start representing clients before the agency, your contacts can help you set up meetings with staff, provide you with information on your case status, and even move a case more quickly to resolution. Your ability to obtain this special treatment will impress your clients and lead to referrals and repeat business.

Q: *I'm concerned I'll be precluded from working on matters my former agency handled, which are exactly the ones where people are most likely to want to hire me. How do I avoid ethics restrictions?*

A: You're right to be concerned about ethics, but be sure you're not reading the restrictions too narrowly. As discussed in *Special Consideration for Government Lawyers*, and

The Revolving Door (Chapter 5), the ABA Model Rules, and most state ethics codes, prohibit former government attorneys from handling matters where they participated "personally and substantially." So if a group of attorneys in your office were assigned to enforcement matters related to Company A, but handled the Company B file, you would be precluded from representing only Company B. In some cases, a government agency may restrict former employees from making an appearance before the agency on any matters (not just those in which they participated substantially) under their official responsibility. The ban on appearances generally lasts one or two years, and typically affect more senior level employees who are responsible for far more files than junior attorneys. Still, even if you're barred from making appearances, you could advise a client on agency policies behind the scenes without making an appearance, or you could offer your expertise to a firm an of counsel basis where the firm's attorneys could make an appearance. See *Giving Notice* (Chapter 5). Where you face a ban, regard it as an opportunity to expand your potential practice areas. Most government agencies have state and federal counterparts, and even if you're banned from appearing before one, you can still appear before the other. For example, if you're barred from appearances before your former employer—say, the federal Equal Employment Opportunity Commission—use your knowledge and credentials as a way to attract clients who need employment counsel before state employment or human rights commissions.

Q: *I struck out interviewing with private law firms after a decade in government. If law firms don't want me, how can I make my government experience attractive to potential clients?*

A: Law firms unfairly assume that a former government employees landed there because they couldn't cut it in private practice, or that they are too accustomed to punching a time clock to adapt to a rigors of the law firm lifestyle. Clients look at it differently. Many prospective clients have great respect for attorneys who put time in government service, and they regard the experience as valuable because it gives you an inside track. When it comes to marketing for clients, you needn't be sensitive about your government background.

From Part-Time to Success *By Carolyn Elefant, Esq.*

Today, more than ever, many resources exist for women who want to reenter the workforce. In New York City, the ABA, in conjunction with many top firms, launched Back to Business Law (*abanet.org/dch/committee.cfm?com=CL999500*), which offers CLE's on cutting-edge issues. In Philadelphia and New York, there's FlexTime Lawyers (*flextimelawyers.com*), that provides networking support for women lawyers working part-time. Other cities are developing similar programs. While useful for CLE's and networking, these resources frequently overlook solo practice as a means for women to (a) remain in the workforce after they've just started families, or (b) to reenter the workforce when their children are more self-sufficient.

I was a prosecutor for several years, so it was logical I would choose defense work when I finally started my own firm. What helped smooth the transition was to make sure I could be around people who knew more than me about defense work. So, once I decided to resign—it was several weeks before the actual date—I immediately sent out two dozen letters to some of the best-regarded criminal-defense practitioners in the area where I wanted to open an office. Most of them worked on their own, or in small-firm setups with an empty space here or there. As a result of space-sharing, I was able to count on wiser individuals for tips and experience on topics I never had to confront as a prosecutor. As it turned out, the arrangement worked both ways: my experience was a boon to them because I could provide insights into a segment of the law-enforcement community that isn't usually available.

State and federal prosecutors don't generally affiliate with a city or county bar association. So, I joined the local bar association as well as a sub-committee tailored toward criminal investigation. With meetings every few months, there were opportunities to mingle with judges, get to know others in this segment of the practice, and to obtain updates on the local rules of practice in state and federal trial courts.

So, how does a former prosecutor get clients right from the start?

- Get appointed to the Criminal Justice Act panel for the federal district in which the principal office is located. Every district has a CJA panel, comprised of attorneys who take cases in which the Federal Defender has a conflict of interest. (The Federal Defender can provide details about panel membership. A prerequisite is proof of training or prior experience in applying or using the United States Sentencing Guidelines.) In state trial courts, door-to-door visits may be required with each judge's secretary to hand out cards and let the support staff know that you're available for conflict appointments. The only downside is that payment for services comes only after the case is closed since your invoice for services cannot, with limited exceptions, be submitted sooner.

Two other methods of steadying the cash flow include review of court "blotter" sheets, and signing up for mandatory arbitration in certain civil cases:

- Some municipal courts permit attorneys or their paralegals to review recent arrests, which include contact information of the defendant. Some of these defendants have not hired counsel yet. Assuming you are clear on ethical rules regarding soliciting new business, a one- or two-page letter can then be sent to that person that explains your ability to help protect his rights.

- Serving as an arbitrator in certain civil cases not only puts a nominal amount in your pocket, but also exposes you to the basics of personal-injury, landlord-tenant and contract-dispute litigation. It is here, in a non-binding setting, that many courts require cases be heard first when the claimed damages don't exceed a pre-set sum such as $20,000 or $25,000. Three-member panels of lawyers sit as a means of alternative-dispute resolution, hearing and deciding several cases per day. I have found it to be invaluable because if I came across certain pleadings or submissions that were well-researched or well-written, then I eventually got copies to use for later reference.

Some attorneys leave government service on short-notice. For those with the luxury of resigning at their pleasure, I suggest starting several weeks before departure to line up office space, figure out how it will be furnished, and order the electronic equipment that best suits their needs. I am a big advocate of locating individuals, or small companies, whose business is building computers and the networks on which they communicate. In my experience, they provide the best personal service, and quickest access when emergency strikes. Also, when you hire a stationer for letterhead and cards, don't forget to include an order for announcements. They are an easy and efficient way to spread the word of your new venture…an indisputable way to attract new clients. A few final pointers:

- Be careful about funneling money into billboards, television, or other expensive advertising media. The transition alone is nerve-wracking without the additional financial strain that comes with little or no client base. Besides, any advertising requires a plan if it's to yield dividends. And such a plan requires a marketing consultant…with attorney experience. Such consultants require a hefty retainer, so you may want to build your financial reserves before considering this option. Make sure you know the Rules of Professional Conduct. In particular: 1) the rules regarding client communications and retainer agreements; 2) the rules about conflict of interest; and 3) handling money: knowing what's yours, what's not, and the differences between the two. These rules probably had no bearing upon your previous life as a prosecutor. They now have everything to do with your being a capable defense attorney and maintaining your ticket.

- Speaking of capability, if you devote your new practice to defending criminal defendants, invest in a membership with the National Association of Criminal Defense Lawyers, and the sister chapter in your state. It's money well spent. Not because it looks good on your resume, but because anyone worth their salt as a defense lawyer associate belongs in these organizations. They devote their careers to this niche, are quick to share their assistance if needed, and can sometimes refer a new matter or two your way. Solidify your status by belonging to NACDL and one of its state affiliates."

Mark A. Sindler (exonerator@earthlink.net) is a criminal defense lawyer in Pittsburgh. 🔵

In the section that follows, Nicole Black, Esq., has put together some of the most-often asked questions about part-time practice to accommodate parenthood, and provided her own thoughtful responses:

Q: *Many experts say that starting a firm is a full-time job. But can I succeed at it part-time?*
A: In order to have a successful and manageable part-time practice, you need to narrow your areas of practice. Litigation is not conducive to part-time practice because of the unpredictable schedule inherent to that area of practice. Areas of practice that are transactional—e.g., real estate, trusts and estates, appeals preparation, and research and writing for other attorneys—are far more manageable as a part-time practitioner. And these areas of practice can often be quite profitable, especially if you minimize your overhead. But whether a part-time practice be successful depends on how define 'success'. If it isn't tied to a large income not commensurate with a reduced schedule, then, yes, you can be successful as a part-time practitioner.

Q: *Some colleagues, even friends, see my home office and part-time schedule, and don't take my success seriously.*
A: What's success? Is it about achieving a balance between work and family, or is it about power and prestige? It's both because there is no one definition of success. But the irony is that a lawyer working at a home office part-time can actually earn more ... or at least as much as ... some law firm associates. So who's the more successful? In my own practice, I perform nearly the same function as I did as an associate in a mid-sized litigation firm ... but I practice on my own terms. I choose the quantity of work I accept, I can turn down assignments, my work schedule is under my control, and my hourly rate far exceeds what I earned at any other point in my legal career (assuming you divide my annual salary for my prior jobs by the number of hours that I worked). So, although some lawyers may be disdainful of my practice since it appears to offer no power or prestige, I know better. I'm in charge of my schedule, my workload, and my hourly rate. I've got a busy practice and a fulfilling professional life. I'm successful by *my definition*, and that's what matters.

Q: *How can I network without sacrificing the time needed for billable work?*
A: Occasional business lunches are a good way to do some person-to-person marketing. But there many other ways to network that don't involve a meal. If your state requires an accumulation of CLE credits to maintain your license, seminars are a good way to fulfill your education obligations and network with other attorneys who practice in the same area of law. Also, join your local bar association and any practice-area committees relevant to your practice. In this way, you can network while brushing up on important local issues. Another networking option are online message boards and listservs such as the ABA's *solosez.net*. And don't forget blogs: not only does a blog highlight your writing skills and your knowledge of your areas of practice, it also allows you to network with attorneys across the country. You'll be astonished at all the many

lawyers you'll meet...virtually and in person...as a result. When I opened up shop as a contract attorney, I started my own blog, *Sui Generis* (*nylawblog.com*), and joined the local bar. In time, I began writing articles about blogging for the local legal newspaper and bar association newsletter. As a result, I was invited to join the Bar Association's Communications Committee.

Q: *I've got young children, and have a part-time practice. But I keep thinking ahead to when my kids are older, and wonder how I should plan for the future?*

A: Right now, the smartest thing to do is to keep on networking, and to stay in the loop in your legal community. The more visible you are, the more often people will think of you when you're ready to increase your hours. I can't say it too often: don't isolate yourself. Join your local bar association, get involved in committees, write articles, start a blog. Make your presence known in whatever way that you can. You never know what will come your way if you make an effort to stay involved in your legal community.

—*Nicole Black (nicoleblackesq.com) is of counsel to an upstate New York law firm, a columnist for the New York Daily Record, and author of Sui Generis, a New York law blog.*

In addition to Nicole's recommendations, here are some additional factors if you're thinking about starting a part-time practice:

How flexible is your day job? Just as you need a predictable practice area to make a part-time practice work, you also need a flexible "day job" with limited hours. For example, some jobs may allow you to work as few as two or three days a week and keep your benefits, leaving other days free for legal work. Or, you might find a day job that allows you to leave early and keep your weekends free. This is especially true for lawyers who teach school. One such lawyer/teacher is Chicago solo Danielle Colyer, a prep school instructor who runs a real estate practice from her home. Though she has an assistant now who shares the workload, Colyer started out reviewing documents in the evenings and dropping them off during her lunch break. These days, she schedules real estate closings after school and on her summer vacation. The subject of an ABA Journal profile in 2007 (read it online at *abanet.org/journal/ereport/jn29solo.html*), Colyer says she's content with her arrangement, but that her part-time legal work did not match her teaching salary until her fourth year of practice.

The time you devote to your day job, even one you enjoy, will affect your practice. Working a second job—particularly if it involves similar skills to your practice (e.g., handling contract work for an attorney or a writing job) can interfere with your efficiency. And while putting in 25 hours at your day job may seem like only half a week, it's also time that a solo with a full-time practice would otherwise devote to marketing or building their firm. If you do decide to moonlight, try to limit your day job to 15 hours...or no more than 20 hours if absolutely necessary...to retain your health insurance benefits.

Where are your loyalties? Often, solos who start out as part-timers—for example, handling contract work for another lawyer—become dependent on their outside income. Consider the case of the solo who agrees to handle 15 hours of contract legal work a week at a rate of $75/hour. Suddenly, the hiring lawyer gets busy and offers the solo another 10 hours of work. The solo, calculating the additional income and goodwill, accepts. Trouble is, the lower-paying contract work prevents the solo from spending time marketing and finding his or her own clients who might pay twice the contract rate…or more. The lesson? If you're handling part time *per diem* work, you need to set a 15-hour limit and stick to it—and be prepared to lose the work if you're not willing to offer more of your time.

Have you explored the risks involved in contract work? Handling contract work for other lawyers, or accepting temporary document-review projects, can raise conflicts concerns. So you should always be sure to run a conflicts check before you accept an assignment for another attorney or firm. At the same time, issues like misappropriation or malpractice liability are not as significant because as a contractor, the scope of your work is strictly defined by the terms of your work arrangement. Moreover, most lawyers and firms who hire lawyers on a temporary or project basis expect them to be handling other outside work anyway.

Should you moonlight while working for a law firm?—Lawyers interested in starting a practice while working for another law firm should proceed with caution, as discussed at length in *Moonlighting for Lawyers: A Kiss of Death*, an article written by Peter Smith and available online at *lawcrossing.com/article/index.php?id=3082*. Smith writes that if you are employed by a firm and procure and service your own clients—even on your own time—you expose your employer to malpractice liability if something goes wrong. Consequently, most law firms strictly forbid outside legal work of any kind, even *pro bono*, without their explicit knowledge and consent. Moreover, if you even inadvertently use firm resources like letterhead, phone lines or the law firm LEXIS account, your employer could report you to the bar for misappropriation of resources. In addition, your outside representation could unknowingly create a conflict with existing law firm clients, another potential ethics violation. In short, don't handle your own clients while still working at a firm unless you disclose the proposed arrangement to your employer and you obtain permission. Of course, don't be surprised if your employer responds by saying that if you want to handle your own clients, you should leave and start your own firm.

"I'm Pregnant, Should I Tell Clients and Opposing Counsel?"

Thoughts on Maternity Leave & New Arrivals, By Carolyn Elefant, Esq.

Q: *I just learned I'm pregnant. Should I tell my clients and opposing counsel?*
A: Unlike other personal issues like marital status or sexual orientation, there's no concealing your condition from clients and colleagues. So, it's appropriate to give a brief

explanation of your expectant status to clients or counsel likely to see you during the pregnancy. Likewise, feel free to announce your good news with those clients and colleagues with whom you have a cordial relationship. Beyond that, discuss your pregnancy only on a "need to know" basis: for example, if you must put a case on hold, or reschedule a hearing to avoid conflicts with your due date or anticipated maternity leave, you need to tell clients of the pregnancy.

Q: *Back at my old law firm, I would have been entitled to paid leave. How do I handle maternity leave as a solo?*

A: The good news is that if, after the birth, you're willing to work a few hours a day or a week, you can extend maternity to six months even a year. The bad news is that you can't expect to take a fully-paid, three-month maternity leave without seriously jeopardizing your practice. Even if you could put all active matters on hold, you would lose substantial ground if you were not willing or able to take calls from, or meet with, new prospects.

- Check your calendar in your fourth or fifth month. Get a continuance if you have an already-scheduled trial or other commitment one month on *either* side of your due date. You don't want to go into labor a month early, on the eve of trial, and then have to deal with the stress of postponement.
- In the last few months before you're due, close out and invoice for as many matters as possible, and move cases forward to a point where they'll be resolved shortly after the baby is born. That way, even though you're not at work, you'll continue to generate some revenue and won't feel pressured to return. If you think you may want to cut back permanently once your baby is born, some changes to your practice may be appropriate. In my own case, I knew that I would not be able to juggle the unpredictable court-appointed criminal cases I had been handling after my first daughter was born, so I closed out my criminal files as quickly as I could.
- Keep the month before your due date—and two months after—clear of major trials or motions that will involve substantial prep time and personal appearances. Many courts will allow you to file notices of unavailability to put a case on hold.
- Your solo practice can't survive if you put all your cases on hold permanently. Transactional attorneys, in particular, may still need to schedule closings to move deals forward, or may have to comply with deadlines set by statute that a court has no authority to suspend. In this case, consider asking one or two trusted colleagues if they can step in and handle a piece of a matter. Incidentally, colleagues will often decline payment for a small favor like getting a filing out or showing up at a scheduling conference. But you need to compensate them for matters involving a significant time commitment. Or, outsource the work to an experienced attorney who can handle depositions, court hearings, and contract negotiation. Even if you're not able to make money from the contract arrangement (because an

experienced contract attorney can charge nearly as much as you charge your clients), at least you would be able to retain the client. For more on outsourcing, see Chapter 12.

- Once the baby is born, make the most of technology. Working the Internet and a smartphone, your clients probably won't even know you're out of the office. You can take an hour or so (when the baby is asleep) to return phone calls or send e-mails. In fact, many lawyer/moms become quite proficient at typing with one hand and nursing or bottle-feeding with the other.

- After two months at home, some moms are quite ready to resume a full schedule; others prefer more time at home. Don't jump in until you're ready. After all, as a solo practitioner, you have the flexibility of easing back into work. For example, you might want to take another two to four months working a few hours a day while the baby naps (or, if you're fortunate, you have parents who live close by and are eager to spend your work time with their new grandchild). One more thing: easing back to work also gives your newborn an opportunity to get used to a new child-care situation.

- The birth of your child is a joyous occasion, and most clients, judges, and lawyers are willing to accommodate requests for extensions and delays. I know because it happened to me: just about the time I had a reply brief due at the D.C. Circuit, I had to have the labor induced. Just before heading to the hospital, I drafted an extension request based on the impending birth. The clerk's office left me a voice-mail that they would hand-carry my request to the judge's office. When I returned from the hospital two days later, the clerk's office called with congratulations...and said my extension request had been granted.

- The birth or arrival of a baby is a special time that passes all too quickly. Enjoy and celebrate the occasion as long as you want. Revenues rise and fall, new clients come and go. How often will you have dedicated time with your new baby? Savor it.

Q: *My solo practice is doing pretty well, but we depend on my wife's job for additional income and health benefits. With our first child on the way, I wonder if our benefits are in jeopardy if she works fewer than four days a week.*

A: Find out how much of your health insurance policy is provided by her employer. Some companies pay the entire premium, others require employees to cover 25 to 60 percent of the cost. If her employer subsidizes only a small percentage, it may not be much more expensive to have your own policy. And, if that is the case—and she works for a company of 20 or more—you can arrange for up to 18 months of coverage through her employer under the federal Consolidated Omnibus Budget Reconciliation Act (COBRA).

Don't Throw in the Towel Yet *By Carolyn Elefant, Esq.*

A few thoughts to consider before throwing in the towel:

Share your difficulty. Though you may feel embarrassed or ashamed, share your struggles with other practitioners. If you can't face colleagues, set up a consultation with your bar's law practice management advisor or send an anonymous SOS to a list-serv. The other day, an anonymous solo posted a "help-me-save-my-practice" e-mail to the *solosez* listserv. Within hours, list members inundated him with suggestions, encouragement, and—most helpful—marketing and management ideas he had never considered. A week later, he reported having implemented some of the changes, and the tone of his follow-up post was decidedly upbeat. In a few months, I fully expect this solo to report that he's turned his business around.

Evaluate what's working and what's not. Look at the cases you've handled during the past year. If you simply haven't found enough clients to pay the bills and you're worried about cash flow, consider a temporary contract assignment or other "fast cash" options (for more details, see Chapter 10). On the other hand, if you're tied up with clients who've promised to pay and haven't, drop the worst offenders rather than continuing to work without pay. Working for free is demoralizing and saps your will to market your practice. When you fire non-paying clients, your morale will improve and you'll have more time to engage in marketing to build your practice.

Sometimes, it's a not lack of clients that account for financial struggles: it's too much overhead. Scrutinize your costs closely: are you paying for Class A office space when you could save several hundred dollars a month in a less fancy building? Is a big chunk of revenue going to staff salaries without return on investment? For example, if an associate's salary and benefits cost you $50,000 but the associate only generates $35,000 in revenues, you're losing money. Many lawyers are reluctant to downsize because they view their fancy building and staff as a symbol of success. And often lawyers are too kind-hearted for their own good, and feel badly about laying off employees, even if it's an economic necessity. At junctures like this, you must evaluate your expenditures from a purely financial perspective, without allowing your personal feelings about status or helping others to intervene. If you can't make these changes on your own, consult with a practice-management consultant for an objective viewpoint.

Have you tried everything? Perhaps you've shrugged aside certain marketing options, thinking *that won't work for me.* Is this a logical evaluation of a particular marketing technique, or is it an excuse to avoid techniques (like cold calling) that make you uncomfortable, or that involve longer term commitment (like blogging) than taking out an ad? If this is about avoidance, it's time to own up and get moving. The future of your firm is on the line; now's not the time for timidity or procrastination.

Set up a plan. A failing practice takes a psychological toll. You feel trapped or stuck in a rut, powerless to make any changes. To break through, create a list of actions to turn things around, such as making some cold calls or touching base with a colleague. If you can't muster up the nerve for daily phone calls, then start by sending out e-mails or attending a networking event. Just do something each day. Your actions will help will go a long way towards getting your practice on the right track.

Give yourself time. Realize that your business will generally ebb and flow until you hit your stride, which may not happen until your third year of practice. So unless you're truly hemorrhaging cash and risk bankruptcy, keep plugging away.

Beware the hard sell. When business is bad, you're particularly vulnerable from consultants and referral services. If you genuinely believe that a consultant can benefit your practice, seek low-cost options. Some consultants offer reasonable group rates, while others will charge a flat fee of a few hundred dollars for a practice tune-up. As for for-fee referral services, try to negotiate a limited trial period of two-to-three months, rather than locking yourself in for a year. The last thing you need now is the added stress of an extra few hundred dollars a month for a referral service that doesn't generate any clients.

You haven't failed. Perhaps you've reached a point where despite your best efforts, you can't find enough business to sustain your practice. Or maybe you found work but you're not earning enough to support your family. You haven't failed. You had the guts to take a leap that few lawyers are willing to take, and you gave it your best shot. Along the way, you taught yourself new skills that you never learned in law school or at your job—drafting a complaint, taking depositions, arguing motions, negotiating contracts. You served clients and solved their problems, perhaps even changed their lives or improved their opinion of lawyers. And you created a something—a law firm—out of thin air, with your law degree and your own two hands. Perhaps your firm did not survive, but no one can ever take away what you accomplished. Everything you learned in the process of creating and running a law firm will stay with you and serve you moving forward, either in a career in law or another profession. That doesn't sound like failure to me.

IN THEIR OWN WORDS

Q: If you could do it all over again, would you start a solo practice?

- Walter James III (class of 1987)—"Yes, in a heartbeat."

- Sergio Benavides (class of 2005)—"Absolutely. Everyone in the world told me that the first year...even the first two years...can be very slow. And they were right. But six months into going solo, my phone rings constantly, and I get a more steady stream of higher quality referrals. I have interesting work, and I enjoy what I am doing. I am the boss, so I can blame no one but myself for when things go wrong."

- Jill Pugh (class of 1994)—"For all the financial uncertainty and moments of being overwhelmed by workload and sometimes isolation, there are so many more moments of satisfaction and freedom. I absolutely would choose to solo again.

- David Abeshouse (class of 1982)—"I'm glad I decided to solo...and I'd do it all over again. My practice and my life are more interesting as a result."

- Art Macomber (class of 2003)—"Yes, emphatically."

- Grant Griffiths (class of 1997)—"YES!!!!!!!"

- Brian Rabal (class of 2005)—"I'll tell you next year."

To read the complete interviews, see Appendix 6. ⬤

Not so many years ago, lawyers who dreamed of becoming solo practitioners were intimidated by the start-up costs.

And for good reason.

As recently as the late 1990's, I remember attending a bar workshop where I learned that new solos needed an initial investment of some $30,000 for Class A office space, administrative help, computing equipment, and a phone system. $30,000! The audience gasped; most of us were new lawyers and scarcely had $3,000 let alone 10 times that amount. Fast forward to 2007; technologic advancements have obliterated all the old financial barriers. But for all the breakthroughs, all the new opportunities, some things are slow to change: there is still a lingering stigma to starting your own law practice. And, in my opinion, the bias starts in law school:

- Even now, few law schools have classes on how to establish a solo practice.
- Law school placement offices, particularly those at top-tier schools, brim with brochures from the AmLaw Top 100 but rarely provide materials on starting your own firm or even make available contact information for alums who might want to serve as mentors.
- Most law professors have never encountered successful solos, since their own experience is often limited to a prestigious federal court clerkship and maybe a short stint at a large law firm.
- The grants or course credits offered to law students who accept summer positions with a public interest group aren't often extended to students who want to intern with a solo, even one representing the same constituency (e.g., clients who qualify for court-appointed counsel fees, or who fall just below the cutoff for legal aid services).
- As for volunteering to work for a solo practitioner, it's even less likely because of the staggering levels of tuition debt with which law students are burdened.

Most law students' perception of, and lack of knowledge about, solo practice remains long after leaving law school. In fact, for many years my only impression of a solo came from a Cornell Law training video describing ethical infractions by harried solo practitioners in small, messy offices. My professor assured us, though, that we would never meet the same fate because the big firms where we were headed would have reliable support staff and oversight that the lowly solo lacked.

Fortunately, cultural attitudes toward solo and small firm practice are improving. Slowly. In an entrepreneurial age, starting your own law firm is now appreciated for what it—an act of entrepreneurialism with an enormous potential for success. In fact, there are many, many examples of former BigLaw attorneys who gained celebrity after starting their own practice. Perhaps the best known is David Boies, who practiced for years at Cravath, and was known only to other large-firm lawyers. After starting his own firm (which started small but has since grown to over 100 attorneys), Boies snagged such high-profile cases as representing the Justice Department in its antitrust action against Microsoft, and for representing former Vice President Al Gore in *Bush v. Gore*, all of which made Boies a household name.

As I wrote in the Preface, solo and small firm practice makes possible now—as never before—the dream of becoming the lawyer you always wanted to be. And even as you contemplate your decision, remember you are not alone. You're part of a growing trend of lawyers who are either rejecting large firm or government practice outright, or are leaving it behind, because they recognize that by harnessing technology they not only can achieve enormous flexibility and provide affordable legal services…but earn a nice living in the process.

In my opinion, large law firms are on a collision course with their own success. Eventually, many of them won't be able to find or retain the talent needed to fuel these mega-firms, and, by then, they will have no choice but to implement real (rather than superficial) changes to retain talent and attract clients. And to whom will BigLaw turn for a model? Why, to entrepreneurial solos who have learned how to enjoy a career in law without sacrificing financial success, work-life balance, or intellectual and personal satisfaction. Which is why your decision to go solo represents more than a personal choice: solo practice serves as an example of, and a catalyst for, change in the legal profession.—*CE*

Chapter 1

1. *Extreme Niche Marketing* (T. Delaney, Small Firm Business Magazine, April 19, 2004).

2. *The Lawyer As a Professional* (Roger Cramton, txethics.org/resources_lawyerprofessional.asp?view=2Cramton).

3. See generally the following—*http://www.nylawyer.com/display.php?file=/wisdom/03/072403* (Holly English column, 7/2005—advising women not to be too insistent on setting limits on part time schedules Firms and Family—These Workplaces Help Balance Career and Home Life, Susan Mandel ABA Journal (Sept. 5, 2003) which describes the experience of a young law firm associate at Arnold & Porter who went to part-time, roughly 40 hours a week *anonymouslawyer.blogspot.com/2004/11/this-morning-sixth-year-associate.html* part time (blog post by fictional law firm partner describing that part time is a "boon" for firm since people work almost the same amount of time at reduced pay with almost no chane of making partner)

4. See Project for Attorney Retention Web site ().

5. *Female Lawyers' Glass Ceiling: Work/Family Divide Keeps Numbers of Women Partners Low* (Rachel Osetrman, New York Times, August 28, 2005).

Chapter 5

1. *Giant Law Firm Settles an Age-Discrimination Suit* (New York Times, Oct. 6, 2007).

2. See ABA Formal Opinon 99-414, *Ethical Obligations When A Lawyer Changes Firms.*

3. *Leaving a Firm: Guidelines for a Smoother Transition* (Dennis Kennedy, Chapter 4 of the ABA's Flying Solo, 4th ed., 2004).

4. Kennedy, id

5. Kennedy, id

6. However, when a work is considered a work made for hire, the author of the work is no longer the individual creator or creators. Instead, the author is considered to be the entity that hired the creator of the work. The circumstances in which a work is considered a work made for hire is determined by the language of the United States Copyright Act: *Works Made for Hire.—(1) a work prepared by an employee within the scope of his or her employment; or (2) a work specially ordered or commissioned for use as a contribution to a collective work, as a part of a motion picture or other audiovisual work, as a translation, as a supplementary work, as a compilation, as an instructional text, as a test, as answer material for a test, or as an atlas, if the parties expressly agree in a written instrument signed by them that the work shall be considered a work made for hire. 17 U.S.C. sec 101.* See also Wikipedia, en.wikipedia.org/wiki/Work_for_hire.

7. *Associate Says Ex-Firm Misused His Name on Web Site* (Amy Zitka, Connecticut Law Tribune, January 11, 2006).

8. *Law.cornell.edu/ethics/comparative/index1.11.* The Cornell LII contains a data base of the Model Rules and a number of state codes, with cross references comparing the provisions)

9. District of Columbia Rules of Professional Conduct, Rule 1.11, Comment [2] (highlighting need for federal and DC government attorneys to comply with federal conflict of interest statutes); see also 18 U.S.C. Chapter 11 (federal conflict of interest statute)

10. See, e.g., *From Public to Private Employment: Companies Seek Exiting Government Lawyers for Hire* Emma Schwartz, Legal Times, August 25, 2005 (describing that after passage of Sarvenes Oxley, law firms and corporations have increased need for SEC attorneys)

Chapter 6

1. *Starting Small, Thinking Big: A Guide to Starting A Practice in the District of Columbia.*

2. IRS Business Web site, *irs.gov/faqs/faq12-1.html.*

3. *Can A Solo Be A Law Firm?* (Washington Lawyer, December 2005).

4. Many of the tips on this list were identified in Wells Anderson and Joe Hartley's *How to Protect Client Confidences in Shared Space* (Appendix A).

5. *Office Sharing* (Jim Calloway, Oklahoma Bar Association).

6. *Associate Says Ex-Firm Misused His Name on Web Site* (A. Zitka, Connecticut Law Tribune, January 11, 2006).

Chapter 8

1. *Enfron Defendant Worked Alongside Attorneys to Win Acquittal* (Brenda Sapin Jeffreys, Texas Lawyer, November 18, 2004).

2. *Firing Clients* (Robert McGarvey, *HomeOfficeMag.com* Feb. 2001).

3. Edward J. Cleary, Director Minnesota Office of Lawyers Professional Responsibility, Bench & Bar of Minnesota, November 1999).

4. See, e.g., *Hiring a Lawyer* (Nolo Press, online at *lawyers.nolo.com/workingFees.cfm*).

5. *Rules of Engagement: Taking the Offense When It Comes to Defense* (Steven Terrell, GP Solo, October/November 2002).

6. *No Retainer = NY Firm: $0; Client: $205,000* (Mark Fass, New York Lawyer February 15, 2006).

7. *Lawyers May Limit Scope of Duty in Matrimonial Cases* (Mary Gallagher, National Law Journal, April 14, 2003).

8. *Thou Shalt Not...* (Steven Lubet, American Lawyer, July 2, 2006).

Appendix 2

1. *Firm Whose Clients Were 'Stolen' Wins $1.4 Million Verdict* (Anthony Lin, New York Law Journal May 28, 2004).

Appendix

Introduction

Naturally, there's no one right way to start and run a new law practice. So, in the appendices that follow we've assembled a variety of options—not rules—related to many of the decisions necessary to begin. We hope these sections provide some useful pros and cons, and we'll leave the decisions to the new boss . . . you!

Business Plans/Mission Statements

For some lawyers, the preparation of a formal business plan is critical to the development of their new practice. It may even be a requirement for a bank or SBA loan application. For other lawyers, though—especially new or aspiring solos unable to identify immediate sources of revenue—a formal business plan might seem like an exercise in futility. Quite the contrary. A "business plan" (which is just business-speak for a simple outline that helps you look ahead, allocate and prioritize resources, and identify future opportunities) will be extremely helpful whatever your circumstances. Nor will it require an MBA. Instead of elaborate formulae, you can base your business plan on your knowledge of your practice area, your conversations with other practitioners, and your research on developing trends and demographics.

In this section you'll find the ingredients of an abbreviated business plan for a hypothetical BigLaw associate named "Ann Gerson", who wants to open a solo practice after five years handling management-side employment law. In this sample, the bold-faced headings are typical for a law firm business plan. At the end of the plan, I've listed some resources that can help:

Executive summary

Draft a description of your proposed firm. For example:

The Gerson Law Firm will provide counsel to employees and management on all matters pertaining to employment law. Our litigation practice will include administrative hearings before the EEOC and State Human Rights Commission, and litigation and appeals in state and federal court. On the transactional side, we will assist with drafting employee manuals, sexual harassment policies, providing sensitivity training seminars, draft no-compete and other contracts, and advise on employment related immigration matters. At Gerson, we believe that first-rate representation comes from an ability to view employment issues from the perspective of both the employee and management employee and employer perspective. Thus, in contrast to other firms that choose sides, The Gerson Law Firm will represent both employer and employee interests. Although our unique approach compels us to diligently check for conflicts and frequently turn down matters, we will pursue this approach because we believe it provides unparalleled benefits to our clients.

Draft a short bio describing your prior employment and any specific problems or questions you solved for other clients. For example:

In September 2007, Ann Gerson, an attorney with a decade of corporate employment experience founded The Gerson Law Offices. Ms. Gerson is committed to providing the highest quality representation in employment law and related matters to the firm's employee and management clients. Following graduation from New York University Law School in 2001, Ms. Gerson embarked on a year-long clerkship for the Honorable Judge Horace Lerner of the Second Circuit, who issued the landmark rulings in employment cases *Rich v. Wright* and *High v. Low*. Thereafter, she served as an associate at BigLaw Firm for five years where she represented corporate clients on employment matters in the health care and high tech fields. Ms. Gerson pioneered use of "bifurcation clauses" in company harassment policies, which according to the Second Circuit's ruling in George v. Jones, insulate management from liability for unauthorized sexual innuendo by individual supervisors. Ms. Gerson left BigLaw Firm to open her own practice. Below is an example of the types of cases handled and results achieved by Ms. Gerson:

- Second-chaired jury trial resulting in verdict in favor of racial discrimination against Microtel Computer Corporation.
- Drafted non-compete contracts for Health Corporation, Inc., which the court enforced in employer's favor in Arbus v. Nickle.
- Testified as expert witness for plaintiffs in employment law malpractice action.

Law firm services
- *Litigation.* Administrative hearings before the EEOC and State Human Rights Commission, and litigation and appeals in state and federal court.
- *Corporate.* Drafting employee manuals, sexual harassment policies, providing sensitivity training seminars, preparation non-compete clauses and other contracts, advise on employment-related immigration matters.
- *Of counsel.* Can serve as counsel in employment-related litigation actions or handle employment matters for corporate clients.

Market identification
- A review of other firm Web sites show that, in addition to Gerson, only four other firms cater to employer and employee-side work. The bulk of firms identified handle general plaintiffs employment matters or class actions; few address problems unique to health care and high tech.
- Few firms handle litigation on contingency; charge hourly rates instead. Opportunities exist for taking smaller contingency matters with clients covering costs.
- Few firms in the geographic market handle whistle-blowing employment issues, particularly in corporate context, i.e., for workers who disclose Sarbanes-Oxley violations or other corporate matters.
- Other possible issue is immigration related to the high-tech field. Question: do

companies need to undertake special measures to guard against discrimination claims when they outsource to save money? What kinds of employment laws apply to outsourced labor? Outsourcing is a huge trend, but few firms have identified this niche even though a need exists for this kind of specialization. Note: In-house counsel lacks this expertise, and few law firms have it either.

- For shorter term work, consider leveraging Second Circuit clerkship expertise. Identify small-to-midsized firms with appeals before Second Circuit, and market brief writing assistance. Contact larger firms to determine whether a need exists for consults on Second Circuit practice.

Reaching clients

- Will target employees through referral networks, also speeches at local women's groups.
- Will establish Web site and/or blog with Q&A on employment issues. Note: try to sign up for column in local paper on Q&A for female employees and issues like harassment and whistle-blowing.
- Will network with solos in complementary areas like family law, bankruptcy and personal injury to engage in cross referrals.
- Will meet clients in virtual office space; also investigate possibility of meeting on weekends so that clients do not have to miss work.

Employer outreach

- Will set up blog dealing with management employment issues.
- Will speak at trade conferences in high tech and healthcare, and on corporate issues.
- Will network with prior law firm; seek referrals from smaller companies.
- Will speak with former clients for leads about colleagues who might be in need of services.
- Author note: in your actual business plan, identify worthwhile trade shows and target publications.

Attorney outreach

- Will continue membership in Labor and Employment bar section, and will volunteer to present panel on new issues.
- May write articles on the Benefits of Outsourcing Appeals or Labor and Employment appeals in the Second Circuit.

Developing new areas

- Will set up networks and strategic alliances with immigration attorneys to increase opportunities for advising on immigration employment matters. Need to look into CLE on immigration law.
- Need to identify contacts that outsource, and to schedule informational interviews

to identify potential needs. Research and conduct additional market research.

- Need CLE on corporate issues and corporate whistle-blowing; contact Professor X to discuss the field and tips on other contacts.

Implementation of Year #1 plan

- January to April 2008. Undertake and implement tasks related to targeting employees and employers.
- March to July 2008. Take immigration CLE, join immigration sections of bar, and make contacts and form strategic alliances.
- June to December 2008. Re-examine success of targeting employees and employers; if successful, begin to move to outsourcing and whistle-blowing specialties.

Financial analysis/projections and billing rates

- High probability that two companies will join The Gerson Firm on a retainer basis for ongoing employment counseling based on a flat rate of $800 per month for five hours of time (including contract review, employee seminar, preparation of contracts, etc). 120 billable hours annually. Total annually: $18,200.
- Will parlay clerkship experience into brief writing for other attorneys at hourly rates of $100-$150/hour. Expect average of a half-dozen to a dozen15-hour tasks annually for rate of $1,500 to $2,250/month. Annual from contract work—$18,000 to $27,000 annually, 90 to 180 billable hours annually
- Small employee matters before EEOC or agencies with settlement value of $10,000 to $25,000; will collect 20 percent contingency or $2,000 to $5,000 per case. Assume four such matters per year, or $8,000 to $20,000. Expect 10 billable hours for each matter or 40 billable hours annually.
- Will try for adjunct position at local law schools for added income, library privileges, and as resume-builder. $2,500 per semester or $5,000 annually 10 hours per months teaching or 60 hours annually.

Total expected income first year—$51,000 to $65,000
Total billable hours annually—300 to 330 hours

Expenses

$200/month for virtual office space—$2,400/year
$2,000/year malpractice insurance—$2,000
$150/month for LEXIS employment law library—$1,800/year
Billing/practice management software (will forego first year while practice is low volume and use available free software or open source)
Computer—$1,500 laptop (w/Adobe, and word processing programs)
Internet access/phone line expenses—$200/month, $1,200/year

Bar membership and trade conferences—$2,000
Web hosting and blogging—$30/month, or $360/year
Web design/production—$1,500
Business stationery—$500
Health insurance (COBRA through employer)—$400/month, $4,800/year
Bar dues/licensing (paid by old law firm for 1st year)

Total—approximately $17,000 at 300–330 hours
Initial Profit (pre-tax)—$34,000 to $48,000
Average hourly rate—$120 an hour (reduced by the teaching position)

Goals for the firm. Make efforts to triple my billable hours to 900/year and to increase average rate to $200/hour within two years for total gross profit of $180,000 and a net of $150,000 (assuming $30,000 in expenses in future years, possibly for office space or part-time support staff). Might also expand the business plan to include Year 2 and Year 3 projections.

Writing the Business Plan. Don't even think about investing in expensive business planning forms or templates to create a business plan until you exhaust some of the free resources available to you. Here are a few:

Bar resources. Check with your bar's LPM advisor to determine if the local bar library has books or models of sample business plans. The Texas Center for Legal Ethics has an excellent, comprehensive business plan form online at , as well as other detailed forms for projecting revenues and expenses at (online Practice Guide with downloadable forms).

The Small Business Administration. (*SBA.gov*) A wealth of information on starting a business but not specific to law practices. At their Web site (*sba.gov/smallbusiness planner/plan/writeabusinessplan/index.html*) you'll find such tools as "essential elements of a good business plan...a step-by-step explanation to help write your plan...sample business plans...an online workshop to improve your plan...and a business plan FAQ." The SBA has many regional offices to provide personal business-startup assistance. Author note: the level of service depends on the staff at your regional office, so even though a colleague may have had a poor experience elsewhere, don't write them off.

Online resources. Bplans.com is a commercial service that sells business planning software and 60 sample plans from other industries. The site does not include a law-specific business plan, but you can adapt the existing templates.

SCORE.org. A non-profit organization whose retired executives are available at no cost to the small business community. Their Web site contains good information, including business plan templates and cost- and revenue-projection spreadsheets. I know several solos who received great help from their local SCORE office.

LexisNexis/Martindale-Hubbell. (*lawyers.com/pdc/tips/plan*) Their online Practice

Development Center offers a free downloadable brochure for solo and small firms on development of a marketing plan, as well as several templates. You can incorporate the marketing plan into a business plan or simply use the marketing plan in lieu of a formal business plan.

The Mission Statement. A mission statement embodies all that you hope to accomplish in starting your firm. It articulates your vision of what you want to create. Most of all, a mission statement serves as a beacon for your practice, a light that helps illuminates your path on those days when the judge tears you apart in court, when opposing counsel drives you to tears with insults, or when a problem client brings a disciplinary action against you.

Here's what a solo blogger known as Greatest American Lawyer says about the importance of drafting a mission statement:

> ... You have to have a long-term vision to feel compelled about what it is that you do each day. You have to know what it is that you are trying to attain. I doubt that the concept of billing clients will ever be enough to drive any person to passion in the workplace. I get up each day and remind myself that I am trying to change the way that law is practiced. Most days that thought fuels the drive and passion that I need to stay focused and driven, and I remain untouched by obstacles which inevitably pop up along the way.
>
> —greatestamericanlawyer.typepad.com/greatest_american_lawyer/2006/01/theimportance.html

Business lawyer and mediator David Abeshouse has a mission statement for his firm and himself as well. David's Web site quotes a survey in the Wall Street Journal, showing that nearly a third of small-business owners say they have little or no trust or confidence in lawyers or the legal profession. The survey also noted that only 22 percent of business disputes are settled by mediation as opposed to 55 percent settled after some court process is involved (source: *bizlawny.com/wst_page9.html*). Thus, David's mission statement went something like this: ... *To improve the percentages of those having trust in lawyers, and to enhance the proportion of disputes appropriately resolved out of court, without litigation.*

Before I opened my own firm, I recognized that individuals, associations, and small and mid-sized businesses have a need for lawyers with the skill, expertise and commitment to tackle at competitive rates sophisticated regulatory problems or complex issues of first impression. Since that time, I have stayed true to my mission, helping clients in the US and abroad to navigate through, and prevail in, regulatory and judicial proceedings without breaking their modest budgets. My own mission statement ties together my disparate practice areas: energy regulatory work before federal agencies, development and environmental counseling to fledgling renewable energy developers, and quality litigation and appellate work representation for clients who've come to me when others wouldn't take their cases.

On those days when my eyes start to glaze over after reading dozens of energy regulatory orders…when I feel angry at misleading pleadings filed by a junior associate at BigLaw…when my clients don't listen to me and get themselves into trouble…when I feel like hanging up my shingle, I remember that every day I stay in business I provide an option to clients that they wouldn't otherwise be available. My mission reminds me I make a difference, and that's enough to get me through another stack of dull, dry orders, and another round of futile e-mails with a difficult client.

Writing the Mission Statement. It's not as difficult as it looks. After all, you already know what motivates you about the law, and what legal issues light your fire. Here are some suggestions to get you started:

What would you most like to change about the law? Perhaps there's something specific about the way law is practiced, or the way clients are treated that you would like to see changed in your firm. Maybe as an associate, you had to grit your teeth when the name-partner blamed you for a mistake that was clearly his fault, and you promised yourself that one day your firm would stay accountable to clients. Or maybe you knew of clients who couldn't get a timely call from the name-partner when they had an important question…and you vowed that if you went solo that client service would be the cornerstone of your firm's mission. From such experiences, mission statements are created.

Read the mission statements of other lawyers. Go to one or more of the Big Four search engines—*Google, Yahoo, MSN,* and *Ask.com*—and search for "mission statements attorney". You'll be inspired at what you find.

A few simple guidelines. Your mission statement should describe what you do, what you stand for, and why you do it. The best statements are just a few sentences long, and they avoid saying how great you are and what a great service you provide. Ask yourself whether you actually believe your mission statement. If you don't, your clients won't either.

Running a Practice

In this section, we've outlined some of the basic equipment, software, and supplies needed to run a practice. The list has been kept purposely short and simple because, starting out, you'll want to remain flexible and keep overhead low. Note: we've also identified *categories* of products rather than making specific recommendations. As your own practice grows, you'll no doubt discover resources specifically suited to your firm's unique needs.

Hardware basics

Mac versus PC. Though Macs are gaining popularity among solo and small firm practitioners, the majority still use PC's for reasons of habit or computing compatibility. For example, the Mac does not support WordPerfect, a word processor favored by many attorneys (though programs such as *Parallels* minimizes some of these issues by allowing Mac users to switch between Windows and Mac operating systems). A Mac is a terrific option for new solos, but you first need to make sure it will support your most important computing needs. If your budget allows, buy a Mac *and* a PC and network the two—a suggestion from law technology consultant Adrianna Linares on her blog (*ihearttech.com/2007/02/i_know_i_dont_t.html*). For additional information, also check Grant Griffiths' Mac Resources at *gdgrifflaw.typepad.com/home_office_lawyer/macs_in_the_law_office/index.html*, or go to *TheMacLawyer.com*.

If you prefer to have just one computer, we recommend a laptop for full portability. You can always connect it to a desktop monitor or docking station if you want a full screen or keyboard for desk use.

Printer. At a minimum, get a laser printer; in fact, a color laser printer if you intend to print your own brochures or stationery. And if you spend a lot of time in court, and you need to produce *praecipes* or other documents on the spot, invest in an inexpensive portable printer.

Copier. Whether you lease or purchase, a commercial-grade photocopy machine is expensive and may be unnecessary. Most shared-space arrangements provide access to a common copier; typically, you are assigned a code to track your usage and billed each month. Note: some virtual office suites include a considerable mark-up—as much as 25 or 50 cents per copy—but the convenience may outweigh the surcharge. For larger copy jobs, of course, there's always Kinkos, Staples, or Office Depot.

Scanner. If you practice regularly before courts or agencies that employ electronic filing systems, get a stand-alone scanner capable of scanning at least 15 pages a minute. If you don't have a paper-heavy practice, then register with one of the online fax providers. Here's how they work—you fax a document to your electronic fax number and receive a copy in electronic format. Using Adobe Acrobat, you can turn the fax image into an electronic document suitable for court filing.

Faxes. If you intend to send and receive a great many faxes, invest in a dedicated phone line. If not, sign up with an online fax service, among them *efax.com, myfax.com* or *trustfax.com* (for a comparison, go to *faxing-service-review.toptenreviews.com).* Once you're registered, you get a fax number whose area code matches your own. Faxes sent to your new number are converted into a PDF file, and e-mailed to you as an attachment. For $10 to $20 per month, you can receive faxes anywhere you have online access. Sending and receiving faxes is easy. If your documents are in electronic format already, you use the fax service's interface to enter and upload the recipient's fax information. If you need to fax documents that exist only in hard copy, you scan the document and send it to your electronic fax number. Note: if you don't have heavy scanning needs, online faxing is a good idea.

PDA. For reasons of mobility and flexibility, most lawyers are moving towards the purchase of a smartphone (e.g., BlackBerry, Treo, iPhone, etc.). Even if you're working out of a home office and your budget is tight, smartphones—with their e-mail, calendaring and contact management—are a smart investment. For additional tech suggestions, see Rick George's essay later in this chapter.

MP3 Players. Whether you purchase an iPod or some other MP3 player, the technology now makes available an avalanche of downloadable legal content. The ABA and just about every other state and local bar association now offers free or modestly priced CLE materials as a podcast. For a list of ABA podcasts, go to *abanet.org/cle/podcast.*

Software basics

Practice management software. also referred to as "case management" or "client management" software—is a catch-all description for a range of products automating various law practice functions: time and billing, conflicts checks, contact management, calendaring, and case management. And now many of the most popular practice management tools (e.g., Time Matters, PC Law, or Amicus) now support multiple functions: they keep time, check conflicts, organize client email and documents in readily accessible databases, track deadlines, and generate client bills. Some solos use these programs, while others choose to create their own management system using tools that are part of MS Office (e.g., Outlook or Excel), free open-source tools (e.g., Google spreadsheets and calendar or *Toggl),* or general purpose, less expensive products (e.g., Chaos Software or Quickbooks).

With all the other expenses associated with a new practice, you may be reluctant to invest in practice management software, or to make time to identify and learn how to use some of the less costly or free products. But such tools are well worth the money *and* the time; in fact, you may be able to download and evaluate some packages for a trial period at no cost! If you do decide to buy or use one or more of the software packages, make your purchase before—or soon after—you open your practice. This way, you will have much more time to learn about each, and to integrate them into your practice.

In the section that follows, solo Sheryl Schelin identifies the most important criteria when selecting and purchasing case management software.

Selection Criteria for Case Management Software *Sheryl Sisk Schelin, Esq.*

What case management software should I buy? Does anyone have thoughts about Time Matters vs. Amicus? Case management or client relation management (CM/CRM) software causes no small amount of stress for many attorneys opening a solo practice. And chances are good that on any given week you'll find the above two questions—or variations thereof—strenuously debated on the ABA's solo listserv. Which solution you choose depends on your needs, your time constraints, your skills, and your budget. Let's look at the advantages and disadvantages of each:

Stand-alone applications. The so-called "out of the box" CM/CRM applications cover a lot of territory. Many of them include rules-based calendaring, file management, document control, contact information, timekeeping, and conflict checking. Others address some of these needs (i.e., case and contact management), and are compatible with other programs that address the others (such as time and billing).

Many of the applications are designed specifically for law firms, and the subsequent modifications and revisions are based on considerable attorney feedback. In theory, this results in a better, more responsive product. But stand-alone applications aren't without disadvantages: in some cases, the cost can be prohibitive...additional licenses drive the cost up further...and the programs have different learning curves, ranging from "one short virtual tour and a glance at the manual" to "hours of specialized training from a $100/hour consultant." And the more robust the program, the more computer resources required; you might need to upgrade your computer just to run the program. Finally, the programs are not completely customizable; while some "tweaks" can be made, it will never meet your needs as well as a program designed for you. Still, given the price and the relatively straightforward installation and implementation process, stand-alone products are probably the most popular solution (a conclusion based solely on anecdotal evidence).

Buying tips for stand-alone solutions:

Step 1: Evaluate your needs and preferences: How comfortable are you with new technology? Will you need a consultant to help master the program and tailor it your practice? Do you need or want a mobile solution or plug-in for your program? Do you have support staff? Are you planning to add them later? What's your budget? Do you want or need a practice area-specific solution?

Step 2: Research the market: The law technology blogs and magazines are your best bet, since they're updated and published more frequently than static Web sites and books, and are more responsive to recent developments. Ask other solos for their recommendations.

Step 3: Identify what is available: Use a spreadsheet format or lists to evaluate each product on paper. Eliminate any program that's significantly outside the needs you identified in Step 1.

Step 4: Try before you buy: Most programs have demos you can request and install for a tryout. If the program you're looking at doesn't have that option, eliminate it from consideration. Give each application demo a good workout. Work a case or matter through start to finish to give all the features a try.

Step 5: Analyze the results: Was it easy to operate? Did you find any glitches that might seem like minor annoyances now but could become a thorn in your side later? Does the product perform as advertised? Is it compatible with your other software and hardware? Are you comfortable with the user-interface? Does the product deliver what you need, and what it promised? Is it workable with your practice area? Does it fit within your budget? Consider initial cost, implementation cost, and the cost of additional licenses, if your firm experiences future growth. Finally, evaluate the company making the product. Do they have experience with law firms, or is this a new market for them? Are they going to be available to help you upgrade three years from now?

Hacked solutions. Hacked solutions require your creative effort, and are potentially more responsive than a stand-alone product. Many potential component applications are either free or very low cost, making this method very attractive to a strapped-for-cash solo. And there is also a certain feeling of accomplishment in a do-it-yourself approach. However, most of these components weren't made specifically for law practice, leaving you with terminology like "sales" and "products" which can complicate the system. These solutions also require both personal effort and varying degrees of technical expertise. You have to know your practice and management systems well to create this sort of solution; which might be hard for new solos, especially those who formerly relied on partners and support staff for many procedural tasks. Finally, some Web-based products are created by new companies that may, or may not, be around for the long haul. You could suddenly find yourself without a critical element in your system due to a business failure.

Creating your own CM/CRM solution. If you wish to take a do-it-yourself approach, here are some suggestions to smooth out the process:

- Map out your case workflow, from first contact through closing out the file.
- List all the pieces of information you need to track—dates, contacts, titles, file numbers, etc.
- Take stock of what you already have and what those applications can do—not just

what you use them for currently (for instance, Outlook has a little-known feature called "Journal" that provides a timekeeping device, which can be associated with various contacts, which in turn can be associated with categories, which could be keyed to file numbers, etc.).

- Identify the available programs that might provide fill a gap, considering the information you identified in steps 2 and 3.
- Give each possible solution a thorough run-through. (tip: create a mock client and matter that you can use to test each candidate application.)
- Analyze the results, and play around with the possibilities until you have a good fit.

—*Sheryl Sisk Schelin* (theinspiredsolo.com) *is a solo lawyer and business coach from South Carolina*

Some additional thoughts on three of the most popular software categories:

Word processing. Lawyers continue to debate the merits of MS Word and Corel WordPerfect. We recommend (a) the word processor with which you're most comfortable, and (b) the one which your clients use. If you can afford it, keep versions of both for greater flexibility: one for clients, the other for any *per diem* work you might do for other attorneys. In this way, you minimize formatting problems when exchanging documents. Note: you might also consider some of the free, open-source word processing programs such as the Open Office suite of products.

Adobe Acrobat. As more courts transition to electronic filing or offer online forms, Adobe Acrobat has become an important tool. If all you want to do is open PDF documents, Adobe's Reader is freely available. But if you need to fill out and save forms, to create a PDF document, or to manipulate PDF files (e.g., to add or delete pages or to combine several PDF documents), you will need Adobe Acrobat. At present, the federal district courts and bankruptcy courts have transitioned to an electronic filing system that only supports PDF files. So if you're planning on federal litigation you'll definitely need the full Adobe package.

Accounting. Some lawyer-specific billing packages include an accounting system or coordinate with *Quickbooks* or other accounting software. If you don't need billing software, you probably can get by with *Quickbooks* or some other small business accounting package. Whatever you use, make sure it allows you to manage your trust accounts in a manner that complies with your jurisdiction's ethics rules. Look to your colleagues, your accountant, or your LPM advisor, for software recommendations. Starting out, you can probably manage your bookkeeping on your own. As your firm grows, you may need a bookkeeper to come in several hours a month. Note: you must maintain strict oversight when granting others access to your books. At the end of the day, you—not the bookkeeper—are accountable for any errors whether negligent or intentional.

Extranets & Project-Collaboration Tools

Extranets. A secure, private network that shares firm information with clients, vendors or other law firms. Extranets (which generally need an IT consultant to set up) are a good investment if you compete with large firms that make them available to their clients, or if you serve a client population that demands easy access to your work product. As a less costly substitute, the project-collaboration tools discussed in this section also let you share information with clients.

Project-collaboration tools. A category of products that facilitates collaboration and the sharing of files or calendars/scheduling data between lawyers and clients, or other lawyers working on the same matter. Examples of project-collaboration tools include *GoogleDocs/spreadsheets* and *Google Calendars* (which allows lawyers to access and view spreadsheets and to share calendars), *Zoho* (which shares documents and appointments), and *Basecamp*, which many solos use to organize and manage files, and to make them accessible to clients. For more information, see Dennis Kennedy's blog post (*denniskennedy.com/blog/2007/02/dennis_kennedys_legal_technology_trends_for_2_1.html*).

Wikis. Among the best-known online collaboration tool, *wikis* allow visitors to post, add or change content. Many wikis (namely, the online encyclopedia known as *Wikipedia.com*) are open to the public. Lawyers use private *wikis* in many ways—from collaborating on books or articles to eliciting feedback from clients. For information on the *wiki* software freely available online, read *Wikis for the Legal Profession* in the February 2007 issue of ABA Law Practice Management (*abanet.org/lpm/lpt/articles/slc02071.shtml*).

Remote access software. Allows you to access information on a computer server from another location. If you work from home, or on a laptop that you tote back and forth, you probably won't need remote access software. If you want to access data from home or office while on the road—or if you want to make files available to staff over the Internet—remote access software is useful. One such product is *GotoMyPC*.

Digital dictation. With a digital recorder, you can dictate anything from short tasks to a full-blown brief. And, since the recording has been saved in digital format, it can be routed online to support staff, to an offsite virtual assistant, or to a transcription-into-text service provider. You can also use voice-recognition software to convert a digital recording into text! Lawyer/blogger Enrico Schaefer has written about how dictating assignments for staff while away from the office (see *greatestamericanlawyer.typepad.com*) significantly improved his productivity.

E-mail. Starting out, you'll need one (if not more) e-mail addresses as well as a mailbox to receive e-mails. There are two types of e-mail: desktop programs (e.g., Microsoft's *Outlook*, Mozilla's *Thunderbird*) which reside on your computer, and Web-based e-mail (e.g., *gmail*, Yahoo) that requires a Web browser to retrieve messages. Because Web browsers are often free, lawyers use Web-hosted e-mail addresses for listserv subscriptions or Web site registration, and a desktop program for business purposes (so that e-mail is automatically stored on their machine).

E-mail address. For law firm business, we suggest using a more professional-looking e-mail address than a Hotmail or AOL account. Choose a domain name and register it with one of online registry services (e.g., *Godaddy.com, Register.com, Network solutions.com*, etc.). Your domain name can include the name of your firm (e.g., *Joneslaw.com*) or a topical name (e.g., *georgiacrimlaw.com*). Once you've registered the domain name, use the tools at the registration site to set up an e-mail address with the domain name in the suffix.

Data storage. In the wake of recent world disasters (natural and manmade), more and more lawyers have taken steps to secure files by uploading them to commercial server providers. Note: if you do use an online data storage company, investigate their practices for keeping data confidential. To be safe, retain files onsite as well. At the very least, use an external hard drive or flash drive.

Firewalls and virus protection. Firewalls are designed to prevent your computer from hostile penetration intent on causing damage or accessing sensitive data. By contrast, virus protection inoculates you from the effects of bugs *already* infecting your system. These days, most computers come with generic virus protection software, but there are other, more robust programs available online for a modest fee. You can also download free firewall software, or purchase more secure programs.

Computer search tools. Have you ever downloaded a document and not stored it immediately in the appropriate file? Or misnamed a document that you needed to find later? There are several available tools to find your documents. Two of the best are GoogleDesktop (available at *Google.com*), and *Copernic* (available at *copernic.com*). Both are free, and both will search file names and document text…even in a PDF format

Resources

American Bar Association. (*mail.abanet.org/archives/lawtech.html*) The ABA's technology Web site is a rich repository of information on technology tools for law firms of all sizes. In Chicago, the ABA also convenes an annual Techshow, where you can test-drive the latest products and services in law firm technology. Techshow sponsors are eager to attract solo and small firm lawyers, and are sensitive to pricing needs. Also consult your state bar's law practice management section, and attend tech seminars sponsored by the state and local bars.

Microlaw.com. Lawyer/marketing consultant Ross Kodner is a well-regarded source on popular law firm technology. See *microlaw.com/tech_center.html*.

Solo blogs. As more and more solos start blogs, they're sharing their own decisions about law office technology. Some of the best solo blogs include *greatestamericanlawyer. typepad.com/greatest_american_lawyer/small_office_technology/index.html*)…Grant Griffiths' Home Office Lawyer (*gdgrifflaw.typepad.com/home_office_lawyer*)…PDF for Lawyers (*pdf forlawyers.com*) with its focus on Adobe, the paperless office and scanning equipment …solo Dennis Kennedy's blog on everything law/tech at *denniskennedy.com/blog/ index.html*…and lawyer/technology consultant Adrianna Linares' I Heart Tech (*iheart tech.com*), which offers entertaining and conversational advice on making the most of your existing software.

- **Voice Over Internet Protocol (VOIP).** Sometime in the future, land-line telephone companies will be moving to the Internet. For now, my favorite online application is *Skype*, because I like getting double use out of my tech dollar. I already pay for broadband Internet access through my DSL connection, and *Skype* leverages that access to permit free telephone calls to any other *Skype* user over the Internet, and unlimited long-distance to any North American telephone for $29.95 a year. A lot cheaper than long distance, and it works great.

- **Mobile communications.** If there is anything a lawyer loves, it is being able to be a lawyer while on the move. Treos, BlackBerries, and other smartphones (from Motorola, Nokia, and HP), are doing more and more these days, and a lawyer can check his e-mail, browse the web, keep up with his calendar and contacts and tasks, instant message his office and secretary, find his way while traveling, look at his documents, scan pages into his computer, dictate memos and email them to his secretary or assistant, all from anywhere in the world. Get mobile; it's where the rest of the world is going.

- **Electronic discovery.** As the new federal electronic discovery rules get adopted by state court systems, as more documents, emails and data get stored electronically…as more data gets stored remotely on servers, and as storage gets more portable and smaller…it is a sure bet that lawyers will have to deal with finding evidence in electronic form, and using it in litigation.

- **Software as a service.** More and more software applications are being hosted at remote computers, and accessed over the Web. As Web use becomes ubiquitous, lawyers and clients will want access to their data and programs wherever they happen to be. One way is to have the software hosted at a remote server, and accessed over the Web. Legal software providers have been slow to adopt this method, due to fears over data and program security. As these fears subside, it's likely that more and more of what you do as a lawyer will be hosted somewhere else. This method of software delivery has, as a main advantage, the fact that no upgrades of the program are necessary, as it is all handled at the host. In addition, the data is likely more secure, and backed up more often, by a host provider.

- **Generic operating systems.** At the time of this writing, Microsoft Vista is the newest operating system but it is not being adopted quickly. In the future, there is a clear trend towards open-source (free) operating systems; most notably, Linux. There are many new distributions of Linux that are as easy to install and use as Windows, and many users are keeping XP on their systems. It is too early to predict the downfall of the Windows operating system; however, the trend is clearly away from proprietary systems.

Rick Georges (FutureLawyer.com) practices real property, corporation, wills, trusts and estates law in St. Petersburg FL, and is the technology writer at Law.com. ●

Independent tech support. CMITsolutions.com (a national chain that outsources IT support for small and medium-size businesses), *CompUSA.com/services* (offers *TechPro* support through some CompUSA outlets), *Firedog.com* (IT support available through some Circuit City outlets), *GeekSquad.com* (IT support available through some Best Buy outlets), *OnForce.com* (it outsources IT support to more than 10,000 tech support vendors around the country), *Staples.com* (offers *EasyTech* support through some Staples outlets), and *YourTechOnline.com* and *PlumChoice.com* (both of which offer remote tech support services by connecting to your computer over the phone).

Telephone Systems. Today, it's possible to reach London, Paris, Dubai, or Beijing for pennies, all with a smartphone capable of sending audio, video, e-mail, and text-messages. No stranger to competition, land-based and mobile operators have begun to aggressively dropping their prices. Suddenly, having a separate phone line for your home office isn't all that expensive. Some thoughts about your telephone service:

- If you have a home office, don't give out your home number for business. Install a separate line or use a cell phone as your primary business line.
- Avoid such bill-busting extras as conference call capacity or fancy voice mail add-ons. With a few hour's notice, you can easily set up multi-party conference calls through such online providers as *unlimitedconferencing.com* or *freeconferencecall.com.* As for voicemail, the Internet once again has come to the rescue. Such online providers such as *ureach.com, grandcentral.com,* or *ringcentral.com,* you're provided with a single phone number that routes calls to other lines, and delivers voice mail to your email box where you can download and store it.

But who will answer the phone? As with so many other issues, lawyers differ sharply about who (or what) should be available when clients or prospective clients call: should you get a receptionist, a personal answering service, or an automated voice-mail system? If yours is a consumer practice (i.e., personal injury, family law), most of your phone traffic will be from prospective clients responding to your Yellow Page or online ad, and who are calling with the expectation of a live response. So, unless you have a receptionist or personal answering service, you risk losing clients who may not want to leave a voice-mail message. On the other hand, if a share of your revenue comes from large-firm referrals, the cost of a shared receptionist or personal answering service, can add to your firm's credibility.

Tips for a receptionist or personal answering service:

- Make sure the receptionist uses your firm's name rather than a generic *law offices* And script out the type of information you need from prospective or existing clients (e.g.,contact information, brief reason for the call), and under what circumstances your calls should be forwarded to you or to your voice-mail.
- Have your calls forwarded to voice-mail when you are unavailable. This eliminates human transcription error, and allows callers to leave a detailed message. Because voice-mail is private, you avoid any possible confidentiality violations that could arise where, for example, a shared receptionist leaves one of your client message in a public area. Voice-mail might also help you escape the fate of one New York personal injury firm that was victimized by a rival associate.[1] His scheme worked like this: he would call his rival's answering service on weekends, impersonate one of the firm's partners and retrieve messages from prospective clients, and then arrange to meet them himself! Eventually, the firm discovered the fraud. The associate was criminally prosecuted and disbarred, and the firm won a $1.4 million judgment from the associate's firm. So, select a secure, reputable answering service or shared receptionist, and have them route calls to a password-protected voice-mail box.

- Keep your receptionist or answering service informed about your schedule so callers understand when you're in court or traveling, and when their call might be returned. It doesn't reflect well on you or the firm when clients are hear you're unavailable or out of the office every time they call.
- For some practices, it may suffice to rely on voice-mail when you're out of the office. Use a professional sounding greeting, and be sure that you clear your messages so that callers aren't greeting with a message that your mail box is full.

The Paperless Office. A "paperless" office refers to one in which documents, records, pleadings are converted and stored in a digital format. As a practical matter, of course, even the most technologically advanced law practices still interpret paperless as "less paper" simply because we're often required to retain certain originals such as wills or notarized documents, or litigation discovery materials.

A few thoughts about going "paperless":

Space saver. Even if your ethics rules require that you retain certain paper files (or if you're just not totally comfortable eliminating hard copies), digitize as many files as you can. From a practical standpoint, it means that many fewer boxes stored in your closet, basement, garage, back room, or offsite locker.

Security. Electronic files are less vulnerable to loss or physical damage than paper files. And, unlike paper documents, it is harder to lose digital files. Even if you place them in the wrong file folder on your computer, you can still find them with a desktop search tool (e.g., Google Desktop or *Copernic*). And if you regularly back up your files...and if you store your back-up in several locations (e.g., on a hard drive, a flash drive, or the laptop you take home at night)...your files will be much more secure than paper files.

Time-saver. Storing files electronically reduces the time spent searching for misfiled papers. When a client calls about a matter, you simply pull up the relevant memo on your computer instead of putting the client on hold or scheduling a time to call back later. In fact, with a paperless office, you can make client files available through an extranet or one of the project-collaboration tools described earlier. Electronic documents also save time in dealing with other lawyers, staff, or virtual assistants. With a few keystrokes, you can send entire files or transmit an assignment to a virtual law clerk.

Hardware/software. Even a few years ago, the cost and complexity of scanning equipment kept the paperless office beyond the reach of many solos. These days, good scanners are inexpensive and as simple to operate as copiers. If you run a paper-heavy practice and scan hundreds of documents, invest in the highest page-per-minute scanning capability you can afford. For lower-volume practices, a scanner that processes 10 to 15 pages a minute will suffice. Another important tool for the paperless office is Adobe Acrobat software (not to be confused with the free Adobe Reader used to view PDF documents). Adobe Acrobat allows you to highlight and to add comments to documents in PDF format (the standard for court filing), to add or delete pages from PDF documents, and to consolidate multiple PDF documents into one uniform document.

The Set-up. You may already have a preferred approach for organizing electronic files, but—at a minimum—you should maintain a separate folder for each client matter, as well as sub-folders for different types of documents (e.g., pleadings, correspondence, templates, etc.). A standard organization format is particularly important if you'll have a clerk or secretary accessing files. This way, they'll always know where to find information. For a detailed tutorial by solo Ernest Sveneson, go to *pdfforlawyers.com/files/handling_cases_electronically.pdf.*

Scanning/saving files. Each time you prepare a document, save an electronic copy in the appropriate file. Likewise, as you receive documents in electronic format via email or e-fax from your client or other lawyers, save them into the appropriate electronic file. When you receive paper documents, get in the habit of scanning them immediately (note; in some paperless offices, no one is permitted to read a document until it's been scanned into the system). If you receive files too large to scan on the spot, hire a virtual clerk to enter them into your system, or send them to a vendor that digitizes documents.

Additional resources. Grant Griffiths on paperless office resources for home office lawyers, online at *gdgrifflaw.typepad.com/home_office_lawyer/paperless_office/index.html*...David Masters, on setting up the paperless office (GP Solo Magazine, December, 2003)...and, *In Search of the Paperless Office* by lawyer/technology consultant Ross Kodner (Wisconsin Bar Journal, March 2007).

Marketing Materials.

Now that you have your own firm, business cards matter more than ever. They're the smallest marketing expense you'll ever have. And, once you're open for business, you don't want to leave the house without them.

Business card graphics. Not so many years ago, a lawyer's business cards were striking for their lack of individuality...mostly black text on white stock. Today, solos and other lawyers are taking the cue from other professions, and our business cards employ color and tasteful graphics. If you want good business cards at little expense, go to one of the office supply chains like Fedex/Kinkos, Staples, or Office Depot. Or go to some of the inexpensive new online sources of business stationery such as *iprint.com* or *vistaprint.com.* If you need design talent, you can link to the work of graphics freelancers all over the country at *craigslist.com, elance.com,* or *guru.com.* Or consult that old standby—the Yellow Pages. Under "graphic design" or "graphic services", you'll find entire columns of designers to prepare your collateral material. Whatever you do, don't design your own cards or get them printed on cheap cardstock.

Business card content. At a minimum, your card needs your name, and your firm's name, address, phone number and e-mail...and a web and/or blog address if have them. If you are licensed in multiple jurisdictions, the card should reflect that, too, so other attorneys can call you with referrals in jurisdictions where they are not licensed. And, if you have practice specialties, be sure to mention them (note: many bars prohibit use of the word "specialize" or "expert", so make sure the card complies with bar regulations). Don't try to squeeze a list of six practice areas on a three-inch card. If you don't have one specific focus, or you have two main practice areas (e.g., securities law and social security appeals), get separate cards.

For my own firm, I have one business card for my energy regulatory practice, and a second for a more general litigation and appeals practice. I distribute the regulatory card at energy trade shows or to other energy lawyers, and keep the other for more general use, e.g., bar networking events or for when I meet people on the street or at a party. Two business cards—one high-end, the other less expensive—also make sense if you attend large networking events where you might distribute dozens of cards at a time. I frequently experiment with new business card designs, and use the duds for drawings for prizes at trade show kiosks. You can stand out from the crowd by coming up with neat ideas for the back of your business card. It might just be a second color, the firm logo, a calendar, or an inspirational quote. People will remember.

Paper. In many practice areas, stationery may not seem as important because so many communications are e-mailed or faxed. If you have a practice that relies heavily on electronic communication, you can probably get by with self-designed letterhead printed as part of the document. Still, professionally printed stationery *is* helpful to impress clients and intimidate opponents. For example, if you'll be going up against large firms in litigation or sending out "cease and desist" letters, quality stationery enhances credibility. Also, stationery imprinted in your firm colors—or with the logo on your Web site and business cards—reinforces your firm's brand.

Web site. From the day you hang your shingle, you should have a Web site and/or blog. A professionally designed site (see Chapter 14) confers instant credibility, and gives clients additional information about you and your practice. Here are a few tips: use a simple Web address; perhaps some variation of your law firm name (e.g., *carolyn elefant.com*), or a simple topical name (e.g., , the name adopted by Virginia solo David Kaufman). And if you're tech savvy and have some extra time, you can design a serviceable site with some of the tools available at *Godaddy.com* or *webpiston.com*. Otherwise, you can find designers at *craigslist.com, elance.com,* or *guru.com*

Legal Research Services

Not so many years ago, law firms maintained large libraries of law reviews, federal and state reporters, specialty practice series, and computerized databases from LEXIS/NEXIS and Westlaw. By contrast, solos had to purchase used books or visit the law library for research because few could afford the major legal databases. The ground began to shift in the mid-1990s, when most courts started releasing decisions on the Web, making them accessible to other online providers seeking to challenge the LEXIS/Westlaw duopoly. Today, thanks to the Internet, legal research options have significantly expanded, narrowing the gap between solos and their BigLaw or government counterparts.

Legal research at the high end. High-end computerized research service is what you find in BigLaw and the government. It's the most expensive service, but provides access to all federal court (including federal district court) and state court databases dating back at least a century; annotated statutes and regulations and specialty libraries like tax or employment; law reviews and journals, and such features as Shepards of Keycite to "shepardize" cases. LEXIS and Westlaw often include so-called "value-adds" as Wright and Moore, American Law Report (ALR), and other treatises. The high-end databases also employ the type of Boolean search tool that lets you search for strings of words and phrases. Though prices have softened, and a more limited version of LEXIS (such as a state library only) is available, the full-service LEXIS and Westlaw is clearly a high-end service. Expect to pay $250 to $450 per month. Note: LEXIS and Westlaw have negotiated rates, especially at the end of the month when the reps try to meet their quotas. Solo Sheryl Schelin says she approached both companies, and was pleased at their response. She posted the following on her blog (*inspiredsolo.com*):

> *I contacted both Westlaw and Lexis, and said, 'Give me a competitive quote for these materials', and I sat back and watched them try to outdo each other. The reps are very knowledgeable about their products, and are genuinely willing to work hard to get the account. Ask for a free password for the entire site; not just what you're evaluating. Ask for free months, or (at least) a discount. Do it nicely and you'll get results.*

Legal research at the mid-level. Personally, I have mixed feelings about mid-range research services. This category typically includes all federal appellate and state libraries, and comprehensive coverage of federal district courts. What it doesn't include are annotated statutes, law reviews, specialized reporters or federal reports like the Bankruptcy Reports of Federal Rules of Decision. Mid-level research services have tools that list where a case has been previously cited. And, while you can review those cases to determine whether the case remains good law, the service (unlike Shepards) won't indicate whether the case has been overruled or appealed. LOISlaw and Fastcase are both mid-level services, and cost about $100 per month on a month-to-month basis. They're not that much cheaper than the low end of the most expensive packages, and yet offer much less in resources. Still, if you don't know how much you will need a service, the flexibility of mid-range packages is appealing. Note: a few bar associations, including the Maryland and Florida bars offer Fastcase research as a no-cost as a benefit of membership.

Budget and free research services. Research services at the low-end include inexpensive—even free—research databases that provide limited service, but should not be overlooked. The best is Versuslaw, whose packages range from $13 to $40 per month. Versuslaw has a Boolean search capability, a database with federal and state appellate cases as well as federal district court cases dating back to 1950. There's no Shepards tool, and some of the cases do not have the official reporter cite. In my opinion, Versuslaw works well for lawyers who subscribe to a specialty or state-specific service, but who want to retain the ability to research the state of law in other jurisdictions. At these prices, Versuslaw is too inexpensive not to have.

Another computerized research service is Casemaker. At present, about two dozen bar associations participate in the Casemaker program, and its service is included in bar membership in participating jurisdictions. It provides access to all cases within the jurisdiction as well as access to cases in participating jurisdictions. Depending upon your practice area and jurisdiction, Casemaker may suffice for your research needs.

Other low-end services include Findlaw, which lets you access federal and state appellate cases for free. Findlaw does not have any search tools; it links to federal and state court Web sites which you must visit individually to find a case. Findlaw isn't appropriate for real legal research, but it's a good tool if you only need to locate a case where you already know the name or docket number.

LEXIS also offers LEXISONE, a free online database of state and federal appellate cases going back 10 years, and which supports the Boolean search techniques used by the full LEXIS service. Another budget option is the LEXIS packages, which let you access a particular library or full service LEXIS for a day, a week or a month. Many of the packages, particularly for a single state or practice area library, are a reasonable $40-$75 per day and $75-$200 per week. Though service is more expensive than regular service, it makes sense when you only have an occasional need to use a certain library. Note: LEXIS now limits some of the best *per diem* packages to members of state bar associations with which LEXIS has negotiated special pricing agreements.

You can check at the LEXISone Web site or contact your state bar association to determine whether your state bar has a participating agreement in place.

Specialty services. If you have a specialized practice area like securities or telecommunications law, you will probably need to research administrative agency decisions in addition to conventional case law. Both LEXIS and Westlaw have these specialty databases, though only LEXIS offers them as a stand-alone package (note: to get the specialty data base from Westlaw, you have to purchase its full service and possibly pay an added fee for the specialty library). There are some work-arounds; none is really satisfactory. For example, you could purchase agency cases on a CD, though you'll need to continue to pay to update the service. Many administrative agencies publish decisions online and have searchable dockets, but they employ rudimentary and unreliable search tools. Bottom line: you're likely to remain captive to LEXIS or Westlaw, at least for your specialty needs, until a better option comes along.

Here are some important issues to consider when choosing a legal research system:

- Practicing in a state-specific area (e.g., Georgia family law, California personal injury law) gives you the most research options. In your jurisdiction, you may have access to Casemaker, in which case any of the low- or mid-range research tools will work. Note: LEXIS offers competitive pricing for new solos who need state-specific access. Its state-specific package provides less coverage than you would get with a low- or mid-range service. But you get the LEXIS features that the other libraries lack...such as Shepard's and annotated statutes and regulations. As a solo myself, I'm bothered by the competitive grip LEXIS and Westlaw continue to have on federal litigation practice. But if you plan on litigating primarily in federal courts, their high-end, full-service may be your best option. As mentioned earlier, mid-level research services do have federal district court coverage. But they don't include Federal Rules of Decision, annotated Federal Rules of Evidence, or Federal Rules of Civil Procedure, all of which are indispensable to federal court practice. For an occasional federal court case, you can get by with a low-end service, perhaps supplemented by research packages. But regular federal court litigation will require LEXIS and Westlaw.
- Some lawyers plan to offer legal research and writing services to other attorneys. If you hold yourself out as a legal research and writing expert, you need to have access to computerized research service. Most lawyers who hire contract attorneys expect full service; they don't want to pay an hourly rate and provide you with legal research service as well. When you're starting out, *per diem* packages may satisfy your research needs because you'll match your costs associated with research to incoming revenues. Once you get your business rolling, you can purchase one of the high-end services.

Research work-arounds. There are many effective, low-cost research tricks that you can use to supplement a research package, or to provide a workaround for inadequate service:

- Many appellate courts have started posting briefs online. Likewise, PACER, the federal court's computerized research data base, allows lawyers to access briefs motions and filings in many cases. You can only search PACER by case name or docket rather than by subject. But if you've seen a news story on a case similar to yours, you can track it on PACER, view the motions, and use the other lawyers' research as a starting point for your own. Note: in the federal court system, only a small percentage of judicial decisions are actually released to computerized databases like LEXIS or Westlaw. Still, these decisions can give you an idea of how a judge might rule... or could be used; not as precedent, but as an example of how another court dealt with an issue of first impression. PACER subscriptions are free; you can sign up for an access ID and password at . You pay eight cents per page, though even if a document is more than 30 pages, PACER will only charge for a maximum of 30 pages.
- Every researcher knows the power of Google's search engine on general topics; don't overlook it for legal research. The next time you need the source of a legal quote, or a case on some substantive area, use Google. Often, it gives me a decent—and surprising—lead on cases that eluded me in computerized data bases.

Your law firm resources. Given that most legal research can be performed on the Internet, today's solos don't need the on-site law library—including full volumes of statutes and case reporters—that our predecessors maintained. Still, you should supplement online research with a small collection of frequently-used materials, among them procedural rules in courts where you practice regularly, CLE materials, journals, treatises, and bar association practice guides. You could purchase form books, but you're better off with computerized forms. Note: from time to time, lawyers offer to hand off old volumes of case reporters or statutes. Most of these materials are hopelessly outdated, and will only take up valuable space on your shelf. If you prefer to read cases in a reporter rather than online, go to a law library and photocopy significant cases to for your files.

Many law libraries, either at the court or at a law school, offer free access to Westlaw or LEXIS. Even beyond free legal research, there are many other benefits to law libraries. And here's a research tip from solo Michael D.J. Eisenberg:

Jenkins Law Library. For less than $100, you can become a member of the Jenkins Law Library (*jenkinslaw.org*), the nation's first law library, and receive 20 minutes a day of online access to full-service LEXIS as a benefit of membership. Twenty minutes may not sound like much, but it's probably enough to shepardize a brief or download several cases for research.

Don't overlook the law library. As computerized legal research becomes pervasive, law libraries seem to have lost some of their cachet. A big mistake; here's why: many times, a legal treatise or volume of ALJ or Corpus Juris Secundum (CJS) will enable you to figure out basic legal standards for general topics, like piercing the corporate veil or the burden of proof in Title VII sexual harassment cases. Also, if you're embarking on research in a broad area that is the subject of countless cases, it's much quicker to read a law review article than to review dozens of cases trying to gain an understanding. But there are several more good reasons—in fact, eight—as described in this essay by University of Washington Law Librarian Mary Whisner:

1. Law librarians, many of whom are legally trained, specialize in legal materials and the needs of legal researchers. Their job is to help you use the library, and to figure out your research puzzles. We keep up with new sources and techniques, and can save you hours in your research. After all, what's more important to you than your time? Librarians also create online guides to help you with your research. I invite you to visit my own library's collection of guides, for instance. We can help your research without ever meeting you... even at 2 a.m.

2. Your local law library is a great resource when you've got a limited budget, limited office space, and you can't afford every practice manual, looseleaf service, formbook, or treatise that could come in handy. And if you find a book or set really useful, you can always order it for your office collection. Even if you're a whizz at online research, some sources are just easier to use in print. In my experience, many people find it helpful using annotated codes in print because of their layout. Sometimes you might even use a database to find a source, but then sit down with the print version and skim the whole chapter you need.

3. Many public law libraries subscribe to databases that lawyers can use free. Some law libraries make them available without charge; others charge on a cost-recovery basis (which is still cheaper than getting your own subscription for occasional use). Even if you subscribe to Westlaw or LexisNexis for access to your own state's laws and cases, wouldn't it be great to be able to use the law library's subscription when you need to research some other state's laws? Here are some of the databases popular with the lawyers who use the University of Washington Law School Library—LegalTrac, an index of legal periodical articles, 1980-present; Hein Online, a collection of PDF documents from a variety of sources, including hundreds of law journals from the 19th Century on; Statutes at Large; the Federal Register; treaties and federal legislative histories; KeyCite, the component of Westlaw that enables researchers to check the history of a case, statute, or other document and find citing references; RIA CheckPoint, a rich source of tax and accounting material; BNA, a wide range of newsletters and databases including BNA publications in tax, labor, and health. As for nonlegal databases, you can search through economics, business, scientific, or medical information. If the law

library doesn't have access, your public library or local university library might.

4. Want a DVD on cross-examination? How about an audiotape to review a subject while you're in your car? Many law libraries have them. Some law libraries (e.g., the State Law Library of Montana) even maintain AV collections you can use for CLE credit.

5. One appeal of solo practice is working in your own environment, and even drafting motions in your robe and slippers. But what if you want a change of scenery? The law library provides you with a fresh place to work—and maybe a fresh outlook. Many county law libraries have conference rooms available for client or colleague meetings, which is great if you don't want visitors to your home office to walk past your ironing board and your lunatic cat en route to your home office. Also, most county law libraries are right in the courthouse. What a great place to gather your thoughts before you argue your motion.

6. When you're working in a firm or government agency, there's a lot to be said for what happens around the water cooler. You can bounce ideas off colleagues and hear about their projects. That's a little harder for solo practitioners. But at the law library, the chances are great for serendipitous meetings with law school classmates, former coworkers, and other acquaintances in the legal community. And who knows...the contacts might even lead to referrals.

7. Did you know that law libraries can also help when you're away from the library, offering such services as telephone or e-mail reference (or even Instant Messaging reference). Many law libraries also offer a document-delivery service, and can send you copies of material. Think of it: if it took an hour of your time to drive to a library for a document, it's a bargain to pay $20 to have it faxed to you.

8. Many law libraries offer training, sometimes with CLE credits. In Seattle for example, the county law library offers classes on Casemaker, Loislaw, LexisNexis, Westlaw, and Word; how to use the Internet for legal research; skip tracing, and more. Generally, the bigger cities have libraries, staffs, and services commensurate with their size. Each state has a state law library (serving state agencies and courts, but often serving attorneys in the state as well), and some federal court law libraries are also open to attorneys. Some cities are served by members-only law libraries (such as the Social Law Library in Boston), while other law school libraries are open to attorneys or alumni of the school, sometimes for a membership fee.

Creating a Sample Forms Library

In recent years, the nation's bar has begun uploading numerous sample forms for the benefit of solo and small firm practitioners; forms to help you manage your firm, to improve your relationship with clients, and to build a form library of your own. Note: the online links in this section come from a variety of jurisdictions. Use the forms as a starting point, but check the rules of your own jurisdiction to make sure the form (especially a retainer letter, fee agreement or "leaving a law firm" letter) contains all of the necessary terms to make it enforceable in the state where you practice.

A few additional thoughts:

- Create a separate forms directory on your computer, and when you find a form you like, download and save it immediately. Many times, a Web address will change or a bar association may decide to remove a form or charge a fee for usage. Some lawyers prefer to print out forms and index the hard copies in a binder. Either way—electronic copy or hard copy—save the electronic version so you won't have to keep re-typing a form every time you use it.
- Take the time to personalize the forms. For a retainer letter, provide a factual background about the case and a description of your office policies (See Ch. 8 for a discussion on retainer letters). For a client intake form, add questions that you've found important to the specific type of case. Sometimes you'll find yourself in a dispute with a client that your retainer letter didn't cover adequately, so modify your retainer going forward to address that type of issue. Even with frequent updates and customization, your forms will save you more time than starting from scratch.
- Go to the Web sites for the courts and government agencies where you practice. Many times, these sites will have a variety of sample forms for practice areas such as litigation (sample complaints, standard interrogatories and document production requests), bankruptcy, family law and appellate practice. Government agencies will also maintain forms that you may need to file for clients to apply for licenses, obtain benefits or appeal adverse rulings, while your state secretary's office will typically have forms for incorporating a business or creating a limited liability company.
- Many state bar associations publish practice guides which include forms, petitions and sample letters for state practice (e.g., sample of notice for municipal liability

cases or freedom of information act requests). If you don't want to purchase the guides (they can be expensive), you can find these guides at your local law library.

- Many times, you can find forms you need by posting an inquiry on a listserv. Some bar associations and private companies (among them, *formpass.com* and *uslegal.com*) sell forms on a "per form" basis or by subscription. Some solos have high praise for the fee-based form sites. However, before committing to a subscription, ask to sign up on a trial basis to see if the service suits your practice. And even if forms purport to comply with state law, you'll want to do your own independent verification nonetheless.

Alabama State Bar. Checklist for Setting Up a New Law Office (*alabar.org/lomap/articles/office_checklist.pdf*).

Delaware State Bar Association. So You Want To Open a Law Office (*dsba.org/AssocPubs/PDFs/lawoffice.pdf*).

South Carolina Bar. Starting a New Practice Checklist and Resources (*scbar.org/pmap/NewPractice.asp*).

State Bar of New Mexico. Checklist for Opening a Law Office (*nmbar.org/Content/NavigationMenu/Attorney_Services_Practice_Resources/Law_Office_Management1/NM_Solo_Handbook/lawpracticeforms.PDF*)

Tennessee Bar Association. TBA Guide to Setting Up a New Practice (*tba.org/tnbarms/tba_settinguppractice/index.html*) **The Florida Bar**—The Florida Bar's Law Office Management Assistance Service New Law Practice /New Office Checklist (*floridabar.org/TFB/TFBResources.nsf/BC390EF1565832AE85256A4F006AEEA8/D67F8164A062252E85256B29004BD7B2/$FILE/soyo-newlawpractchecklist.pdf*).

The Institute of Continuing Legal Education. How-To Kit: Open a Law Practice (*icle.org/newlawyers/content/2001tk3803.htm*).

The Missouri Bar. Checklist for Starting a Law Practice (*members.mobar.org/pdfs/lpm/checklist.pdf*).

The Texas Center For Legal Ethics And Professionalism. Master Checklist for Setting up a New Practice (*txethics.org/book/ch4_01.pdf*).

Virginia State Bar. Checklist for Opening Your First Law Office (*vsb.org/publications/brochure/firstlaw.html*).

Planning forms

The Texas Center for Legal Ethics and Professionalism. Developing a Law Firm Business Plan (*txethics.org/TCLEPCOURSE2005/omlp/sec3.6.pdf, and txethics.org/resources_opening.asp*). Includes forms for creating a budget and financial projections.

Leaving your law firm

New York State Bar Association. Letter from Firm and Departing Attorney (*nysba.org/Content/NavigationMenu/Attorney_Resources/Law_Practice_Management l/Departing_a_Law_Firm/LetterfromFirmandDepartingAttorney.pdf*).

New York State Bar Association. Departing a Law Firm (*nysba.org/Content/Navigation-Menu/Attorney_Resources/Law_Practice_Management l/Departing_a_Law_Firm/Departing_a_Law_Firm.htm*).

State Bar of Wisconsin. Sample Letter to Clients Regarding File Retention (*wisbar.org/AM/Template.cfm?Section=Wisconsin_Lawyer&TEMPLATE=/CM/Content Display.cfm&CONTENTID=35460*).

The Florida Bar. Unilateral Letter to Client from a Departing Attorney (*floridabar.org/TFB/TFBResources.nsf/Attachments/52868823D8DBFCE685256B29004B D7C2/$FILE/LOMAS-Sample%20Unilateral%20Letter.pdf?OpenElement*).

Engagement letters

Louisiana State Bar Association. Sample Engagement Letter (General), at *lsba.org/publications/l-letter_engagement.doc*.

New York State Bar Association. Sample Engagement Letter/New Client (*nysba.org/Content/NavigationMenu/Attorney_Resources/Practice_Management/SAMPLE ENGAGEMENTLETTER.pdf*.

South Carolina Bar. Sample Engagement Letters (*scbar.org/PMAP/transitions/Client EngagementLettersPartner.htm*).

Tennessee Bar Association. Engagement Letter New Client (*tba.org/tnbarms/tba_settinguppractice/engagementletter.doc*).

The Mississippi Bar. Engagement Letter—New Client (*msbar.org/admin/spotimages/80.pdf*).

Fee agreements

Louisiana State Bar Association. Fee Agreement and Authority to Represent (Contingency Fee), at *lsba.org/publications/Fee_Agreement_Contingency_Fee l.doc*.

Louisiana State Bar Association. Fee Agreement and Authority to Represent (Flat Fee), at *lsba.org/publications/3-agreement_flat_fee.doc*.

Louisiana State Bar Association. Fee Agreement and Authority to Represent (Hourly with Advance), at *lsba.org/publications/3-agreement_hourly_with_advance.doc*.

California Family Law Institute. Sample Legal Services Arbitration Agreement, at *cfli.com/sample-retainer.html*.

'Lectric Law Library. Sample Fee Agreement Based on Hourly Rate for Services, at *lectlaw.com/forms/f028.htm*.

The State Bar of California. Sample Written Fee Agreement Forms, at *calbar.ca.gov/calbar/pdfs/MFA/Sample-Fee-Agreement-Forms.pdf*.

Disengagement letters

Louisiana State Bar Association. Sample Disengagement Letter (Non-Payment), at *lsba.org/publications/7-letter_disengagement_non-payment.doc.*

   Milwaukee Bar Association. Professionalism Committee, Simple End of Representation Letter, at *milwbar.org/pdf/formletter_13.PDF.*

   New York State Bar Association. Sample Disengagement Letter—Termination of Engagement, at *nysba.org/Content/NavigationMenu/Attorney_Resources/Practice_Management/SAMPLEDISENGAGEMENTLETTER.pdf.*

   State Bar of Georgia. Sample Disengagement Letter. Closing Letter, at *gabar.org/public/pdf/lpm/dlcls.pdf.*

   State Bar of Michigan. Sample Disengagement Letter. Lost Client, at *michbar.org/pmrc/articles/0000081.doc.*

   Tennessee Bar Association. *Disengagement Letter, Closing Letter, at tba.org/tnbarms/tba_settinguppractice/disengage.doc.*

Non-engagement letters

   Louisiana State Bar Association. Sample Non-Engagement Letter (General), at *lsba.org/publications/1-letter_nonengagement.doc.*

   Milwaukee Bar Association. Professionalism Committee, Non-Engagement Letter (Firm Decision Not to Take Case), *at milwbar.org/pdf/formletter_3.PDF.*

   Oklahoma Bar Association. Nonengagement Letter, at *okbar.org/members/map/forms/Nonengagement%20Letter%201.pdf.*

   State Bar of Georgia. Sample Non-engagement Letter, at *gabar.org/public/pdf/lpm/nl.pdf.*

   Tennessee Bar Association—Non-Engagement Letter, at *tba.org/tnbarms/tba_settinguppractice/nonengagement.doc.*

Client intake

   AllLaw.com. Business Client Intake Form, at *alllaw.com/forms/Business/business_intake.*

   Center for Criminal Justice Advocacy. Client Interview in Criminal Cases, at *criminaldefense.homestead.com/ClientInterview.html.*

   Louisiana Indigent Defense Assistance Board. Client Interview Sheet, at *lidab.com/Updated%20Forms/Initial%20Client%20Interview%20Form.htm.*

   Louisiana State Bar Association. Establishing the Attorney-Client Relationship Checklist, at *lsba.org/publications/1-checklist_establishing_attorney-client_relationship.doc.*

   Louisiana State Bar Association. Office of Loss Prevention, Client Management Sample Forms, at *gilsbar.com/downloads/ClientManagementForms.pdf.*

   Oklahoma Bankruptcy Attorney. Bankruptcy Client Interview Form, at *oklahomabankruptcyattorney.net/downloads/Bankruptcy_Client_Interview.doc.*

   Oklahoma Bar Association. Sample Office Intake Forms, at *okbar.org/members/map/articles/intake.htm.*

   The Maryland State Bar Association. Client Intake Form, at *msba.org/departments/loma/articles/characteristics/intake.htm.*

Opening and closing files

Louisiana State Bar Association. Checklist for Closing Files, at *lsba.org/publications/5-checklist_closing_files.doc*

Louisiana State Bar Association—Checklist for Opening Files, at *lsba.org/publications/Section_5_replacement_file_Checklist_for_Opening_Files.doc.*

Tennessee Bar Association. File Closing Checklist, at *tba.org/tnbarms/tba_settinguppractice/fileclosingchecklist.doc.*

Tennessee Bar Association. File Opening Checklist, at *tba.org/tnbarms/tba_settinguppractice/fileopeningchecklist.doc.*

The Florida Bar. Lomas Checklist Law Office Closure or Law Firm Dissolution, at *floridabar.org/TFB/TFBResources.nsf/Attachments/880FD7AAEF47C80D8525713700 537065/$FILE/Checklist%20for%20closing%20law%20office%20or%20dissolving%20law %20firm.pdf?OpenElement.*

Paperless law office

Freedman Consulting. The Paperless Office: Real or Legend? at *pa-lawfirm consulting.com/pdfs/technology/THE_PAPERLESS_OFFICE.pdf.*

Richard Keyt. A Simple Inexpensive Way to Create a Paperless Law Office, at *key law.com/tech/paperless.htm.*

State Bar of Wisconsin. In Search of the Paperless Office, at *wisbar.org/AM/Template.cfm?Section=Law_practice_management2&CONTENTID=64829&TEMPLATE=/C M/ContentDisplay.cfm.*

Practice management forms

Louisiana State Bar Association. Practice Aid Guide: The Essentials of Law Office Management, at *lsba.org/publications/practice_aid_guide.asp.*

Oklahoma Bar Association. Management Assistance Program Forms for Download, at *okbar.org/members/map/forms.htm.*

State Bar of Georgia. Forms, at *gabar.org/programs/lawpracticemanagement/forms.*

The Milwaukee Bar Association. Professionalism Committee Standard Form Letters, at *milwbar.org/legalresources/formletter.htm.*

Of counsel forms

Georgia Bar's Law Practice Management Office. A sample agreement at *gabar.org/public/pdf/lpm/oca.pdf.*

Closing a law practice

American Bar Association. Consent to Close Office, at *abanet.org/legalservices/helppreservists/forms/consenttocloseoffice.pdf.*

New York State Bar Association. For Solos: Planning Ahead Guide, at *nysba.org/template.cfm?Section=For_Solos_Planning_Ahead_Guide&Template=/ContentManagement/*

ContentDisplay.cfm&ContentID=65809.

State Bar of New Mexico. Law Office Management: Closing a Practice, at *nmbar.org/Content/NavigationMenu/Attorney_Services_Practice_Resources/Law_Office_Management1/NM_Guide_to_Closing_a_Law_Office/NM_Guide_to_Closing_a_Law_Office.htm.*

Form packages

Texas Center for Legal Ethics and Professionalism. Opening A Law Practice, *txethics.org/resources_opening.asp* (30 forms and checklists ranging from sample business plans, financial projection forms, checklists for website design, starting a firm, etc.) txethics.org/resources_opening.asp.

The Missouri Bar. ClientKeeper Software, at *mobar.org/bef032af-349c-4473-aaf3-3bcfcc8de2f4.aspx.* Various forms dealing with client relations, including retainer and engagement letters, fee agreements and other samples).

Where to Go (When You Don't Know Where to Go)

Sooner or later, all of us encounter legal issues we're not equipped to answer. Of course, when you worked at a firm or for a government agency, you could always go to a colleague, or check an in-house form file or brief data base, or assign a junior attorney to research the issue. And if an ethics question came up, you could ask your supervisor to deal with it, or you took it to the managing partner. Now that you have your own firm, where do you turn when you have questions on substantive law …ethics…or practice management?

Law practice management offices. Many bar organizations have practice management offices staffed by former practicing attorneys. LPM advisors can field many of the nuts-and-bolts questions about starting a firm—where to find office space; required registrations; how to purchase malpractice insurance, etc. Some LPM offices even have a list of mentor attorneys to whom you can call—and possibly meet with—for detailed advice about starting a firm. Don't be shy; take advantage of the bar's LPM resources. After all, your bar dues pay for them.

Ethics hotlines. Has a client ever threatened you with a grievance after you've demanded payment for an overdue bill for the umpteenth time? Or maybe opposing counsel has accused you of ethical misconduct to intimidate you from vigorously pursuing your client's case? If so, there's no need to suffer alone. Call your bar ethics hotline. Your inquiry probably won't immunize you from future bar action, but at least you'll get some guidance in confidence…and a little peace of mind.

Colleagues. Your law school pals and former colleagues, and those with whom you now share office space, may be your greatest resource for questions of substantive law, ethics, or practice management. Beyond that, develop a list of colleagues with different specializations to whom you can turn for help. Networking events are a great way to line up such a go-to list. When you meet an attorney who practices in an area that might one day be relevant to your practice, ask if it would be OK to call if the need arose. Most lawyers will agree to help, but there will be those who imply that you should pay for their advice. Move on; there are plenty of others willing to help—if only as a matter of professional courtesy—and they're the ones who deserve your business.

The Internet. The Internet is indispensable now as a ready source for answers. Bar association listservs, such as the ABA's *solosez.net* with its nearly 2,300 members, are a good way to get varying responses to an inquiry…often within an hour of posting it. These days, most local bars as well as specialty bars (i.e., bars for specific practice areas like elder law or trusts) run listservs free to members. Bloggers are another useful, and as-yet overlooked resource. Most of today's bloggers are willing to share their expertise, if only because they're constantly seeking new material about which to write, and responding to queries serves that end. Dennis Kennedy (*denniskennedy.com/blog*), a prominent tech blogger, is particularly generous with his "all request days," during which he responds to reader queries on anything from advice on a particular type of software to the future of BigLaw practice.

Ask the court clerk (nicely). Lawyers have different approaches to obtaining information from clerks...some less effective than others. For example, criticizing the court's system or expressing annoyance at the long wait to receive help doesn't produce the best results. Generally, a friendly, deferential attitude—combined with an earnest explanation of a desire to adhere to the court's rules—works best. Set ego aside; it's all about getting the right answer. And remember, you still must corroborate the information that clerks provide, so keep a copy of the rules handy when you seek help, and ask the clerk to cite the specific rule that supports their answer.

Government personnel. Government personnel are also a valuable resource. Don't assume that you need to speak with an attorney to get answers. Depending on the question, nonlegal staff can also provide valuable information. Many agencies also have hotlines. As is true of court clerks, the quality of government agency staff varies, so when you find a helpful person, record their contact information for future use.

Mentors. Some bars have mentor programs, assigning new attorneys or solos to more experienced practitioners. A mentor may not be able to answer all your questions, but they should be able to direct you to an appropriate resource. Where your bar association doesn't have a formal mentoring program, cultivate your own mentor; perhaps a more experienced practitioner in your field or even a colleague from your former firm.

Solo By Choice: Individual Profiles

The individual solo profiles shown here, and excerpted throughout the book, were compiled in the summer of 2006, and portions of the biographical data (e.g., resume and practice specialties) may not reflect the current status of the individual's law practice. In alphabetical order, the solos profiled are David Abeshouse (class of 1982), Anonymous (class of 1993), Sergio Benavides (class of 2005), Heidi Bolong (class of 1987), Traci Ellis (class of 1990), Denny Esford (class of 2003), Mark Del Bianco (class of 1980), Grant Griffiths (class of 1997), Walter D. James III (class of 1987), Sara Fern Meil (class of 2003), Jill Pugh (class of 1994), Brian Rabal (class of 2005), Scott Wolfe (class of 2005), and Spencer Young (class of 1995):

David Abeshouse

Education—Vanderbilt School of Law; class of 1982

Resume—Practicing law for 24 years; associate in medium and small suburban law firms, and medium New York firm, partner/medium suburban firm

Solo practice—6 years in solo suburban practice

Practice specialties—Business litigation, arbitration, and mediation (i.e., commercial litigation and ADR)

Bottom line—*I'm glad I decided to solo. My practice and life are more interesting as a result.*

Q: *With all your legal experience, what appealed to you about solo'ing?*
A: One of the factors was the merger of a law firm in which I was a partner. It preceded my departure by a few years, but it was definitely a precipitating factor. Also, I realized that...for the good of my career...I needed to be more of a rainmaker than a worker bee, but I was working so hard that I lacked the time and opportunity. And I wanted to sink or swim on my own, do things in my own fashion, rather than have to abide the partnership meeting/committee/sub-committee process of decision-making. And then there were family considerations: I wanted the flexibility to participate more in my children's activities.

Q: *What do you remember about your first day as a solo?*
A: Exhilaration, energy, anticipation, relief, and excitement (combined with dread, concern, and anxiety). Happily, the former prevailed over the latter.

Q: *How did you find your first clients?*

A: I took them with me when I left the firm; more accurately, they came with me when I left.

Q: *As a parent, what it's like to solo?*

A: Now that my office is closer to home, I can zip in and out of the office to go to my kids' games, concerts, and the like, without being beholden to the expectations of others in my firm, and without spending as much time commuting.

Q: *What role does a spouse/partner play in one's solo practice?*

A: If they're not supportive, it's much less likely to work.

Q: *What role does risk play in solo practice?*

A: A solo has to be able to stomach a fair bit of risk, because you ultimately have only yourself to rely upon. And that doesn't change over time, although there are ways to make things easier (by using outsourcing judiciously).

Q: *What would you tell a roomful of new grads?*

A: I feel it was important that before I went solo I had a good grounding in the substantive law via work experience, practice skills in general, and practice management. I'm sure I would have made many more mistakes if I solo'ed right from law school, and I would have missed out on some excellent experiences. There are those who feel a new grad can solo. But I believe it's much harder to concentrate one's career in a given area or two (unless you had a previous career in a related area). And I also believe that a broad general practice is far more difficult to succeed in than is a practice with one or two focal areas of expertise.

Q: *How did other lawyers respond to your decision to solo?*

A: In the first couple of years, I had many offers of partnership from friends and colleagues, some of whom believed that soloing is too hard to do. But I was committed to it for at least three years, and told them I'd let them know later. Now, six years later, I'm still soloing, and enjoying it…although it's very demanding and makes taking a vacation—even a full weekend off—difficult.

Q: *What advice do you have for other solos?*

A: The works of respected practice-management and marketing authors, such as Jay Foonberg, Ed Poll, and Jennifer Rose. Read legal blogs, friends and colleagues who already are solos, and to marketing consultants like Allison Shields, Stephen Fairley, and Trey Ryder.

Q: *Given what you've learned, would you still decide to solo?*
A: Yes. My practice and life are more interesting as a result.

Q: *What questions should new or prospective solos consider?*
A:

- Do you have at least a six-month cash reserve for home and practice expenses, or can you borrow it based on available credit?
- Do you have the requisite mentality (attitude, motivation, energy, commitment) and skills (self-reliance; ability to juggle wearing many varied hats) to persist?
- Do you have the collegiality of other lawyers available to you to avoid legal loneliness, and to secure the opportunities to "partner" informally with colleagues to achieve results for your clients?

Anonymous

Education—Duke, class of 1993
Resume—Former partner, AmLaw 100 firm (New York)
Solo practice—Began 2005
Practice specialties—Corporate, securities, M&A
Bottom line—*If you think you might want to solo, go for it now (or early in your career), before the golden handcuffs go on.*

Q: *Why did you decide to start a solo practice?*
A: I was not happy with big firm life, even as a partner; the demands were too great, too arbitrary. I wanted a change.

Q: *What was it like in the beginning?*
A: I took it slow. I decided to take the New Jersey bar (I was admitted in New York), so the first two months were more of a 'getting my Web site ready, getting a marketing plan together, e-mailing people, etc.', rather than working. I also remember not putting on a suit.

Q: *How did you find your first clients?*
A: Almost all of my clients have come from big firm lawyers I know and/or investment bankers I worked with previously.

Q: *If you are a parent, what is it like to solo?*
A: It's great. I work about four blocks from home. I go to all of my kids' events, and surprise them and pick them up at school, etc.

Q: *What role does risk play in solo practice?*

A: It's risky. Luckily for me, my wife is a big firm partner, so we have a cushion. But it's still tough. It's very different not knowing what that next paycheck will be.

Q: *How did you bring in a stream of revenue in the beginning?*

A: I had some carry-over work from my old firm, which helped some.

Q: *What were you least prepared for?*

A: I thought I would get more referrals than I have gotten.

Q: *What would you tell a roomful of new grads?*

A: If you think you might want to solo, go for it now (or early in your career), before the golden handcuffs go on. (But whenever you decide to go solo), treat every encounter as a marketing opportunity.

Q: *What advice do you have for other solos?*

A: Just as marketing is crucial, so is networking with other lawyers (from a personal sanity standpoint and also because you will learn and get clients from them). Join the two solo listservs—*solosez* and *solomarketing.*

Q: *How helpful was it to have prior experience before opening your own practice?*

A: Very helpful. Clients are more willing to go with me than a solo with 'lesser' credentials.

Q: *How did other lawyers respond to your decision to go solo?*

A: They thought I was absolutely nuts.

Sergio Benavides

Education—University of San Francisco School of Law; class of 2005

Solo Practice—Two years.

Practice specialties—Employee wage claims, general business transactions and litigation; intellectual property issues and legal structure setups for small business

Bottom line—*Working for a law firm is no guarantee of a career or a great salary. Everyone is expendable, and loyalty is at a minimum. I prefer to guarantee my future by creating it and being responsible for it myself.*

Q: *How did you know solo'ing would be the right thing to do?*

A: I researched it for the last year of law school, and took a class on law practice. I also spoke with numerous solos, went to conferences, read books, joined attorney associations for solos, and joined listservs online.

Q: *What did you hope to achieve with a solo practice?*

A: The freedom to choose my workload…have schedule flexibility and expanded opportunities to undertake all kinds of legal work…a chance to keep all the profits…and to avoid law office politics.

Q: *What was it like in the beginning?*

A: Slow and difficult. I brought in some revenue by offering to do flat-fee investigations for some clients.

Q: *And did things improve?*

A: There was a lot of frustration. I remember having to go through tons of bad intake consultations, and dealing with free-loaders who wanted free legal advice. And then I had some clients agree to representation only to back out at the last minute.

Q: *What were you least prepared for when you began?*

A: Litigation. I am still learning every day. Also, I wasn't prepared for simple, day-to-day office management/secretarial skills.

Q: *What would you tell new grads?*

A: Keep your overhead low, build a good support network, and make sure you've got enough savings to survive the slow times.

Q: *Marketing wisdom*

A: Make friends with lawyers in all practice areas. Take them to coffee, to lunch. If you take them out and give them a nice lunch, even attorneys making $200, $300 an hour will be willing to chat about your legal work from time to time. Think of it as an investment. You want to get on their radar, so they take your phone calls, answer your questions, and refer you work. Also, make thank-you calls and send thank-you notes. During the holidays, I send Starbucks gift cards. What lawyer doesn't love coffee?

Q: *Given what you've learned, would you still solo?*

A: Absolutely. Everyone in the world told me that the first year, even the first two years, would be slow…and they were right. But now after six months, my phone rings constantly, and I get a steady stream of referrals.

Q: *What should new or prospective solos be asking themselves?*

A:

- Do I know what kind of lawyer I want to be?
- Am I self-motivated?
- Am I extroverted, or at least not be afraid of meeting new people all the time?
- Do I have the energy to constantly go out and sell myself and my practice through networking?

- Do I have a reliable support network of attorney friends, colleagues, and family?
- Do I have enough savings or loan money to help me weather the slow periods?
- Do I have access to attorney mentors who will help me when I need it?

Heidi Bolong

Education—JD/MBA University of Washington; class of 1987

Resume—1987-2004, big city/small city large firm, and in-house; resumed full-time practice in 2005

Solo Practice—One year

Practice specialties—Estate planning, elder law, probate, small-business advising

Bottom line—*Underestimate your revenue and overestimate your expenses...and figure out what your unique selling position will be.*

Q: *What do you remember about your first day as a solo?*
A: I was scared. I didn't know what I was doing, and I didn't know if I could do it.

Q: *What it's like being a solo and a mom?*
A: Great! I have the flexibility without having to ask permission.

Q: *Who helped the most when you started out?*
A: My parents...and the listserv members at *solosez.net*.

Q: *What role do spouses/partner play?*
A: Can't imagine solo'ing without the emotional and financial support of my husband.

Q: *What was it like financially in the beginning?*
A: It was hard. I had very few clients because I hadn't moved from another practice, and...because I'd been teaching the previous seven years...most of the local attorneys didn't even know I was still in town. On top of that, I'm introverted, so networking is even more difficult for me.

Q: *What would you tell a roomful of new grads?*
A: Market yourself. Do a business plan. Underestimate your revenue and overestimate your expenses. Figure out what your unique selling position will be.

Q: *What's the biggest goof you ever made?*
A: A year ago, I spent many hours developing a plan for a doctor-client, who dangled the promise of introductions to other physicians. Afterward, he said he wanted to think about the plan, and then left without paying a cent of my fee. Whenever possible now, I get the money up front.

Q: *What advice have you for new or prospective solos?*

A: Think about what you have to offer your clients that no one else can...and get paid up front.

Q: *What should new solos be asking themselves?*

A: What niche will they focus on, and can they afford the start-up costs and the expense of living six months without revenue?

Traci Ellis

Education—Ohio State University; class of 1990

Resume—Practiced law 16 yrs

Work—Medium firm, in-house at Fortune 500 firm, small privately held company

Soloing —1 year

Practice specialty—General business & real estate law

Bottom line—*Soloing is hard; even harder if you don't have any competency yet in a practice area. But if you've got a stomach for risk...and have a good support system...go for it.*

Q: *Why did you want to solo?*

A: I wanted freedom from the corporate structure...to run my business in a more relaxed atmosphere...and to remove limitations from my earning capacity.

Q: *How did you explain your decision?*

A: I told the company's CEO that I felt led to pursue entrepreneurial ventures.

Q: *What was that first day like?*

A: Fear. I remember thinking to myself, *'What have I done? I've just walked away from a six-figure salary plus bonuses!'*

Q: *How does soloing work as a parent?*

A: I love it. My office is less than 10 minutes from my home, and five minutes from each of my kids' schools. A few weeks ago, I went to my middle school son's school play *in the middle of the day*. Other times, I've taken 'forgotten' homework to school during the day. I couldn't have done that before going solo because I had less freedom to leave the office during the day...and I was 30–40 minutes away from home and the kids' schools.

Q: *Is your husband supportive of your solo'ing?*

A: I couldn't do it without him. He is my biggest supporter, cheerleader & encourager. This means even more to me because my decision to leave my corporate job not only impacted me, but him as well. To pull a six-figure salary out of the household income with very little lead time and planning put pressure on him to cover all of the household expenses and sometimes put cash into my business as well.

Q: *What role does risk play in solo'ing?*
A: I think you have to a risk-taker to own your own business...any business...but especially a law practice. In addition to cash-flow fluctuations, there is the added risk of malpractice claims by disgruntled clients.

Q: *Was it difficult to achieve a revenue stream in the beginning?*
A: I wouldn't say I've achieved a revenue 'stream' yet...it's more like a revenue 'ëdrip'. I've done very little marketing, and my business is growing by word of mouth. The one exception: I've written a couple of articles for a real estate investor publication on legal issues related to real estate investing, and have gotten a few clients from that. Every month that one of my articles appears, I get three or four calls, which has resulted in a few new clients.

Q: *What have the first few months been like?*
A: My solo practice is quite new, so these first few months are very fresh in my mind. I spent a lot of time thinking about client perception...whether I should work out of my home, or jump into an office lease, whether I should I have high-quality letterhead or just print it out myself. I wanted to 'ëlook successful' right from the start because I felt (and still feel) that for my practice areas, ppl have a certain expectation of what an attorney 'ëlooks like', and I needed to meet or exceed those expectations. Ultimately, I decided to lease office space, and I was fortunate to find inexpensive Class B office space that looks very nice. I'm not paying anywhere close to what I would have had to pay for a Class A space, but I'm in a nice building just off a main thoroughfare in town.

Q: *What were least prepared for?*
A: Accounting. I purchased an integrated practice management & accounting software package, but the accounting still frustrates me.

Q: *What would you tell new law grads?*
A: I would tell them the truth: solo practice is hard...and probably harder if you're a new grad and don't have any competency in any practice area. I would tell them that marketing is key but expensive...that clients are demanding...cash flow is unpredictable...and that the higher overhead the more stressful it is. But...and this is a big but...if you have the stomach for the risk, and have a good support system behind you, then go for it. The freedom, the sense of accomplishment, and the earning potential, all make it worthwhile. I don't regret my decision one bit, even knowing that I've got to make payroll (I couldn't do it all and well; I had to hire an assistant), make the rent, pay the phone bill, order supplies...even while three clients haven't paid their bills.

Also, I would tell new grads to absolutely have a written business plan but not to write it in stone. It should be frequently updated and you have to be flexible.

Q: *Biggest goof so far?*
A: I make sure I get the retainer check up front. But in my second month, in an effort to provide good client service to a client whose matter had an extremely tight deadline, I did the work very quickly and was completed before the bank notified me that the client's check had bounced! When I notified the client, she left a message that her wedding was just a month away and that expenses were eating into her cash flow and she would pay me when she returned from the honeymoon. Boy, I didn't see that one coming. Fortunately, I'm a quick learner. Now I wait for the check to clear. If it's an urgent matter that requires immediate work, I request a money order, cash, or a cashier's check unless I know the client well.

Q: *Any marketing tips?*
A: The best marketing I've done has been to write articles for a publication read by my target clients. It's free publicity, and I always get calls. I suggest that solos find those publications (relevant to their practice) and get published. It's free marketing…and it works.

Q: *If you had it to do over again, would you still solo?*
A: Absolutely, unequivocally yes.

Denny Esford

Education—Chicago/Kent School of Law; class of 2003
Resume—Contract lawyer in large firm litigations
Solo Practice—Two years
Practice specialties—Civil litigation including contract, business torts and non-patent IP
Bottom line—*The longer you wait to solo the harder the transition will be.*

Q: *What were some of the factors that led you to open a solo practice?*
A: I had no other choice. I graduated in the middle of the pack, and, as a new lawyer at age 46—with a wife, two teenage girls and a mortgage—no one would hire me unless I was willing to work for $30 to $40k.

Q: *What do you remember about your first day as a solo?*
A: I went directly into contract work to supplement my income, so I just remember being fortunate to have the ability to pay my bills while building a practice.

Q: *Who helped you most when you started out?*

A: A mentor I met during a law school internship, and a couple of other attorneys I do litigation work for periodically. They all have been good sources of substantive help with the law and moral support. I also recently signed on with *solosez.com* to get quick answers, and to point me in the right direction when I am stumped or feeling a bit overwhelmed.

Q: *What role has marriage played in your practice?*
A: My wife works as a university lab tech to help pay the bills, and most importantly, to provide us with affordable and comprehensive family health care.

Q: *What do you remember of your first few months solo'ing?*
A: Getting used to the fear that my contract assignments would end suddenly without replacements. That didn't happen. My first assignment did end quickly and suddenly, but it was replaced in a week, and I have been working continuously ever since.

Q: *What would you tell a roomful of new grads about solo'ing?*
A: The longer you wait, the harder the transition will be.

Q: *What should new or prospective solos ask themselves?*
A: Are you well-capitalized? As a new solo, you should not underestimate the cost of running your business.

Mark Del Bianco

Education—Yale School of Law, class of 1980
Resume—Justice Department; a small international trade firm, and Skadden Arps D.C., from 1992–2003.
Years in Solo practice—3+ years
Practice specialties—Communications and internet
Bottom line—*Getting good clients is all about networks—hometown, college, law school, government, firm, etc.*

Q: *Why did you decide to start a solo practice?*
A: The dot-com crash decimated Skadden's telecom practice, and other firms were not interested in attorneys with my level of experience (e.g., my age) unless you had a million dollars of portable business.

Q: *How did you find your first clients?*
A: I took a couple of small clients with me. Others came from referrals from colleagues or from my Web site.

Q: *What do you remember about your first day on your own?*
A: Nothing…except the worry.

Q: *What's it like to solo as a parent?*
A: (When I began solo'ing) my youngest was a junior in high school, and I had two in college. It worked out well because I had time to see all my daughter's games, and do many things with her during her senior year.

Q: *What aspect(s) of solo'ing were you least prepared for?*
A: The constant marketing.

Q: *What role does a spouse/partner play in one's solo practice?*
A: A very big role. My wife and I have a routine where each weekend we talk about what marketing I've done over the past week, and (what) plans (I have) for the next week.

Q: *What role does risk play in solo practice?*
A: If you (or more importantly, your spouse) have little appetite for risk, you'll never become a solo. The big firm or government paycheck is just too stable and hard to give up.

Q: *What would you tell a roomful of new grads?*
A: Getting good clients is all about networks; hometown, college, law school, government, firm, etc. Unless you have two or three good, separate networks, making it as a solo is very difficult. Which means that unless you spend a lot on advertising, you may have to spend a decade or more building up your networks before going out on your own.

Q: *How did other lawyers respond to your decision to go solo?*
A: Most were surprised; some thought I was crazy. A lot of them at larger firms were jealous.

Grant Griffiths

Education—Washburn University School of Law; class of 1997
Resume—Solo and small firm environments for 10 years
Solo Practice—5 years
Practice specialties—Family law with some criminal defense work
Bottom Line—*With four children, I didn't want big firm life to interfere with being a parent. Being a solo allows me to do those things I want and need to do with them.*

Q: *What were some of the factors that led you to open a solo practice?*
A: I wanted to be the one that made the choice as to whether to take a case or not, and not because some law firm partner told me I had to.

Q: *How did you feel on your first day?*

A: Scared to death! I remember looking in the mirror and wondering where I was going to get the money to put food on the table and pay my overhead.

Q: *What do you remember of those first few months?*

A: There is so much to cope with when you are a solo right out of law school. Sometimes I felt like I had no idea what I was doing. Not that it can't be done. Just that you have to be careful not to allow yourself to be overwhelmed... or think you have to do everything yourself. That was my mistake. My advice: find a good paralegal or assistant. And, if you have a spouse/partner, listen to them and allow them to help. Don't do what I did ...don't let your pride get in the way of accepting help and advice.

Q: *How did you bring in a stream of revenue in the beginning?*

A: I took every court-appointed criminal case I could get... minor divorce cases that the large firms in my area did not want to mess with... I also developed a referral relationship with some of the other more established solos and small firms.

Q: *What would you tell a roomful of new grads?*

A: Take classes in accounting and/or management, and find good help and pay them well.

Q: *What marketing wisdom have you for other solos?*

A: I think that if a solo will pick a certain area of practice and blog about it, they will not only gain knowledge themselves. They will gain new clients.

Q: *Given what you've learned, would you still decide to solo?*

A: YES!

Walter D. James III

Education—University of Nebraska School of Law; class of 1987

Resume—1987-2004, large firm practice

Solo Practice—Three years.

Practice specialties—Environmental law

Bottom line—*I decided to solo because I got tired of the hours, the commute, and not getting compensated for the amount of business I was bringing in.*

Q: *What was your first day of solo'ing like?*

A: I had a four-hour conference call that first day. When I finished, I realized I had almost paid my entire overhead for the month!

Q: *What it's like to solo as a parent?*

A: It's the best. My daughter's school is a half-block away, and sometimes I'm able to have lunch with her and pick her up from school. And, on some days, she just stops in after school. As a solo, I am able to spend time with my two kids and not feel guilty about it.

Q: *Outside your family, who helped you most when you started out?*

A: A couple of lawyer friends of mine helped me decide which software to get, what hardware to buy, what to lease, and how to get a line of credit. Those guys were also great from a morale standpoint as well.

Q: *What were the first few months like?*

A: The only thing I can recall was saying to myself, 'ë*Why didn't you do this five years ago?*'

Q: *What were you least prepared for when you began?*

A: Accounting.

Q: *What would you tell new grads about solo'ing?*

A: It gets better every day.

Q: *What advice have you for new or prospective solos?*

A: Keep marketing. Never…ever…rest on your laurels.

Q: *Given what you've learned, would you still decide to solo?*

A: Yes, in a heartbeat.

Sarah Fern Meil

Education—Columbia Law School; class of 2003
Solo practice—One year
Resume—Wachtell, Lipton, Rosen & Katz (associate '03-'06)
Practice specialties—Employee rights law
Bottom line—*You can take on the big firms and you can beat them.*

Q: *What did you know about solo practice before starting?*

A: I knew enough to know that I didn't know much. But what I *did* know is that lawyers all over the country were practicing as solos ,and they were somehow making it work.

Q: *How did you find your first clients?*

A. My first clients were friends of my parents. My first paying clients were referrals from other attorneys.

Q: *How did you bring in a stream of revenue in the beginning?*
A: I saved enough money so that I did not need to bring in a stream of revenue in the beginning. But I was also lucky to pay my rent from the start because of some estate-planning work and a few appearances for a local solo.

Q: *What would you tell a roomful of new grads?*
A: Follow your heart. Seriously. It's a clichéÈ for a reason.

Q: *How did other lawyers respond to your decision to go solo?*
A: Some were supportive. Some feigned support. Some laughed. Most didn't care.

Q: *Has your education and prior experience helped or hurt you in opening your practice?*
A: Working in a big corporate firm helped me to realize that I didn't want to (continue to) work in a big corporate firm. But if I never had that experience, I might have doubted my decision to solo. I now have fewer doubts.

Q: *What advice do you have for other solos?*
A: I'm probably not qualified to give advice to anyone. But I guess it's this: '*You can take on the big firms and you can beat them*'.

Jill Pugh

Education—Northwestern School of Law/Lewis & Clark College; class of 1994
Resume—Began as a contract lawyer, and later worked for another solo and a small firm
Solo Practice—1996/resumed solo practice in 2001
Practice specialties—Employment law; representing employees and small businesses management
Bottom line—*For all the financial uncertainty and moments of being overwhelmed by workload and isolation, solo'ing offers so many more moments of satisfaction and freedom.*

Q: *What did you know about solo'ing before you began?*
A: I knew virtually nothing about it the first time; the second time around I had more business savvy, and I knew I needed a better mix of contingency vs. hourly cases. I also knew that I did not care for law firm culture. If I was going to work the long hours of a litigation attorney, I wanted to be able to decide what cases I would take, and to reap the benefits without having them go to a partner who was playing golf while I worked all weekend!

Q: *What it's like to solo as a parent?*

A: I don't have children, but I can speak to the benefits/issues of solo practice as a primary caregiver for my mother as she battled cancer. My father did not have the flexibility to leave work to take her to her chemotherapy sessions, so I took on that responsibility. I am certain I would have been fired by a firm for the amount of time I had to be away from work during the last two years of my mother's life. As my own boss, though, I could take off during the day, and then come back and work late into the night after I had taken her home. Trying to schedule depositions and hearings around her appointments was a challenge, but I was almost always amazed at how cooperative most of my opposing counsel were during this time.

Q: *Who helped you most when you started out?*

A: I was fortunate to have several mentors who were seasoned employment law attorneys. When I moved back, I met them and took everyone I could think of out for coffee and lunch to network and to try to find a job. If I was advising someone just starting, out, I advise them to find mentors in solo practice *regardless of their practice area.*

Q: *What role has marriage played in your career?*

A: My first husband was not supportive at all. He didn't take any responsibility for household chores, so I was pretty much in charge of everything. It was a terrible drain and hindered my ability to grow my practice. My second husband has been very supportive; he helps me with marketing, technology and business issues, and makes sure the household chores are done. I have so much more energy to devote to my practice with a supportive husband!

Q: *What role does risk play in solo practice?*

A: Risk and solo practice are synonymous. As rewarding as a solo practice is, it is incredibly unpredictable and inherently risky. You bear the brunt of bad court decisions (especially in a contingency-fee practice), and you bear the risk of clients who fail to pay.

Q: *What were you least prepared for?*

A: The first time out, I was least prepared to handle depositions. I had never attended a deposition, much less taken one, and I had no idea what I was doing! I also had never gone to court, and had to call up lots of seasoned practitioners to find out the rules of the game.

Q: *What would you tell new grads?*

A: The biggest struggle for a solo practitioner is isolation. If you are a loner, I do not think you can truly succeed as a solo. You must have people with whom you can brainstorm, and to whom you can turn for help. The Internet and online listservs makes this easier…but there is no substitution for human contact. Not only do you need it to build your referral base, you need it so you have a shoulder to cry on when a judge or a client does something really stupid.

Q: *What marketing wisdom have you for other solos?*
A: Without engaging in any marketing at all, I somehow managed to keep my doors open the entire first time I was a solo, and for the first three years the second time. Now, I make an effort to cultivate relationships. At least once a week, I have lunch (or coffee) with a colleague, or a potential referral source. I track personal and professional information for everyone I come into contact with, so that if I run across something that might be helpful or of interest I can forward it to them. Volunteering to chair the employment law section of my state's trial lawyer association has been a wonderful opportunity to meet more experienced employment law attorneys and raise my profile. And providing helpful information to the various listservs to which I belong has also garnered me lots of referrals.

Q: *Given what you know, would you still decide to solo?*
A: Absolutely. For all the financial uncertainty and moments of being overwhelmed by workload and sometimes isolation, there are so many more moments of satisfaction and freedom.

Q: *What questions should new or prospective solos ask themselves?*
A: Can I create structure for myself? Working solo means you have to be able to create "rules" for yourself, create systems to get the work done, to monitor your business. You and only you set your schedule, and you have to stick to it.

- *Do I know how much money I need to cover my basic living expenses?* How much money will it cost me to run my law practice? Where will I find that money if I don't make it right away?
- *Am I a people-person?* You have so much more client contact as a solo; you also must make human contact to get new business; you should make human contact to make sure your legal skills are up to date.
- *Can I handle long stretches by myself without any other people around?* As a true solo, with no support staff, it is only you and the computer until midnight working on that summary judgment motion.
- *Am I technologically savvy?* It is impossible to run a solo office and be computer illiterate.
- *Am I detail-oriented?* Again, especially if you have no support staff, do you have the patience and attention to detail to proof read all letters and pleadings before they leave your office? Do you have the attention to detail to be sure you read the local rules regularly, even the silly ones about the top margin and font size?

- *Do I have a personal support network?* In this profession in general, it is soooo easy to burn out, and even more so I think if you are going it alone. You must take time to stop and smell the roses (or play rugby or travel or whatever relaxes you) or you will go crazy.

Brian Rabal

Education—Thomas M. Cooley Law School (Michigan); class of 2005
Solo practice—Two years
Practice specialties—Family law, criminal, and civil litigation
Bottom line—*Shake hands with as many people as you can.*

Q: *What were some of the factors that led you to open a solo practice?*
A: The ability to spend more time with family, the costs of commuting, flexibility, and the fact that I have never been good with office politics.

Q: *How did you explain your decision to colleagues?*
A: I explained that I could rent an office for less than I was paying for gas to commute.

Q: *What do you remember about your first day as a solo?*
A: Sitting in my office alone with no prospects for work.

Q: *What it's like to solo as a parent/single parent?*
A: It certainly makes school events, doctor visits, etc. easier to attend. I feel that I am able to spend more time with the family. However, I think that it sometimes hurts my practice because I will allow the kids to come to the office, which effects my work.

Q: *The role of risk*
A: Huge. I am giving up consistent income in an attempt to somehow make it.

Q: *What legal or practice skills were you least prepared for when you began?*
A: Lack of understanding of civil procedure, filing requirements (e.g., cover sheet, how many copies of pleading required, etc.)

Q: *What would you tell a roomful of new grads?*
A: That you have no guarantee of clients. That if you don't have a network of individuals to help you, it sometimes takes all day to do or to figure out how to do even the simplest things.

Q: *What are you learning about marketing for solos?*
A: Shake hands with as many people as you can. Join civil, social and fraternal organizations.

Q: *What should new or prospective solos be asking themselves?*
A: Are you willing to live on nothing for the first few months?

Q: *Given what you've learned, would you still decide to solo?*
A: I'll tell you next year.

Scott Wolfe

Education—Loyola University New Orleans School of Law; class of 2005
Solo—Two years
Practice specialties—Construction and business law
Bottom line—*... To be a successful solo really comes down to an ability to be one's own boss, and to feel confident enough to put one's money and future on the line.*

Q: *What had you heard about solo'ing before you started?*
A: That it wasn't something one should do right out of law school. That going solo requires some real-life lawyering experience

Q: *But you decided to solo right away anyway... why?*
A: I have a strong background in business. My family is full of entrepreneurs, and, throughout high school, college, and law school, I was self-employed. My personality has never allowed me to work for any companies or organizations, and I knew even when I was starting law school that I would solo. Beyond that, I made the decision for the standard reasons: the ability to make my own schedule... the power of controlling my job security and destiny... the benefit of not having a promotional ceiling... the rewards of being in business for yourself, etc.

Q: *How did you explain your decision to colleagues?*
A: My law school friends, and my friends in the legal community, were very skeptical about my decision. But I made it clear that because of my personality and my business background, I thought I would be more successful as a solo than in a firm environment.

Q: *What was it like in the beginning?*
A: I spent a lot of time worrying about the appearance of my letterhead, business cards, Web site, etc. I also felt a little uneasy about announcing myself to others as an attorney... especially as a solo practitioner. As time went on, though, I grew comfortable in my own skin. I became more confident in the services I provided, and confident in my image. I may not be a large firm, but I still present myself as a professional organization. I think it's important for sole practitioners to have a polished image as a solo firm. It gives us the best of both worlds, and just maybe helps take the edge off some of the hesitation we have when introducing ourselves to larger clients and/or firms as a solo.

Q: *Who helped you most when you started out?*

A: My attorney friends; especially one who represented my father in the past. He fielded all of my questions, and was a great ear for all of my rookie problems. Also, I subscribed online to a few solo listservs. I can ask practically any legal question, and get a quality answer within minutes.

Q: *What role do spouses/partners play in a solo practice?*

A: I'm not married, but my girlfriend and I live together. Without her support, starting up a solo practice *and* maintaining a relationship, would have been extraordinarily difficult. Because of her help, I was able to put off hiring a secretary during my start-up period.

Q: *What were your first few months like?*

A: Scared, self-conscious. I had a feeling that maybe my firm wasn't good enough to take clients. But I got over that in two or three months. My practice got its start in post-Katrina New Orleans, when many attorneys were still displaced, and there was a lot of business coming into the city to help in the rebuilding. I took a few insurance dispute cases on contingency, and I was able to use that client base to find other clients who needed LLCs, contracts, and the like. I also had two quick settlements that put some breath into my firm's lungs, and from there I consciously grew my non-contingency work.

Q: *What were you least prepared for?*

A: I was very prepared for the *business* side of law... accounting, bookkeeping, marketing, client management, case load, and I had an intimate understanding of the bottom line. But I was least prepared for the legal side. I just didn't know what to do. I knew how to figure out proper venue and jurisdiction, but I had no idea how to actually file the paper with the clerk of court's office. And I didn't know how to properly request service—either in the sheriff's office or on a petition. Many times when I would file a motion, I would question whether it needed to be served or mailed, and whether I needed to include order or not.

Q: *What would you tell new grads?*

A: Think carefully whether you are the *solo type*. Not only should new grads prefer to be their own boss, but they must also be disciplined for it. There are a lot of benefits to being a solo practitioner... and a lot of responsibilities. The legal and business requirements will come with time and effort, but I think that to be a successful solo comes down to an ability to be one's own boss, and to feel confident enough to put your money and future on the line.

Q: *How have other lawyers responded to your decision to solo?*

A: Some laughed, others were doubtful. I guess they felt I didn't have a chance. But at a CLE conference, I happened to lunch with an Eastern District US Judge. When he asked where I practiced, I expected the kind of skepticism I'd heard before. But he wasn't skeptical. He seemed impressed by my decision to solo, and said something like, *'It's sad that you just don't see that kind of thing anymore'*. That was one of the most supportive responses I got after making my decision to go solo out of law school.

Q: *Do you have any marketing advice for other solos?*
A: The law is as much a business as it is a profession. I suggest solos read some of the business, marketing, and advertising books they see at bookstores. Not just the ones for attorneys and attorney marketing (although those are helpful), but just some general business books. I think that one of the big mistake solos make is in advertising. They're an easy sell for ad sales people. Putting up a billboard will not make you rich, and sending out direct mail or buying a Yellow Page ad won't do much good. Your first goal should be to create a brand. So, if you do plan on billboards, make sure they look like your Web site, your newspaper ads, your e-marketing campaign, and your stationery. And then hit all of the media avenues open to you, hit them consistently, and hit them with the same message/design. The key to effective advertising is figuring out how to make your ads seemingly everywhere on your budget. And your ad budget should be 10 percent of the money you pull in. If done right, it'll be worth it.

Q: *What should new or prospective solos ask themselves?*
A: Am I willing to work occasional Saturday nights and Sunday mornings…am I disciplined enough to keep my own schedule…am I organized enough to manage a complicated business…why do I want to solo…what are my goals…and, what is my exit strategy?

Spencer Young
Education—JD/MBA Golden Gate University School of Law (class of 1995)
Resume—1996-2001 small firm and large firms; 2002-2004, non-profits and government.
Solo practice—January, 2006
Practice specialties—All plaintiff's/employment, confidentiality, elder law, personal injury
Bottom line—*Go solo only if you have the guts, and you want to be your own boss.*

Q: *What did you know about solo'ing before you started?*
A: That people not as bright or hard working as myself were making it happen…that solo'ing was high risk with high reward…that it would be expensive if done the wrong way (e.g. taking on too much overhead or not partnering on expensive cases)…and that it offers a lot of freedom to structure your life the way you want.

Q: *Why did you want to solo?*

A: A desire to get paid completely and fully for my own efforts...for freedom in my day...to be able to take cases I chose...to test my business and legal skills...and to experience the risk/reward/rush of running my own business.

Q: *How did you explain your decision to colleagues?*

A: I tell them about my need for autonomy...and that most weeks I earn the same or better salary in half the time without having a boss bark at me.

Q: *What role do spouses/partner play in a solo practice?*

A: My partner plays a very important role. In the crucial first few months, she supported me and helped me believe in myself. Now that I have significantly built my business by settling/winning some cases, I have another source of confidence. But when it really mattered, my partner was able to make me believe when I thought (my decision to solo) was a wash.

Q: *How did you make a living in the beginning?*

A: Contract lawyering, contract lawyering, contract lawyering. After that: referral services and charging $150–$250 a pop for initial consultations.

Q: *What do you remember of your first few months?*

A: I remember being constantly concerned whether it was going to work...and generally feeling just about as alive as I've ever felt aside from participating in live or extreme sports.

Q: *What were you least prepared for when you began?*

A: The run-of-the-mill procedural stuff; the stuff they don't teach you in law school. Some of it is practice-area specific (e.g., can you mail serve a respondent in a marriage dissolution); other stuff is general (e.g. what the different terms used in court are), and then there are the filing procedures (e.g. two-hole punching the original), etc. Also, I had no idea how time-consuming it was to track bills, deductions, expenses etc. Sometimes it seems like that's half the job. It reminds me what one of my mentors told me. He said, "ëSpencer, start solo'ing when you're young. If I had learned how to run the business aspect of solo'ing at your age, I'd be a millionaire now."

Q: *What would you tell a roomful of new grads?*

A: Work in different environments before you solo. Don't solo by default (e.g., lay-off), or even for the money. Do it because you like the profession, you have the guts, you want to be your own boss, and you can deal with the ramifications of that decision.

Q: *How did other lawyers respond to your decision to solo?*
A: Shocked that I did it at age 29. And then when I tell them about my latest settlement, how great it was to help the client…and how I got the entire one-third myself…then they have a palpable sense of jealousy and confusion on their face. Others just say 'good for you', and are genuinely happy I made the decision.

Q: *What's the biggest goof you ever made?*
A: That's easy; I challenged a judge's ruling on a point of law that I knew absolutely nothing about. I was winging a hearing for a client who contacted me in a rush. I asked the judge why she was ruling against me on an issue, and she just about tore me in half because her courtroom was packed, and I obviously had no idea what I was talking about. It was hilarious and pathetic. I got out of it by shutting up immediately, and continuing my line of questioning.

Q: *What should prospective solos ask themselves?*
A: Why do you want to go solo? For the money? If yes, you may fail, and when things get tough you're likely to quit for a steady job. But if you're goal is to help people and take charge of your life, you're more likely to push through the hard times.

- Do you have the people-skills to be your own marketing agent, or do you have the money to pay someone else to do it? If neither, think twice about solo'ing.
- Do you have the contacts to help you answer questions along the way? This is absolutely crucial; I do not know if I would have made it without my mentors and contacts.
- Are you comfortable making yourself work, or do you need a boss and a network of people guiding you along? If you tend to slack off, and need someone else's approval and guidance, a solo practice is probably not for you.

CAREER RESOURCES FOR A LIFE IN THE LAW

Solo By Choice
How to Be the Lawyer You Always Wanted to Be
> By Carolyn Elefant • $45 / 312 pages. (January 2008)

Lawyers at Midlife
A Personal & Financial Retirement Planner for Boomer Attorneys
> By Michael Long & John Clyde • $35 / 224 pages. (March 2008)

Should You Really Be a Lawyer?
A Decision-Making Guide to Law School and Beyond
> By Deborah Schneider & Gary Belsky • $25 / 248 pages (2nd edition, March 2008)

What Can You Do With a Law Degree?
Career Alternatives Inside, Outside & Around the Law
> By Cheryl Heisler • $30 / 352 pages (6th edition, 2008)

Where in the World Do You Want to Practice Law?
Career Advice From 24 Leading International Lawyers
> $30 / 250 pages (October 2008)

Running From the Law
Why Good Lawyers Are Getting Out of the Legal Profession
> By Deborah Arron • $17 / 192 pages (3rd edition)

The Complete Guide to Contract Lawyering
What Every Lawyer & Law Firm Should Know About Temporary Legal Services
> By Deborah Arron & Deborah Guyol • $30 / 288 pages (3rd edition)

Should You Marry a Lawyer?
A Couple's Guide to Balancing Work, Love & Ambition
> By Fiona Travis, Ph.D. • $19/ 168 pages

Order individual copies and boxed sets at info@DecisionBooks.com

Date: 6/27/22

**PALM BEACH COUNTY
LIBRARY SYSTEM**

**3650 Summit Boulevard
West Palm Beach, FL 33406**

TOP 10
ORLANDO

Top 10 Orlando Highlights

The Top 10 of Everything

CONTENTS

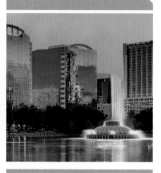

Orlando Area by Area

Streetsmart

Within each Top 10 list in this book, no hierarchy of quality or popularity is implied. All 10 are, in the editor's opinion, of roughly equal merit.

Throughout this book, floors are referred to in accordance with American usage; i.e., the "first floor" is at ground level.

Title page, front cover and spine *Sunset on the boardwalk by The Villages, Sumter County* ***Back cover, clockwise from top left*** *Downtown cityscape; Cocoa Beach pier; lush golf course; boardwalk by The Villages; ICON Orlando™*

The rapid rate at which the world is changing is constantly keeping the DK Eyewitness team on our toes. While we've worked hard to ensure that this edition of Orlando is accurate and up-to-date, we know that opening hours alter, standards shift, prices fluctuate, places close and new ones pop up in their stead. So, if you notice we've got something wrong or left something out, we want to hear about it. Please get in touch at **travelguides@dk.com**